"THE MAN WHO THOUGHT HIMSELF A WOMAN"

HIMSELF A WOMAN"

and

Other Queer Nineteenth-Century Short Stories

Q19: The Queer American Nineteenth Century
Christopher Looby, Series Editor

Queer is a good nineteenth-century American word, appearing almost everywhere in the literature of the time. And, as often as not, the nineteenth-century use of it seems to anticipate the sexually specific meanings the word would later accrue. Sometimes *queer* could mean simply *odd* or *strange* or *droll*. But at other times it carried within itself a hint of its semantic future, as when Artemus Ward, ostensibly visiting a settlement of "Free Lovers" in Ohio, calls them "some queer people," or when the narrator of Constance Fenimore Woolson's "Felipa" refers to the eponymous child, who wears masculine clothing, as "a queer little thing," or when Herman Melville, writing of the master-at-arms Claggart in *Billy Budd*, tells us that young Billy, sensitive to Claggart's attentively yearning yet malicious behavior toward him, "thought the master-at-arms acted in a manner rather queer at times." *Q19: The Queer American Nineteenth Century* makes available again a set of literary texts from the long American nineteenth century in which *queer* appears in all its complex range of meanings—as in George Lippard's *The Midnight Queen*: "'Strange!' cried one. 'Odd!' another. 'Queer!' a third."

"The Man Who Thought Himself a Woman"

and

Other Queer Nineteenth-Century Short Stories

———•———

Edited and with an introduction by
Christopher Looby

PENN

University of Pennsylvania Press
Philadelphia

Publication of this volume was aided by gifts from the UCLA Friends of English and the UCLA Dean of Humanities.

Published by
University of Pennsylvania Press
Philadelphia, Pennsylvania 19104-4112
www.upenn.edu/pennpress

Printed in the United States of America on acid-free paper
10 9 8 7 6 5 4 3 2 1

Cataloging-in-Publication Data is available from the Library of Congress
ISBN 978-0-8122-2366-8

Contents

INTRODUCTION

———•———

Queer Short Stories in Nineteenth-Century America

*The short story is an American invention, and arguably
the most important literary genre to have emerged
in the United States.* —Alfred Bendixen

There is something queer about the short story. —Axel Nissen

If the short story is an original American literary form, as Alfred Bendixen has claimed, and if the short story is in some way queer, as
Axel Nissen has argued, then it would seem to follow that there is
something fundamentally queer about the most distinctively American
literary genre.[1] American writers didn't invent the short story out of
nothing, of course. The short story as we know it had precursors in
other prose forms—character sketches, moral anecdotes, illustrative
material in sermons, inset narratives or digressive episodes in novels,
to name a few—but it seems to have emerged in distinction from these
other kindred forms, and as a genre with its own formal specificity and
dedicated purpose, more or less when Washington Irving composed the
stand-alone tales "Rip Van Winkle" and "The Legend of Sleepy Hollow"
(both 1820).

Like any genre, the short story exists in a differential relationship
to other genres; in the case of the short story, most obviously in a con-
trastive relationship to the novel, as two prose fiction forms

distinguished from each other according to their relative lengths. Nissen's argument for the queerness of the short story begins with the idea that the novel and the short story define each other by their differences, one the longer "major" genre and the other the shorter "minor" one, and he suggests that this binary opposition operates in a dynamic conceptual field structured by other binaries like man/woman, heterosexual/homosexual, central/marginal, and normal/abnormal.[2] The short story, as the "minor" genre, is implicitly allied (Nissen claims) with the disvalued halves of those other binaries: thus the short story is to the novel as woman is to man, abnormal is to normal, and queer is to straight. It might be hypothesized, then, that the short story as a genre emerged historically and developed formally in large part in order to explore and depict queer realms of experience for which the novel was felt to be, at least in some ways, unsuited. It would be no accident, therefore, that the short story was invented, developed, and came to flourish in the century that saw the modern sexual system (eventually organized around the homo-hetero binary) fitfully emerge and unevenly develop. Some historians of sexuality have seen early forms of sexual types (like the homosexual) appear on the scene in the eighteenth century; others have said that it was not until the word "homosexual" was coined in the 1860s that we can legitimately observe persons who answered to this description; still others have claimed that it was the trial of Oscar Wilde in the 1890s that truly marks the historical consolidation of homosexual identity. For the purposes of this collection of short stories, the dating of this process of emergence is not crucial; what is more important is that it was a *process*, uneven and elusive, and that many of these stories testify to that very unevenness and elusiveness.

Any number of scholars and critics have written about the relationships between sexual marginality or dissidence, on the one hand, and deviant narrative structures on the other. These critics often argue that many of the standard features of narrative genres, not exclusively but especially the novel (for example, orderly sequentiality, linear development over time, family continuity over generations, satisfactory ideological closure) are inherently normalizing in their tendencies.[3] It would stand to reason, then, that a historically new narrative form (say, the short story) might find much of its purpose in representing characters and situations that did not conform to the deep structures of normative temporality that were otherwise ingrained in the existing literary culture. Perhaps the short story, not dedicated to creating long normalizing narratives, discovered and offered new queer expressive opportunities. And perhaps queer experience sought and found a natural home in the short story form.

Many of the classic American short stories that have been said (by Bendixen and others) to inaugurate the genre, such as Washington Irving's famous two, already mentioned, and Edgar Allan Poe's "Ligeia" (1838), "The Man of the Crowd" (1840), and "The Purloined Letter" (1844), have been the frequent objects of queer critical commentary.[4] (Rather than reprint very many of these widely available canonical stories here, this anthology inclines toward the relatively unfamiliar.) And among the most celebrated later nineteenth-century American writers of short stories, such as Ambrose Bierce, Alice Brown, Willa Cather, Kate Chopin, Rose Terry Cooke, Mary E. Wilkins Freeman, Bret Harte, Nathaniel Hawthorne, Henry James, Sarah Orne Jewett, Herman Melville, Elizabeth Stuart Phelps, Harriet Prescott Spofford, Charles Warren Stoddard, Octave Thanet (Alice French), Mark Twain, Edith Wharton, and Constance Fenimore Woolson—many of whom are represented in the present anthology—it is not difficult to discover an argument for the queerness (understood in one way or another) of many of their tales.[5] Perhaps it is no coincidence that the nineteenth century—the century when, it has been said, sexuality as such (and various taxonomized sexual identities) were invented—is the period when American short stories were invented, and when they were the queerest.[6]

They were queerest, in part, of necessity—simply because they date from a time when fixed itineraries of sexual desire and settled categories of sexual identity had not yet been fully constituted, and so the errant desires and feelings the stories portrayed would not necessarily correspond to what later became the standard types of erotic orientation (for example, straight, gay). As the genre has continued to flourish in the twentieth and twenty-first centuries, its queerness has only become more evident, as a very partial list of names can only begin to suggest—Sherman Alexie, Sherwood Anderson, James Baldwin, Paul Bowles, Truman Capote, William Faulkner, Charlotte Perkins Gilman, Ernest Hemingway, Langston Hughes, H. P. Lovecraft, Flannery O'Connor, Annie Proulx, James Purdy, Eudora Welty, Tennessee Williams. But many of these writers' short stories seem less queer in the semantically unstable nineteenth-century sense than gay or lesbian as the twentieth century largely understood those terms: they tend to have internalized the "deployment of sexuality," as Foucault called it, the disciplinary structure that insists that each person belongs natively to a particular sexual category.[7]

Such lists of writers as those assembled above will immediately betray the fact that defining what counts as "queer" is a vexing question—a question for which this anthology certainly does not propose a definitive answer. Instead, this collection wants to enlarge the boundaries of the queer (or even start to dissolve them)—or, to be more historical, to recover a sense of the relative unboundedness of the nineteenth-century range of queer experience. This collection therefore does not require that the author of a given story be gay, lesbian, bisexual, transgender, or queer under some other description (although many of the writers could be described in these terms); it does not require that there be uncontestably queer characters in the stories (whatever that might mean); nor does it insist that same-sex or otherwise nonnormative passionate relationships must appear therein (although, of course, they often do). In nineteenth-century America the categories of sexual identity and erotic practice were much less crisply defined than they later became, so choosing stories on the basis of rigid criteria from later eras would be both unduly restrictive and historically incorrect. Rather, this anthology means to *pose the question* of literary queerness in several unprescriptive ways. To that end it is organized into four sections under different overlapping rubrics: queer *places*, queer *genders*, queer *attachments*, and queer *things*. Instead of locating queerness only as a quality of persons, that is, it proposes that queerness can be found elsewhere too.

This collection of stories first asks whether a *place*, such as a region or a city, a landscape or a built structure—a raucous tavern, a lush island in the Pacific, a strange house, a remote valley, a foreign city—can be queer. Or whether one's spatial location within (or without), emotional relationship with, or visceral response to that place can be considered queer. Many of these stories find queerness to be site-specific. It may seem obvious that one's *gender* can be queer—the complex relationship of gender nonconformity to dissident sexualities is well known—but the queerness of one's relationship to one's own

gender (desired or hated, owned or disowned, freely chosen or coer-
cively assigned, deeply ambivalent) is what many of the stories explore.
Then: can the forms of our *attachments* be themselves queer, even if
in other respects (in the joining, say, of a man and a woman) the attachment may be utterly normal? Can a woman's relationship to a man
be queer? Conversely, can a woman's passionate relationship to another woman be normal? Quite a few of the stories here appear to find
same-sex passions to be unremarkable but opposite-sex romance to be
odd or even perverse. And finally this collection asks: can one's relationship to *things*—nonhuman animals, inanimate objects, architectural features, foodstuffs, flowers—be queerly intense or perversely
consuming? Some people's strongest attachments, obviously, are not to
other persons or bodies but to nonhuman objects of one kind or another. Can that count as queer? The stories in this collection entertain
and explore all of these questions and more.

As a result of this intentional dilation of the range of the queer,
some of the stories may seem, to some readers, not really very queer
at all. Where is the *sex*, these readers might ask. It's a reasonable question, to be sure. This collection understands sex and sexual pleasure
(or displeasure, or indifference) not to be strictly segregated from
other forms of sensuous pleasure or embodied experience but always
to be in a lively interanimating relationship to them. A crucial aspect
of the modern sexual system that was consolidated in the nineteenth
century was its reduction of sexual expression to a limited repertoire
of genitally centered acts and sensations: everything outside this repertoire was not sex. That reduction has come to seem quite strange
and deformative in retrospect. One critic has recently written of sexual
celibacy, for instance, that while it can be understood as the opposite
of (or absence of) sexuality, it can also be taken as a kind of sexuality
in its own right.[8] Other critics have understood the polymorphous per-
versity and relative disinhibition of children to be fundamentally
queer.[9] With such bracing stipulations in mind, this collection of stories
features excitable nuns, passionate children, and many other sorts of
rebellious or nonconforming people who might all be counted as in
some sense queer because of their slantwise relationship to norms of
gendered bodily propriety: bachelors and spinsters, drunks and gamblers, coquettes and playboys, murderers, thieves, and other criminals,
bad husbands, reluctant wives, ungrateful children, irresponsible

parents, fops, dandies, loungers, artists, travelers, overeaters, artists—rogues, we might say, of all kinds.[10] Are they all queer, or would this be to stretch even this elastic category—meant, to be sure, as a kind of anti-category—beyond its breaking point?

Certain of the stories included here will seem, to some readers, quite familiarly queer: they match up fairly closely with our categories of gay or lesbian, queer, bisexual, or transgender identity, feeling, or attachment. But it is important that they don't tend to match up exactly: things were quite different in the nineteenth century. For example, Japhet Colbones (in "The Man Who Thought Himself a Woman"), Felipa (in the story of that name), Nancy Jackson (in Twain's story), and Ah Wee (in "The Haunted Valley") all evidently cross-dress, but they don't seem to be of the same sort with one another, never mind of a kind with the transgender lives that we encounter or live today. What all of these stories do, in one fashion or another, however, is *pose* the question of queerness—of desires, feelings, sensations, inhibitions, urges, and affiliations (or disaffiliations) that escape narrow categorical description.

It's noteworthy that in fact in many of the stories some psychic phenomenon or moment of experience is explicitly tagged as outside the normal range of everyday phenomena: inexplicable, unprecedented, opaque, even supernatural. When John Lankton, a dissipated young man who is the hero of Walt Whitman's "The Child's Champion," first lays loving eyes on a twelve-year-old boy named Charley, the baffled narrator can only helplessly ask, "Why was it that from the first moment of seeing him, the young man's heart had moved with a strange feeling of kindness toward the boy?" (8). There is no rational explanation for it: the sudden emotion, the narrator avers, is merely "wondrous" (8). Likewise George, in Elizabeth Stoddard's "Out of the Deeps," upon seeing his cousin's wife Charlotte alive after thinking her dead, disconcertedly experiences "a host of sensations which he believed no man had ever felt before" (180). Martin Morse, in Bret Harte's "In the Tules," to take another example, experiences utterly "unaccountable feelings" (193) for the mysterious stranger, Captain Jack, who exerts such a "complete fascination" (191) over him. The eponymous twin brothers of Bayard Taylor's "Twin-Love," David and Jonathan, appear to communicate telepathically over vast distances in order to redress their mistaken submission to regrettable social norms.

The elusiveness or inscrutability of queer feelings or urges (even one's own feelings, illegible to oneself) are often registered in these stories. In Charles Warren Stoddard's "A South-Sea Idyl" the narrator, who cannot sleep, observes uncertainly (or coyly?) of himself, "I think I must have been excited" (17). In Constance Fenimore Woolson's "Felipa" the narrator, Catherine, observing the curiously unsettled relationship between her friend Christine and Christine's suitor Edward, says parenthetically, "I call them lovers for want of a better name, but they were more like haters: however, in such cases it is nearly the same thing" (43). When Constance suddenly kisses Undine (and then repeats the act) in Octave Thanet's "My Lorelei," she cannot confidently parse her own intentions: "Almost involuntarily, I drew her to me and kissed her" (62). Noticing of a surprised Undine that the "faintest flush had tinged her cheek," the second kiss cannot be so ambiguously detached from Constance's will (62). Tiddy Colbones, in "The Man Who Thought Himself a Woman," has "a peculiar feeling" at the dinner table one evening, an ominous feeling "that something seemed to choke me"; her sister-in-law Drusy at the same moment "grew dizzy, too" and has "felt queer ever since" (106). These inexplicable sensations turn out to be omens of terrible tragedy. When the lovely Helena suddenly returns to her aunt's provincial New England home after being away for many years, in Sarah Orne Jewett's "Martha's Lady," the servant Martha can barely speak, "there [is] such a ringing in her ears"; her employer, Miss Pyne, is "a little puzzled by something quite unusual in Martha's face" (218). The unnamed little girl in Sadakichi Hartmann's "Schopenhauer in the Air" rises "slowly" from the gutter and moves in a kind of trance with the crowd that surrounds her, proceeding "slowly, as if by mere accident, in the same direction" as the others until she finds "herself at the end of the wharf, looking down into the water, lapping against the framework like the soft caresses of living hands" (281). When Adrienne Farival in Kate Chopin's "Lilacs" catches the first whiff of those flowers every spring she almost compulsively returns to the convent where she had once been a schoolgirl (292) and annually enjoys a sort of queer hiatus in her otherwise worldly existence.

Many of the stories themselves include intradiegetically what I would like to call queer inset texts. It is as if they are drawing attention to the queerness of their own literary projects, one short story exhibiting within itself an—even shorter!—model of its own queer narrative

ambitions. In Bierce's "The Haunted Valley," for instance, the narrator—
an unnamed urbane traveler in the American west—reproduces on the
page as best he can what he calls the "exaggerated eccentricity" of a
nearly unreadable grave marker inscription that one semiliterate
character called Whisky Jo has composed as the epitaph for another,
named Ah Wee:

> AH WEE—CHINAMAN.
> Aig unnone. Wirkt last fur Wisky Jo. This monment is ewreck-
> ted bi the saim to keep is memmerry grean an liquize a wornin
> to Slestials notter take on ayres like Wites. Dammum! She wus
> a good eg. (29)

Fully decoding this epitaph, characterized by its misspelling and dialect, requires the complete context of the story, naturally; but I would
like it to stand here, detached from that context and with its obscurity
thereby heightened, as an emblem of the queer short story itself, with
its vexed relationship to legibility as such. The cosmopolitan narrator,
with his command of proper English, confesses to "amazement" as he
reads the epitaph, and calls attention to "the meagre, but conscientious
description of the deceased, the insolent frankness of confession, the
grotesque and ambiguous anathema, and last, but not least, the ludicrous transition of gender and sentiment" (29). Did Whisky Jo love or
hate Ah Wee (or is that too reductive a question)? Is the deceased "Celestial" (a term that once was used to refer to Chinese people) still resented for putting on airs like whites? Or is Ah Wee still longed for, and
his (or her?) memory kept green with devotion? In the epitaph the
word "is" (that is, "his") precedes the word "memmery," but then "She"
is used in the final sentence. Was Ah Wee, after all, male or female (or
is that also too simple a question)? Did Whisky Jo even know, in fact—
or care—whether Ah Wee was a man or a woman? Did Ah Wee cross-
dress, and is that the reason for Whisky Jo's confusion (or, for that
matter, the ground of his attraction)? The story is perhaps most queer
because it does not make it easy (may in fact make it impossible) to
resolve any of these questions. But its very obscurity entices the reader,
enlists the reader in an attempt to penetrate a realm of experience that
is at once alien and alluring.

Among other such queer intradiegetic texts is the diary kept by

Constance Lynde, excerpts from which purportedly constitute Octave Thanet's "My Lorelei," with their glaring five-year gap (68), after which the interrupted story of a brief same-sex passion is completed in distant retrospect. There are the letters Nancy Jackson writes to her mother from sad involuntary exile in Mark Twain's "How Nancy Jackson Married Kate Wilson"—writes, we are told, in "a disguised hand" (126), to match the gender disguise she has been compelled to assume. There is the unseen poem called "Urania," written by the bachelor florist John Thompson in Samuel L. Knapp's "The Bachelors" (91); the deeply ambiguous suicide note left by Japhet Colbones in "The Man Who Thought Himself a Woman" (108); the brief missive written by Li Chung O'Yam in Sui Sin Far's "The Heart's Desire," bound under the wing of a carrier dove and sent to invite Ku Yum to join her in the palace (221). These and others are embedded emblems, so to speak, of the queer work of writing that these stories perform. It is tempting to think of the short stories gathered here as themselves texts meant to be found or returned to after a temporal hiatus, or letters sent with a yearning hope but no assurance of receipt, or notes posted to an unimaginable future.[11]

Although they are not represented within their stories as *written* tales, we might also add to this list of queer inset texts the gaudy lies that Paul tells in Willa Cather's "Paul's Case," the telepathic summons Jonathan sends to David (already mentioned) in Bayard Taylor's "Twin-Love," the painful confessions made by Sarah to Mrs. Dunbar in Mary Wilkins Freeman's "Two Friends" and by George to his cousin Horace in Elizabeth Stoddard's "Out of the Deeps," and, especially, the "quare things" Dave says to his fellow slaves in Charles Chesnutt's "Dave's Neckliss," such as the preposterous claim that hams grow on trees (274). These might all be counted as queer literary productions, and they might instruct us as readers in how to approach the stories of which they form parts.

Queer Places

In the first section of this anthology, five stories are grouped under the rubric "queer places" in order to highlight the ways in which queerness may be present not just in a person but in a geographical place, or a region, or a local setting. In Walt Whitman's "The Child's Champion" (1841), the queer place is a rowdy New York tavern and then the cozy bedroom of an inn. (It might also be the quaint Hudson Valley environs, which had already been invested by one of the short story's inventors, Washington Irving, with queer atmospherics. This region will appear once more in "The Man Who Thought Himself a Woman.") In Charles Warren Stoddard's "A South-Sea Idyl" (1869) it is an island in the Pacific—"How queer the whole atmosphere of the place was!" (17), he exclaims. In Ambrose Bierce's "The Haunted Valley" (1871) it is a desolate and violent western landscape, and a particular secluded topographical depression. In Constance Fenimore Woolson's "Felipa" (1876) it is "a wild place" (37) on the coast of Florida. And in Octave Thanet's "My Lorelei" (1880) it is a "queer" town (56), Heidelberg, in a romantically picturesque Germany. All of these queer locations are evidence of the *spatial* unevenness of nineteenth-century sexual formations. Another writer, born in the nineteenth century and pseudonymously known as Earl Lind or Ralph Werther, who was the author of *Autobiography of an Androgyne* (1918) as well as its sequel, *The Female-Impersonators* (1922), later claimed that, having traveled extensively in the United States as well as in Europe, and having "explored the Underworld in many cities of both continents," he had found that "in America's smaller cities west of the meridian of Kansas City, the sexual Underworld is more bold . . . than anywhere else in the United States or Europe."[12] Charles Warren Stoddard, meditating on the same east-west geographical axis, wrote on March 2, 1869, to Walt Whitman from Honolulu, describing his delightful "intercourse with these natives": "For the first time in my life I act as my nature prompts me. It would not answer in America, as a general principle, not even in California where men are tolerably bold."[13]

It is worth noting that a good number of the stories gathered here either locate their action or have a publication provenance "west of the meridian of Kansas City": Bierce's "The Haunted Valley" and Stoddard's "A South-Sea Idyl" were both first printed in the *Overland Monthly*, a San Francisco literary journal (edited by Bierce); Thanet's "My Lorelei" appeared in *The Western* (a St. Louis magazine); Twain's "How Nancy Jackson Married Kate Wilson" is conspicuously set in his usual southwestern American region; in Bayard Taylor's "Twin-Love" one of the twin brothers, David, goes "westwards" for a time into physical and emotional exile in "the outer line of settlement," where he led "a wild and lonely life" (171); and Bret Harte's "In the Tules," while first published in London, set its action in California. It is hard not to think that Harte, late in his career, living in England and publishing this tale of intense but virtually indescribable male-male passionate attachment in the *Strand Magazine* (London) in 1895—a few months after Oscar Wilde was notoriously prosecuted, convicted on charges of "gross indecency," and imprisoned—would advert pointedly to an earlier, less punitive time and, tellingly, to a distant place—what Stoddard referred to as "California where men are tolerably bold."

Queer Genders

In the next section, "Queer Genders," each of the five stories may be said to confound our usual sense of gender identity in some fashion. Samuel L. Knapp's "The Bachelors" (1836) features three young men who pledge to each other to remain unmarried; two of them keep their promise, while one does not. Adult masculinity was often in the nineteenth century felt to be imperfect or incomplete if it did not entail marriage: we might therefore think of "married" and "unmarried" as categories of gender. The anonymous 1857 story, "The Man Who Thought Himself a Woman," may seem to give itself away in its title as a story of what we now call a transgendered person. But its mapping of the gender landscape is in many ways different from ours, and deeply confounding: Japhet Colbones likes the company of women and likes feminine occupations such as sewing and embroidery, but those traits do not effectively disqualify him for marriage and fatherhood. Mary Wilkins Freeman in "Two Friends" (1887) depicts a lifelong domestic attachment between two women, one of whom does "the rough work, the man's work," the other "the woman's work" (113), but in other ways their roles do not line up with this conventionally gendered division of labor. Mark Twain's grim and merciless tale "How Nancy Jackson Married Kate Wilson," probably written between 1900 and 1903 but left unpublished during his lifetime, tells the story of a young woman coerced into permanently masquerading as a man; it might be said to highlight the essentially coercive nature of gender roles as such. Willa Cather's celebrated "Paul's Case" (1905) may seem most familiar to us, featuring, as it does, a young protagonist perceived to be effeminate, having certain tastes that have been associated with homosexuality, and exhibiting behaviors that came to be signifiers of gay identity; but one thing that is striking about this story is how it refrains from classifying Paul narrowly, how it depicts a world that doesn't know quite what to make of him (as he doesn't really know what to make of himself).

The stories in this section on "queer genders," might just as well have been listed under "queer places," to be sure. The anonymous streets, as well as the hotels and the concert halls of the big city, seem infused with queer energy in "Paul's Case"; the Irvingesque Rattle-Snake Village of "The Man Who Thought Himself a Woman" is a setting that kindly tolerates the "queerities, quips, and quirks" (96) of its inhabitants; the garden, conservatory, and greenhouse of Thompson, one of Knapp's bachelors, "who was in advance of all the florists in the country" (90), is an extraterritorial environment of freedom where at least some of the rules of ordinary life are suspended. Indeed, it might be noted here as an aside that flowers play an important role in many of the stories throughout this volume: someone has planted and tended to "a clump of unmistakable garden-violets" (29) by the grave of the ambiguous Ah Wee in Bierce's "The Haunted Valley," Cather's Paul is often associated with flowers, Jewett's Martha is taught how to arrange flowers by Helena, the "rarest flowers" (220) bloomed only for Li Chung in Sui Sin Far's "The Heart's Desire," a girl named after a flower (Lilly) eats candy flowers in Alcott's "The Candy Country," and the heroine of Chopin's "Lilacs" is intoxicated by the odor of the flowers that give the story its name.

Queer Attachments

"Queer attachments" is the rubric that helps organize the third section of stories. Each of these stories depicts unusual configurations of persons, forms of attachment (or disattachment) that are marked as somehow odd or idiosyncratic. Bayard Taylor's "Twin-Love" features identical twins, named by their mother after the biblical pair David and Jonathan, whose passionate attachment to one another at first apparently excludes the possibility of any other strong relationship. But their deep bond eventually comes to include a woman, Ruth, who is officially married to Jonathan but, in a sense, is united to (and queerly unites) them both. "'Ruth is ours, and I bring her kiss to you,' Jonathan said, pressing his lips to David's" (168). Elizabeth Stoddard's "Out of the Deeps" depicts two men, one of whom, George (a bachelor), professes to love his cousin Horace's wife Charlotte; when she is (temporarily, erroneously) believed to have died in a shipwreck, the memory of this mutual love proves an uneasy basis for the men's ongoing attachment to one another. When Charlotte is found to be alive after all (and her shocked husband thereupon deteriorates and dies), mutual admiration of her then forms the ground for the surviving bachelor's new bond with yet another man, Charlotte's rescuer. Bret Harte's "In the Tules" features an indescribable relationship, mostly conducted in absentia, between two men, and the previously mentioned "unaccountable feelings" (193) that the one has for the other. Part of what is queer about Martin Morse is his strong preference for solitude and social disconnection; another part of what is queer about him is the intensity of his feelings for a man who exists, more or less, only in his imagination. Likewise, in Sarah Orne Jewett's "Martha's Lady" (1897) Martha spends her life devotedly loving a woman whom she knew only briefly and who has now been absent for more than forty years. Some queer theorists have argued for the "antisocial" essence of queerness.[14] David's frontier exile in "Twin-Love," Morse's "habits of loneliness and self-reliance [which] made him independent of his neighbours" (186), Martha's radical social isolation in Jewett's story, and Li Chung O'Yam's alienated life "in a sad, beautiful old palace" (220) might all be counted as instances of queer antisociability. Certain other queer critics and psychoanalytic theorists would advise us that erotic desire is always mediated by representation—that even though we may think we love a person, in truth we always principally love an idea of that person. Both "In the Tules" and "Martha's Lady" explore attachments that are no less powerful for being drastically attenuated, essentially notional, and severely asymmetrical. Sui Sin Far's exquisitely short tale "The Heart's Desire" (1908) is a gemlike parable about forming one's own improvised attachments regardless of what society prescribes for you. An unhappy little princess living alone in a palace, Li Chung O'Yam is first offered a father, then a mother, then a brother—but none of these is at all what she truly wants. She takes matters into her own hands: "Trouble not your minds. I will find my own hearts-ease," she tells her attendants (221). What she finds is another little girl with whom to live "happily together" (221).

Many of these stories featuring "queer attachments" might also have been grouped under "queer places" or "queer genders," to be sure. These orienting rubrics are meant to be suggestive but not limiting. The underpopulated marshy landscape of the flood-prone Sacramento River Valley and the roistering Gold Rush camps of "In the Tules," for example; the magnificent but lonely palace of "The Heart's Desire"; the elegant spinster household and provincial New England village of "Martha's Lady"—all of these places seem imbued with queer energy, or enabling of queer adventure. Martha's tomboyish tree climbing; Captain Jack's finely scented clothes; Li Chung's bold assertiveness—these all seem to transgress gender norms in subtler or less subtle ways. Conversely, we might add to the roster of "queer attachments" some that are grouped elsewhere in this volume, for instance Woolson's "Felipa," in which the eponymous small boyish girl falls in love not with Christine or Edward singly but with the two of them as a couple. As Catherine narrates, "The child had a curious habit of confounding the two identities which puzzled me then as now" (47). We might note that threesomes or triangulated configurations of desiring persons abound throughout this collection: there are Whisky Jo, Ah Wee, and the odd third party named Gopher, for instance, in "The Haunted Valley"; there are Nancy Jackson, her sadistic tormentor the "sour bachelor" Thomas Furlong (122), and Nancy's mother who jilted Furlong many years before; the two friends of Mary Wilkins Freeman's story enjoy a friendship uncomfortably haunted by the unspoken presence of John Marshall, Abby's former suitor.

Queer Things

In the final group of stories, arranged under the title "Queer Things," queerness is relocated from the space of interpersonal relationships to the realm of attachment (or aversion) to things: here, unusual architectural features (a gigantic chimney in Melville's tale), pastries and other sweets (in Alcott's "The Candy Country"), smoked meats (a tantalizing ham in "Dave's Neckliss"), and a "single grape, slightly rotten on one side, that had dropped into the gutter" (in Hartmann's "Schopenhauer in the Air," 279), as well as the lavish bunches of lilacs, along with other household objects—the rich accouterments of the heroine's dissipated urban life and the contrasting spare furnishings and devotional objects of the nunnery—in Chopin's story.

Again, other stories that happen to be placed elsewhere in this volume might very easily have qualified for the "queer things" section. Alongside Melville's "I and My Chimney," featuring queer architecture, we might very well have placed Bierce's "Haunted Valley" on account of the "hermaphrodite habitation" (24) in which Whisky Jo lives, or "The Man Who Thought Himself a Woman," for the "uncouth, irregular" structure (94) that Japhet Colbones's great-great-grandfather built for his solitary residence when, in his old age, a strange "freak" led him to abandon wife and family, forswear social and kinship relations altogether, and live by himself in a hut in the woods. Then there is Felipa's strong bond with her dog Drollo, her "second self" (38), not to mention her attachment to a crude doll or "fetich" (39) and the "secret lair" (39) she has constructed as a home for her doll, which serves also as her own antisocial hut in a thicket of weeds, and to which she brings "portions of her meals or a new-found treasure—a sea-shell, a broken saucer, or a fragment of ribbon" (39). Queer things can be identified virtually everywhere. Among the more obvious, of course, are Japhet Colbones's secretly gathered feminine habiliments in "The Man Who Thought Himself a Woman"; also in the category of clothing are the lovingly made adornments that Sarah creates for Abby in "Two Friends." Intoxicating drinks make frequent appearances, along with the disinhibition that alcohol is known to produce: in Whitman's "The Child's Champion," in Bierce's "The Haunted Valley," Harte's "In the Tules," Hartmann's "Schopenhauer in the Air," and in Chopin's "Lilacs," to name a few. In Thanet's "My Lorelei" there is the engagement ring that Undine returns with understated drama to her fiancé; in Jewett's "Martha's Lady" there is the piece of wedding cake, the handkerchief, and the small lovely toilet implements that Helena sends to Martha, who lovingly cherishes them for decades. These things are all invested with the queer desires that they betoken.

One serious matter that ought to be acknowledged candidly, when thinking of this collection as a whole, is that many of these stories involve grave violence, ranging from frightening but nonlethal and finally inconsequential bodily violence ("The Child's Champion"), to stabbing ("Felipa") and murder ("My Lorelei," "The Haunted Valley," "How Nancy Jackson Married Kate Wilson," "In the Tules"), as well as extrajudicial lynching ("In the Tules"). There is also the strangely ambiguous case of "The Candy Country," in which a child eats apparently human creatures who are made of sugar and other delectable substances. Several of the stories involve attempted suicide ("Felipa") or completed suicide ("The Man Who Thought Himself a Woman," "Paul's Case," "Dave's Neckliss," "Schopenhauer in the Air"). Some of the stories involve psychological or physical coercion or punishment of a cruel or abusive kind ("Dave's Neckliss" stands out here). Such scenarios can be unsettling, even seriously disturbing to many readers. And there is a long and dubious tradition, beginning at least in the nineteenth century and certainly continuing well into the twentieth, of queer fictions resolving the intractable social and psychological dilemmas of their characters by killing them off or, just as often, having them kill themselves.[15] Much could be said about the complicated social and historical circumstances that frame the prevalence of such horrifying violent events in queer literary texts and in fictions that feature queer protagonists. On the one hand, these dire plot turns and narrative outcomes bear stringent witness to the real historical violence that has often been visited upon erotic and gender nonconformists in queer-hating societies. But these stories can also be unsettling because in some sense they seem to be visiting that violence upon their characters themselves.

Among the many challenges these stories present, in different ways, to contemporary readers, perhaps the most troubling is this: they often feature, in ways that are finally not resolvable, both queer-affirmative and queer-negative elements. That is, they include scenarios that bear witness to the deep suffering that has been imposed upon queer dissidents by societies that have despised and harmed them. But they also feature scenarios that describe and preserve queer forms of life and queer collective worlds that history may have largely left behind but that are not—by dint of the fact that they are attested to here—necessarily lost forever. Another way to put this is that the stories can appear to show that the world in the past was less rigidly and punitively organized around enforceable structures of sexual normativity—the nineteenth century can look in retrospect like a time of relative freedom around questions of bodies and pleasures—while at the same time they appear to document the infliction of harm on sexual nonconformists. Thus these stories all feel as though they can be read both "symptomatically" (as historical evidence of social injustice) and "reparatively" (as offering usable resources for beneficial social change).[16]

Such deep ambiguities raise as well some difficult questions about how these stories were received in their time. Did readers recognize such queer ambiguities when the stories were first published? It is notoriously hard to find reliable substantive evidence of how readers in the past responded to literary works; perhaps this collection will lead some of its own readers to pursue research along these lines. With respect to the contemporary reception of the stories collected here, in some cases inferences can be made on the basis of the revisions their own authors made to them, and a good many of these revisions are recorded in the notes to this volume. Walt Whitman revised "The Child's Champion" in such a way as to suggest that he grew wary of the homoerotic feelings he had dramatized, and it appears that he sought to disguise those feelings at least partly in later reprintings. On the other hand, Sarah Orne Jewett made some small but telling revisions to the ending of "Martha's Lady" between its first publication in 1897 and its next printing in 1899, changes that arguably bring its same-sex passion into higher relief. Willa Cather revised "Paul's Case" in ways that may also bear upon her careful negotiation of the cultural boundaries around queer expression. We might also infer—although it is what might be called a strong inference—that Octave Thanet never reprinted "My Lorelei" after its first rather obscure appearance because she came to rue its somewhat explicit depiction of a same-sex passion. Mark Twain never published "How Nancy Jackson Married Kate Wilson" while he was alive: is this evidence of his recognition that its content somehow violated the boundaries of acceptable erotic expression in its day? One of the most intriguing cases here is that of Bayard Taylor's "Twin-Love." On the one hand, it was published in 1871 in a completely respectable mainstream elite periodical, the *Atlantic Monthly*. Readers today will wonder quite naturally whether any of its readers then considered it queer that two twin brothers should share a bed into adulthood, profess to be emotionally sufficient unto themselves, suffer a traumatic separation when one of them marries a woman, then miraculously and happily reunite and resume their intimacy with the blessing of the wife—who contentedly dies to make their exclusive devotion once again possible. Later on, in 1936, Taylor's biographer Richmond Beatty would describe the story as "rather suspicious in its implications" and would assert inaccurately that David and Jonathan's father sensed "a more than normal intimacy between them."[17] Yet another scholar—at yet another chronological remove—would observe that "what readers of the *Atlantic* made of it can only be conjectured," judging "Twin-Love" on his own account to be "most peculiar" and averring that it skirted "the edge of suggestive sexuality."[18] Such scattered treatments of an obscure short story by a now little-known author demonstrate that at least some readers sensed—some years after its publication—at least something queer about it, even as they attested to the enduring difficulty of saying exactly what that queerness amounted to. "Twin-Love" made a strong claim in 1871 for the moral propriety and emotional beauty of the brothers' love: "It is no blame in us to love one another," David avers to his brother's wife, Ruth (169). After Ruth's death "they still walk hand in hand, still sleep upon the same pillow, still have their common wardrobe" (173–74). Taylor's story ends by invoking "the touching mystery of their nature" (174). We might well choose to respect that refusal to explain or decipher something announced as ineradicably mysterious.

It can occasionally feel today—although historical predictions are dicey—as though the modern sexual regime of homo-hetero disciplinarity is finally fading away, and that bodies and pleasures might really be reconfigured in less prescriptive ways in the impending future. In this regard these stories offer us a weird and intransigent mixture of bated hope and wary admonition.

EDITOR'S NOTE

Each of the texts included in this volume has been reproduced from its first publication, whether in a periodical or (in the case of Knapp's "The Bachelors") from its first printing in a book. The texts have not been modernized, except for the closing up of contractions (for example, *do n't, it 's, there 's,* and so on) in "The Child's Champion," "The Man Who Thought Himself a Woman," "Twin-Love," "Martha's Lady," "The Candy Country," and "Dave's Neckliss." The use of single and double quotation marks has been made consistent throughout the volume. A small number of obvious typographical errors have also been silently corrected. Illustrations, decorative titles, and ornamental typography that accompanied some of the texts in their original versions (Harte's "In the Tules," Far's "The Heart's Desire," Alcott's "The Candy Country," and Chopin's "Lilacs") have not been reproduced here.

PART I

QUEER PLACES

The Child's Champion

Walt Whitman

Just after sunset one evening in summer—that pleasant hour when the air is balmy, the light loses its glare, and all around is imbued with soothing quiet—on the door-step of a house there sat an elderly woman waiting the arrival of her son. The house was in a straggling village some fifty miles from the great city, whose spires and ceaseless clang rise up, where the Hudson pours forth its waters. She who sat on the door-step was a widow; her neat white cap covered locks of gray, and her dress though clean, was patched and exceeding homely. Her house, for the tenement she occupied was her own, was very little, and very old. Trees clustered around it so thickly as almost to hide its color—that blackish gray color which belongs to old wooden houses that have never been painted; and to get to it, you had to enter a little ricketty gate, and walk through a short path, bordered by carrot-beds, and beets, and other vegetables. The son whom she was expecting was her only child. About a year before, he had been bound apprentice to a rich farmer in the place, and after finishing his daily tasks, he was in the habit of spending half an hour at his mother's. On the present occasion, the shadows of the night had settled heavily before the youth made his appearance; when he did, his walk was slow and dragging, and all his motions were languid, as if from great weariness. He opened the gate, came through the path, and sat down by his mother in silence.

"You are sullen, to-night, Charley," said the widow, after a minute's pause, when she found that he returned no answer to her greetings. As she spoke, she put her hand fondly on his head; it was as wet as if it had been dipped in the water. His shirt, too, was soaked; and as she passed her fingers down his shoulder, she felt a sharp twinge in her heart, for she knew that moisture to be the hard wrung sweat of severe toil, exacted from her young child, (he was but twelve years old,) by an unyielding task-master.

"You have worked hard to-day, my son."

"I've been mowing."

The widow's heart felt another pang. "Not all day, Charley?" she said in a low voice, and there was a slight quiver in it.

"Yes, mother, all day," replied the boy; "Mr. Ellis said he couldn't afford to hire men, for wages is so high. I've swung the scythe ever since an hour before sunrise. Feel of my hands." There were blisters on them like great lumps.

Tears started in the widow's eyes. She dared not trust herself with a reply, though her heart was bursting with the thought that she could not better his condition. There was no earthly means of support on which she had dependence enough to encourage her child in the wish she knew was coming; the wish—not uttered for the first time—to be freed from his bondage.

"Mother," at length said the boy, "I can stand it no longer. I cannot and will not stay at Mr. Ellis's. Ever since the day I first went into his house, I've been a slave, and if I have to work there much longer, I know I shall run away, and go to sea, or somewhere else. I'd as lieve be in my grave as there." And the child burst into a passionate fit of weeping.

His mother was silent, for she was in deep grief herself. After some minutes had flown, however, she gathered sufficient self-possession to speak to her son in a soothing tone, endeavoring to win him from his sorrows, and cheer up his heart. She told him that time was swift; that in the course of years he would be his own master; that all people had their troubles; with other ready arguments, which though they had little effect in calming her own distress, she hoped would act as a so-lace on the disturbed temper of the boy. And as the half hour to which he was limited had now elapsed, she took him by the hand and led him to the gate to set forth on his return. The child seemed pacified, though occasionally one of those convulsive sighs that remain after a fit of weeping, would break from his throat. At the gate, he threw his arms round his mother's neck; each pressed a long kiss on the lips of the other, and the youngster bent his steps toward his master's house.

As her child passed out of sight, the widow returned, shut the gate, and entered her lonesome room. There was no light in the old cottage that night; the heart of its occupant was dark and cheerless. Sore agony, and grief, and tears, and convulsive wrestlings were there. The thought of a beloved son condemned to labor—labor that would bend down a man—struggling from day to day under the hard rule of a soulless gold-worshipper; the knowledge that years must pass thus; the sickening idea of her own poverty, and of living mainly on the grudged charity of neighbors—these racked the widow's heart, and made her bed a sleepless one. O, you, who, living in plenty and peace, fret at some little misfortune or some trifling disappointment—behold this spectacle, and blush at your unmanliness! Little do you know of the dark trials (compared to yours as night's great veil to a daylight cloud) that are still going on around you; the pangs of hunger—the faintness of the soul at seeing those we love trampled down, without our having the power to aid them—the wasting away of the body in sickness incurable—and those dull achings of the heart when the consciousness comes upon the poor man's mind, that while he lives he will in all probability live in want and wretchedness.

The boy bent his steps to his employer's as has been said. In his way down the village street, he had to pass a public house, the only one the place contained; and when he came off against it, he heard the sound of a fiddle, drowned however at intervals by much laughter and talking. The windows were up; and, the house standing close to the road, Charles thought it would be no harm to take a look and see what was going on within. Half-a-dozen foot-steps brought him to the low casement, on which he leaned his elbow, and where he had a full view of the room and its occupants. In one corner was an old man known in the village as Black Dave: he it was whose musical performances had a moment before drawn Charles's attention to the tavern; and he it was who now exerted himself in a most violent manner to give, with divers flourishes and extra twangs, a tune popular among that thick-lipped race whose fondness for melody is so well known. In the middle of the room were five or six sailors, some of them quite drunk, and others in the earlier stages of that process; while on benches around were more sailors, and here and there a person dressed in landsmen's attire, but hardly behind the sea-gentlemen in uproariousness and mirth. The individuals in the middle of the room were dancing—that is, they were going through certain contortions and shufflings, varied occasionally by exceeding hearty stamps upon the sanded floor. In short, the whole party were engaged in a drunken frolic, which was in no respect different from a thousand other drunken frolics, except perhaps that there was less than the ordinary amount of anger and quarrelling. Indeed, every one seemed in remarkably good humor. But what excited the boy's attention more than any other object, was an individual seated on one of the benches opposite, who though evidently enjoying the spree as much as if he were an old hand at such business, seemed in every other particular to be far out of his element. His appearance was youthful; he might have been twenty-one or two. His countenance was intelligent—and had the air of city life and society. He was dressed not gaudily, but in all respects fashionably, his coat being of the finest black broadcloth, his linen delicate and spotless as snow, and his whole aspect a counterpart to those which may be nightly seen in the dress circles of our most respectable theatres. He laughed and talked with the rest; and it must be confessed his jokes, like the most of those that passed current there, were by no means distinguished for their refinement or purity. Near the door, was a small table covered with decanters, and with glasses, some of which had been used but were used again indiscriminately, and a box of very thick and long cigars.

"Come, boys," said one of the sailors, taking advantage of a momentary pause in the hubbub to rap his enormous knuckles on the table, and call attention to himself; the gentleman in question had but one eye, and two most extensive whiskers. "Come, boys, let's take a drink, I know you're all a getting dry, so curse me if you shant have a suck at my expense."

This polite invitation was responded to by a general moving of the company toward the little table, holding the before-mentioned decanters and glasses. Clustering there around, each gentleman helped himself to a very respectable portion of that particular liquor which suited his fancy; and steadiness and accuracy being at that time by no means distinguishing traits of the arms and legs of the party, a goodly amount of fluid was spilled upon the floor. This piece of extravagance excited the ire of the personage who was treating; and his anger was still further increased when he discovered two or three loiterers who seemed disposed to slight his civil request to drink.

"Walk up boys, walk up. Don't let there be any skulkers among us, or blast my eyes if he shant go down on his marrow bones and gobble up the rum we've spilt. Hallo!" he exclaimed, as he spied Charles, "Hallo! you chap in the window, come here and take a sup."

As he spoke, he stepped to the open casement, put his brawny hands under the boy's armpits, and lifted him into the room bodily.

"There, my lads," he said to his companions, "there's a new recruit for you. Not so coarse a one either," he added as he took a fair view of the boy, who, though not what is called pretty, was fresh, and manly looking, and large for his age.

"Come youngster, take a glass," he continued; and he poured one nearly full of strong brandy.

Now Charles was not exactly frightened, for he was a lively fellow and had often been at the country merry-makings, and with the young men of the place who were very fond of him; but he was certainly rather abashed at his abrupt introduction to the midst of strangers. So, putting the glass aside, he looked up with a pleasant smile in his new acquaintance's face.

"I've no need of anything now," he said, "but I'm just as much obliged to you as if I was."

"Poh! man, drink it down," rejoined the sailor; "drink it down, it won't hurt you." And by way of showing its excellence, the one-eyed worthy drained it himself to the very last drop. Then filling it again he renewed his hospitable efforts to make the lad go through the same operation.

"I've no occasion; beside, it makes my head ache, and I have promised my mother not to drink any," was the boy's answer.

A little irritated by his continued refusals, the sailor, with a loud oath, declared that Charles should swallow the brandy whether he would or no. Placing one of his tremendous paws on the back of the boy's head, with the other he thrust the edge of the glass to his lips, swearing at the same time, that if he shook it so as to spill its contents, the consequences would be of a nature by no means agreeable to his back and shoulders. Disliking the liquor, and angry at the attempt to overbear him, the undaunted child lifted his hand and struck the arm of the sailor with a blow so sudden, that the glass fell and was smashed to pieces on the floor, while the liquid was about equally divided between the face of Charles, the clothes of the sailor, and the sand. By this time the whole of the company had their attention drawn to the scene. Some of them laughed when they saw Charles' undisguised antipathy to the drink; but they laughed still more heartily when he discomfited the sailor. All of them, however, were content to let the matter go as chance would have it—all but the young man of the black coat, who had before been spoken of. Why was it that from the first moment of seeing him, the young man's heart had moved with a strange feeling of kindness toward the boy? He felt anxious to know more of him—he felt that he should love him. O, it is passing wondrous, how in the hurried walks of life and business, we meet with young beings, strangers, who seem to touch the fountains of our love, and draw forth their swelling waters. The wish to love and to be beloved, which the forms of custom, and the engrossing anxiety for gain, so generally smother, will sometimes burst forth in spite of all obstacles; and, kindled by one, who, till the hour was unknown to us, will burn with a lovely and a pure brightness. No scrap is this of sentimental fiction; ask your own heart, reader, and your own memory, for endorsement to its truth.

Charles stood, his cheek flushed and his heart throbbing, wiping the trickling drops from his face with a handkerchief. At first, the sailor, between his drunkenness and his surprise, was pretty much in the condition of one who is suddenly awakened out of a deep sleep, and cannot call his consciousness about him. When he saw the state of things however, and heard the jeering laugh of his companions, his dull eye, lighting up with anger, fell upon the boy who had withstood him. He seized the child with a grip of iron; he bent Charles half way over, and with the side of his heavy foot, gave him a sharp and solid kick. He was about repeating the performance, for the child hung like a rag in his grasp; but all of a sudden his ears rang as if pistols had snapped close to them; lights of various hues flickered in his eye, (he had but one, it must be remembered,) and a strong propelling power, caused him to move from his position, and keep moving until he was brought up by the wall. A blow—a cuff, given in such a scientific and effectual manner, that the hand from which it came was evidently no stranger to the pugilistic art—had been suddenly planted on the ear of the sailor. It was planted by the young stranger of the black coat. He had watched with interest the proceedings of the sailor and the boy: two or three times he was on the point of interfering, but when he witnessed the kick, his rage was uncontrollable. He sprung from his seat like a mad tiger. Assuming, unconsciously, however, the attitude of a boxer, he struck the sailor in a manner to cause those unpleasant sensations just described; and he would probably have followed up his attack in a method by no means consistent with the sailor's personal ease, had not Charles, now thoroughly terrified, clung round his leg, and prevented his advancing. The scene was a strange one, and for a moment quite a silent one. The company had started from their seats and held startled but quiet positions; in the middle of the room stood the young man, in his not at all ungraceful posture, every nerve strained, and his eyes flashing very brilliantly. He seemed to be rooted like a rock, and clasping him with an appearance of confidence in his protection, hung the boy.

"Dare! you scoundrel!" cried the young man, his voice thick with agitation; "dare to touch this boy again, and I'll batter you till no sense is left in your body."

The sailor, now partially recovered, made some gestures from which it might be inferred that he resented this ungenteel treatment.

"Come on, drunken brute!" continued the angry youth; "I wish you would—you've not had half what you deserve."

Upon sobriety and sense more fully taking their seats in the brain of the one-eyed mariner, however, that worthy determined in his own mind, that it would be most prudent to let the matter drop. Expressing, therefore, his conviction to that effect, adding certain remarks to the purport that he "meant no harm to the lad," that he was surprised at such a gentleman getting so "up about a little piece of fun," and so forth. He proposed that the company should go on with their jollity just as if nothing had happened. In truth, he of the single eye was not a bad hearted fellow; the fiery enemy, whose advances he had so often courted that night, had stolen away his good feelings, and set busy devils at work within him, that might have made his hands do some dreadful deed, had not the stranger interfered.

In a few minutes the frolic of the party was upon its former footing. The young man sat down on one of the benches, with the boy by his side; and, while the rest were loudly laughing and talking, they two held communion together. The stranger learned from Charles all the particulars of his simple story—how his father had died years since—how his mother had worked hard for a bare living, and how he himself for many dreary months had been the bond-child of a hard-hearted, avaricious master. More and more interested, drawing the child close to his side, the young man listened to his plainly told history; and thus an hour passed away. It was now past midnight. The young man told Charles that on the morrow he would take steps to have him liberated from his servitude; for the present night, he said, it would perhaps be best for the boy to stay and share his bed at the inn; and little persuading did the child need to do so. As they retired to sleep, very pleasant thoughts filled the mind of the young man; thoughts of a worthy action performed; of unsullied affection; thoughts, too—newly awakened ones—of walking in a steadier and wiser path than formerly. All his imaginings seemed to be interwoven with the youth who lay by his side; he folded his arms around him, and, while he slept, the boy's cheek rested on his bosom. Fair were those two creatures in their unconscious beauty—glorious, but yet how differently glorious! One of them was innocent and sinless of all wrong; the other—O to that other, what evil had not been present, either in action or to his desires!

Who was the stranger? To those who, from ties of relationship or otherwise, felt an interest in him, the answer to such a question was not a pleasant theme to dwell upon. His name was Lankton—parentless—a dissipated young man—a brawler—one whose too frequent companions were rowdies, black-legs, and swindlers. The New-York police officers were not altogether strangers to his countenance; and certain reporters who note the transactions there, had more than once received gratuities for leaving out his name from the disgraceful notoriety of their columns. He had been bred to the profession of medicine: beside that, he had a very respectable income, and his house was in a pleasant street on the west side of the city. Little of his time, however, did Mr. John Lankton spend at his domestic hearth; and the elderly lady who officiated as housekeeper was by no means surprised to have him gone for a week or a month at a time, and she knowing nothing of his whereabout. Living as he did, the young man was an unhappy being. It was not so much that his associates were below his own capacity, for Lankton, though sensible and well-bred, was by no means talented or refined—but that he lived without any steady purpose—that he had no one to attract him to his home—that he too easily allowed himself to be tempted—which caused his life to be of late one continued scene of dissatisfaction. This dissatisfaction he sought to drive away (oh! foolish youth!) by mixing in all kinds of parties and places where the object was pleasure. On the present occasion, he had left the city a few days before, and was passing the time at a place near the village where Charles and his mother lived. He had that day fallen in with those who were his companions in the tavern spree—and thus it happened that they were all together; for Lankton hesitated not to make himself at home with any associates that suited his fancy.

The next morning, the poor widow rose from her sleepless cot, and from that lucky trait in our nature which makes one extreme follow another, she set about her daily toil with a lightened heart. Ellis, the farmer, rose too, short as the nights were, an hour before day; for his God was gain, and a prime article of his creed was to get as much work as possible from every one around him. He roused up all his people, and finding that Charles had not been home the preceeding night, he muttered threats against him, and calling a messenger, to whom he hinted that any minutes which he stayed beyond a most exceeding short period, would be subtracted from his breakfast time, dispatched him to the widow's to find what was her son about.

What was he about? With one of the brightest and earliest rays of the warm sun a gentle angel entered his apartment, and hovering over the sleepers on invisible wings, looked down with a pleasant smile and blessed them. Then noiselessly taking a stand by the bed, the angel bent over the boy's face, and whispered strange words into his ear: thus it came that he had beautiful visions. No sound was heard but the slight breathing of those who slumbered there in each others arms; and the angel paused a moment, and smiled another and a doubly sweet smile as he drank in the scene with his large soft eyes. Bending over again to the boy's lips, he touched them with a kiss, as the languid wind touches a flower. He seemed to be going now—and yet he lingered. Twice or thrice he bent over the brow of the young man—and went not. Now the angel was troubled; for he would have pressed the young man's forehead with a kiss, as he did the child's; but a spirit from the Pure Country, who touches anything tainted by evil thoughts, does it at the risk of having his breast pierced with pain, as with a barbed arrow. At that moment a very pale bright ray of sunlight darted through the window and settled on the young man's features. Then the beautiful spirit knew that permission was granted him: so he softly touched the young man's face with his, and silently and swiftly wafted himself away on the unseen air.

In the course of the day Ellis was called upon by young Lankton, and never perhaps in his life was the farmer more puzzled than at the young man's proposals—his desire to provide for a boy who could do him no pecuniary good—and his willingness to disburse money for that purpose. In that department of Ellis's structure where the mind was, or ought to have been situated, there never had entered the slightest thought assimilating to those which actuated the young man in his proceedings in this business. Yet Ellis was a church member and a county officer.

The widow too, was called upon, not only that day, but the next and the next.

It needs not to particularize the subsequent events of Lankton's and the boy's history: how the reformation of the profligate might be dated to begin from that time; how he gradually severed the guilty ties that had so long galled him—how he enjoyed his own home, and loved to be there, and why he loved to be there; how the close knit love of the boy and him grew not slack with time; and how, when at length he became head of a family of his own, he would shudder when he thought of his early danger and escape.

Loved reader, own you the moral of this simple story? Draw it forth—pause a moment, ere your eye wanders to a more bright and eloquent page—and dwell upon it.

A South-Sea Idyl

Charles Warren Stoddard

There was a little brown rain-cloud, that blew over in about three minutes; and Bolabola's thatched hut was dry as a hay-stack in less than half that time. Those tropical sprays are not much, anyhow; so I lounged down into the banana patch, for I thought I saw something white there—something white and fluttering—moving about. I knew pretty well what it was, and didn't go after it on an uncertainty.

The Doctor looked savage. Whenever he slung those saddle-bags over his left shoulder, and swung his right arm clean out from his body, like the regulator of a steam-engine, you might know that his steam was pretty well up. I turned to look back, as he was strapping up his beast of burden, till the poor animal's body was positively waspish; then he climbed into his saddle, and sullenly plunged down the trail toward the precipice, and never said "Good-by," or "God bless you," or any of those harmless tags that come in so well when you don't know how to cut off your last words.

I solemnly declare—and this without malice—the Doctor was perfectly savage.

Now, do you know what demoralized that Doctor?—how we came to a misunderstanding?—or why we parted company? It was simply because here was a glorious valley, a mild, half-civilized people, who seemed to love me at first sight. I don't believe I disliked them, either. Well! they asked me to stop with them, and I felt just like it. I wanted to stop and be natural; but the Doctor thought otherwise of my intentions—and that was the row.

The next thing I knew, the Doctor had got up the great precipice, and I was quite alone with two hundred dusky fellows, only two of whom could speak a syllable of English, and I the only representative of the superior white within twenty miles. Alone with cannibals— perhaps they were cannibals. They had magnificent teeth, at any rate, and could bite through an inch and a half sugar-cane, and not break a jaw.

For the first time that summer, I began to moralize a little. Was it best to have kicked against the Doctor's judgment? Perhaps not! But it is best to be careful how you begin to moralize too early: you deprive yourself of a great deal of fun in that way. If you want to do any thing particularly, I should advise you to do it, and then be sufficiently sorry to make it all square.

I'm not so sure that I was wrong, after all. Fate, or the Doctor, or something else, brought me first to this loveliest of valleys, so shut out from every thing but itself, that there were no temptations which might not be satisfied. Well! here, as I was looking about at the singular love-liness of the place—you know this was my first glimpse of it; its abrupt walls, hung with tapestries of fern and clambering convolvulus; at one end two exquisite water-falls, rivaling one another in whiteness and airiness—at the other the sea, the real South Sea, breaking and foam-ing over a genuine reef, even rippling the placid current of the river, that slipped quietly down to its embracing tide from the deep basins at these water-falls—right in the midst of all this, before I had been ten minutes in the valley, I saw a straw hat, bound with wreaths of fern and *maile;* under it a snow-white garment, rather short all around, low in the neck, and with no sleeves whatever.

There was no sex to that garment; it was the spontaneous offspring of a scant material and a large necessity. I'd seen plenty of that sort of thing, but never upon a model like this, so entirely tropical—almost Oriental. As this singular phenomenon made directly for me, and hav-ing come within reach, there stopped and stayed, I asked its name, using one of my seven stock phrases for the purpose; I found it was called Kana-ana. Down it went into my note-book; for I knew I was to have an experience with this young scion of a race of chiefs. Sure enough, I have had it. He continued to regard me steadily, without embarrassment. He seated himself before me; I felt myself at the mercy of one whose calm analysis was questioning every motive of my soul. This sage inquirer was, perhaps, sixteen years old. His eye was so earnest and so honest, I could return his look. I saw a round, full, rather girlish face; lips ripe and expressive—not quite so sensual as those of most of his race; not a bad nose, by any means; eyes perfectly glorious—regular almonds—with the mythical lashes "that sweep," etc., etc. The smile which presently transfigured his face was of that nature that flatters you into submission against your will.

Having weighed me in his balance—and you may be sure his instincts didn't cheat him (they don't do that sort of thing)—he placed his two hands on my two knees, and declared, "I was his best friend, as he was mine; I must come at once to his house, and there live always with him." What could I do but go? He pointed me to his lodge, across the river, saying, "There was his home, and mine." By this time, my *native* without a master was quite exhausted. I wonder what would have happened if some one hadn't come to my rescue, just at that moment of trial, with a fresh vocabulary? As it was, we settled the matter at once. This was our little plan—an entirely private arrangement between Kana-ana and myself: I was to leave with the Doctor, in an hour; but, at the expiration of a week, we should both return hither; then I would stop with him, and the Doctor could go on!

There was an immense amount of secrecy, and many vows, and I was almost crying, when the Doctor hurried me up that terrible precipice, and we lost sight of the beautiful valley. Kana-ana swore he would watch continually for my return, and I vowed I'd hurry back: and so we parted. Looking down from the heights, I thought I could distinguish his white garment; at any rate, I knew the little fellow was somewhere about, feeling as miserably as I felt—and nobody has any business to feel worse. How many times I thought of him through the week! I was always wondering if he still thought of me. I had found those natives to be impulsive, demonstrative, and, I feared, inconstant. Yet why should he forget me, having so little to remember in his idle life, while I could still think of him, and put aside a hundred pleasant memories for his sake? The whole island was a delight to me. I often wondered if I should ever again behold such a series of valleys, hills, and highlands in so small a compass. That land is a world in miniature, the dearest spot of which, to me, was that secluded valley; for there was a young soul watching for my return.

That was rather a slow week for me, but it ended finally; and just at sunset, on the day appointed, the Doctor and I found ourselves back on the edge of the valley. I looked all up and down its green expanse, regarding every living creature, in the hope of discovering Kana-ana in the attitude of the watcher. I let the Doctor ride ahead of me on the trail to Bolabola's hut, and it was quite in the twilight when I heard the approach of a swift horseman. I turned, and at that moment there was a collision of two constitutions that were just fitted for one another; and all the doubts and apprehensions of the week just over were indignantly dismissed, for Kana-ana and I were one and inseparable, which was perfectly satisfactory to both parties!

The plot, which had been thickening all the week, culminated then, much to the disgust of the Doctor, who had kept his watchful eye upon me all these days—to my advantage, as he supposed. There was no disguising our project any longer, so I out with it as mildly as possible. "There was a dear fellow here," I said, "who loved me, and wanted me to live with him; all his people wanted me to stop, also; his mother and his grandmother had specially desired it. They didn't care for money; they had much love for me, and therefore implored me to stay a little. Then the valley was most beautiful; I was tired; after our hard riding, I needed rest; his mother and his grandmother assured me that I needed rest. Now, why not let me rest here awhile?"

The Doctor looked very grave. I knew that he misunderstood me—placed a wrong interpretation upon my motives; the worse for him, I say. He tried to talk me over to the paths of virtue and propriety; but I wouldn't be talked over. Then the final blast was blown: war was declared at once. The Doctor never spoke again, but to abuse me; and off he rode in high dudgeon, and the sun kept going down on his wrath. Thereupon I renounced all the follies of this world, actually hating civilization—feeling entirely above the formalities of society. I resolved on the spot to be a barbarian, and, perhaps, dwell forever and ever in this secluded spot. And here I am back to the beginning of this story, just after the shower at Bolabola's hut, as the Doctor rode off alone and in anger.

That resolution was considerable for me to make. I found, by the time the Doctor was out of sight and I was quite alone, with the natives regarding me so curiously, that I was very tired, indeed. So Kana-ana brought up his horse, got me on to it in some way or other, and mounted behind me to pilot the animal and sustain me in my first bareback act. Over the sand we went, and through the river to his hut, where I was taken in, fed and petted in every possible way, and finally put to bed, where Kana-ana monopolized me, growling in true savage fashion if any one came near me. I didn't sleep much, after all. I think I must have been excited. I thought how strangely I was situated: alone in a wilderness, among barbarians; my bosom friend, who was hugging me like a young bear, not able to speak one syllable of English, and I very shaky on a few bad phrases in his tongue. We two lay upon an enormous old-fashioned bed with high posts—very high they seemed to me in the dim rushlight. The natives always burn a small light after dark; some superstition or other prompts it. The bed, well stocked with pillows, or cushions, of various sizes, covered with bright-colored chintz, was hung about with numerous shawls, so that I might be dreadfully modest behind them. It was quite a grand affair, gotten up expressly for my benefit. The rest of the house—all in one room, as usual—was covered with mats, on which various recumbent forms and several individual snores betrayed the proximity of Kana-ana's relatives. How queer the whole atmosphere of the place was! The heavy beams of the house were of some rare wood, which, being polished, looked like colossal sticks of pea-nut candy. Slender canes were bound across this frame-work, and the soft, dried grass of the meadows was braided over it—all completing our tenement, and making it as fresh and sweet as new-mown hay.

The natives have a passion for perfumes. Little bunches of sweet-smelling herbs hung in the peak of the roof, and wreaths of fragrant berries were strung in various parts of the house. I found our bed-posts festooned with them in the morning. Oh! that bed. It might have come from England in the Elizabethan era and been wrecked off the coast; hence the mystery of its presence. It was big enough for a Mormon. There was a little opening in the room opposite our bed: you might call it a window, I suppose. The sun, shining through it, made our tent of shawls perfectly gorgeous in crimson light, barred and starred with gold. I lifted our bed-curtain and watched the rocks through this window—the shining rocks, with the sea leaping above them in the sun. There were cocoa-palms so slender they seemed to cast no shadow, while their fringed leaves glistened like frost-work as the sun glanced over them. A bit of cliff, also, remote and misty, running far into the sea, was just visible from my pyramid of pillows. I wondered what more I could ask for to delight the eye. Kana-ana was still asleep, but he never let loose his hold on me, as though he feared his pale-faced friend would fade away from him. He lay close by me. His sleek figure, supple and graceful in repose, was the embodiment of free, untrammeled youth. You who are brought up under cover, know nothing of its luxuriousness. How I longed to take him over the sea with me, and show him something of life as we find it. Thinking upon it, I dropped off into one of those delicious morning naps. I awoke again presently: my companion-in-arms was the occasion this time. He had awakened, stolen softly away, resumed his single garment—said garment and all others he considered superfluous after dark—and had prepared for me, with his own hands, a breakfast, which he now declared to me, in violent and suggestive pantomime, was all ready to be eaten. It was not a bad bill of fare: fresh fish, taro, poe, and goat's milk. I ate as well as I could, under the circumstances. I found that Robinson Crusoe must have had some tedious rehearsals before he acquired that perfect resignation to Providence which delights us in book form. There was a veritable and most unexpected table-cloth for me alone. I do not presume to question the nature of its miraculous appearance. Dishes there were—still, dishes, if you're not particular as to shape or completeness; forks, with a prong or two—a bent and abbreviated prong or two; knives that had survived their handles; and one solitary spoon. All these were tributes of the two generous people, who, for the first time in their lives, were at the inconvenience of entertaining a distinguished stranger. Hence this reckless display of table-ware. I ate as well as I could, but surely not enough to satisfy my crony; for, when I had finished eating, he sat about two hours in deep and depressing silence, at the expiration of which time, he suddenly darted off on his bareback steed and was gone till dark, when he returned with a fat mutton slung over his animal. Now, mutton doesn't grow wild thereabout, neither were his relatives shepherds; consequently, in eating, I asked no questions, for conscience' sake.

The series of entertainments offered me were such as the little valley had not known for years: canoe rides up and down the winding stream, bathings in the sea and in the river, and in every possible bit of water, at all possible hours; expeditions into the recesses of the mountains, to the water-falls that plunged into cool basins of fern and cresses, and to the orange grove, through acres and acres of guava orchards; some climbings up the precipices; goat hunting, once or twice, as far as a solitary cavern, said to be haunted—these tramps always by daylight; then a new course of bathings and sailings, interspersed with monotonous singing and occasional smokes under the eaves of the hut at evening.

If it is a question how long a man may withstand the seductions of nature, and the consolations and conveniences of the state of nature, I have solved it in one case; for I was as natural as possible in about three days.

I wonder if I was growing to feel more at home, or more hungry, that I found an appetite at last equal to any table that was offered me? Chickens were added to my already bountiful rations, nicely cooked by being swathed in a broad, succulent leaf, and roasted or steeped in hot ashes. I ate it with my fingers, using the leaf for a platter.

Almost every day, something new was offered at the door for my edification. Now, a net full of large guavas or mangoes, or a sack of leaves crammed with most delicious oranges from the mountains, that seemed to have absorbed the very dew of heaven—they were so fresh and sweet. Immense lemons perfumed the house, waiting to make me a capital drink. Those superb citrons, with their rough, golden crusts, refreshed me. Cocoa-nuts were heaped at the door; and yams, grown miles away, were sent for, so that I might be satisfied. All these additions to my table were the result of long and vigorous arguments between the respective heads of the house. I detected trouble and anxiety in their expressive faces. I picked out a word, here and there, which betrayed their secret sorrow. No assertions, no remonstrances on my part, had the slightest effect upon the poor souls who believed I was starving. Eat I must, at all hours and in all places; and eat, moreover, before they would touch a mouthful. So nature teaches her children a hospitality which all the arts of the capital can not affect.

I wonder what it was that finally made me restless and eager to see new faces? Perhaps my unhappy disposition, that urged me thither, and then lured me back to the pride of life and the glory of the world. Certain I am that Kana-ana never wearied me with his attentions, though they were incessant. Day and night he was by me. When he was silent, I knew he was conceiving some surprise in the shape of a new fruit, or a new view to beguile me. I was, indeed, beguiled; I was growing to like the little heathen altogether too well. What should I do when I was at last compelled to return out of my seclusion, and find no soul so faithful and loving in all the earth beside? Day by day, this thought grew upon me, and with it I realized the necessity of a speedy departure.

There were those in the world I could still remember with that exquisitely painful pleasure that is the secret of true love. Those still voices seemed incessantly calling me, and something in my heart answered them of its own accord. How strangely idle the days had grown! We used to lie by the hour—Kana-ana and I—watching a strip of sand on which a wild poppy was nodding in the wind. This poppy seemed to me typical of their life in the quiet valley. Living only to occupy so much space in the universe, it buds, blossoms, goes to seed, dies, and is forgotten.

These natives do not even distinguish the memory of their great dead, if they ever had any. It was the legend of some mythical god that Kana-ana told me, and of which I could not understand a twentieth part; a god whose triumphs were achieved in an age beyond the comprehension of the very people who are delivering its story, by word of mouth, from generation to generation. Watching the sea was a great source of amusement with us. I discovered in our long watches that there is a very complicated and magnificent rhythm in its solemn song. This wave that breaks upon the shore is the heaviest of a series that preceded it; and these are greater and less, alternately, every fifteen or twenty minutes. Over this dual impulse the tides prevail, while through the year there is a variation in their rise and fall. What an intricate and wonderful mechanism regulates and repairs all this!

There was an entertainment in watching a particular cliff, in a peculiar light, at a certain hour, and finding soon enough that change visited even that hidden quarter of the globe. The exquisite perfection of this moment, for instance, is not again repeated on to-morrow, or the day after, but in its stead appears some new tint or picture, which, perhaps, does not satisfy like this. That was the most distressing disappointment that came upon us there. I used to spend half an hour in idly observing the splendid curtains of our bed swing in the light air from the sea; and I have speculated for days upon the probable destiny awaiting one of those superb spiders, with a tremendous stomach and a striped waistcoat, looking a century old, as he clung tenaciously to the fringes of our canopy.

We had fitful spells of conversation upon some trivial theme, after long intervals of intense silence. We began to develop symptoms of imbecility. There was laughter at the least occurrence, though quite barren of humor; also, eating and drinking to pass the time; bathing to make one's self cool, after the heat and drowsiness of the day. So life flowed out in an unruffled current, and so the prodigal lived riotously and wasted his substance. There came a day when we promised ourselves an actual occurrence in our Crusoe life. Some one had seen a floating object far out at sea. It might be a boat adrift; and, in truth, it looked very like a boat. Two or three canoes darted off through the surf to the rescue, while we gathered on the rocks, watching and ruminating. It was long before the rescuers returned, and then they came empty-handed. It was only a log after all, drifted, probably, from America. We talked it all over, there by the shore, and went home to renew the subject; it lasted us a week or more, and we kept harping upon it till that log—drifting slowly, O, how slowly! from the far mainland to our island—seemed almost to overpower me with a sense of the unutterable loneliness of its voyage. I used to lie and think about it, and get very solemn, indeed; then Kana-ana would think of some fresh appetizer or other, and try to make me merry with good feeding. Again and again he would come with a delicious banana to the bed where I was lying, and insist upon my gorging myself, when I had but barely recovered from a late orgie of fruit, flesh, or fowl. He would mesmerize me into a most refreshing sleep with a prolonged and pleasing manipulation. It was a reminiscence of the baths of Stamboul not to be withstood. Out of the sleep I would presently be wakened by Kana-ana's performance upon a rude sort of harp, that gave out a weird and eccentric music. The mouth being applied to the instrument, words were pronounced in a guttural voice, while the fingers twanged the strings in measure. It was a flow of monotones, shaped into legends and lyrics. I liked it amazingly; all the better, perhaps, that it was as good as Greek to me, for I understood it as little as I understood the strange and persuasive silence of that beloved place, which seemed slowly, but surely weaving a spell of enchantment about me. I resolved to desert peremptorily, and managed to hire a canoe and a couple of natives, to cross the channel with me. There were other reasons for this prompt action.

Hour by hour I was beginning to realize one of the inevitable results of Time. My boots were giving out; their best sides were the uppers, and their soles had about left them. As I walked, I could no longer disguise this pitiful fact. It was getting hard on me, especially on the gravel. Yet, regularly each morning, my pieces of boot were carefully oiled, then rubbed, or petted, or coaxed into some sort of a polish, which was a labor of love. Oh, Kana-ana! how could you wring my soul with those touching offices of friendship!—those kindnesses unfailing, unsurpassed!

Having resolved to sail early in the morning, before the drowsy citizens of the valley had fairly shaken the dew out of their forelocks, all that day—my last with Kana-ana—I breathed about me silent benedictions and farewells. I could not begin to do enough for Kana-ana, who was, more than ever, devoted to me. He almost seemed to mistrust our sudden separation, for he clung to me with a sort of subdued desperation. That was the day he took from his head his hat—a very neat one, plaited by his mother—insisting that I should wear it, (mine was quite in tatters) while he went bare-headed in the sun. That hat hangs in my room now, the only tangible relic of my prodigal days. My plan was to steal off at dawn, while he slept—to awaken my native crew, and escape to sea before my absence was detected. I dared not trust a parting with him, before the eyes of the valley. Well, I managed to wake and rouse my sailor boys. To tell the truth, I didn't sleep a wink that night. We launched the canoe, entered, put off, and had safely mounted the second big roller just as it broke under us with terrific power, when I heard a shrill cry above the roar of the waters. I knew the voice and its import. There was Kana-ana rushing madly toward us; he had discovered all, and couldn't even wait for that white garment, but ran after us like one gone daft, and plunged into the cold sea, calling my name, over and over, as he fought the breakers. I urged the natives forward. I knew if he overtook us, I should never be able to escape again. We fairly flew over the water. I saw him rise and fall with the swell, looking like a seal, for it was his second nature, this surf-swimming. I believe in my heart I wished the paddles would break or the canoe split on the reef, though all the time I was urging the rascals forward; and they, like stupids, took me at my word. They couldn't break a paddle, or get on the reef, or have any sort of an accident. Presently we rounded the headland—the same hazy point I used to watch from the grass house, through the little window, of a sunshiny morning. There we lost sight of the valley and the grass house, and every thing that was associated with the past—but that was nothing. We lost sight of the little sea-god, Kana-ana, shaking the spray from his forehead like a porpoise; and this was all in all. I didn't care for any thing else after that, or any body else, either. I went straight home and got civilized again, or partly so, at least. I've never seen the Doctor since, and never want to. He had no business to take me there, or leave me there. I couldn't make up my mind to stay; yet, I'm always dying to go back again.

So I grew tired over my husks: I arose and went unto my father. I wanted to finish up the Prodigal business: I ran and fell upon his neck and kissed him, and said unto him: "Father, *if* I have sinned against Heaven and in thy sight, I'm afraid I don't care much. Don't kill any thing: I don't want any calf. Take back the ring, I don't deserve it; for I'd give more this minute to see that dear, little, velvet-skinned, coffee-colored Kana-ana, than any thing else in the wide world—because he hates business, and so do I. He's a regular brick, father, molded of the purest clay, and baked in God's sunshine. He's about half sunshine himself; and, above all others, and more than any one else ever can, he loved your Prodigal."

The Haunted Valley

Ambrose Bierce

A half-mile north from Jo. Dunfer's, on the road from Hutton's to Mexican Hill, the highway dips into a sunless ravine, which opens out on either hand, in a half-confidential manner, as if it had a secret to impart at some more convenient season. I never used to ride through it without looking first to the one side and then to the other, to see if the time had arrived for the promised revelation. If I saw nothing—and I never did see any thing—there was no feeling of disappointment, for I knew the disclosure was merely withheld temporarily, for some good reason which I had no right to question. That I should one day be taken into full confidence, I no more doubted than I doubted the existence of Jo. Dunfer himself, through whose premises the *cañon* ran. It was said that Jo. had once undertaken to erect a cabin in some remote portion of it, but for some reason had abandoned the enterprise—almost any reason, I should think, would have been a valid one—and constructed the present hermaphrodite habitation, half residence and half groggery, upon an extreme corner of his estate; as far away as possible, as if on purpose to show how radically he had changed his mind.

This Jo. Dunfer—or, as he was familiarly known in the neighborhood, Whisky Jo.—was a very important personage in those parts. He was apparently about forty years of age, a long, shock-headed fellow, with a corded face, a gnarled arm, and a knotty hand like a bunch of prison-keys. He was a hairy man, with a stoop in his walk, like that of one who is about to spring upon something and rend it. Next to the peculiarity from which he had derived his local appellation, his most obvious characteristic was a deep-seated antipathy to the Chinese. I saw him once in a towering rage because one of his herdsmen had permitted a travel-heated Asian to slake his thirst at the horse-trough in front of the saloon end of Jo.'s establishment. I ventured to faintly remonstrate with Jo. for his unchristian spirit, but he merely replied that "ther wusn't no mention of Chinamen in the Noo Test'ment"; and strode away to wreak his anger upon his little, White man-servant, whom, I suppose, the inspired scribes had likewise neglected to mention by name. Some days afterward, finding him sitting alone in his bar-room, I cautiously approached the subject, when, greatly to my relief, the ends of his long mouth drew round into a good-natured grin, and with an air of conscious condescension, he explained:

"You youngsters are too good to live in Californy: you'd better all of ye git back to New England, fur none of ye don't understand our play. People who are born with autermatic gold spoons, nine hundred fine, a-shovelin' choice viuns into ther mouths, can afford to hang out liberary ideas about Chinagration" (by which poor Jo. meant Chinese immigration, and in which he included every thing relating to that people); "but us that has to rustle round on the outside fur our hash, hain't got no time for foolishness."

And this long consumer, who had never struck a stroke of honest work in all his life, sprung the lid of a Chinese tobacco-box, and with his thumb and forefinger forked out a wad like a miniature hay-cock. Holding this reinforcement within supporting distance, he fired away with renewed confidence:

"I tell ye, youngster, ther a bad lot, and ther agoin' fur every thing green in this country, except yourself" (here he encountered a stubborn chuckle, and pushed his reserve into the breach) "like a herd of 'Gyptian locusses! I had one of 'em to work fur me, five years ago, and I'll tell ye all about it, so't ye ken see the bearin's of this whole question.

"I didn't pan out well, them days: drank more'n wus good fur me, and hadn't no nice discriminatin' sense of my duty as a free W'ite citizen; so I got this pagan as a kind of cook, and turned off a Mexican woman—as nice a Greaser as ye ever seen. But when I got religi'n, over at the Hill, and they talked of runnin' me fur the Legislater, my eyes wus opened. But what wus I to do? If I made him sling his kit and mosey, somebody else 'd take him, and mightn't treat him well. *What wus I to do?* What 'd any Christian do, 'specially one new to the business?"

Jo. paused for a reply, with an expression of grave thoughtfulness, but an indescribable air of uneasiness; as of one who has arrived at a correct result in the solution of a problem, by some short-cut of his own, but is not quite satisfied with the method. He finally rose, and swallowed a tumblerful of bad whisky from a full bottle on the counter, and resumed his seat and his story:

"Besides, he wa'n't of no account: didn't know nothin', and wus always takin' on airs. They all do it. I stood it as long as a *riata,* but 'twa'n't no kind of use. Still, I couldn't quite make up my mind to discharge him, and I'm glad now I didn't, fur the example of what follers would 'a been lost. I'm *mighty* glad!" And Jo.'s glee was solemnly celebrated at the decanter.

"Once—'twus nigh onto five years ago, come next October fifteenth—I started in to stick up a shanty. 'Twus 'fore this 'un wus built, and in another place; it don't signify where, 'cause 'tain't of no importance. I set Ah Wee and a little W'ite, named Gopher, to cuttin' the timber. I didn't expect Ah Wee to be of much account, 'cause he wus so little, with a face 'most as fair as yourn, and big, black eyes that somehow I seem to see 'em yet."

While delivering this trenchant thrust at syntax and sense, Mr. Dunfer fixedly regarded a knot-hole in the thin board partition, as if that were one of the eyes whose size and color had incapacitated his servant for active usefulness.

"Now, you youngsters won't believe any thing ag'in' the infernal yeller devils," he suddenly flamed out, with an appearance of rage which somehow failed to impress me; "but I tell ye that that Chinaman was the perversest scoundrel you ever dreamed of!"

I was about to explain that perverse scoundrels were not a staple article in my nightly visions, when Jo. rose excitedly, dashed in another brimming tumbler of whisky, and resumed, standing:

"That miser'ble, pig-tail Mongolianer went to hewin' away at the saplin's all round the stems, girdleways. I p'inted out his error as patiently as I could, an' showed him how to cut 'em on two sides, so's to make 'em fall right; but no sooner did I turn my back onto him, like this"—and he turned it upon me, amplifying the illustration by taking in some more liquor—"than he wus at it ag'in. It wus jest this way: while I looked at him, *so*"—regarding me rather unsteadily, and with evident complexity of vision—"he wus all right; but when I looked away, *so*"—taking a long swig at the decanter—"he wus all wrong. Then I'd gaze at him reproachful-like, *so,* an' he'd reform."

Probably Mr. Dunfer honestly intended the regard he turned upon me as a merely reproachful one, but it was singularly well calculated to arouse the gravest apprehension in the breast of any unarmed person so reproached, and as I had lost all interest in his interminable narrative, I rose to go. Before I had fairly risen, he had again turned to the counter, and with a barely audible "So," had emptied the bottle at a gulp. Heavens! what a yell! It was like a Titan in his last, strong agony. Jo. staggered back after emitting it, as a cannon recoils from its own thunder, and then dropped into his chair, as if he had been stricken down like a beef—his eyes drawn sidewise toward the wall, with a stony stare that made my flesh creep on my bones. Looking in the same direction, I saw, with a quick chill of the scalp, that the knot-hole in the wall had indeed become a human eye—a full, black eye, that glared into my own with an entire lack of expression more awful than the most devilish glitter. I involuntarily covered my face with my hands, to shut out the horrible illusion, if such it was, and the little White manservant, coming into the room at that moment, broke the spell, and I walked out of the room with a sort of dazed fear that *delirium tremens* was contagious. My horse was hitched at the watering-trough, and, untying him, I mounted and gave him his head, too much troubled in mind to note whither he took me.

I did not know what to think of all this, and, like every one who does not know what to think, I thought a great deal, and, naturally, to very little purpose. The only reflection that seemed at all satisfactory, and which, singularly enough, was uppermost in my mind, was one that was not at all connected with Jo. Dunfer and his pointless narrative; and this was, that on the morrow I should be some miles away, with a strong probability of never returning.

A sudden coolness brought me out of my abstraction, and, looking up, I found myself entering the deep shadows of the ravine. The day was stifling; and this transition from the silent, visible heat of the parched fields to the cool gloom, heavy with the pungency of cedars, and vocal with the melody of the birds that had been driven to its leafy asylum, was exquisitely refreshing. I looked for my mystery, as usual, but not finding the ravine in a communicative mood, dismounted, led my sweating animal into the undergrowth, tied him securely to a tree, and sat down upon a rock to meditate. I began bravely, by analyzing my pet superstition about the haunted valley. Having resolved it into its constituent elements, I arranged them in convenient troops and squadrons, and, collecting all the forces of my logic, bore down upon them from impregnable premises with the thunder of irresistible conclusions, and a great noise of chariots and general intellectual shouting. Then, when my big mental guns had overturned all opposition, and were growling almost inaudibly away on the horizon of pure speculation, the routed enemy straggled in upon their rear, massed silently into a solid phalanx, and captured me, bag and baggage. An indefinable dread came upon me, and I rose to shake it off, and began thridding the narrow dell by an old, grass-grown cow-path that seemed to flow along the bottom, as a kind of substitute for the brook that Nature had neglected to provide.

The trees among which the path straggled were very ordinary, well-behaved plants, a trifle perverted as to bole, and eccentric as to bough, but with nothing unearthly in their general aspect. A few loose bowlders, which had detached themselves from the sides of the depression to set up an independent existence at the bottom, had dammed up the pathway, here and there, but their stony repose had nothing in it of the stillness of death. There was a kind of death-chamber hush in the valley, it is true, and a mysterious whisper above: the wind was just fingering the tops of the trees—that was all.

It is strange that in all this time I had not once thought of connecting Mr. Dunfer's drunken narrative with what I now sought; and it was only when I came upon a clear space and stumbled over the level trunks of some small trees, that the revelation came to me. This was the site of the abandoned "shanty," and the fact was the more forcibly impressed upon me by quickly noting that some of the rotting stumps were hacked all round, in a most unwoodman-like manner, while others were cut square, and the butt-ends of the corresponding trunks were hewn to that blunt wedge form which is given by the axe of a master. The opening was not more than ten yards in diameter, and upon one side was a little knoll—a natural hillock—some ten feet across, bare of shrubbery, but covered with green grass. Upon this, standing up rigidly a foot or two above the grass, was a head-stone! I have put a note of admiration here, not to indicate any surprise of my own, but that of the reader. For myself, I felt none. I regarded that lonely tombstone with something of the same feeling that Columbus must have had when he saw the hills of San Salvador. Before approaching it, I completed leisurely my survey of the stumps, and examined critically the prostrate trunks. I was even guilty of the affectation of winding my watch, at an unusual hour and with uncommon care and deliberation. Then I lighted a cigar, and found a quiet satisfaction in the delay. All these unnecessary, but only possible, preliminaries being arranged, I approached my mystery.

The grave—a rather short one—was in somewhat better repair than seemed right, considering its age and surroundings; and I actually widened my eyes at a clump of unmistakable garden-violets, showing evidence of comparatively recent watering. The stone was a rude-enough affair, and had clearly done duty once as a door-step. In its front was carved, or rather dug, an inscription, the exaggerated eccentricity of which I can not hope to reproduce without aid from the engraver. It read thus:

AH WEE—CHINAMAN.

Aig unnone. Wirkt last fur Wisky Jo. This monment is ewreckted bi the saim to keep is memmerry grean an liquize a wornin to Slestials notter take on ayres like Wites. Dammum! She wus a good eg.

It would be difficult to adequately convey my amazement at this astonishing epitaph. The meagre, but conscientious, description of the deceased, the insolent frankness of confession, the grotesque and ambiguous anathema, and last, but not least, the ludicrous transition of gender and sentiment, marked this as the production of one who must have been at least as much demented as bereaved. I felt that any further discovery would be a pitiful anti-climax, and, with an unconscious regard for dramatic effect, I turned squarely about and walked away.

"Gee-up there, old Fuddy-duddy!" This unique adjuration came from the lips of a queer little man, perched atop of a light wagonful of fire-wood, behind a brace of fat oxen, who were hauling it easily along, with a simulation of herculean effort that had evidently not imposed upon their driver. As that gentleman happened at the moment to be staring me squarely in the face, and smiting his animals at random with a long pole, it was not quite clear whether he was addressing me or one of them; or whether his beasts were named Fuddy and Duddy, and were both subjects of the imperative verb "to gee-up." Anyhow, the command produced no visible effect upon any of us, and the queer little man removed his eyes from my face long enough to spear Fuddy and Duddy alternately with his wand, remarking quietly, but with some feeling, "Dern your skin!"—as if they enjoyed that integument in common. So far, my request for a ride had elicited no further attention than I have indicated, and, finding myself falling slowly astern, I placed one foot upon the inner circumference of a hind wheel, and was slowly elevated by an aspiring spoke to a level with the hub, whence I boarded the concern, *sans cérémonie,* and scrambling forward, seated myself beside the driver—who took no notice of me until he had administered another indiscriminate castigation to his cattle, accompanied with the advice to "buckle down, you derned Incapable!" Then, while this dual incapable was, by courtesy, supposed to be reveling in the happiness of obedience to constituted authority, the master (or rather the former master, for I could not suppress a whimsical feeling that the entire establishment was my lawful prize) trained his big, black eyes upon me with an expression strangely, and somewhat unpleasantly, familiar, laid down his rod—which neither blossomed nor turned into a serpent, as I half expected—folded his arms, and gravely demanded, "W'at did you do to W'isky?"

My natural reply would have been that I drank it, but there was something about the query that suggested a hidden significance, and something about the man that did not encourage a shallow jest. And so, having no other answer ready, I merely held my tongue, but felt as if I were resting under an imputation of guilt, and that my silence was being construed into a confession. Just then a cold shadow fell upon

my cheek, and caused me to look up. We were descending into my ravine! I can not describe the sensation that came upon me: I had not
seen it since it unbosomed itself four years ago, and now I felt like one
to whom a friend has made some sorrowing confession of crime long
past, and who has basely deserted him in consequence. The old memories of Jo. Dunfer, his fragmentary revelation, and the unsatisfying
explanatory note by the head-stone, came back with singular distinctness. I wondered what had become of Jo., and—I turned sharply round
and asked my prisoner. He was intently watching his cattle, and, without withdrawing his eyes, replied:

"Gee-up, old Terrapin! He lies alongside uv Ah Wee, up the *cañon*.
Like to see it? They al'ays comes back to the spot: I've been expectin'
you. H-woa!"

At the enunciation of the aspirate, Fuddy-duddy, the incapable terrapin, came to a dead halt, and, before the echo of the vowel had died
away up the ravine, had folded up all his eight legs and lain down in
the dusty road, regardless of the effect upon his derned skin. The queer
little man slid off his seat to the ground, and started up the dell without
deigning to look back to see if I was following. But I was.

It was about the same season of the year, and at near the same
hour of the day of my last visit. The jays clamored loudly, and the trees
whispered darkly, as before; and I somehow traced in the two a fanciful analogy to the open boastfulness of Mr. Jo. Dunfer's mouth and the
mysterious reticence of his manner, and to the mingled insolence and
tenderness of his sole literary production—the Epitaph. All things in
the valley seemed unchanged, excepting the cow-path, which was almost wholly upgrown with rank weeds. When we came out into the
"clearing," however, there was change enough. Among the stumps and
trunks of the fallen saplings, those that had been hacked "China fashion" were no longer distinguishable from those that were cut "Melican
way." It was as if the Old World barbarism and the New World civilization had reconciled their differences by the arbitration of an impartial
decay—as one day they must. The knoll was there, but the Hunnish
brambles had overrun and all but obliterated its effete grasses; and the
patrician garden-violet had capitulated to his plebeian brother—or
perhaps had merely reverted to his original type. Another grave—a
long and robust mound—had been made beside the former one, which
seemed to shrink from the comparison; and in the shadow of a new

head-stone, the old one lay prone upon the ground, with its marvelous inscription wholly illegible by reason of the dead leaves drifted over it. In point of literary merit the new epitaph was altogether inferior to the old, and was even repulsive in its terse and savage jocularity. It read:

"JO. DUNFER.—DONE FOR!"

By the air of silent pride with which my guide pointed it out, I was convinced that it was a conception of his own; but I turned from it with indifference, and tenderly brushing away the leaves from the tablet of the dead pagan, restored the mocking inscription of four years ago, which seemed now, fresh from its grave of leaf-mold, to possess a certain pathos. My guide, too, appeared altered, somehow, as he looked at it, and I fancied I detected beneath his whimsical exterior a real, earnest manhood. But while I regarded him, the old far-away look, so subtly forbidding and so tantalizingly familiar, crept back into his great eyes, and repelled while it attracted. I resolved, if possible, to end this scene, and clear up my mystery:

"My friend," said I, pointing to the smaller grave, "did Jo. Dunfer murder this Chinaman?"

He was leaning against a tree, and looking across the little clearing into the top of another, or through it into the sky beyond, I don't know which. He never moved a muscle of his body, nor trembled an eyelash, as he slowly replied:

"No, sir; 'e justifiably hommycided 'im."

"Then he did really kill him?"

"Kill 'im? I think 'e did—rather. Don't every body know that? Didn't 'e stan' up before the Corriner an' confess it? An' didn't the joory render out a verdick uv 'come to 'is death by a healthy Christian sent'ment workin' in the Caucasian breast?' An' didn't the church at the Hill cashier 'im fur it? An' didn't the indypendent voters 'lect 'im Jestice o' the Peace, to git even on the gospelers? I don't know w'er' you wus brought up!"

"But did Jo. actually do this because the Chinaman could not, or would not, learn to cut down trees in the manner he prescribed?"

"Yes; it stan's so on the reckerd. That wus the defense 'e made, an' it got 'im clear. Stan'in' on the reckerd, it is legle and troo. My knowin' better don't make no difference with legle trooth. It wa'n't none o' my fun'ral, an' I wusn't invited. But the real fact is (and I wouldn't tell it to no other livin' soul, nor at any other livin' place—and you ought'o knowed it long ago) that Jo. wus jealous o' me!" And the little wretch actually swelled out, and made a comical show of adjusting a merely hypothetical cravat, noting the effect in the palm of his hand, which he held up before him to represent a mirror.

"Jealous of *you!*" I repeated, with ill-mannered astonishment.

"Yes, jealous o' *me!* W'y, ain't I nice!"—assuming a mocking attitude of studied grace, and twitching the wrinkles out of his threadbare waistcoat. Then suddenly changing his expression to one of deep feeling, and dropping his voice to a low pitch of singular sweetness, he continued:

"Yes; Jo. thought dead loads o' that Chinaman. Nobody but me ever knowed how 'e doted onto 'im. Couldn't bear 'im out uv 'is sight—the derned fool! And w'en 'e come down to this clearin', one day, an' found me an' Ah Wee neglectin' our respective work—him to sleep an' me to grapple a tarantula out uv 'is sleeve—W'isky laid hold o' my axe and let us have it. I dodged jist then, fur the derned spider had bit me, but Ah Wee got it bad in the breast an' stiffened out. W'isky wus jist a-weighin' me out another one, w'en 'e seen the spider fastened onto my finger, an' 'e knowed 'e'd made a derned jack uv 'isself. So 'e knelt down an' made a dernder one. Fur Ah Wee give a little kick an' opened up 'is eyes—'e had eyes like mine—an' puttin' up 'is hands, drew W'isky's big head down, an' held it there w'ile 'e stayed—w'ich wusn't long, fur a tremblin' run all through 'im, an' 'e give a long moan an' went off."

During the progress of this story, the narrator had become transfigured. Gradually the comic—or, rather, sardonic—element had been eliminated, and, as with bowed head and streaming eyes he painted that strange death-scene, it was with difficulty that I repressed an audible sob. But this consummate actor had somehow so managed me that the sympathy due to his *dramatis personœ* was really bestowed upon himself. I don't know how it was done, but when he had concluded, I was just upon the point of taking him in my arms, when suddenly a broad grin danced across his countenance, and with a light laugh he continued:

"W'en W'isky got 'is knob out o' chanc'ry, 'e wus about the worst lookin' cuss you ever seen. All 'is good close—'e used to dress flashy them times—wus sp'ilt. 'Is hair wus tusseled, and 'is face—w'at I could see uv it—wus so w'ite that chalk 'ud 'a made a black mark on it. 'E jist stared once at me, 's if I wa'n't no account, an' then—I don't know any more, fur ther wus shootin' pains a-chasin' each other from my bit finger to my head, an' the sun went down behind that hill.

"So the inquest wus held without my assistance, an' W'isky went before it an' told 'is own story; an' told it so well that the joory all laughed, an' the Corriner said it wus a pleasure to hev a witness as hadn't any nonsense about 'im. It took W'isky six weeks, workin' at odd spells 'tween drinks, to gouge that epitaph"—with a diabolical grin: "I gouged his'n in one day.

"After this 'e tuk to drinkin' harder an' harder, an' got rabider an' rabider anti-coolie, but I mus' say I don't think 'e wus ever exackly glad 'e snuffed out Ah Wee; or that, 'f 'e'd had it to do over ag'in, 'e'd a even soop'rintended the job in person. He mayn't 'a suffered as me an' you would, but 'e didn't use to brag so much about it w'en 'e wus alone, as w'en 'e could git some goose like you to listen to 'im."

Here the historian twisted his face into an expression of deep secretiveness, as of one who might tell more if he chose, and executed a wink of profound significance.

"When did Jo. die?" I inquired, thoughtfully. The answer took away my breath:

"W'en I looked in at 'im through the knot-hole, and you'd put suthin' in 'is drink—you derned Borgy!"

Recovering somewhat from my amazement at this astounding charge, I was half minded to throttle the audacious accuser, but was restrained by a sudden conviction that came upon me in the light of a revelation. Mastering my emotion—which he had not observed—I fixed a grave look upon him, and asked earnestly, and as calmly as I could:

"And when did you become insane?"

"Nine years ago!" he shrieked, springing forward and falling prone upon the smaller of the two graves; "nine years ago, w'en that great broote killed the woman who loved *him* better than she did *me!*—me who had disguised myself an' follered 'er from 'Frisco, w'er' he won 'er from me at poker!—me who had watched over 'er fur years, w'en the scoundrel she b'longed to wus ashamed to acknowledge 'er an' treat 'er well!—me who, fur 'er sake, kep' 'is cussed secret fur five years, till it eat 'im up!—me who, w'en you p'isened the broote, fulfilled 'is only livin' request o' me, to lay 'im alongside uv 'er an' give 'im a stone to 'is head!—me who had never before seen 'er grave, 'cause I feared to meet 'im here, an' hev never since till this day, 'cause his carcass defiles it!"

I picked up the struggling little maniac, and carried him fainting to his wagon. An hour later, in the chill twilight, I wrung Gopher's hand and bade him farewell. As I stood there in the deepening gloom, watching the blank outlines of the receding wain, a sound was borne to me upon the evening wind—a sound as of a series of rapid thumps—and a voice cried out of the night:

"Gee-up there—you derned old Geranium!"

FELIPA

———•———

Constance Fenimore Woolson

Christine and I found her there.

She was a small, dark-skinned, yellow-eyed child, the offspring of the ocean and the heats, tawny, lithe and wild, shy yet fearless—not unlike one of the little brown deer that bounded through the open reaches of the pine barren behind the house. She did not come to us—we came to her: we loomed into her life like genii from another world, and she was partly afraid and partly proud of us. For were we not her guests?—proud thought!—and, better still, were we not women? "I have only seen three women in all my life," said Felipa, inspecting us gravely, "and I like women. I am a woman too, although these clothes of the son of Pedro make me appear as a boy: I wear them on account of the boat and the hauling in of the fish. The son of Pedro being dead at a convenient age, and his clothes fitting me, what would you have? It was manifestly a chance not to be despised. But when I am grown I shall wear robes long and beautiful like the señora's." The little creature was dressed in a boy's suit of dark-blue linen, much the worse for wear, and torn.

"If you are a girl, why do you not mend your clothes?" I said.

"Do you mend, señora?"

"Certainly: all women sew and mend."

"The other lady?"

Christine laughed as she lay at ease upon the brown carpet of pine needles, warm and aromatic after the tropic day's sunshine. "The child has divined me already, Catherine," she said.

Christine was a tall, lissome maid, with an unusually long stretch of arm, long sloping shoulders and a long fair throat: her straight hair fell to her knees when unbound, and its clear flaxen hue had not one shade of gold, as her clear gray eyes had not one shade of blue. Her small, straight, rose-leaf lips parted over small, dazzlingly white teeth, and the outline of her face in profile reminded you of an etching in its distinctness, although it was by no means perfect according to the rules of art. Still, what a comfort it was, after the blurred outlines and smudged profiles many of us possess—seen to best advantage, I think, in church on Sundays, crowned with flower-decked bonnets, listening calmly serene to favorite ministers, unconscious of noses! When Christine had finished her laugh—and she never hurried anything, but took the full taste of it—she stretched out her arm carelessly and patted Felipa's curly head. The child caught the descending hand and kissed the long white fingers.

It was a wild place where we were, yet not new or crude—the coast of Florida, that old-new land, with its deserted plantations, its skies of Paradise, and its broad wastes open to the changeless sunshine. The old house stood on the edge of the dry land, where the pine barren ended and the salt marsh began: in front curved the tide-water river that seemed ever trying to come up close to the barren and make its acquaintance, but could not quite succeed, since it must always turn and flee at a fixed hour, like Cinderella at the ball, leaving not a silver slipper, but purple driftwood and bright sea-weeds, brought in from the Gulf Stream outside. A planked platform ran out into the marsh from the edge of the barren, and at its end the boats were moored; for although at high tide the river was at our feet, at low tide it was far away out in the green waste somewhere, and if we wanted it we must go and seek it. We did not want it, however: we let it glide up to us twice a day with its fresh salt odors and flotsam of the ocean, and the rest of the time we wandered over the barrens or lay under the trees looking up into the wonderful blue above, listening to the winds as they rushed across from sea to sea. I was an artist, poor and painstaking: Christine was my kind friend. She had brought me South because my cough was troublesome, and here because Edward Bowne recommended the place. He and three fellow-sportsmen were down at the Madre Lagoon, farther south: I thought it probable we should see him, without his three fellow-sportsmen, before very long.

"Who were the three women you have seen, Felipa?" said Christine.

"The grandmother, an Indian woman of the Seminoles who comes sometimes with baskets, and the wife of Miguel of the island. But they are all old, and their skins are curled: I like better the silver skin of the señora."

Poor little Felipa lived on the edge of the great salt marsh alone with her grandparents, for her mother was dead. The yellow old couple were slow-witted Minorcans, part pagan, part Catholic, and wholly ignorant: their minds rarely rose above the level of their orange trees and their fish-nets. Felipa's father was a Spanish sailor, and as he had died only the year before, the child's Spanish was fairly correct, and we could converse with her readily, although we were slow to comprehend the patois of the old people, which seemed to borrow as much from the Italian tongue and the Greek as from its mother Spanish. "I know a great deal," Felipa remarked confidently, "for my father taught me. He had sailed on the ocean out of sight of land, and he knew many things. These he taught to me. Do the gracious ladies think there is anything else to know?"

One of the gracious ladies thought not, decidedly: in answer to my remonstrance, expressed in English, she said, "Teach a child like that, and you ruin her."

"Ruin her?"

"Ruin her happiness—the same thing."

Felipa had a dog, a second self—a great gaunt yellow creature of unknown breed, with crooked legs, big feet and the name Drollo. What Drollo meant, or whether it was an abbreviation, we never knew, but there was a certain satisfaction in it, for the dog was droll: the fact that the Minorcan title, whatever it was, meant nothing of that kind, made it all the better. We never saw Felipa without Drollo. "They look a good deal alike," observed Christine—"the same coloring."

"For shame!" I said.

But it was true. The child's bronzed yellow skin and soft eyes were not unlike the dog's, but her head was crowned with a mass of short black curls, while Drollo had only his two great flapping ears and his low smooth head. Give him an inch or two more of skull, and what a creature a dog would be! For love and faithfulness even now what man can match him? But, although ugly, Felipa was a picturesque little object always, whether attired in boy's clothes or in her own forlorn bodice and skirt. Olive-hued and meagre-faced, lithe and thin, she flew over the pine barrens like a creature of air, laughing to feel her short curls toss and her thin childish arms buoyed up on the breeze as she ran, with Drollo barking behind. For she loved the winds, and always knew when they were coming—whether down from the north, in from the ocean, or across from the Gulf of Mexico: she watched for them, sitting in the doorway, where she could feel their first breath, and she taught us the signs of the clouds. She was a queer little thing: we used to find her sometimes dancing alone out on the barren in a circle she had marked out with pine-cones, and once she confided to us that she talked to the trees. "They hear," she said in a whisper: "you should see how knowing they look, and how their leaves listen."

Once we came upon her most secret lair in a dense thicket of thorn-myrtle and wild smilax, a little bower she had made, where was hidden a horrible-looking image formed of the rough pieces of saw-palmetto grubbed up by old Bartolo from his garden. She must have dragged these fragments thither one by one, and with infinite pains bound them together with her rude withes of strong marsh-grass, until at last she had formed a rough trunk with crooked arms and a sort of a head, the red hairy surface of the palmetto looking not unlike the skin of some beast, and making the creature all the more grotesque. This fetich was kept crowned with flowers, and after this we often saw the child steal-ing away with Drollo to carry to it portions of her meals or a new-found treasure—a sea-shell, a broken saucer, or a fragment of ribbon. The food always mysteriously disappeared, and my suspicion is that Drollo used to go back secretly in the night and devour it, asking no questions and telling no lies: it fitted in nicely, however, Drollo merely performing the ancient part of the priests of Jupiter, men who have been much admired. "What a little pagan she is!" I said.

"Oh no, it is only her doll," replied Christine.

I tried several times to paint Felipa during these first weeks, but those eyes of hers always evaded me. They were, as I have said before, yellow—that is, they were brown with yellow lights—and they stared at you with the most inflexible openness. The child had the full-curved, half-open mouth of the tropics, and a low Greek forehead. "Why isn't she pretty?" I said.

"She is hideous," replied Christine: "look at her elbows."

Now, Felipa's arms *were* unpleasant; they were brown and lean, scratched and stained, and they terminated in a pair of determined little paws that could hold on like grim Death. I shall never forget coming upon a tableau one day out on the barren—a little Florida cow and Felipa, she holding on by the horns, and the beast with its small fore feet stubbornly set in the sand; girl pulling one way, cow the other; both silent and determined. It was a hard contest, but the girl won.

"And if you pass over her elbows, there are her feet," continued Christine languidly. For she was a sybaritic lover of the fine linens of life, that friend of mine—a pre-Raphaelite lady with clinging draperies and a mediæval clasp on her belt. Her whole being rebelled against ugliness, and the mere sight of a sharp-nosed, light-eyed woman on a cold day made her uncomfortable for hours.

"Have we not feet, too?" I replied sharply.

But I knew what she meant. Bare feet are not pleasant to the eye now-a-days, whatever they may have been in the days of the ancient Greeks; and Felipa's little brown insteps were half the time torn or bruised by the thorns of the chapparal. Besides, there was always the disagreeable idea that she might step upon something cold and squirming when she prowled through the thickets knee-deep in the matted grasses. Snakes abounded, although we never saw them; but Felipa went up to their very doors, as it were, and rang the bell defiantly.

One day old Grandfather Bartolo took the child with him down to the coast: she was always wild to go to the beach, where she could gather shells and sea-beans, and chase the little ocean-birds that ran along close to the waves with that swift gliding motion of theirs, and where she could listen to the roar of the breakers. We were several miles up the river, and to go down to the ocean was quite a voyage to Felipa. She bade us good-bye joyously; then ran back to hug Christine a second time, then to the boat again; then back.

"I thought you wanted to go, child?" I said, a little impatiently, for I was reading aloud, and these small irruptions were disturbing.

"Yes," said Felipa, "I want to go; and still—Perhaps if the gracious señora would kiss me again—"

Christine only patted her cheek and told her to run away: she obeyed, but there was a wistful look in her eyes, and even after the boat had started her face, watching us from the stern, haunted me.

"Now that the little monkey has gone, I may be able at last to catch and fix a likeness of her," I said: "in this case a recollection is better than the changing quicksilver reality."

"You take it as a study of ugliness, I suppose?"

"Do not be so hard upon the child, Christine."

"Hard? Why, she adores me," said my friend, going off to her hammock under the tree.

Several days passed, and the boat returned not. I accomplished a fine amount of work, and Christine a fine amount of swinging in the hammock and dreaming. At length one afternoon I gave my final touch, and carried my sketch over to the pre-Raphaelite lady for criticism. "What do you see?" I said.

"I see a wild-looking child with yellow eyes, a mat of curly black hair, a lank little bodice, her two thin brown arms embracing a gaunt old dog with crooked legs, big feet and turned-in toes."

"Is that all?"

"All."

"You do not see latent beauty, proud courage, and a possible great gulf of love in that poor wild little face?"

"Nothing of the kind," replied Christine decidedly. "I see an ugly little girl: that is all."

The next day the boat returned, and brought back five persons— the old grandfather, Felipa, Drollo, Miguel of the island and—Edward Bowne.

"Already?" I said.

"Tired of the Madre, Kitty: thought I would come up here and see you for a while. I knew you must be pining for me."

"Certainly," I replied: "do you not see how I have wasted away?"

He drew my arm through his and raced me down the plank-walk toward the shore, where I arrived laughing and out of breath.

"Where is Christine?" he asked.

I came back into the traces at once: "Over there in the hammock. You wish to go to the house first, I suppose?"

"Of course not."

"But she did not come to meet you, Edward, although she knew you had landed."

"Of course not, also."

"I do not understand you two."

"And of course not, a third time," said Edward, looking down at me with a smile. "What do quiet, peaceful little artists know about war?"

"Is it war?"

"Something very like it, Kitty. What is that you are carrying?"

"Oh! my new sketch. What do you think of it?"

"Good, very good. Some little girl about here, I suppose?"

"Why, it is Felipa!"

"And who is Felipa? Seems to me I have seen that old dog, though."

"Of course you have: he was in the boat with you, and so was Felipa, but she was dressed in boy's clothes, and that gives her a different look."

"Oh! that boy? I remember him. His name is Philip. He is a funny little fellow," said Edward calmly.

"Her name is Felipa, and she is not a boy or a funny little fellow at all," I replied.

"Isn't she? I thought she was both," replied Ned carelessly, and then he went off toward the hammock. I turned away after noting Christine's cool greeting, and went back to the boat.

Felipa came bounding to meet me. "What is his name?" she demanded.

"Bowne."

"Buon—Buona: I cannot say it."

"Bowne, child—Edward Bowne."

"Oh! Eduardo: I know that. Eduardo—Eduardo—a name of honey."

She flew off singing the name, followed by Drollo carrying his mistress's palmetto basket in his big patient mouth; but when I passed the house a few moments afterward she was singing, or rather talking volubly of, another name—"Miguel," and "the wife of Miguel," who were apparently important personages on the canvas of her life. As it happened, I never really saw that wife of Miguel, who seemingly had no name of her own; but I imagined her. She lived on a sand-bar in the ocean not far from the mouth of our river; she drove pelicans like ducks with a long switch, and she had a tame eagle; she had an old horse also, who dragged the driftwood across the sand on a sledge, and this old horse seemed like a giant horse always, outlined as he ever was against the flat bar and the sky. She went out at dawn, and she went out at sunset, but during the middle of the burning day she sat at home and polished sea-beans, for which she obtained untold sums: she was very tall, she was very yellow, and she had but one eye. These items, one by one, had been dropped by Felipa at various times, and it was with curiosity that I gazed upon the original Miguel, the possessor of this remarkable spouse. He was a grave-eyed, yellow man, who said little and thought less, applying *cui bono?* to mental much as the city man applies it to bodily exertion, and therefore achieving, I think, a finer degree of inanition. The tame eagle, the pelicans, were nothing to him, and when I saw his lethargic, gentle countenance my own curiosity about them seemed to die away in haze, as though I had breathed in an invisible opiate. He came, he went, and that was all: exit Miguel.

Felipa was constantly with us now. She and Drollo followed the three of us wherever we went—followed the two also whenever I stayed behind to sketch, as I often stayed, for in those days I was trying to catch the secret of the barrens: a hopeless effort, I know it now. "Stay with me, Felipa," I said; for it was natural to suppose that the lovers might like to be alone. (I call them lovers for want of a better name, but they were more like haters: however, in such cases it is nearly the same thing.) And then Christine, hearing this, would immediately call "Felipa!" and the child would dart after them, happy as a bird. She wore her boy's suit now all the time, because the señora had said she "looked well in it." What the señora really said was, that in boy's clothes she looked less like a grasshopper. But this had been translated as above by Edward Bowne when Felipa suddenly descended upon him one day and demanded to be instantly told what the gracious lady was saying about her; for she seemed to know by intuition when we spoke of her, although we talked in English and mentioned no names. When told, her small face beamed, and she kissed Christine's hand joyfully and bounded away. Christine took out her beautiful handkerchief and wiped the spot.

"Christine," I said, "do you remember the fate of the proud girl who walked upon bread?"

"You think that I may starve for kisses some time?" said my friend, going on with the wiping.

"Not while I am alive," called out Edward from behind. His style of courtship *was* of the sledge-hammer sort sometimes. But he did not get much for it on that day; only lofty tolerance, which seemed to amuse him greatly.

Edward played with Felipa very much as if she was a rubber toy or a trapeze performer. He held her out at arm's length in mid-air, he poised her on his shoulder, he tossed her up into the low myrtle trees, and dangled her by her little belt over the claret-colored pools on the barren; but he could not frighten her: she only laughed and grew wilder and wilder, like a squirrel. "She has muscles and nerves of steel," he said admiringly.

"Do put her down: she is too excitable for such games," I said in French, for Felipa seemed to divine our English now. "See the color she has."

For there was a trail of dark red over the child's thin oval cheeks which made her look strangely unlike herself. As she caught our eyes fixed upon her she suddenly stopped her climbing and came and sat at Christine's feet. "Some day I shall wear robes like the señora's," she said, passing her hand over the soft fabric; "and I think," she added after some slow consideration, "that my face will be like the señora's too."

Edward burst out laughing. The little creature stopped abruptly and scanned his face.

"Do not tease her," I said.

Quick as a flash she veered around upon me. "He does not tease me," she said angrily in Spanish; "and, besides, what if he does? I like it." She looked at me with gleaming eyes and stamped her foot.

"What a little tempest!" said Christine.

Then Edward, man-like, began to explain. "You could not look much like this lady, Felipa," he said, "because you are so dark, you know."

"Am I dark?"

"Very dark; but many people are dark, of course; and for my part I always liked dark eyes," said this mendacious person.

"Do you like my eyes?" asked Felipa anxiously.

"Indeed I do: they are like the eyes of a dear little calf I once owned when I was a boy."

The child was satisfied, and went back to her place beside Christine. "Yes, I shall wear robes like this," she said dreamily, drawing the flowing drapery over her knees clad in the little linen trousers, and scanning the effect: "they would trail behind me—so." Her bare feet peeped out below the hem, and again we all laughed, the little brown toes looked so comical coming out from the silk and the snowy embroideries. She came down to reality at once, looked at us, looked at herself, and for the first time seemed to comprehend the difference. Then suddenly she threw herself down on the ground like a little animal, and buried her head in her arms. She would not speak, she would not look up: she only relaxed one arm a little to take in Drollo, and then lay motionless. Drollo looked at us out of one eye solemnly from his uncomfortable position, as much as to say, "No use: leave her to me." So after a while we went away and left them there.

That evening I heard a low knock at my door. "Come in," I said, and Felipa entered. I hardly knew her. She was dressed in a flowered muslin gown which had probably belonged to her mother, and she wore her grandmother's stockings and large baggy slippers: on her mat of curly hair was perched a high-crowned, stiff white cap adorned with a ribbon streamer, and her lank little neck, coming out of the big gown, was decked with a chain of large sea-beans, like exaggerated lockets. She carried a Cuban fan in her hand which was as large as a parasol, and Drollo, walking behind, fairly clanked with the chain of sea-shells which she had wound around him from head to tail. The droll tableau and the supreme pride on Felipa's countenance overcame me, and I laughed aloud. A sudden cloud of rage and disappointment came over the poor child's face: she threw her cap on the floor and stamped on it; she tore off her necklace and writhed herself out of her big flowered gown, and running to Drollo, nearly strangled him in her fierce efforts to drag off his shell chains. Then, a half-dressed, wild little phantom, she seized me by the skirts and dragged me toward the looking-glass. "You are not pretty either," she cried. "Look at yourself! look at yourself!"

"I did not mean to laugh at you, Felipa," I said gently: "I would not laugh at any one; and it is true I am not pretty, as you say. I can never be pretty, child; but if you will try to be more gentle, I could teach you how to dress yourself so that no one would laugh at you again. I could make you a little bright-barred skirt and a scarlet bodice: you could help, and that would teach you to sew. But a little girl who wants all this done for her must be quiet and good."

"I am good," said Felipa—"as good as everything."

The tears still stood in her eyes, but her anger was forgotten: she

improvised a sort of dance around my room, followed by Drollo dragging his twisted chain, stepping on it with his big feet, and finally winding himself up into a knot around the chair-legs.

"Couldn't we make Drollo something too? dear old Drollo!" said
Felipa, going to him and squeezing him in an enthusiastic embrace. I
used to wonder how his poor ribs stood it: Felipa used him as a safety-
valve for her impetuous feelings.

She kissed me good-night and then asked for "the other lady."

"Go to bed, child," I said: "I will give her your good-night."

"But I want to kiss her too," said Felipa.

She lingered at the door and would not go; she played with the
latch, and made me nervous with its clicking; at last I ordered her out.
But on opening my door half an hour afterward there she was sitting
on the floor outside in the darkness, she and Drollo, patiently waiting.
Annoyed, but unable to reprove her, I wrapped the child in my shawl
and carried her out into the moonlight, where Christine and Edward
were strolling to and fro under the pines. "She will not go to bed, Christine, without kissing you," I explained.

"Funny little monkey!" said my lily friend, passively allowing the
embrace.

"Me too," said Edward, bending down. Then I carried my bundle
back satisfied.

The next day Felipa and I in secret began our labors: hers consisted
in worrying me out of my life and spoiling material—mine in keeping
my temper and trying to sew. The result, however, was satisfactory,
never mind how we got there. I led Christine out one afternoon: Edward followed. "Do you like tableaux?" I said. "There is one I have
arranged for you."

Felipa sat on the edge of the low, square-curbed Spanish well, and
Drollo stood behind her, his great yellow body and solemn head serving
as a background. She wore a brown petticoat barred with bright colors, and a little scarlet bodice fitting her slender waist closely; a che-
misette of soft cream-color with loose sleeves covered her neck and
arms, and set off the dark hues of her cheeks and eyes; and around her
curly hair a red scarf was twisted, its fringed edges forming a drapery
at the back of the head, which, more than anything else, seemed to
bring out the latent character of her face. Brown moccasins, red stockings and a quantity of bright beads completed her costume.

"By Jove!" cried Edward, "the little thing is almost pretty."

Felipa understood this, and a great light came into her face: forgetting her pose, she bounded forward to Christine's side. "I am pretty, then?" she said with exultation: "I *am* pretty, then, after all? For now you yourself have said it—have said it."

"No, Felipa," I interposed, "the gentleman said it." For the child had a curious habit of confounding the two identities which puzzled me then as now. But this afternoon, this happy afternoon, she was content, for she was allowed to sit at Christine's feet and look up into her fair face unmolested. I was forgotten, as usual.

"It is always so," I said to myself. But cynicism, as Mr. Aldrich says, is a small brass field-piece that eventually bursts and kills the artilleryman. I knew this, having been blown up myself more than once; so I went back to my painting and forgot the world. Our world down there on the edge of the salt marsh, however, was a small one: when two persons went out of it there was a vacuum at once.

One morning Felipa came sadly to my side. "They have gone away," she said.

"Yes, child."

"Down to the beach to spend all the day."

"Yes, I know it."

"And without me!"

This was the climax. I looked up. The child's eyes were dry, but there was a hollow look of disappointment in her face that made her seem old: it was as though for an instant you caught what her old-woman face would be half a century on.

"Why did they not take me?" she said. "I am pretty now: she herself said it."

"They cannot always take you, Felipa," I replied, giving up the point as to who had said it.

"Why not? I am pretty now: she herself said it," persisted the child. "In these clothes, you know: she herself said it. The clothes of the son of Pedro you will never see more: they are burned."

"Burned?"

"Yes, burned," replied Felipa composedly. "I carried them out on the barren and burned them. Drollo singed his paw. They burned quite nicely. But they are gone, and I am pretty now, and yet they did not take me! What shall I do?"

"Take these colors and make me a picture," I suggested. Generally, this was a prized privilege, but to-day it did not attract: she turned away, and a few moments after I saw her going down to the end of the plank walk, where she stood gazing wistfully toward the ocean. There she stayed all day, going into camp with Drollo, and refusing to come to dinner in spite of old Dominga's calls and beckonings. At last the patient old grandmother went down herself to the end of the long plank walk where they were with some bread and venison on a plate. Felipa ate but little, but Drollo, after waiting politely until she had finished, devoured everything that was left in his calmly hungry way, and then sat back on his haunches with one paw on the plate, as though for the sake of memory. Drollo's hunger was of the chronic kind: it seemed impossible either to assuage it or to fill him. There was a gaunt leanness about him which I am satisfied no amount of food could ever fatten. I think he knew it too, and that accounted for his resignation. At length, just before sunset, the boat returned, floating up the river with the tide, old Bartolo steering and managing the brown sails. Felipa sprang up joyfully: I thought she would spring into the boat in her eagerness. What did she receive for her long vigil? A short word or two: that was all. Christine and Edward had quarreled.

How do lovers quarrel ordinarily? But I should not ask that, for these were no ordinary lovers: they were decidedly extraordinary.

"You should not submit to her caprices so readily," I said the next day while strolling on the barren with Edward. (He was not so much cast down, however, as he might have been.)

"I adore the very ground her foot touches, Kitty."

"I know it. But how will it end?"

"I will tell you: some of these days I shall win her, and then—she will adore me."

Here Felipa came running after us, and Edward immediately challenged her to a race: a game of romps began. If Christine had been looking from her window, she might have thought he was not especially disconsolate over her absence; but she was not looking. She was never looking out of anything or for anybody. She was always serenely content where she was. Edward and Felipa strayed off among the pine trees, and gradually I lost sight of them. But as I sat sketching an hour afterward Edward came into view, carrying the child in his arms. I hurried to meet them.

"I shall never forgive myself," he said: "the little thing has fallen and injured her foot badly, I fear."

"I do not care at all," said Felipa: "I like to have it hurt. It is *my* foot, isn't it?"

These remarks she threw at me defiantly, as though I had laid claim to the member in question. I could not help laughing.

"The other lady will not laugh," said the child proudly. And in truth Christine, most unexpectedly, took up the rôle of nurse. She carried Felipa to her own room—for we each had a little cell opening out of the main apartment—and as white-robed Charity she shone with new radiance. "Shone" is the proper word, for through the open door of the dim cell, with the dark little face of Felipa on her shoulder, her white robe and skin seemed fairly to shine, as white lilies shine on a dark night. The old grandmother left the child in our care and watched our proceedings wistfully, very much as a dog watches the human hands that extract the thorn from the swollen foot of her puppy. She was grateful and asked no questions; in fact, thought was not one of her mental processes. She did not think much: she only felt. As for Felipa, the child lived in rapture during those days in spite of her suffering. She scarcely slept at all—she was too happy: I heard her voice rippling on through the night, and Christine's low replies. She adored her beautiful nurse.

The fourth day came: Edward Bowne walked into the cell. "Go out and breathe the fresh air for an hour or two," he said in the tone more of a command than a request.

"But the child will never consent," replied Christine sweetly.

"Oh yes, she will: I will stay with her," said the young man, lifting the feverish little head on his arm and passing his hand softly over the bright eyes.

"Felipa, do you not want me?" said Christine, bending down.

"He stays: it is all the same," murmured the child.

"So it is. Go, Christine," said Edward with a little smile of triumph.

Without a word Christine left the cell. But she did not go to walk: she came to my room, and throwing herself on my bed fell in a moment into a deep sleep, the reaction after her three nights of wakefulness. When she awoke it was long after dark, and I had relieved Edward in his watch.

"You will have to give it up," he said as our lily came forth at last with sleep-flushed cheeks and starry eyes shielded from the light. "The spell is broken: we have all been taking care of Felipa, and she likes one as well as the other."

Which was not true, in my case at least, since Felipa had openly derided my small strength when I lifted her, and beat off the sponge with which I attempted to bathe her hot face. "They" used no sponges, she said, only their nice cool hands; and she wished "they" would come and take care of her again. But Christine had resigned in toto. If Felipa did not prefer her to all others, then Felipa could not have her: she was not a common nurse. And indeed she was not. Her fair beauty, ideal grace, cooing voice and the strength of her long arms and flexible hands were like magic to the sick, and—distraction to the well; the well in this case being Edward Bowne looking in at the door.

"You love them very much, do you not, Felipa?" I said one day when the child was sitting up for the first time in a cushioned chair.

"Ah, yes: it is so delicious when they carry me," she replied. But it was Edward who carried her.

"He is very strong," I said.

"Yes, and their long soft hair, with the smell of roses in it too," said Felipa dreamily. But the hair was Christine's.

"I shall love them for ever, and they will love me for ever," continued the child. "Drollo too." She patted the dog's head as she spoke, and then concluded to kiss him on his little inch of forehead: next she offered him all her medicines and lotions in turn, and he smelled at them grimly. "He likes to know what I am taking," she explained.

I went on: "You love them, Felipa, and they are fond of you. They will always remember you, no doubt."

"Remember!" cried Felipa, starting up from her cushions like a Jack-in-the-box. "They are not going away? Never! never!"

"But of course they must go some time, for—"

But Felipa was gone. Before I could divine her intent she had flung herself out of her chair down on to the floor, and was crawling on her hands and knees toward the outer room. I ran after her, but she reached the door before me, and, dragging her bandaged foot behind her, drew herself toward Christine. "You are *not* going away! You are not! you are not!" she sobbed, clinging to her skirts.

Christine was reading tranquilly: Edward stood at the outer door mending his fishing-tackle. The coolness between them remained unwarmed by so much as a breath. "Run away, child: you disturb me," said Christine, turning over a leaf. She did not even look at the pathetic little bundle at her feet. Pathetic little bundles must be taught some time what ingratitude deserves.

"How can she run, lame as she is?" said Edward from the doorway.

"You are not going away, are you? Tell me you are not," sobbed Felipa in a passion of tears, beating on the floor with one hand, and with the other clinging to Christine.

"I am not going," said Edward. "Do not sob so, you poor little thing!"

She crawled to him, and he took her up in his arms and soothed her into stillness again: then he carried her out on to the barren for a breath of fresh air.

"It is a most extraordinary thing how that child confounds you two," I said. "It is a case of color-blindness, as it were—supposing you two were colors."

"Which we are not," replied Christine carelessly. "Do not stray off into mysticism, Catherine."

"It is not mysticism: it is a study of character—"

"Where there is no character," replied my friend.

I gave it up, but I said to myself, "Fate, in the next world make me one of those long, lithe, light-haired women, will you? I want to see how it feels."

Felipa's foot was well again, and spring had come. Soon we must leave our lodge on the edge of the pine barren, our outlook over the salt marsh, our river sweeping up twice a day, bringing in the briny odors of the ocean: soon we should see no more the eagles far above us or hear the night-cry of the great owls, and we must go without the little fairy flowers of the barren, so small that a hundred of them scarcely made a tangible bouquet, yet what beauty! what sweetness! In my portfolio were sketches and studies of the barrens, and in my heart were hopes. Somebody says somewhere, "Hope is more than a blessing: it is a duty and a virtue." But I fail to appreciate preserved hope—hope put up in cans and served out in seasons of depression. I like it fresh from the tree. And so when I hope it *is* hope, and not that well-dried, monotonous cheerfulness which makes one long to throw the persistent smilers out of the window. Felipa danced no more on the barrens; her illness had toned her excitable nature; she seemed content to sit at our feet while we talked, looking up dreamily into our faces, but no longer eagerly endeavoring to comprehend. We were there: that was enough.

"She is growing like a reed," I said: "her illness has left her weak."

"-Minded," suggested Christine, smiling.

At this moment Felipa stroked the lady's white hand tenderly and laid her brown cheek against it.

"Do you not feel reproached," I said.

"Why? Must we give our love to whoever loves us? A fine parcel of paupers we should all be, wasting our inheritance in pitiful small change! Shall I give a thousand beggars a half hour's happiness, or shall I make one soul rich his whole life long?"

"The latter," remarked Edward, who had come up unobserved.

They gazed at each other unflinchingly. They had come to open battle during those last days, and I knew that the end was near. Their words had been cold as ice, cutting as steel, and I said to myself, "At any moment." There would be a deadly struggle, and then Christine would yield. Even I comprehended something of what that yielding would be. There are beautiful velvety panthers in the Asian forests, and in real life too, sometimes.

"Why do they hate each other so?" Felipa said to me sadly.

"Do they hate each other?"

"Yes, for I feel it here," she answered, touching her breast with a dramatic little gesture.

"Nonsense! Go and play with your doll, child." For I had made her a respectable, orderly doll to take the place of the ungainly fetich out on the barren.

Felipa gave me a look and walked away. A moment afterward she brought the doll out of the house before my very eyes, and, going down to the end of the dock, deliberately threw it into the water: the tide was flowing out, and away went my toy-woman out of sight, out to sea.

"Well!" I said to myself. "What next?"

I had not told Felipa we were going: I thought it best to let it take her by surprise. I had various small articles of finery ready as farewell gifts which should act as sponges to absorb her tears. But Fate took the whole matter out of my hands. This is how it happened. One evening in the jessamine arbor, in the fragrant darkness of the warm spring night, the end came: Christine was won. She glided in like a wraith, and I, divining at once what had happened, followed her into her little room, where I found her lying on her bed, her hands clasped on her breast, her eyes open and veiled in soft shadows, her white robe drenched with dew. I kissed her fondly—I never could help loving her then or now—and next I went out to find Edward. He had been kind to me all my poor gray life: should I not go to him now? He was still in the arbor, and I sat down by his side quietly: I knew that the words would come in time. They came: what a flood! English was not enough for him. He poured forth his love in the rich-voweled Spanish tongue also: it has sounded doubly sweet to me ever since.

"Have you felt the wool of the beaver?
Or swan's down ever?
Or have smelt the bud o' the brier?
Or the nard in the fire?
Or ha' tasted the bag o' the bee?
Oh so white, oh so soft, oh so sweet is she!"

said the young lover again and again; and I, listening there in the dark fragrant night, with the dew heavy upon me, felt glad that the old simple-hearted love was not entirely gone from our tired metallic world.

It was late when we returned to the house. After reaching my room I found that I had left my cloak in the arbor. It was a strong fabric: the dew could not hurt it, but it could hurt my sketching materials and various trifles in the wide inside pockets—*objets de luxe* to me, souvenirs of happy times, little artistic properties that I hang on the walls of my poor studio when in the city. I went softly out into the darkness again and sought the arbor: groping on the ground I found, not the cloak, but—Felipa! She was crouched under the foliage, face downward: she would not move or answer.

"What is the matter, child?" I said, but she would not speak. I tried to draw her from her lair, but she tangled herself stubbornly still farther among the thorny vines, and I could not move her. I touched her neck: it was cold. Frightened, I ran back to the house for a candle.

"Go away," she said in a low hoarse voice when I flashed the light over her. "I know all, and I am going to die. I have eaten the poison things in your box, and just now a snake came on my neck and I let him. He has bitten me, I suppose, and I am glad. Go away: I am going to die."

I looked around: there was my color-case rifled and empty, and the other articles were scattered on the ground. "Good Heavens, child!" I cried, "what have you eaten?"

"Enough," replied Felipa gloomily. "I knew they were poisons: you told me so. And I let the snake stay."

By this time the household, aroused by my hurried exit with the candle, came toward the arbor. The moment Edward appeared Felipa rolled herself up like a hedgehog again and refused to speak. But the old grandmother knelt down and drew the little crouching figure into her arms with gentle tenderness, smoothing its hair and murmuring loving words in her soft dialect.

"What is it?" said Edward; but even then his eyes were devouring Christine, who stood in the dark, vine-wreathed doorway like a picture in a frame. I explained.

Christine smiled softly. "Jealousy," she said in a low voice. "I am not surprised." And of her own accord she gave back to Edward one of his looks.

But at the first sound of her voice Felipa had started up: she too saw the look, and wrenching herself free from old Dominga's arms, she threw herself at Christine's feet. "Look at *me* so," she cried—"me too: do not look at him. He has forgotten poor Felipa: he does not love her any more. But *you* do not forget, señora: *you* love me—*you* love me. Say you do or I shall die!"

We were all shocked by the pallor and the wild hungry look of her uplifted face. Edward bent down and tried to lift her in his arms, but when she saw him a sudden fierceness came into her eyes: they shot out yellow light and seemed to narrow to a point of flame. Before we knew it she had turned, seized something and plunged it into his encircling arm. It was my little Venetian dagger.

We sprang forward; our dresses were spotted with the fast-flowing blood; but Edward did not relax his hold on the writhing wild little body he held until it lay exhausted in his arms. "I am glad I did it," said the child, looking up into his face with her inflexible eyes. "Put me down—put me down, I say, by the gracious señora, that I may die with the trailing of her white robe over me." And the old grandmother with trembling hands received her and laid her down mutely at Christine's feet.

Ah, well! Felipa did not die. The poisons wracked but did not kill her, and the snake must have spared the little thin brown neck so despairingly offered to him. We went away: there was nothing for us to do but to go away as quickly as possible and leave her to her kind. To the silent old grandfather I said, "It will pass: she is but a child."

"She is nearly twelve, señora. Her mother was married at thirteen."

"But she loved them both alike, Bartolo. It is nothing: she does not know."

"You are right, lady: she does not know," replied the old man slowly; "but *I* know. It was two loves, and the stronger thrust the knife."

My Lorelei

A Heidelberg Romance

FROM THE DIARY OF MRS. LOUIS DANTON LYNDE

Octave Thanet

Heidelberg, *July* 9, 1874.—Louis is still at Frankfort. There are in-conveniences in being in love with one's husband, when he has to spend half his time in Frankfort "on business." However, I will not grumble, since but for this same "business" we could not have afforded Europe for years.

We have been here two weeks; we expect to be here two months. The town is a queer, quaint, many-gabled, abominably paved place, with the famous Heidelberger Schloss shouldering its red walls through the trees of the western hills, like the Middle Ages looking down on us. When the sun sets, its rugged towers are outlined against a golden background, such as Fra Angelico gives his Madonnas. Our hotel fronts the Anlage, a charming street, of which only one side is bordered with cream-colored brick, while the other rolls back in wooded hills, where the White Caps hold their Kneipen, and the band plays on summer nights. Louis's Prussian friend, Count Von Reibnitz, recommended the hotel; indeed, he honors it with his own long-descended presence. He is a tall young man, of a florid complexion and a frank expression. He has regular features, and a great, sun-burned, white mustache, which he waxes at the ends. I cannot believe that his shoulders are so square and his waist so slender without some assistance from art. His regiment is stationed in Schwetzingen, but for some occult reason he seems to spend a great deal of his time here.

Ted Tresham is here also,—my good-natured, good-looking, and, I fear, slightly good-for-nothing cousin, whom I haven't seen for two years. His engagement does not seem to have sobered him particularly. Probably, it is merely a family affair; Miss Tresham is so rich, and his second cousin, besides. She is staying here with her aunt, Mrs. Guernsey, waiting for Uncle Tresham. When he comes, they are going home, and the young people are to be married in December. I have always had a curiosity to see Undine Tresham, and now that I have opportunities, I improve them. She is worth seeing: when I look at her I am reminded of a German Lorelei, and I don't think it is the name altogether which suggests the comparison. No: for there are the deep, calm eyes (quite indescribable eyes); the waving, soft, brown hair, the mysterious smile,—all that delicate and elusive loveliness which the poets give to those strange creatures who attract a passion which they cannot return. She has two marked dimples and a blue vein on her cheek. Her white teeth make her smile dazzling. And she has the very sweetest voice I ever heard. Yet, I doubt my cousin may have made a great mistake. This, too, though Miss Tresham is undeniably clever, and her manners are as charming as her face. Will Coombs was in love with her once. He never asked her to marry him; she was "too jolly heartless," he said. Will has a keen streak running through his nonsense, and I fancy he was right about Undine Tresham. Graceful and cordial and winning as she is, there is an intangible mist of coldness about her, a curious remoteness, a persistent light-heartedness, that seems to spring, not from ignorance or hardness, but from sheer incapacity to feel. For instance, I cannot for my life imagine those beautiful eyes of hers filled with tears! All this from two weeks' acquaintance and Will's wild talk; decidedly, I am not timid in inference.

July 10.—I know a countess. She is the first countess of my acquaintance, therefore valued. Her name is Dunin Slepshks Wall—something! Mamma has it all neatly written out on a slip of paper, which she carries about with her, that she may be able to address the gnädige frau properly. *I* shall call her "countess." It is short, but at the same time imposing, and I have observed that they always address people so in novels. She is an amiable old woman, who rouges, and smokes cigarettes after dinner. Once she was a celebrated beauty, and she is still a brilliant talker—when she does not speak English. Unhappily, her politeness leads her to always converse with me in my own tongue. I can't tell her I don't understand English; so I sit at *table-d'hote* in a desperate state of mind, listening to her unintelligible fluency, and making frantic guesses at her meaning. Mamma can't understand her at all, and she thinks the poor woman is deaf; and when mamma looks helpless and unhappy, and murmurs, "I beg your pardon?" she yells the remark over again. Her seat at *table-d'hote* is next mine, and opposite we have two Americans. The elder is a middle-aged woman; the younger, a girl of perhaps twenty-three. They are interesting, after a fashion,—that is, the girl is; for the woman looks like nothing so much as a weak water-color, she is so faded, indistinct, and neutral-tinted. But the girl is a beauty! How Titian would rave over her crispy, red-gold hair, and topaz-brown long-lashed eyes, and creamy-white skin, with the pink glowing under the white on her oval cheeks! To me she seems like one of his gorgeous Venetian dames come to life again, with his own luxuriant grace of contour in her figure, and his own alluring splendor of coloring in her face. I suppose nine persons out of ten would call Miss Grace Wilmott (that is her name, and the water-color's title is Mrs. Moore) a magnificently handsome woman, but I don't like her; to be frank, I don't like Titian. Somehow it is an oppressive kind of beauty; there is a trifle too much of her, and then— her ribbons are never quite fresh! "Such things are women," Louis would say, and he would add that I was prejudiced because she flirts with Ted Tresham. Yesterday she blushed when he came into the room. He took the vacant seat beside her (it is not his seat at all), and one of her dimpled white hands stole under the table. I know from the sheepish look in the corner of Theodore's eye that he squeezed it! Undine and Mrs. Guernsey were not present. I wonder if he cares for his future wife; she, I fancy, is not likely to break her heart for any one. Still, it is impossible not to like her, she is so amusing, and her manners are perfect; with her aunt, for example, nothing could be better. Mrs. Guernsey is odd and fussy, and what must seem even more inexplicable to Undine, fervently enthusiastic; yet she never loses her temper, is always willing to come home before the dew falls, carries as many extra shawls as her aunt suggests, and listens with never-failing patience to the moral reflections. Far be it from me, however, to speak one slighting word of the excellent Mrs. Guernsey; she is a boon! Like mamma, she is a hungerer and a thirster for information. *I* am not. It is consequently an immense relief to have flung in our power, as it were, a comrade for mamma who is continually and indefatigably improving the time. They go off together on little instructive sprees.

July 15.—What a fascination there is about this quiet little town! Nothing is new, no one is excited; even the corps students get drunk decorously. I seem to have stepped out of the bustle and hurry and struggle of modern life. It is bliss, after Chicago. Yesterday we spent the day at the castle; there I saw a young man and a young woman sitting under the lindens. They sat there all day; half a dozen times we came back to them; always in the same attitudes,—she knitting some blue woollen article, he sitting on the grass at her feet. Occasionally he would take her hand and hold it for a few moments, smiling. He had providently spread a gay handkerchief on the grass, for his clothes were new, beyond a doubt; and he looked tranquilly and unreservedly happy. They said little; but several times the *restauration* waiters brought them beer, and at noon, they ate a great deal of bread and cheese and a large sausage, which they appeared to have brought with them. When night fell, and we went homeward, we overtook them walking hand in hand among the trees. They looked supremely satisfied with life; possibly a trifle stolid, but innocent as Arcadia. Undine glanced up at them as they passed. "They are happy," she said; "probably they are very lately married; but fancy two Americans spending a day in such a way!"

"I don't like American lovers," said I.

We all went up to the castle together,—Undine, Ted, mamma, and I. We rode up the hill in the most degraded manner on diminutive donkeys, with a man walking behind to guide the beasts by the tail! I shall not tell Louis.

The road climbs the steepest of hills through old Heidelberg, which is picturesque and ruinous to the last degree.

All the inhabitants (save a few very bad children, who try to frighten tourists' donkeys) are over eighty, and wear ragged, dingy, blue garments.

At the castle gateway we dismounted and dismissed our donkeys. The gateway itself is a commonplace modern structure, with an iron ring let into the stone on one side. Ted explained that this was the celebrated "wishing ring." One must knock three times with it, wishing the same thing each time; then he must enter and make the circuit of the grounds in absolute silence, going out through the same gateway. If these directions are followed to the letter, whatever he has wished shall surely come to pass. Instantly out came mamma's Baedecker and glasses. "Has any one ever tried it?" she asked, eagerly.

"Hundreds," said Ted; "only ten have succeeded, though. One of these was a woman."

"Ach, *so?*" said Undine, with the absurd German inflection.

"Actually," said Ted. "I don't wonder you are surprised, but it really happened. She gagged herself with her handkerchief, and had her husband tie her hands, so she managed to walk all around and out safely, but the instant he took the handkerchief out, she gave a kind of gasping scream, and fell down dead!"

"What did she do that for?" said mamma, rather startled.

"Why, you see, she had so much to say that it killed her trying to say it all at once! What are you going to do, Undine?"

Undine, who had laid her hand on the ring, said she was going to wish.

"What will you wish for, liebchen?" said Ted, carelessly. "What have you left to want?"

She lifted her eyes to his; certainly they are the most beautiful eyes in the world. There was a little vibration in her sweet, slow voice, "I don't know, Ted"; she answered, "every thing has come to me before I have had time to want it; I can only wish to keep."

At that moment it occurred to me that I had made a little mistake about my Lorelei. Such a thought had no business to make me melancholy, but it did. I walked by Undine's side, almost as silent as she. For that matter, Ted was the only lively member of the party, since mamma was absorbed in comparing the realities with Baedecker's flights of fancy,—naturally a serious occupation,—and Undine never opened her lips. Finally, she walked out of the gate, and came back smiling. "It *is* a strain, Ted," she confessed. "I hope I shall be immortalized in the castle traditions. I feel very much exhausted; would you mind going to the *restauration* and having a cup of coffee, Mrs. Burt?"

Ted suggested champagne, but Undine asked him solemnly if he had ever tried the *restauration* champagne, and when he admitted his ignorance, she said, "The coffee is the worst of its kind, but the champagne is simply beyond words."

I am bound to say (after taking both) I think she told the truth. The *restauration* is a wooden building, glaringly modern and out of place so near the grand old ruin. Ugly wooden tables are scattered among the trees, and depressed-looking men, in shabby dress-coats, bear trays in the usual precarious manner, to the people who are seated around the tables. We soon left this scene of festivity and repaired to the museum. There mamma was in her glory. She put me to open shame, standing before some wooden-looking portraits, her bonnet perched disreputably on one side of her head, and audibly reading Baedecker's descriptions. We lost her three times in twenty minutes, and each time we found her thus. The weapons, also, seemed to exert an unaccountable fascination over her. She would take the daggers down from the wall, and run her fingers along the edge,—positively, it looked as though she meant to steal the things!

"Why, my dear," she said, to my remonstrances, "we are all alone in the room, and nobody seems to take the least care of any thing here."

Nobody did seem to take any care, but, nevertheless, I was relieved when we got her safely out of the museum. I hope we did our duty by Heidelberg Castle. Ted took us everywhere. We saw the rent tower, and the tuns, and the great chapel, and a darksome hole which Ted called the monk's chapel; but I think the monks had more sense. Finally, we came out on the terrace.

The sun had sunk below the horizon; only a few crimson streaks, like the careless strokes of an emptied brush, stained the yellow glow in the west. Far below us was spread the town, a huddle of pointed roofs and church spires; directly beneath, the Neckar ran noiselessly over its rocks; to the right and to the left stretched the hills. The near hills were green, and checkered with corn-fields and vineyards; but in the distance the dark purple outlines looked darker against the yellow sea of light. The shadows of the ruined towers lay long and heavy on the grass. Away to the right, a solitary nightingale was singing; and as we stood listening for a moment, vaguely awed by the beauty and the melancholy of the scene, some students, out of sight, began Heine's song:—

Du hast Diamanten und Perlen,
　Hast Alles was Menschenbegehr,
Und hast die schönsten Augen,—
　Mein Liebchen, was willst du mehr?

In the friendly dimness I saw Ted's arm steal around his cousin's waist. He hummed the refrain,—

Und du hast die schönsten Augen,—
　Mein Liebchen, was willst du mehr?

"What I wished at the gate, Ted," said Undine.

"And what was that?" said Ted, lowering his voice. "A heart, by chance?"

"No," said Undine, quietly; "I have more than I need now. But, Ted, we really ought to go. Aunt Eliza will be worried. She has a wild notion that donkeys run away. She says there is viciousness in their eyes!"

We rode home gaily enough; but that evening, passing Undine's door, it opened and she came out; by the lamp-light her face looked pale. For the first time, she seemed to me not the beautiful, cold lorelei about whom I was weaving a fanciful romance, but a girl who had no mother, and who was too rich to have many friends. Almost involuntarily, I drew her to me and kissed her. The faintest flush tinged her cheek. I can't describe how oddly she looked at me, saying, "Then, I don't chill you, Constance."

"Not to mention," said I, laughing. Then I kissed her again. It is possible she was pleased at something; it is possible she was hurt at something. I half believe she is as puzzled over the pleasure or the pain, as I am puzzled over that curious look in her eyes.

July 18.—Louis has returned.

July 21.—Yesterday Louis said, "Con, Ted will get himself into a row if he doesn't mind his pace better. I caught him walking on the Anlage with that Miss Wilmott, this evening. It doesn't look well in an engaged man." Decidedly, it does not. Lately Ted's devotion to that girl has been scandalous, even judged by American ideas. Where foreigners must place Miss Wilmott, I don't venture to imagine.

July 26.—Yesterday I was reading *Undine* to Louis, and Von Reibnitz. Undine's namesake, and the countess came in together during the reading, and would not allow me to stop. The countess, who had never read De la Motte Fouqué's charming tale, quite flattered one by her excitement over its ending. "Ah, bah!" she exclaimed, "but then Undine vas a eediot! Thou art but small like her, my friend."

"She should haf some oder man to take her away from dat villain fool," muttered Von Reibnitz. He looked at Undine as he spoke.

I believe I know now why he spends so much time in Heidelberg. Poor young man! Yesterday, after some imperious drill had torn him from us, the countess burst into a kind of Greek chorus of praise; she grew so enthusiastic that she even abandoned her cherished English, and recounted his virtues in French. Not the least of these seemed to be that his mother was the countess's twelfth cousin. For a brief period this brave, this noble young man, this best of sons, had slightly,—but the most slightly, view you,—admired "Mlle. Grase"; but who could care for her long? "Dear friends, behold the true Bertulda, so weak, so selfish—bah, so pretty!"

She made such a crowning offence of the last adjective that I laughed outright. Nevertheless, the countess is a shrewd old woman.

July 30.—For my sins, Bertulda has taken a fancy to me. She does not improve on acquaintance.

August 2.—Undine bewilders me. Does she care for Ted? If she does, how can she watch Grace Wilmott's audacious flirtation with that odd air of amusement? She has a curious smile, appearing on singularly incongruous occasions; it is almost as if she were smiling at herself. Once I asked her about her name. "My father gave it to me," she said. "It is after an aunt of mine who had a family reputation for fortitude, and my father called me after her because I never cried. You know my mother died when I was born, and there was only he to decide. He died when I was three; I don't even remember how he looked, but I have an idea I should have liked him."

"Didn't you cry often when you were a child?"

"No, somehow I never *wanted* to cry. I really don't remember crying hard but once. That was because I had no little sister. It was amusing."

"It doesn't strike me as amusing."

"You don't know the circumstances. I wasn't more than eight years old. There was a horrid little girl who lived near us,—a dreadfully disagreeable little girl,—who was always chewing gum, and when she tired of that, used to flatten the gum on my hair. It was her crude sense of humor, I suppose; but youth is not tolerant, and it was no end of trouble getting the gum out of my hair! Well, she, this unpleasant little girl, Malie Hungerford, had the sweetest little baby sister in the world. I thought it a great shame that Malie should have three sisters, while I had not even a brother. I was very fond of little Lulu, so I stole her."

"Stole her!"

"Yes, stole her out of the cradle while the nurse was talking to her friend, the ice-man, and Malie was chewing gum somewhere else; stole her, and carried her to an old woman who was to take care of her for me for a dollar a week, my Roman sash, and my new wax doll. You can fancy the conclusion of the story, of course. The old woman was a cunning old woman. She carried the baby home, running all the way. An indignant delegation of Hungerfords waited on my aunt. Poor Aunt Eliza! She began to cry, while I simply stared. 'Oh, Undine! how *could* you act so?' she said, the Hungerfords all the time glaring at me solemnly. 'I wanted a little sister,' said I. 'But, my dear,' said Mrs. Hungerford,—she was a very large woman, Constance, very tall and very stout, and she always grew red in the face when she became moral and instructive,—'my dear,' said she, 'God gives little brothers and sisters—' 'Then won't He please give me one,' I interrupted, not meaning to be rude, but only awfully in earnest. 'No, He won't,' screamed Malie; 'and you can't have any, *never!*' But I didn't look at her. '*Can't* I?' I said to Mrs. Hungerford. 'Why, no, my dear,' she said, you can't. But you may have dear little friends, who will love you very much.' Then I cried."

"Did you always want a sister?"

"Not so much when I saw more of sisters, but I have times of wanting her still."

"Undine," said I, "suppose you try *me;* I never had a sister either, and I love you."

"Do you?" she said, looking at me with her lovely, unfathomable eyes. "I am glad. You will make a nice sister."

At least, dear, though I did not say it to you, I shall make a faithful one.

August 6.—Louis again away, Constance a martyr to Bertulda. Hardly a day passes that she does not come into my room, clad in an untidy blue cashmere wrapper, fling herself upon my lounge, and *confide.* The other day she told me how hard it was to earn her living as a companion (Mrs. Moore never denies her any thing), how sad and lonely she felt, and how much she longed for sympathy. She wept a few tears on a torn handkerchief, which she deluged with my cologne; then she took the cologne off with her to bathe her head. Of course, it has not returned. Farewell, a long farewell to all my sweetness, for she borrowed my other perfumery Thursday. Sometimes her feelings overcome her, and she cries on my handkerchiefs; that is why my stock is getting low. Grief always makes her hair come down, and she puts it up with my hair-pins. Whenever she needs a pin, she carefully selects a black pin from the cushion. There are chords—! and black pins in a foreign country touch one of mine.

August 10.—Ted has taken Mrs. Guernsey to Baden for a few days.

August 15.—Yesterday we had a most disagreeable adventure. We were to drive to Neckar Steinoch, and take dinner at a quaint little inn lauded by Von Reibnitz. Mamma, the countess, and I were to go in a carriage; Von Reibnitz and Undine were to ride. It was a lovely plan, but Bertulda spoiled it all! At the last moment, she wheedled an invitation out of mamma's soft heart. "Poor motherless child!" said mamma. "And you know, Connie, there is a vacant seat in the carriage." So she came. She looked as handsome as a snake, in a blue Chambéry gauze, and a Paris hat trimmed with roses. We took dinner in the garden of the inn. The garden slopes down into the river, and from where we sat we could see trimly checkered hills and vineyards, and, peeping through the trees, a ruined tower, from which once a robber baron descended on peaceful travellers, but which now holds nothing more warlike than flocks of swallows. On the steepest of the hills, a few wretched houses were clustered about a slender church-spire, and a foot-path crawled up to them through stunted vineyards. Von Reibnitz told us that a colony of *cretins* dwelt there. They support themselves chiefly by begging, and I should judge that the whole colony had turned out in our honor. Horrible-looking beings they were,—dwarfed, maimed, deformed in strange and hideous fashions, scarred with loathsome diseases,—living hints of the appalling possibilities of our race. One bolder than the others followed us to the carriage, and clung to the door. He was a repulsively ugly man, who limped, and had somehow lost two fingers of his left hand. Bertulda was nearest to him; she shuddered, and called out in her bad German, "*Gahen snell! ich haben nix!*" The creature only grinned, and clutched her arm. She wrenched it away, screaming to the coachman to strike the man with his whip. The coachman gave a half-reckless stroke behind him, and the *cretin* at that instant swaying forward with the motion of the carriage, the lash cut him full in his face. It was an ugly thing to see! Uglier, perhaps, though, to see his arms tossed up and his body curve backward as the sudden lurch of the carriage tumbled him into the road! The frightened horses broke into a gallop, while mamma shrieked, the countess, I fear, swore, and Bertulda gazed piteously—at her own arm! I looked back. The *cretin* was standing in the centre of the road, covered with dust. There was a wet, red line across his cheek; he wiped it with his ragged sleeve. Undine had thrown him a gold piece, but it glittered unnoticed at his feet. Not so much as glancing down, he looked from his stained sleeve to us, muttering to himself. Then a cloud of dust made a dingy ghost of him, and Undine and Von Reibnitz clattered up to the dro-schky. They were assailed by a little storm of questions. "Was the poor fellow hurt?" cried mamma. "Vat did he saying?" said the countess. "Did he pick up his money?" I asked.

"Oh, no, Mrs. Burt, he wasn't hurt badly," said Undine; "he was saying he would murder Miss Wilmott, madam. No, Connie, he didn't—what is the matter, Miss Wilmott?"

Bertulda was looking desperately frightened; her nerves were so shaken, in fact, that we had to stop and avert the hysterics with cham-pagne. She had taken as much champagne as was good for her already, and the consequent spectacle was not edifying. I wish Ted had seen her.

August 16.—Yesterday Undine gave me an elegant dressing-case. I told her she gave me too many presents. She opened her eyes, "Are you not my sister?" she said. I am out of all patience with Ted. How can a man, fortunate enough to have won such an exquisite being as Undine, descend to Grace Wilmott's *beauté de diable?* Because he is a *man,* I suppose. Yesterday night they went to the cemetery,—"to hear the nightingales sing." Nice, cheerful place for a romantic stroll! As the countess says, *"Blague!"*

September 12.—Ted has a duel on his hands. Walk with Miss Wilmott—rude student—Grace frightened—student knocked down—challenge! The student says he knew Grace before,—had walked with her himself; Grace says it is a wicked lie. Maybe it is, and maybe it isn't. All this, with many unnecessary comments, was confided to me last night. It goes without saying that Undine is not to know.

September 13.—An awkward thing has just happened. Undine and I, going into the reading-room, came suddenly upon Grace Wilmott, sobbing on Ted Tresham's shoulder. "The devil!" said he. Upon my word, I don't blame him. Bertulda sank into a chair, and made a great fuss with her handkerchief. Undine, quite silent, stood in the doorway, looking from one to the other. She was dressed for dinner; the sunlight burnished the dull olive tints of her dress, there was a lace scarf flung about her shoulders, and the opals at her white throat flickered like flame. She had never looked more beautiful. I wonder if Ted didn't think so, too; anyhow, he stared at her with all his eyes. Before he could speak, she stepped between him and Grace. "Excuse me," she said, and there was not a quiver in her sweet voice, "I did not know any one was here. Before I go, let me return something that belongs to Mr. Tresham." She slipped a ring from her finger, laid it on the table near Ted, and turning, passed out of the room. There didn't seem any thing for me to do save go; so, I went—in another direction.

As for my cousin Theodore Tresham, * * * He has just been to see me. I am happy to say he looked infinitely uncomfortable. He burst out at once; he knew he had been a cursed fool, but it wasn't as bad as I thought; he swore he didn't know Miss Wilmott was in the room when he came into it; she had heard of the duel, and she felt sorry, and so— and so—"By Jove, I don't know how it *did* happen!" groaned Ted.

I said I thought I *did*; that was a nice girl to lose Undine for!

"Leave her out, can't you?" he said, gloomily. "You women are always so infernally hard on each other."

"Is Undine hard on her?"

Ted stood up; he looked more of a man than I had ever seen him. "Constance," he said, "I love Undine. And she knows it. Whatever follies and idiotic fancies for other women I may have, I always come back to her. I *have* to! She knows that, too. Tell her I am ashamed of myself, and it is the last time she shall need to forgive me. Tell her I'll do any thing she wants, if she will only let me speak to her one single time."

Well, I promised; for who dares decide what will make a woman happy? Ted as a husband I should not fancy myself, but Undine may.

Later.—I went down stairs to Undine, and conscientiously began Ted's apologies. She stopped the first of them with, "Do you think, Connie, you can invent more excuses for Ted than I?"

She had been so composed, so free from any show of either anger or grief, that I had begun to hope (yes, to *hope,* though Ted is my cousin) that she did not really care for him. In my disappointment, I said the silliest thing possible,—I told her she was far too good for him. She laughed, then she sighed; I had never heard her sigh before, and the soft little sound affected me strangely.

"I don't know about that," she said; "and besides, Constance, we don't love people because they are good, but because we can't help it."

Nothing appropriate occurring to me to say, I said nothing; but I felt, with rush of thankfulness so intense that it was pain, how much I respected Louis. Just at this point in the conversation, it was ordained that Mrs. Guernsey should come in and tell me most of the history of Heidelberg Castle. I have just escaped.

To-morrow the countess and her son are going to take mamma and me to Schwetzingen. The son is a mild-mannered young man, who is the best swordsman in Heidelberg. A wretched old German, with a villainous voice, promenades beneath my window, singing over and over again the first two lines of the Lorelei:—

"Ich weiss nicht was soll es bedeuten,
    Das ich so traurig bin!"

I am tired; I am out of spirits; I wish I could sleep a long, long time.

*   *   *   *   *   *   *   *   *   *

Heidelberg, *September* 25, 1879.—How still the life stands in an old German town. I look from my window on the same shady streets, corps students, yellow-brown dogs sniffing at their masters' heels, English tourists in astonishing plaids and grays, American tourists in sombre black, honest *haus fraus* knitting in the shade, all the same. I might have left them yesterday,—and it is yesterday five years. Five years ago, I put this old journal in the pocket of my trunk, thinking then that I never should write in it again. I did not take it out again until yesterday. The trunk was too large for ordinary use, and it stood unmolested in the garret. At first I shrank from seeing the book, and yet, at the same time, shrank from destroying it; after awhile, I believe I forgot about it; but when I took the old trunk out for this journey, I remembered, and yesterday I read the journal through. Every thing comes back so freshly here, where I knew Undine, and I am glad at last that it should come. Perhaps some day I shall be glad that I have told the end of the story which I began in so unconscious and light-hearted a fashion five years ago. I might, for example, give this journal to Theodore Tresham. I have been trying to renew the old time in every way I know. This morning I climbed up to the castle; I wandered through the bare rooms and ruined arches, and I stood for a moment beneath the gateway where Undine wished "to keep." Nothing there has changed: the waiters at the *restauration* seem to wear the self-same shabby dress-coats; the very coffee was cold—as it used to be.

One thing I have not done: I have not gone to Schwetzingen, although a very pleasant party went to-day, and urged us to accompany them. But I did not go; I do not think I shall ever see Schwetzingen again. Yet it was a pleasant enough day which we spent there five years ago. I forget what we did; I only remember now the look of Louis's face as he walked into the little dining-room of the Golden Stag, where we all were, and the sound of his voice, saying, "Con, you were always brave; there has been a bad accident to Miss Tresham, and she wants you." At least I was brave enough not to make any trouble. While they were putting the horses into the lightest carriage they could find,—Von Reibnitz's dog-cart,—for there was no railroad then from Schwetzingen, Louis told me all he knew; afterwards I heard the rest. It seems Undine and Mrs. Guernsey had gone up to the castle, and were out on the terrace, when they heard wild screams, and almost instantly Grace Wilmott darted up to them, pursued by a horrible-looking man brandishing a dagger. Louis did not know then, but it was the *cretin* of Neckar Steinoch; for weeks he had been tracking Grace, with the strange cunning of his distorted wits, and he had found her alone among the ruins. The dagger belonged to the museum, and I suppose he stole it. Grace had fled the instant she saw him; she rushed to Undine, stumbled, and fell at her feet. The fall probably saved her, for the *cretin* had caught her dress and struck one furious blow; before he could strike again, Undine had flung her arms about him. Slender as they were, they clung like steel: though he shifted his dagger to his left hand and stabbed her, they never loosened their grasp. "Run!" she cried to the helpless, shrieking creature by her side; "run, I can't hold him long!" Bertulda,—well, she *was* Bertulda,—she saved herself. Mrs.

Guernsey's screams brought a dozen people to the spot, Louis among them. He had returned unexpectedly from Frankfort, and still wore his travelling revolver; drawing it, he pushed it under Undine's arm, within an inch of the man's breast, and fired. The *cretin* rolled over on the stones, and was dead in five minutes. But his rusty dagger had done its work. They carried my poor girl to the hotel, and Louis went for me. It was Von Reibnitz who brought him the horse.

Our drive home is like a nightmare to me. When we reached the hotel, a man ran out of the shadow of the blue and white awnings and held out his hand to help me from the carriage. "Yes," he said, answering the question I had not courage to ask; "they think she may live until morning, but there is no—no hope!" Then I saw it was Ted,—for at first the sun had shone in his face, and I was half dazed; now I could see how white and haggard his gay, careless face was, with red circles about the eyes, as if he had been crying. "O Constance," he cried, wringing my hand hard, "for God's sake, get me a chance to see her; Mrs. Guernsey is angry, and won't let me in!"

I suppose I must have promised; somehow I got away, and hurrying down the dark hall, almost ran into Grace Wilmott. Her eyes were red and swollen,—it was always such an easy thing for her to cry! She sobbed out an entreaty for me to stop.

"O Mrs. Lynde, is she really going to die? Indeed, it wasn't my fault! And every body blames me! Oh, please stop! Oh, what shall I do?"

I did stop. It was dark in the hall, but there was some light, and I hope she saw my face. I pointed over my shoulder. "Mr. Tresham is *there"* I said, and I left her; it was our last conversation. Mrs. Guernsey was waiting. She led me into the room. There was a table, covered with papers, drawn up to the bed, and beside it stood a tall man in black. Through the triangle made by his bent arm, I caught a glimpse of soft, brown hair; he moved, and I saw Undine's face. I went up to her,—what does it matter how I felt? I think it was then Mrs. Guernsey and the doctor went softly out of the room. Undine feebly put her hand on mine. "I knew you would come, Connie," she said; "my dear love, how hard you must have driven!"

I tried to speak,—to tell her it would hurt her to talk. She smiled and said, "Nothing will hurt me now. Connie, I wanted to speak to you alone, on business. I have left half my property to Ted; then I have left something to Aunt Eliza,—all she would take, you know she is rich; and

I have left some fifty thousand in legacies to some poor people I have known; the rest I have given to you. You are my sister, Constance; you will take my money, wont you? It makes me happy to think of your having it."

"Oh, why did you save that girl?" I cried. "Oh, how can I bear it?"

Undine smiled again,—the curious smile which used to puzzle me. "Why?" she repeated. "I'm sure I don't know, myself. Yet, I suppose I would do it over again, were it to do. It seems absurd, rather, doesn't it?"

I could not speak. "How still it is!" said Undine. "Is it really so still, or is it—Connie, do you mind going to the window to see?"

I went to the window. There was straw scattered over the street, and Von Reibnitz stood like a sentinel at the corner. When I told Undine, she sighed. "How good he is!" she murmured, "I wish—" She did not finish the sentence, but a moment later she asked me to thank Von Reibnitz, and to give him a chain she had worn, which he had once admired. "Some day, I hope," she said, "he will give it to some pretty German girl, who will love him as the countess says 'the best of sons' deserves." It was a little while after this, she asked me if I had seen Ted. I told her what he had said. "Did he think I could die without seeing him?" she said. "My poor boy! But, for all that, he will marry Grace Wilmott."

"He can never look at her again!" I cried. Heaven knows, I believed it at the time!

She leaned her head half wearily on my shoulder. "I believe I could have kept him had I lived," she said; "but a memory is so weak. Constance."

"Yes, dear."

"Do you believe spirits can see those they used to love?"

"Oh, God knows, my darling, I cannot tell you. You will be happy, however it is!"

"Do you think so?" she answered, dreamily. "I have always been a kind of pagan, and I don't—feel—quite—certain."

What could I say to her? I sat silent, with a heavy heart, while one by one the street lights sprang out of the darkness, and by their gleam I took my last look of my darling's face.

They were singing over among the hills the same little love-song of Heine's, which I heard, for the first time, the day we visited the castle:—

"Du hast Diamanten und Perlen,
　　Hast Alles was Menschenbegehr,
Und hast die schönsten Augen—
　　Mein Liebchen, was willst du mehr?"

She turned those "loveliest eyes" wistfully up to mine. *"You* will always love me Con, wont you? Now call Ted. Kiss me first." Even as I kissed her, I felt her lips stir with a smile. "Connie, do you remember the day at the castle, when I wished? Well, the ring is a true fairy, for I wished Ted might love me as long as I lived,—and he will."

I laid her gently back on the pillows, but I could not see her face through my tears. I did not need to call Ted: he was watching at the door. I could hear him rush past me and fling himself on his knees before Undine, begging her, in a broken voice, to forgive him,—only to forgive him. "I never loved Grace; I never loved any one but you! You said I always came back—O my God! Constance! Constance, come here!"

Yes, he might kiss her hands and her hair, show his useless remorse in any frantic way he would,—it did not matter what he did any more, for Undine lay there with her last smile forever fixed on her beautiful mouth; as if dead she smiled at his pain, as living she smiled at her own.

All this is five years away. We left Undine in the pretty little cemetery where Ted and Grace Wilmott went to hear the nightingales sing. Last night I heard them singing by her grave.

Poor Von Reibnitz was killed in the Franco-Prussian war. He left me a little pet dog, which, as I am not fond of dogs, has been something of a trial to me.

The countess is on her Polish estates with her son. She writes me occasionally, and often alludes to her Heidelberg experience. I have no doubt she makes a capital tragic tale of it: she was always a fine talker in every language but English.

Ted Tresham married Grace Wilmott within six months after his cousin's death. I hear queer stories of his wife's extravagance and flirtations, and I take a grim satisfaction in the hearing. Our own intercourse with Ted naturally ceased with his marriage, but business matters have made a few interviews necessary. He seems subdued and changed, and looks ten years older. He has never mentioned Undine's name.

As for me, Undine's legacy has prospered with us. I am more in love with my husband than ever. My dear mother is still with us. On the whole, I am a very happy woman,—but I have never made another friend.

PART II

QUEER GENDERS

THE BACHELORS

Samuel L. Knapp

"One impulse of a vernal wood
    May teach you more of man—
Of moral evil, and of good—
    Than all the sages can."

The knowledge of human nature cannot be acquired by simply surveying the mass of mankind. We must study the characters of individuals, and draw our general inferences from a careful examination of the whole details. By such a process we shall find that the laws of nature and the commands of heaven are in harmony, and cannot be opposed with impunity. The heart that is cased in flint to the common observer, often beats with an irregular motion, and has its aches, that are ill-concealed under the mask of indifference.

JOHN THOMPSON, HENRY GILBERT, and MONTJOY TILESTON RUSSELL, were nearly of the same age—born in the same city—educated in the elementary branches of knowledge in the same school—and graduated from college in the same class. They were bright boys—emulous of distinction—and held, if not an equal rank with each other, surely a high one in their class. In the course of obtaining their education, they were constantly associated together, and a strong friendship grew up between them, which they fondly believed that nothing but death could destroy. They agreed to settle in their native city. Thompson studied the law—Gilbert, physic—and Russell entered the counting-room of his father, and prepared himself to become a merchant—one acquainted with the history and geography of nations, with the nature and amount of their products and commerce. After a few years, he became a partner in the house of which his father was the head, and was considered as an active, intelligent young merchant. The lawyer and doctor began business under good auspices, particularly the former. He was well read, sagacious, and full of confidence. He studied his causes well, and was in general very successful—for he would not condescend to be a tool against his judgment for any one. The doctor was learned in his profession, and refined in his manners. He would not use a harsh word to the humblest patient, nor flatter the most exalted. If he did not advance so rapidly as many dashing young men have done, still it may be said, that what he gained, he never lost. His delicacy was only surpassed by his firmness—and that never had a particle of asperity in it.

These young gentlemen had made it a rule with themselves to meet once a week, to enjoy a banquet of conversation; and to which feast, like Scarron's, each guest brought his own dish. This habit was kept up for several years with great constancy, and to their mutual advantage. Sometimes a few friends were admitted to join this trio—and this was considered a great favor.

At a time between the embargo of 1807 and the war of 1812, the prices of merchandize underwent many fluctuations, in the successive shocks given to commerce by the numerous acts of national legislation. At a time when new changes were anticipated, the young merchant was not at his weekly supper as usual. The other two went out to find him. He was still at his desk, but engaged to be with them in the course of an hour or two. When he arrived he told them that he anticipated that great changes were about to take place in the prices-current, and that he had prevailed upon a young man who had just come into possession of a great estate, to venture an hundred thousand dollars to be used by him at half profits. He dwelt so long on the subject, and gave such satisfactory reasons for his belief of great gains, that his friends were convinced that he had a splendid prospect before him; and after some further preliminary remarks, the professional gentlemen prepared to put something into the speculation. This, Russell agreed to take, upon conditions that they should receive all the profits—saying, that if he was successful, he should make enough out of what he now had of his own and of others, and that he would not trade for his own benefit on the money of his friends. The lawyer and doctor, by pledging their bank stock and mortgaging some paternal real estate, raised fifteen thousand dollars each. This was done forthwith, and the money was put into the hands of their friend the merchant. Some weeks elapsed before the waters began to move. The first purchase made by Russell was of all the spices, drugs, and coffee he could find at fair prices. The next, was to enter into contracts, which were made binding, for an immense quantity of distilled spirits, at numerous distilleries. This being done, he repaired to the city of New York, to watch the operation of the great speculators in Wall street. This was managed so adroitly, that his views were not suspected until he was well acquainted with the signs of the flood from the first rise until it would return to its neap. He then left that city for his own. All his transactions were carried on without bustle, and succeeded to his wishes.

At a supper on one of their usual nights of meeting, Russell assured his friends that each of them were now worth an hundred thousand dollars in addition to their former fortunes; and that he had been equally successful himself, but that he should now discontinue his exertions—believing that speculation had reached its height. The professional men were delighted with the news, and earnestly desired their mercantile friend to cease his operations;—they did not wish for more. Elated with success, they pushed round the bottle, until they were all a little flushed with wine and the thoughts of their prosperity. At this crisis, one of them proposed that they should adopt a plan of life that would insure them the title of "THE IMMORTAL THREE." "Name it!—name it!" were heard from the other two. "Then," said he, "let us make up our minds to live bachelors until we go to our graves." "Agreed!—agreed!" was the response—and, before the clock struck twelve that night, they had signed a paper, (of which each took a copy,) that he should forfeit the pledge of honor which held them together, whoever might enter the bonds of matrimony, or suffer any woman to call him *husband.* They then talked over the course of life they intended to pursue. "I," said the lawyer, "will forthwith close my professional business, or, at least, as soon as possible—buy me a farm, and become an agriculturist, a horticulturist—and my chief delight shall be in a garden. In viewing nature and her delightful products I will spend my days; and repose, when I choose, on a bed of flowers."—"I," said the doctor, "will never again administer a tincture, or a pill, or grasp the amputating knife. I will retire from corporal and mental miseries, and confine myself to philosophical research. The microscope, the developements of chemistry, and the pure mathematics, shall delight me by day, and the still greater wonders of the telescope by night."—The merchant pondered for awhile, but at last shaped his course. "My fame shall be that of a traveller," said he; "I will emulate Mandeville, surpass Bruce, and rival Ledyard. I will hunt the chamois on the Alps—shoot the condor on the Andes—and drink at the sources of the Mississippi and the Nile. I will engrave my name on the top of the highest Pyramid—and bring up a gem from the deepest cavern in the mines of Golconda."

The genius of revelry was the ascendant of this midnight hour; and when the morning sun arose, each was ready to shed tears at his rash pledge—but neither would be foremost in acknowledging his folly and recanting his error. The lawyer was the first to set about performing his part. He bought a large, fine farm, well wooded and watered, of an excellent soil—and commenced his labors. He laid out his grounds on the most approved methods—and, by dams, sluices, &c. prepared to irrigate a greater portion of his fields. He collected a rare stock of cattle, and kept them under the full force of feed. His farm soon became a pattern one—and all in the neighborhood were his imitators, as far as they could be. His poultry-yard swarmed with every species of domestic fowl that ever made a supper for Lucullus, or was ever eaten with curry at the feast of an Asiatic satrap. Every day in the year he could command from his own premises all the luxuries of life—in which he took more pleasure in seeing than in devouring. He supplied the sick with an hundred little dainties from his field or larder, and his wine was a cordial ready to flow when the village physician prescribed it for any of his poor patients. His fields were the object of admiration—but it was on his garden that he spent the most of his time, and where he exercised his highest faculties. The copious stream which ran through his grounds was made to pass in three channels—being separated before they entered the walls of the garden. Trees were planted on the banks of each current, excepting in the proper places for bridges and openings. The grounds were wavy by nature, which offered great capacities for picturesque landscapes. The fruit-trees were numerous of every kind that the climate would bear. His green-house and conservatory were large, and filled with plants and flowers from every clime. In a beautiful clump of trees he erected a temple for a study, and there read the classics and all the modern works of taste and talent. It was indeed a treat to be invited to spend a few days at his hospitable mansion. His library was extensive, and contained many curious works on all subjects, and which far exceeded any other private library in the country, in works on agriculture, gardening, and on all these kindred subjects. He had classed them and arranged them himself, and made an index to these works with his own hand—which gave great facilities in readily finding whatever was wanted by the cultivator. In his winter's leisure he amused himself in collecting facts to show the progress of agriculture in every part of the globe, in every age of the history of man, and which went far to prove that the food for the population of the world grew more abundant as the human race increased. The easterly side of his farm was bounded on a lake of large dimensions, filled with a great variety of excellent fish. His friends always found the finest table at his house that the country could afford. Here was happiness one would think sufficient for any mortal.

Gilbert purchased himself a farm on a small scale—-just large enough to raise a subsistence for himself and household. He erected an observatory, furnished himself with costly astronomical intruments, and in the lower part of his tower he provided rooms for philosophical experiments, and spent more hours in his laboratory than in his observatory. He turned from experiments to abstract sciences; and, at the same time, he kept a meteorological table, and measured the fall of rain and snow with accuracy; and once a quarter gave a paper to the Philosophical Society, on some scientific subject—being the result of ingenious experiments and sound reflections.

He made a curious almanack each year, and presented it to a shoemaker in the neighborhood who had to support fifteen children. This son of Crispin rode into fame by his learned neighbor's science, and had numerous letters addressed to him from distant places—all of which Gilbert regularly answered, until Melchisedek Buswell became renowned in every quarter of the globe, as one of the first mathematicians and astronomers of the day—when, perhaps, the utmost extent of Buswell's knowledge was no more than to work out that tremendous question, "How many barley-corns does it take to reach round the world?"

He often visited his friend Thompson, and heard him talk of grain, cattle, trees, shrubs, and flowers, and probably partook, in some slight degree, of his friend's delight—but, after all, could not help thinking how undignified was Thompson's pursuits compared with his own. What pleasure could a wheat-field give, compared with some new discovery in the heavens?

The two friends often heard from Montjoy, who was careful to send them every rare book on mathematics, astronomy, agriculture, or botany; and also, every rare plant and every new mathematical instrument. They were in the habit of corresponding most frequently with each other, which made no small item in their duties and their happiness.

Gilbert offered to instruct young men who were going to sea, in the lunar and sideral calculations, without fee or reward—only stipulating, that when they became master-mariners, they should pay to the Female Orphan Asylum the usual fee for a common course of instruction in navigation. This was readily complied with. If he was not happy to the extent of the measure of the lot of some mortals, he was free from anxiety and ambition. Now-and-then a writer would attack some of his favorite theories; and this would give him some pain, notwithstanding all that he wrote was under feigned names. At times he grew weary of his pursuits, and would turn to works of taste for relief. These would engage him for a few days only; and even during that time he would forget the beauty of a figure of rhetoric, to pursue some problem which had started up in his mind as he was dwelling on Shakspeare or Milton. He contrived to keep up with the news of the day, but took no part in politics—for he found that political excitement was the bane of science and an enemy to letters. He had his political views, and gave his vote, but never attempted to influence the minds of others, or to seek for public honors for himself. He associated with but few, and was familiar with no one but his friend Thompson—yet he was kind to all. The professional men of the village usually dined with him once a week. He paid his physician as the Chinese do, by the year—deducting all the term of his sickness, if he should chance to be unwell. With but few singularities, he moved onward with the current of time—devoting six hours each day to his mathematical and astronomical studies. The good people considered him as rather belonging to the stars than to earth; but as he paid his taxes cheerfully, and injured no one, they thought him no bad citizen.

Montjoy Tileston Russell, after visiting most of the great cities in Europe, turned his attention to Asia and Africa. He sailed for the Cape of Good Hope, and spent some months in examining that country with more attention than any American traveller had done before his time. From thence, he made a voyage to Bengal, and visited a large portion of that immense country. He took passage in an English vessel bound to Bombay. In this place, he became acquainted with the Recorder, Sir James Mackintosh, one of the most accomplished men of his time: with him, he passed several hours every day. He had bills of exchange on John Long, Esq., a merchant of extensive business in Bombay, and became intimately acquainted with his family. Mr. Long was an Englishman, who had resided many years in Spain, and had married a Spanish lady of great beauty and talents. They had been blessed with several children: the sons were in the king's service—an only daughter was still unmarried, and lived at home, having just left school in England. She united the Spanish dignity with the English complexion, and was in every respect a fine woman. She spoke the English, Spanish, French, and Italian languages, with purity and ease. She became quite interested in the recital of Russell's travels in various parts of the world, but could not help intimating that such a life of peril could not be a happy one; and expressed a fear for his safety, when he told her that in a few weeks he was to sail for Mocha, and from thence he was going to explore the coast of the Red Sea, taking the track of the Israelites through the wilderness to Judea, and then winter in Grand Cairo. Finding an American ship in the port, he collected all the rare plants he could find, and sent them to his friend Thompson, with a sketch of his travels. In making up his packages of flowers and seeds, he was assisted by Cynthia Long, who had become quite enamored with the study of botany. He hastened his departure, for he felt himself getting deeply in love with his fair friend, and seemed to flatter himself that there might be some reciprocity between them: but then, his pledge of honor to live a bachelor came across his mind, and he grew sick at the thoughts of it. "What evil genius," he would often say to himself, "came over me at that fatal hour? Would to God, that we had all been made bankrupts by our speculations, which we considered so fortunate at the time, and then we should have never found ourselves miserable by this foolish pledge!" With these feelings, he tore himself away from his friends, and sailed for Mocha, hardly caring for his fate. He reached his port of destination, without any remarkable occurrence. From Mocha, he started with a caravan to the interior of the country. For some time, he went on as well as one could expect in such company, partly uncertain of his course, and more uncertain of his treatment. When they stopped, he was in misery from the want of tents, and from want of proper food; and where to rest his head, he did not often know. But this he could bear, thinking that at some time his journey would end, and he should be happy in thinking that he had done bravely. At length, one afternoon, when they had encamped near a spring of water, and were enjoying themselves with the prospect of pursuing their journey as soon as the moon arose—this was just before midnight—the camels were laden, and the whole ready to depart, when some one of the horses became restive, and would not touch his provender, keeping his head close to the ground, as if hearing something afar off. The leaders hastened his orders to depart. All were mounted, and had proceeded about a mile, when a band of enemies on horses and dromedaries dashed in upon them, making a desperate charge. The Arabs were brave, and fought as long as they could. Russell, thinking it was for life and liberty, made a most desperate fight; but all was in vain. The assailants were numerous, and their conquest was easy. Two of the caravan escaped: the rest were killed, wounded, or taken prisoners. Russell fell under the sabres of his foes, with many wounds; but none of them were mortal. He had several cuts in the breast and arms, and was exhausted from loss of blood.

As soon as the fight was over, the assailants, knowing the importance of their prisoner, bound up his wounds with bruised poppies, and gave him barley-water to raise his exhausted spirits. They laid him in their tents, on the skin of a camel, and treated him with great attention from mere mercenary motives. This first night was an awful one to him: he saw the stars performing their destined courses, while the moon was riding in majesty over his head. The silence was distressing. No sound broke the stillness of the night: the long, sighing breaths of the camel and dromedary alone were heard; for the Arabs were all in profound repose. One constellation sunk after another, until the morning sun arose. He was unable to drag one limb after another—but they must go on. They tied him to a bed on the back of a camel, and pushed onwards, fearing to remain in the same situation, apprehending a vigorous pursuit. This situation was not so distressing as he expected, for their progress was slower than common, and their regard for his comfort greater than he anticipated. His reflections were, however, any thing but pleasant. Talking to himself, he said, "Why should I have left my native land, where fame and even pleasure awaited me, to roam in this barbarous country, to satisfy my curiosity, without doing much good to my fellow-men? Why should I have left the charms of civil and social life, to wander among savage men? I could have slept in quiet in my own bed, in the land of my nativity, and have received every attention that wealth and respect could have commanded, and now I am a slave—a wounded man; and Heaven only knows if ever I am again to see the faces I once looked upon, and loved! This is travelling to satisfy the restlessness of the mind." With these thoughts he passed the night, drawing no other consolation than that which arose from believing that his wounds were not mortal.

By many marches, he was conveyed to the much distinguished residence of the tribe to whom he was now a prisoner. They knew his situation in life, and were determined not to lose their prize. When he reached the usual abode of the Arab women, he was treated with no ordinary kindness, for they all understood that he would be ransomed at a high price. From the strength of his constitution, and the simplicity of his living, he began to recruit, and in a few weeks was nearly well again; but not a word was dropped about his ransom. Still, he was comparatively happy, from the attentions he received among his new acquaintances. The chief Arab's daughter made him delicate cakes of pease meal and barley, and gave them to him daily, when the father was absent. This was done with a tenderness that won his heart. He would often say to himself, "Oh woman! how kind thou art in all tribes and people, while savage man acts like a hard master—aye, and often like a brute!" The mother and daughter would steal to his tent, and give him goats' milk and little cheeses, when the lordly chief was fast asleep. He said to himself, "I do not deserve this! Have I not entered into a league to abjure the marriage tie? Why do they harass me with their kindness? it is only a satire on my outrageous pledge! But they know it not." The chief began to think of making him a son-in-law; but to every intimation of this kind he was dumb, and appeared not to understand the hints given him.

The long absence of the traveller from Bombay, without any direct intelligence from him, at first began to alarm his friends, and at length rumors of his death were prevalent. It was stated that he had fallen in an attack upon the caravan, who had pledged themselves for his safety at Mocha. Those who escaped stated that they saw him fall under the sabres of two fierce Arabs, while fighting manfully for his life. No hopes remained for his safety, among his friends in general at Bombay. But his female friend, Cynthia Long, could not be satisfied that her friend Russell was dead. She mourned his fate, with others, but still could not give him up entirely. She could not feel that the gallant and accomplished Russell was dead; and she dwelt upon the subject, until she saw him in imagination, a slave, going through every scene of degradation. In this frame of mind, she applied to an old Arab, who kept a sort of *Café* at the corner of one of the streets near her father's residence, to learn if he knew any thing of the course her friend had taken. He was well acquainted with his whole route, and told her that, in his opinion, Russell was still alive, as his ransom must have been the principal object of the expedition to attack the caravan. The bargain was soon made between old Hassan and Cynthia. She was to furnish him with money, and he was to set out immediately, to find the Captain. Cynthia, without hesitation, pawned her jewels, and raised two thousand dollars, in gold sequins, for the enterprize. Hassan received his instructions, and was off the next morning. He went to Mocha—learned all about the caravan that was cut up in its course to Jerusalem. He followed the track, faithful to his promise, in the garb of a poor Arab, until he found his long-sought object. He entered the tent where Russell was a prisoner, and now felt that half was done, and more, when he was assured that he was in fine health. Hassan had come a mendicant to the wealthy Arab's tent, and took no notice of his slave. After some inquiries, he stated to the chief that great concern had been felt at Mocha for a traveller who had joined a caravan to search for medicinal herbs in that region; and suggested that a liberal sum would be given for his ransom, if he could be found. The avaricious feelings of the chief were excited; and believing that his slave was the traveller, seemed to listen to the suggestions of the mendicant: which ended at length in a determination to go with his slave to a place near Mocha, to see if the ransom could be obtained. They were soon on their way. Hassan had declared on his word, as a Mussulman, that he had heard a merchant of distinction—Tariff Ben Hafiz—offer a thousand dollars for the ransom of the traveller, and he thought he would give more. Within a short distance from the city, they stopped, and Hassan repaired at once to Mocha. In a few days, Hafiz appeared—a merchant, whose garb bespoke him a man of consequence. The money—fifteen hundred dollars—was paid, and a bill of sale was given. "Go, traveller," said Hafiz, "and enjoy yourself among the daughters of your land, and make no farther attempt to explore these dangerous paths. Curiosity is a vice, when it is attended by too much danger. Go, cultivate your maize—extend your commerce; but leave the desert for those who were born near it, and must cross it." "I am willing and able to repay you my ransom," said Russell. "I know it," said Hafiz. Meet me at Bombay: I will there take my right, and only that. An Arab may be a robber, but never a usurer. There, sir, I shall exact the last sequin I shall pay. This, however, you must add to your ransom—these sequins—that you may go to Bombay as a gentleman. On my pledge, I will be there as soon as you are, and demand my advance": and waving his hand with Oriental grace and dignity, bade the traveller adieu.

A vessel soon sailed from Mocha to Bombay, on board of which a humble Arab occupied a place in the steerage, and on the voyage fell dangerously sick. He was an old man. Russell became acquainted with his case; for there are none so ready to become acquainted with the miseries of others, as those who have suffered themselves. Russell attended the old man's couch with every medicine considered proper in his case; and when it was allowed him to recruit by delicate food, Russell brought it to him at the proper hours. It was received with great gratitude; but at the same time, in a manner that seemed to say that I have done this thing to others. The attachment between the patient and the nurse seemed to grow daily; and Russell made the old Arab promise him that he would call on him when they arrived at Bombay, and renew their intercourse. The sick man was at home at Bombay; and mentioned not only Sir James Mackintosh, but also Mr. Consul Long and his daughter Cynthia, among his friends. "Then," said Russell, "you are my friend—I am his friend." "And they are more your friends," said Hassan, "than you will ever know." The manner in which this was said was so peculiar, Russell noticed it, but could not precisely comprehend what was meant by the expression, the Asiatics are so full of enigma. Once or twice, the old Arab spoke of Cynthia Long, in a manner that stumbled Russell. "Can this old fellow," said he, mentally, "have a passion for this young lady?"

On the arrival of the vessel at Bombay, Russell was received by all his friends as one raised from the dead. He stated the whole history of the adventure, and all agreed that it was *passing strange*. Every day he became more and more interested in Cynthia, and thought less of his idle pledge. To ease his own mind on the subject, he consulted the rector of the Episcopalian church on a supposed case of conscience, stating his own exactly. The rector laughed at him, to think a man of sense could have any scruples on such a question. The vow, when made to the Lord, was not even required to be paid, if any thing injurious to another might flow from the fulfilment of it. The pledge of honor, even among men of the world, was not binding in a court of honor, unless it would enhance another's happiness, or shed some new rays of glory on one's country or his own fame. Sir James being present, placed the subject on the right grounds, as he did every thing; and Russell made up his mind to make proposals to Cynthia, having a belief that he could obtain the consent of her parents. He waited now only for the appearance of the Arabian merchant, whose visit he so much desired: for he was not apprized of the sum paid for his ransom; but thought that it must have been great, as his owner held him at a high price, in comparison with others their prisoners, to slave-traders who had made offers for him. No Tariff Ben Hafiz came. Russell requested Mr. Long to take from the fund in his hands twice the sum he had ever known paid for the ransom of any captive, and sequester it for the payment to the merchant when he might arrive. In a few days an opportunity occurred for Russell to offer himself. In wandering about the botanical garden, then under the supervisorship of Sir James, Russell took up a violet of the tricolor purple kind, and gave it to Cynthia. They had been talking of the Oriental language of flowers. She placed it on her bosom. He said no more. On their return, he made his wishes known to the parents of Cynthia, and presented them with further credentials than he had before exhibited, and found that his suit was prosperous. He now prepared to be married by the consent of all parties, and to return to his native country, having made a free and candid statement of his whole course of life.

Mr. Long, having determined to give his daughter a splendid set of diamonds on her marriage, repaired to Samuel the Israelite, who was the first jeweller of Bombay, for a set of diamonds. He was told by Samuel that he had a set that he could furnish at a low price, as he had received them as a pledge for a certain sum of money from a young lady of the city, who had come to him in disguise. They were pledged for two thousand dollars. Mr. Long was astonished to see that these gems bore his own daughter's initials. He said, "I will take them to my house, Samuel, and see if they will suit." He entered the house with a slow and measured step; and opening the casket in a significant manner, enquired how these jewels suited. Cynthia raised herself with more than ordinary majesty, and said, "Father, they are the only jewels I ever wish to accept. They were once mine: I pawned them to redeem a friend from slavery and death—that friend is before you." The Anglo-Iberian maid quailed not before her father's stern look. "I sent Hassan on the errand of enquiry. He also was the Arab merchant who purchased Mr. Russell, and my jewels were the means to save my friend from captivity. Condemn me who will. It was Hassan who ordered him to come to Bombay—I gave no such orders. I supposed that he would have taken some other course, and that I never should have seen him again." Russell rushed forward, and took her in his arms, and exclaimed, "My guardian angel! nothing but the decrees of heaven shall part us hereafter." The father and mother were in ecstasy. The story took wing; and old Hassan was, at once, put into a noble *café*, and amply paid for his services. Mr. Long gave his daughter to his American friend, and Sir James was the friend of the bridegroom; and the casuistic parson joined Montjoy Tileston Russell, the American traveller, to Cynthia Long, the Anglo-Iberian maid, who had, in the generosity of her nature, saved her friend from captivity. The whole city rejoiced at the event; and as the happy pair returned from church, the populace strewed flowers in their pathway. In a few weeks, a ship was bought, and Russell and his lady were ready to depart for America. The ship had a full cargo of goods. Mr. Long gave a supper to his friends, and Sir James was there, in the full glow of his intellectual powers, and old Hassan was invited to the feast. It was one of mind and feeling. Sir James was full of playfulness, and had many allusions to the union of the two countries. He gave many splendid anticipations of future events; and said, the mother and the daughter were one day to be the arbiters of the world. Old Hassan whispered in Cynthia's ear, that he wished to leave Asia for America; and Russell declared that nothing would give him more pleasure, than to take the old man out with him. The voyage was soon got up, and all was in readiness. The parting was painful: but a woman goes with one she loves to any clime or country, with a blindness that proves her love. This has been, is, and for ever will be the law of nature. All Bombay were on the shore, when Russell and his spouse departed. The clergyman waved his hands and blessed them, as he saw them depart. All said, "God bless the new-married couple!" The voyage was a pleasant one, and they reached the shores of the United States without any disaster. Russell was known to be one of the three bachelors, and every one was waiting to witness the effect on the other two. They, too, heard the story, and were silent. Not a word escaped their lips. Thompson and Gilbert, perhaps, had some conversation among themselves; but whatever it might have been, it never reached the world. They still persevered in their course, without any observations on the dereliction of their friend. Russell felt an awkwardness in his situation, as it regarded his friends, but made no explanations.

Thompson still was delighted with his employment as an agriculturist, but more particularly as a gardener of Flora. His garden, conservatory, and green house, attracted the attention not only of his neighbors, but also of every traveller. Those who came with a line from a friend, were invited to partake of refreshments in his hospitable mansion, and all had an opportunity of visiting his grounds. He was in advance of all the florists in the country. He had a larger collection of roses than any other person, and a greater variety of exotics of every kind. But the flower he loved the most was the tricolored violet, called *heart's ease, forget-me-not*, and sometimes *a pansey*. This little flower throughout Europe and Asia, for countless ages, has been an emblem of affection.

Gilbert still pursued his course of study—furnishing the periodicals with articles on astronomy, for his amusement; but he sometimes felt that man was born to live on the earth, and rest securely while connected with his fellow-man. Often he was found to acknowledge that he was fatigued when he returned from his flights through the heavens, and he was obliged to rest himself by indulging in the reveries of fancy. One of his favorite amusements was to people the planets with beings of his own creation. He wrote a poem which he called "*Urania*," describing the inhabitants of his beloved Venus—with their beautiful change of seasons, their refined manners and high poetical character, their freedom from political feuds, and the perpetual sunshine of the soul which reigned among them. He dwelt on this subject until he loved to watch that lovely star that shines brightest in the heavens, whether she belonged to the evening shades or to the morning's dawn. He dwelt upon the heavens, until, like our first parents in the bower of Eden, he communed with celestial spirits—and, although no Eve was with him, could say to these creatures of his imagination,—

> ———"How often, from the steep
> Of echoing hill or thicket, have we heard
> Celestial voice to the midnight air;
> Sole, or responsive each to other note,
> Singing the Great Creator! Oft in bands,
> While they keep watch, or nightly rounding walk,
> With heavenly touch of instrumental sounds,
> In full harmonious number join'd, their songs
> Divide the night, and lift our thoughts to heaven."

He carried his devotion to his loved star, and to the whole host of the skies, so far, that some began to think him so much under the influence of the moon or stars, that he was not competent to take care of himself. Among them was an only nephew—a profligate young man, who had squandered his own property, and was now waiting for his uncle's. In an evil hour he petitioned the Judge of Probate to appoint him guardian to his uncle. The Judge knew the astronomer, and indignantly refused to consider the application. The young man's prospects were ruined for ever. This eagerness to inherit, is often the cause of never inheriting. This act of his nephew so severely wounded Gilbert's pride, that he could not contain himself within any bounds of prudence, and his rage at the insult was almost sufficient to induce those unacquainted with him, to suppose there was some aberration of mind in his conduct. The ingratitude of his nephew stung him to the heart, and he began to think that the pursuits of science were vain, if they led to such disasters. He communed with Thompson on his mortification, who gave him good counsel, and recommended him to pursue for some time the general wanderings of literature in his delightful garden. This offer was accepted—and, for several of the summer months, he took up his abode with his friend.

Russell was happy in his family, and for awhile successful in his business; but, after several years, finding his property in some measure reduced, by losses at sea, he closed his business, and retired into the country, some eight or ten miles from his former friends; but, as they seldom visited their neighbors, he did not see them—until the time we have mentioned of their being together after the wound had been given to the feelings of Gilbert by his nephew—and then the meeting was accidental. Riding around the country with his whole family in a large carry-all, the driver took such roads as he thought would give them the best view of the country. Thompson's garden was to be seen from the street—and the children cried out to the driver to stop, and let them see *Paradise*. This compliment was heard by the owner of the premises—and he raised his head from the flowers he was examining, and saw Russell and his family, and noticed the impatience of the children to walk in the garden—and, stepping up to the wall, invited the children to come in; and, opening the gate himself, came up to the carriage and offered Mrs. Russell his hand, to conduct her to the garden. She did not know the gentleman. As he entered the enclosure, he with great embarrassment stammered out—"Russell, will you not do me the honor of looking at these flowers with your children?" He descended from the carriage, and entered the garden. Thompson gazed on him a moment, and then rushed into Russell's embrace. They forgave each other; no explanations were necessary. The wife, from what she had heard from her husband when they were married, instantly understood the whole matter—and hastened to find her strolling children. Gilbert had seen the interview from the summer-house, and flew out to meet them. He read all at a glance, and declared that it was the happiest moment of his life. As soon as the three friends were a little more composed, they went in search of Madam Russell.

Thompson and Gilbert were introduced to the wife of their friend—an elegant and accomplished woman. She received them as old friends, and in ten minutes the children were climbing up to get into the arms of their new friends. They were invited to stay and dine—which invitation was accepted—and a happy time they had of it. The two bachelors were delighted to find the second and third sons were named for them—the first being called after the maternal grandfather.

They lived for several years in almost daily intercourse. The bachelors came to dine with Russell, and they became more attached to each other than they had ever been in their youthful days. Calling to mind who it was that had made their fortunes, they secured the inheritance of a good portion of their estates to Russell's children—who, in every respect, deserved their good fortune. On the marriage of Russell's eldest daughter, her grandfather (Mr. Long) and his wife, who had several years before returned to England, were present, having come to this country to see their children and grandchildren. The bachelors were present, and enjoyed the scene, perhaps, more than either the parents or grandparents. Sitting at the supper-table after the others had retired, Thompson gave the substance of this narrative to the writer of this tale—closing it with this emphatic remark—"That *no man was ever happy, even in Paradise, or in the loftiest flights of the imagination, or in the depths of science, who neglected to follow the laws of nature and the commands of God.*"

THE MAN WHO THOUGHT
HIMSELF A WOMAN

—◦—

Anonymous

Japhet Colbones was a very odd individual. All his ancestors were odd individuals, as far back as they can be remembered. His great-grand-father, at the age of seventy-one, built a hut in a patch of thick woods, leaving a handsome and comfortable home, a wife, children, and grand-children, to live alone by himself. He even forbade the visits of his family, though a favorite daughter ventured sometimes to present herself on the forbidden premises, till one day he brought out his gun and threatened to shoot her if she came again. At long intervals he would return to his old home, but he required to be received in all respects as a stranger. Dire was his wrath if any one called him "father"; and the little tow-headed urchins on the premises were taught, with their catechism, not to notice the old man whenever they should see him, nor, on peril of their lives, to call him by the endearing cognomen of grand-daddy.

Nobody could account for this freak taken in his old age. His forest residence was uncouth, irregular—lighted by an unsheltered opening, filled with logs and coarse contrivances for furniture. There, in his rude fire-place he cooked the game that he killed, with his own hands. Whenever he was out of necessary food he supplied himself from his well-filled larder at home, the servants or the daughters knowing what provision he wanted by the particular basket or utensil he carried.

It was useless for the old wife, poor thing! to follow him mutely, the longing in her heart to comfort and to live with him, plainly written on her face. He deigned to take no notice of her whatever, except to frown if he met her eye; and thus he lived till he died.

The son, grand-father to Japhet, was not a whit behind his father in his oddities. He caused a coat to be made wherein were introduced seven different colors, and would not kill or allow to be killed on his premises, any thing that had life. Consequently his family were Grahamites against their will. Cats and dogs swarmed in all directions, and it took nearly every thing that was raised to keep his constantly-multiplying herds. None who lived in Rattle-Snake Village can have forgotten the extraordinary sensation caused by his death, nor with what gusto scores of useless animals were sacrificed to the manes of the departed oddity.

Number three, father of Japhet, was in his way an original and an eccentric. His tastes travelled bookward. Not an auction took place in the neighboring city that he did not attend, and purchase every leather-covered and worm-eaten volume that could be found, oftentimes paying the most ridiculous prices, extorted by those who took advantage of his weakness. He is living now, a pale, loose-jointed man, a little weak in the knees, with an abundant shock of iron-gray locks; large, flatulent-looking blue-white eyes, a prominent nose, and a peaked chin. In his house books abounded. Not a closet, chest, trunk, drawer, or shelf but was filled with flapping leaves. The children kicked and tore them about the premises, for the old man seemed to set no store by them after he had made them his own by way of purchase. All the sentimental maids and youths came to 'Squire Colbones for mental aliment, and I am not sure that the collection was the choicest in the world. Many of them were never returned; and as Mrs. Colbones said, when the 'Squire grumbled, she was sure it was a mercy, for they eat, and drank, and slept on books now; and if they were all returned they'd have to build additions every year for the sake of getting a room to themselves.

All the male members of the Colbones family, were, as it is generally expressed, "lacking somewhere." The women were generally good, harmless creatures, with few idiosyncrasies, and feeble mental constitutions, willing to put up with the queer freaks of the masculines, and always ready with a defence or an excuse when they were particularly disagreeable. They did hope, however, the four maiden aunts belonging to the last generation but one, that Japhet, the most promising scion of the family and the only son of his father, (seven daughters preceding him,) would be free from all singularities, queerities, quips, quirks, and oddities; and while they watched him with fearful misgivings, they yet said to themselves and to each other: "He looks so differrent from the Colbones, and so much like the Rashers, (his mother's side,) that I guess there won't be any streaks in him." Japhet was rather a fine-looking boy. The only draw-back to his good appearance was a head of somewhat unwieldy size, and whitish blue eyes, exactly like his father's. With books, of course, he was on intimate terms, they having been his playthings from his earliest years—indeed, he was seldom seen without them. Manfully he mastered his "abs" and "ebs," and hurried forward to the first class in the primary school. So rapid was his progress, that every body marvelled, and an itinerant phrenologist examined his cranium for nothing, because, he said: "One did not often meet with such splendid development of brain." Forthwith he declared that Japhet must go to college; that he shouldn't wonder if the boy was a marvel; yes, indeed, he fully expected to ask him for an office when he should advance to the dignity of being President of the United States. The elder Colbones was in raptures, and almost went to the city heels over head in his anxiety to buy more books, that the sciences and ologies might be crammed into that capacious brain. Only one person professed to have no faith in the predictions of the man with the skulls, old goody Granger—the matron of the poor-house.

"La!" she would say, putting her thumbs on her hips, "do you s'pose a Colbones'll ever come to any thing? Talk about his brain; any body might see it was rickety. Take my word for 't, he'll be as much of a fool as the rest on 'em."

Suddenly, when he was fourteen, Master Japhet refused to go to school any longer. His mother coaxed him, his father beat him, but all to no purpose. He had learning enough, he said; he meant to go to farming, or any thing else he liked. He had his way; left the red schoolhouse; made up faces at the teacher when he asked him why; bought himself yarn and knitting-needles, and pestered his mother till she taught him how to knit. From knitting he went to embroidery, and during the long winter evenings made fancy seats for chairs, table-covers, and every thing else he could think of, saying that he was pre-paring himself for future housekeeping. His family grew accustomed to his odd ways, and his sisters happy that instead of teasing them as other brothers did their sisters, he sat down with them like a real good boy, and when they were in a quandary, helped them out. Japhet was something of a genius, in his way, in devising patterns and drawing them; and he often made a sixpence in this manner. As he grew older he became more and more fond of his needle and of in-door employ-ment. The moment his labor was over in the field, he would hie to his own little room, and there, cutting out articles to please his fancy, stitch away at them with all the ardor of a young mother shaping a dress for her first-born. Singular as it may seem, he was not ashamed to have his handiwork shown at the county fair, with his name attached, and contemplated a handsome quilt, which he had contributed, with as much satisfaction as a first-rate machinist gazes at his complicated cogs and wheels, shafts and pulleys.

Every body laughed at Japhet, though they said it was to be ex-pected, coming from so odd a family. The girls made all manner of sport of him, especially Nanny Halliday and Nelly Gray, two young la-dies who were quite near neighbors of the odd family, and to whom Japhet distributed his smiles and nodded his capacious head.

"Don't you say another word to me about Japhet Colbones," cried Nanny, in great wrath, to some one who quizzed her. "Good laws! ketch me to have a woman for a husband when there are plenty of men about."

"But jest see what a grand farm you'd get, Nanny," pursued her tormentor; "and if ever you got tired cutting out, makin' and mendin', why, you could jest hand the needle-book over to your husband, and he'd do it tidy as a mitten."

"Oh! do hush," cried Nanny with spirit, her red cheeks growing redder; "I wouldn't have Japhet Colbones if there wasn't another fellow in the world."

Just then Tiddy Grant came into the little cottage. Tiddy was twenty-four, lean, poor, and worked very hard. Her face had a sort of sharp prettiness that sometimes falls to the lot of thin people. She had been washing, and came to rest herself in talking with her neighbors.

"Poh!" she exclaimed, overhearing the last remark, "you're a great fool then, if he's asked you, I'm sure. Catch me to refuse a young man that's got nothing suspicious about him but a few little oddities. I'm sure Japhet's a very good farmer, and a very good-looking man too; and as for his sewing propensities, I know some men that had better be using needle and thread than be lounging in bar-rooms and making their wives miserable."

Little she thought that Japhet, now a young man of nineteen, was hidden in the next room, and that he had indulged in another odd freak in prevailing upon an old friend to propose for him in this novel manner.

"Bless us, Japhet!" exclaimed his sisters as he came down the next morning in his newest suit of blue, with bright buttons, "an't you going to work?"

"I'm going to get married," said Japhet shortly.

Such a look of consternation! The girls caught their breath and stared at him stupidly.

"For pity's sake, who to?" queried the oldest.

"Tiddy Grant," he responded, pulling up his dicky before the little glass.

"Oh! g-r-a-c-i-o-u-s!" cried his eldest sister again. "Why she's an old maid."

"So are you!" responded the young man quietly.

"Well, if I am, I arn't going to get married to a little boy," retorted his sister sharply.

"Nor an't she," replied Japhet, giving a final look at the glass.

"I don't believe it; it's only one of his odd freaks," said another sister, watching him as he went down the road.

"It'll be just like him exactly, to bring that mean, poor-spirited thing here this very day," exclaimed another; "and we can't have a wedding, or company, or any thing."

"Like's not he'll find her at the wash-tub, and marry her in a check apron," said the younger sister, who had never liked Tiddy, because she was poor and mean in her appearance.

Off posted Japhet to the little brown cottage where lived Tiddy Grant. At a long table her mother and herself were ironing, for they took in washing for their living. Both paused when they saw the young man; and Tiddy, bethinking herself of yesterday's speech, blushed till she looked almost handsome.

"It's a nice day!" said Japhet.

"Very," echoed mother and daughter.

"A fine day to be married in," suggested the young man.

Tiddy looked up in astonishment and then looked down in confusion.

"If you'll have me Tiddy, say 'Yes,' and put your bonnet on; we'll go right to the minister's."

The poor girl was confounded; she never had received an offer before in her life. So she stood awkwardly, catching by the table; then in her consternation, took hold of a hot iron, cried, "Oh!" and sank upon a seat paralyzed.

"I an't got much time," said Japhet very coolly, rising; "and I'm determined to be married to-day or never. If you'll have me, here I am; but you must make haste or we shan't be home in time for dinner."

"Law, Tiddy, are you dumb?" exclaimed old Mrs. Grant in an agony of fear that her daughter would lose the chance; "do say 'Yes!' and done with it."

"Yes, and done with it," murmured Tiddy faintly.

"Well, now don't lose any time; I've got some hoeing to do to that patch of corn at the left of the house. I'll wait till you put on your bonnet and shawl."

Tiddy walked in a dream to the door to go up-stairs. Then turning irresolutely, she said, timidly: "What will your sisters think?"

"Law! Tiddy, do hurry!" cried old Mrs. Grant, while Japhet said quite coolly: "I never ask them what they think, or any body else."

Another moment of indecision, and Tiddy was arraying herself in her best gown—a shilling print—trembling, half-laughing, half-crying. It was so strange! so odd! but then every body knew Japhet came of an odd family.

Japhet got home with his wife just as his father drove up with a new cart-load of books. Sisters and mother looked daggers at the double infliction. Old Mr. Colbones glanced suspiciously at Tiddy Grant, now Tiddy Colbones.

"Now you can all have your look, and say your say," exclaimed Japhet; "Tiddy is my wife. I've jest been and married her, and brought her home to dinner; I hope it's most ready."

The elder Colbones spoke not a word, but sending for some one to unload his books, he went complacently into the house. Poor Mrs.

Colbones, on the contrary, fretted and fumed. "What did Japhet want to be such a confounded fool for? Wasn't the house already full from cellar floor to clapboard with trash?—and now he must go to bringing more."

Tiddy had not been in her new home a week before the sisters of the new bridegroom held a consultation, with the doors shut.

"I'm sure no such thing ever happened before," whispered the eldest, "and I'm almost confident that huzzy has taken it."

"And don't you think," said Sarah, the next eldest, "two pair of my very finest stockings are gone."

"And my nicest, newest flannel petticoat," chimed in another.

"And my blue and green striped calico!"

"Did mother tell you she missed two of her best caps?"

"No! the laws, you don't say so!"

"Yes, and like's not the huzzy has carried them to the old woman's, at home," chimed in another.

"Well, I declare! to think that our Japhet should go and marry a thief!"

All this while, poor Tiddy was scrubbing away down-stairs, (for work was her life,) helping her new mother-in-law. She had really found in Japhet a tolerable companion and a very industrious husband. She had not yet become sufficiently accustomed to her sisters to like their ways; she even felt nervous and uncomfortable in their presence. How would her indignation have been roused could she have known that they suspected her of stealing! She noticed their growing coldness, their avoidance of her, and spoke to her husband about it. His only reply was: "I'm going to build a house; wait awhile."

With his father's aid, Japhet set himself to work in earnest, and near the close of the harvest he had ready a pretty little cottage, with a garden spot attached, and a fine orchard in the rear. The land was his father's gift; the house he built with his own money, and furnished it neatly. By this time Tiddy was looked upon with less suspicion by the members of the odd family. They had searched her drawers in her absence, and found means to inspect even the old widow's wardrobe. Finding none of the missing clothes, they contented themselves with calling it a mystery, or supposing that in their absence some strolling thief had robbed them. As the family was over large, Tiddy suggested to her husband, that two of his sisters should come and stay with them, adding that "she might be glad of their services before a great while."

"Do just as you please," was his reply.

So Drusy, the eldest, and Fanny, the next in age, were invited to become inmates of the new house. The girls very willingly accepted the offer, as their father was disclosing some new freak of eccentricity every day. He had recently had every door taken from its hinges, and the house was uncomfortably cold, until he had a mind to put them on again.

Some years had passed, and Tiddy had often congratulated herself on her good fortune. She was the mother of two handsome little girls, who were the delight of their parents; and Japhet, though very odd and singular, had developed no very unusual trait of character. Drusy and Fanny, still unmarried, lived with them yet.

One pleasant morning Drusy came down stairs in no very amiable mood.

"I can't find my best black silk!" she cried in consternation; "the one I earned myself. I've looked for it high and low. And my nice tucked skirt is gone, too; and Fanny's pink pelerine and best bonnet. What shall we do? I'm sure they were all in my drawers yesterday!"

Tiddy was astonished as well as they. She left her work, and commenced searching. In every nook and corner of the house they hunted, turned chests wrong side out, emptied drawers, stripped closets, but nothing could they find of the missing articles. There was no other recourse for Drusy, the poor thing, but to cry; and at it she went, bemoaning her ill-fortune in the most extravagant manner.

It certainly was very mysterious. None but the usual inmates had been in the house. Tiddy searched her own part of the premises as faithfully as every other. But what would she want of the dress or the vandyke? She could get such things whenever she wished; and Drusy did not even suspect her this time: but how had it happened? By witchcraft? The Colbones were very superstitious, and they shuddered to go to bed after this strange mishap. Drusy declared that she heard footsteps every night; and waking up her sister the night after the accident, both lay listening and trembling, for there certainly was a sound as of some one moving around the house.

"As sure as you live, Fanny, the house is haunted," whispered Drusy.

"For pity's sake, don't!" cried Fanny, pulling the bed-quilt over her head.

"I've heard that sometimes them that's gone get a spite against you, and torment you almost to—"

"Drusy! hold your tongue! I wish you hadn't waked me up," chattered Fanny under the bed-clothes.

"I was only wondering," persisted Drusy, who had a love for the horrible, "if old Grandpa Colbones—"

"I'll scream murder if you don't keep still!" cried Fanny, now trembling so that the bed shook.

"Well, anyhow, there's a noise down stairs. There, don't you hear it? Like somebody marching."

Poor Fanny was striving to be oblivious to every thing, but it would not do; she was thoroughly frightened.

"O Drusy!" she moaned, "if there should be robbers! Japhet has got money in the house; and they might come in and murder us in our beds. O Drusy! did you lock the door?"

Yes: Drusy never went to bed without locking doors and windows, and shaking every dress and stocking out, to be sure there was nobody inside. She would have gone to her brother's room, but that it was across the entry, and she was a coward. Beside, she was sure she had heard the same sounds before, and they were yet unharmed.

Fanny declared the next day that she would go back to her father's house, for she was scared almost out of her seven senses. Tiddy was astonished. Tiddy had heard nothing; but then, she addded, with a laugh, a whole regiment of soldiers might come in the house, and she never should know it, she was so sound a sleeper.

It was very strange, she said, an hour after, she could not find her best shawl, high nor low; and two very fine night-dresses were gone. She had been hunting for them quietly, though she very well knew where she had left them. She had but one place for them. Wasn't it strange?

Drusy wondered, Fanny wondered; but Japhet said not a word, and soon went out as usual.

"How dreadfully stupid Japhet looks of mornings!" said Drusy, who began to question and to be suspicious of every body.

"He's such a hard sleeper!" responded Tiddy; "why, I can hardly get him awake by breakfast-time! I have to pound him and pull him and turn him!"

"He used to be up earlier," said Drusy thoughtfully.

In the course of the day a neighbor came in and brought her knitting-work.

"Has Japhet taken to peddling?" she asked with a little laugh.

"Taken to peddling!" echoed Tiddy and both the sisters: "what can you mean?"

"Why, he goes through the village every day with a great tin box," replied the woman; "and actually as many as a dozen people have asked me if he has gone to peddling."

"I'm sure I don't know what you mean!" said Tiddy; "I didn't know he carried any box of the kind."

"Very strange!" said Drusy and Fanny; but they determined to "wait for the wagon." When they heard it coming they hurried to a chamber at the back of the house, overlooking the barn. Sure enough, there was Japhet, just lifting from his wagon with no little difficulty a great tin box such as peddlers carry. The sisters looked at each other: what did it mean?

"Between you and me," whispered Drusy, "I shouldn't wonder if he grew strange as he grew older; you know they say all the others did: but what can he have in that box?"

"I'm sure I can't think," replied Fanny; "and do look: if he arnt locking up the carriage-house! Laws, Drusy! I thought of going in and trying to find out what it can be."

"So did I," responded Drusy; "but it's no use now. He's got some odd idea in his head, and I suppose he'll keep it there."

Tiddy Colbones manifested no little astonishment when Drusy and Fanny told her what they had seen, and what they had heard; and for the moment seemed a little uneasy.

"Perhaps it's empty, and he's only taken the notion to carry the box with him because it looks sort of business-like," she suggested.

"I'm sure it isn't empty!" exclaimed Drusy, "for he lifted it as if it was a heft. Dear me! what can it be?"

"Did you bring any thing from town, Japhet?" asked Tiddy that evening at supper.

He looked up as if astonished at the question.

"To be sure I did: I brought myself," he answered.

"Oh!" and his wife made no other reply; only Drusy and Fanny exchanged glances with her.

That night, by previous arrangement, Drusy and Fanny were to occupy the chamber adjoining Tiddy's sleeping-room. A small window or movable frame opened from one chamber to the other, and under that Tiddy had affixed a string in such a way that a slight pull upon it would awaken her, if her slumber were ever so deep. For a long while the redoubtable spinster kept awake, her fears excited at the slightest sound; but finally drowsiness overcame her, and her eyes obstinately refused to keep open.

For some hours she slept heavily; but at the accustomed time awoke, as had become a usual habit with her.

There were the sounds again; the going down-stairs, lifting the latch, the fumbling and stepping about. Drusy pulled the string. In a few moments Tiddy's night-capped head appeared at the door.

"It is Japhet, as I suspected," she said, whispering. "He's not in my room. Come; we won't light a lamp, but go softly down-stairs. You foolish thing, to tremble so! it's only one of his freaks, and harmless, I suppose, at that. Come; are you ready?"

Drusy delayed as long as she could, fidgeting about the shawl she had prepared beforehand, and shivering, she said, at the cold; then, taking care to keep behind Tiddy, crept down-stairs.

There seemed to be an illumination. The hall was quite light. Tiddy stood on the stair, and reached over to the glass top of the door. For a moment she stood gazing; then, sinking back, she began laughing immoderately to herself; her queer contortions, as she beckoned Drusy to look, and the efforts she made to keep from betraying herself, making her, in her night-cap and uncouth attire, appear quite ridiculous.

Drusy stood on tip-toe, taking in the whole scene and its ludicrousness at a glance. Japhet was standing before the looking-glass, his box open beside him. He was arrayed in woman's clothes almost from head to foot, and was just then pulling and straightening out the ruffles on a cap which Drusy recognized as the one her mother had lost some years before. The gown, with its bright blue and white pattern, was familiar to her; and now he was throwing over the pelerine that they had missed so lately. Every thing he had on seemed to have undergone a change—to have been widened, enlarged, and otherwise altered.

After he had sufficiently admired himself, he spread out his gown, took his handkerchief in his hand, and began to walk back and forth with as much of the air and gait of a woman as he could assume. Then he would take out his knitting, smile amicably, sit down with finikin niceness, and knit, holding his head affectedly now this way, now that, with many an accomplished smirk.

Poor Drusy did not feel like laughing, for she saw now where her nice black silk had gone, and sundry other of her valuables, and she began forming a plan in her mind how she should avail herself of them, when Japhet arose, and appeared to be coming toward the door, whereupon the two women fled up-stairs.

The next night, and the next, they watched, and saw the same scene acted over with but few variations. Sometimes the beautiful black silk, altered and disfigured; sometimes other missing dresses were donned; and the imaginary woman kept on knitting, smirking, and smiling, till the two hours he had allotted himself were over.

Many were the plans the three women formed to get possession of the box, but they could seem to make none of them available; and they dared not hint to Japhet what they knew.

One beautiful bright day in August, when the rich harvests, rudely wrested from the bosom of nature, covered the land, and the heavens smiled in a blue and quiet serenity, Japhet lingered about the house till the breakfast-dishes were placed away, and the usual domestic work was begun. All at once the man of few words spoke:

"Tiddy! take the children, and go and spend the day at father's."

"Oh! I can't, Japhet; there's the churning, and little bits of things to do that I have let go till now. But I'll get them all through, and go to-morrow, Japhet."

"Drusy and Fanny," said the oddity, looking about, "dress the children, and go with Tiddy to spend the day at father's."

Nothing more was to be said. Tiddy had never dreamed of having a way of her own; so she smothered down her disappointment, and prepared for the visit. They all set off very soon, Japhet standing at the door as they went, saying, that if he didn't call for them before dark they needn't come home that night.

"If you don't come for me by five," spoke up Tiddy with more self-will than she had ever dared before, "I shall come home."

He jerked his head in his odd way, and off they went.

The day passed, pleasantly. The old man and his old wife were social in their queerness; for association with her husband for over forty years had made Mrs. Colbones almost as strange as he. But toward five Tiddy began to grow uneasy.

"I feel worried and unhappy," she said to Drusy; "I wish Japhet would come."

"Why should you feel worried?" asked Drusy, her own face somewhat clouded.

"I don't know," was the reply; "but just as I got up from the dinner-table, something seemed to choke me: did you see me catch hold of my throat? and I have had a peculiar feeling ever since."

"And just then I grew dizzy, too," said Drusy; "I didn't like to tell you, but *I've* felt queer ever since."

"How foolish we are," said Tiddy, trying to laugh; "there's the cart now: and there's—oh! no, it isn't; it's a neighbor. Let us get the children and ourselves ready; for if he isn't here by five, I shall certainly go home."

They all sat waiting till after the clock struck five. Then they started, Tiddy saying, in a faint sort of way, that they should probably meet Japhet on the road, and they might as well be occupied with something: it was only half a mile.

Quite silent, listening to the pretty prattle of the little girls, they arrived at the house. It was shut up, and looked strangely lonesome. They rapped at the door. No answer. Pretty soon the girl they had left at home came flying over from a neighbor's.

"Mr. Colbones told me I might go for the day, after you were gone," she said, laughing. Apparently she had been enjoying herself very much.

"But the work?" said Tiddy reproachfully.

"I know: but he wouldn't let me stay. When I told him what you expected, he just took me by the arm and put me out."

"Where in the world is he?" cried Tiddy, now alarmed, shaking the door.

"I'm sure I don't know," replied the girl; "gone off somewhere, I suppose. I'll get in the cellar-way, and let you in." And so she did.

Once in the house, Tiddy felt oppressed with a strange awe. She went into the parlor, and started back with a scream. All the chairs in the house had been brought in and ranged in double rows around the room, as if for a funeral, while the large hall-table was set in the centre, spread with a white cloth, and occupied only by the great Bible and hymn-book.

"What does this mean?" asked Tiddy, sinking down, her strength entirely gone. The children laughed with glee, and began to play meeting.

"It's surely a sign!" cried Drusy, her cheeks whitening, while Fanny shivered as with an ague.

"Where *is* that man? oh! dear! where *can* he be?" cried Tiddy, in great distress. "Drusy! you go hunt. Mary! (to the girl) go round to all the neighbors." Then, proceeding to the foot of the stairs, she shouted his name; but there was no answer.

"I don't know why, but I dread to go up-stairs," said Tiddy falteringly. "Look; he has shut up every blind."

"There's no use in feeling so; we might as well go up," said Drusy, summoning a show of courage. "I don't believe he's in the house, nor haven't from the first. That fixing in the parlor, and shutting up the blinds, was just one of his freaks. I knew he would grow odder as he grew older; all the Colbones do. Come; we might as well have it over with." So saying, she resolutely mounted into the chamber.

Every thing there was in scrupulous order; though the rooms, upon such an unexpected summons, had been left somewhat untidy. He was in none of the sleeping-apartments, and Tiddy breathed more freely. Drusy now boldly opened the door leading to the great garret. The red rays of the fast-setting sun streamed down the narrow stairs. She went up slowly, one at a time, and when well at the top, gave one sweeping glance about. Then, in a loud voice she cried: "Here he is, Tiddy: the wicked fellow! trying to scare us all out of our senses. O Japhet!"

By this time Tiddy had flown up with Fanny, and now approached the figure that sat in the shadow. Bonnet, cap, pelerine, gloves, black-silk gown, a bag in its hand, fantastic bows pinned all over it: it was a most fearfully grotesque object. Tiddy, calling him by name, went nearer and nearer, and still nearer; then, with a shriek: "O Drusy!" she cried, "he's stone dead!" and fell down fainting.

It was quite true. This was the oddest freak yet, of the odd man. He had managed to hang himself in a sitting posture, and his face was calm and placid. In the bag in his hand was a paper on which were written the words:

"I think I am a woman. I have been seven years making me a perfect suit of garments appropriate for my sex. As I have passed so long, falsely, for a man, I am ashamed to show myself in my true colors; therefore, I hang myself. The property all to go to the woman I have called my wife. It is now twelve o'clock. I have prepared every thing for the funeral, and desire that I may be laid out in the clothes I have on.   JAPHET COLBONES."

Poor Tiddy was almost distracted. In spite of his strange ways, she had loved her husband deeply, and the manner of his death made the bereavement much more dreadful. Crowds came flocking to see the strange sight; and the wonder grew when it was seen that he had taken the greatest pains to leave out not the smallest minutia of a woman's wearing-apparel.

And thus, according to the term of his singular request, he was placed in his coffin in Drusy's black silk; the only difference in the terms being that the bonnet and shawl were taken off, and the gold rings and jewelry with which he had adorned his neck and fingers.

"There's the last of the Colbones, likely," whispered one neighbor to another. "The women will die old maids, and Tiddy's two children are girls: an't it lucky?"

Tiddy was left with a handsome property; but she could no longer bear to live in the house where he had died. So she bought a little cottage for herself and her mother, and very kindly took Drusy and Fanny to live with her.

Old Mr. Colbones still mourns that he has no sons to leave his books to; and it is whispered that if he should die before his wife, there will probably be a great bonfire somewhere in the vicinity.

Two Friends

━━━◆━━━

Mary Wilkins Freeman

"I wish you'd jest look down the road again, Mis' Dunbar, an' see if you see anything of Abby comin'."

"I don't see a sign of her. It's a real trial for you to be so short-sighted, ain't it, Sarah?"

"I guess it is. Why, you wouldn't believe it, but I can't see anybody out in the road to tell who 'tis. I can see somethin' movin', an' that's all, unless there's somethin' peculiar about 'em that I can tell 'em by. I can always tell old Mr. Whitcomb—he's got a kind of a hitch when he walks, you know; an' Mis' Addison White always carries a parasol, an' I can tell her. I can see somethin' bobbin' overhead, an' I know who 'tis."

"Queer, ain't it, how she always carries that parasol? Why, I've seen her with it in the dead of winter, when the sun was shinin', an' 'twas freezin' cold; no more need of a parasol—"

"She has to carry it to keep off the sun an' wind, 'cause her eyes are weak, I s'pose."

"Why, I never knew that."

"Abby said she told her so. Abby giggled right in her face one day when she met her with it."

"She didn't!"

"She did—laughed right out. She said she couldn't help it nohow:

you know Abby laughs terrible easy. There was Mis' White sailin' along with her parasol h'isted, she said, as fine as a fiddle. You know Mis' White always walks kind of nippin' anyhow, an' she's pretty dressy. An' then it was an awful cold, cloudy day, Abby said. The sun didn't shine, an' it didn't storm, an' there wa'n't no earthly use for a parasol anyway, that she could see. So she kind of snickered. I s'pose it struck her funny all of a sudden. Mis' White took it jest as quick, Abby said, an' told her kind of short that her eyes were terrible weak, an' she had to keep 'em shaded all the time she was outdoors; the doctor had give her orders to. Abby felt pretty streaked about it. You don't see her comin' yet, do you?"

"No, I don't. I thought I see somebody then, but it ain't her. It's the Patch boy, I guess. Yes, 'tis him. What do you think of Abby, Sarah?"

"Think of Abby! What do you mean, Mis' Dunbar?"

"Why, I mean, how do you think she is? Do you think her cough is as bad as 'twas?"

Sarah Arnold, who was a little light woman of fifty, thin-necked and round-backed, with blue protruding eyes in her tiny pale face, pursed up her mouth and went on with her work. She was sewing some red roses on to a black lace bonnet.

"I never thought her cough was very bad anyhow, as far as I was concerned," said she, finally.

"Why, you didn't? I thought it sounded pretty bad. I've been feelin' kind of worried about her."

" 'Tain't nothin' in the world but a throat cough. Her mother before her used to cough jest the same way. It sounds kind of hard, but 'tain't the kind of cough that kills folks. Why, I cough myself half the time."

Sarah hacked a little as she spoke.

"Old Mis' Vane died of consumption, didn't she?"

"Consumption! Jest about as much consumption as I've got. Mis' Vane died of liver complaint. I guess I know. I was livin' right in the house."

"Well, of course you'd be likely to know. I was thinkin' that was what I'd heard, that was all."

"Some folks did call it consumption, but it wa'n't. See anything of Abby?"

"No, I don't. You ain't worried about her, are you?"

"Worried?—no. I ain't got no reason to be worried that I know of.

She's old enough to take care of herself. All is, the supper table's been settin' an hour, an' I don't see where she is. She jest went down to the store to git some coffee."

"It's kind of damp to-night."

" 'Tain't damp enough to hurt her, I guess, well as she is."

"Mebbe not. That's a pretty bonnet you're makin'."

"Well, I think it's goin' to look pretty well. I didn't know as 'twould. I didn't have much to do with."

"I s'pose it's Abby's."

"Course it's Abby's. I guess you wouldn't see me comin' out in no such bonnet as this."

"Why, you ain't any older than Abby, Sarah."

"I'm different-lookin'," said Sarah, with a look which might have meant pride.

The two women were sitting on a little piazza at the side of the story-and-a-half white house.

Before the house was a small green yard with two cherry-trees in it. Then came the road, then some flat green meadow-lands where the frogs were singing. The grass on these meadows was a wet green, and there were some clumps of blue lilies which showed a long way off in it. Beyond the meadows was the southwest sky, which looked low and red and clear, and had birds in it. It was seven o'clock of a summer evening.

Mrs. Dunbar, tall and straight, with a dark, leathery face whose features were gracefully cut, sat primly in a wooden chair, which was higher than Sarah's little rocker.

"I know Abby looks well in 'most everything," said she.

"I never saw her try on anything that she didn't look well in. There's good-lookin' women, but there ain't many like Abby. Most folks are a little dependent on their bonnets, but she wa'n't, never. Sky blue or grass green, 'twas all one; she'd look as if 'twas jest made for her. See anything of her comin'?"

Mrs. Dunbar turned her head, and her dark profile stood out in the clear air. "There's somebody comin', but I guess it ain't— Yes, 'tis, too. She's comin'."

"I can see her," said Sarah, joyfully, in a minute.

"Abby Vane, where have you been?" she called out.

The approaching woman looked up and laughed. "Did you think

you'd lost me?" said she, as she came up the piazza step. "I went into Mis' Parson's, an' I staid longer'n I meant to. Agnes was there—she'd jest got home—an'—" She began to cough violently.

"You hadn't ought to give way to that ticklin' in your throat, Abby," said Sarah, sharply.

"She'd better go into the house out of this damp air," said Mrs. Dunbar.

"Land! the air won't hurt her none. But mebbe you had better come in, Abby. I want to try on this bonnet. I wish you'd come too, Mis' Dunbar. I want you to see if you think it's deep enough in the back."

"There!" said Sarah, after the three women had entered, and she had tied the bonnet on to Abby's head, picking the bows out daintily.

"It's real handsome on her," said Mrs. Dunbar.

"Red roses on a woman of my age!" laughed Abby. "Sarah's bound to rig me up like a young girl."

Abby stood in the little sitting-room before the glass. The blinds were wide open to let the evening light in. Abby was a large, well-formed woman. She held her bonneted head up, and drew her chin back with an air of arch pride. The red roses bloomed meetly enough above her candid, womanly forehead.

"If you can't wear red roses, I don't know who can," said Sarah, looking up at her with pride and resentment. "You could wear a white dress to meetin' an' look as well as any of 'em."

"Look here, where did you git the lace for this bonnet?" asked Abby, suddenly. She had taken it off and was examining it closely.

"Oh, 'twas some I had."

"See here, you tell the truth now, Sarah Arnold. Didn't you take this off your black silk dress?"

"It don't make no odds where I took it from."

"You did. What made you do it?"

"'Tain't worth talkin' 'bout. I always despised it on the dress."

"Why, Sarah Arnold! That's jest the way she does," said Abby to Mrs. Dunbar. "If I didn't watch her, she wouldn't leave herself a thing to put on."

After Mrs. Dunbar had gone, Abby sat down in a large covered rocking-chair and leaned her head back. Her eyes were parted a little, and her teeth showed. She looked ghastly all at once.

"What ails you?" said Sarah.

"Nothin'. I'm a little tired, that's all."

"What are you holdin' on to your side for?"

"Oh, nothin'. It ached a little, that's all."

"Mine's been achin' all the afternoon. I should think you'd better come out an' have somethin' to eat; the table's been settin' an hour an' a half."

Abby rose meekly and followed Sarah into the kitchen with a sort of weak stateliness. She had always had a queenly way of walking. If Abby Vane should fall a victim to consumption some day, no one could say that she had brought it upon herself by non-observance of hygienic rules. Long miles of country road had she traversed with her fine swinging step, her shoulders thrown well back, her head erect, in her day. She had had the whole care of their vegetable garden, she had weeded and hoed and dug, she had chopped wood and raked hay, and picked apples and cherries.

There had always been a settled and amicable division of labor between the two women. Abby did the rough work, the man's work of the establishment, and Sarah, with her little, slim, nervous frame, the woman's work. All the dress-making and millinery was Sarah's department, all the cooking, all the tidying and furbishing of the house. Abby rose first in the morning and made the fire, and she pumped the water and brought the tubs for the washing. Abby carried the purse, too. The two had literally one between them—one worn black leather wallet. When they went to the village store, if Sarah made the purchase, Abby drew forth the money to pay the bill.

The house belonged to Abby; she had inherited it from her mother. Sarah had some shares in the village bank, which kept them in food and clothes.

Nearly all the new clothes bought would be for Abby, though Sarah had to employ many a subterfuge to bring it about. She alone could have unravelled the subtlety of that diplomacy by which the new cashmere was made for Abby instead of herself, by which the new mantle was fitted to Abby's full, shapely shoulders instead of her own lean, stooping ones.

If Abby had been a barbarous empress, who exacted her cook's head as a penalty for a failure, she could have found no more faithful and anxious artist than Sarah. All the homely New England recipes which Abby loved shone out to Sarah as if written in letters of gold.

That nicety of adjustment through which the appetite should neither be cloyed by frequency nor tantalized by desire was a constant study with her. "I've found out just how many times a week Abby likes mince-pie," she told Mrs. Dunbar, triumphantly, once. "I've been studyin' it out. She likes mince-pie jest about twice to really relish it. She eats it other times, but she don't really hanker after it. I've been keepin' count about six weeks now, an' I can tell pretty well."

Sarah had not eaten her own supper to-night, so she sat down with Abby at the little square table against the kitchen wall. Abby could not eat much, though she tried. Sarah watched her, scarcely taking a mouthful herself. She had a trick of swallowing convulsively every time Abby did, whether she was eating herself or not.

"Ain't goin' to have any custard pie?" said Sarah. "Why not? I went to work an' made it on purpose."

Abby began to laugh. "Well, I'll tell you what 'tis, Sarah," said she, "near's I can put it: I've got jest about as much feelin' about takin' vittles as a pillow-tick has about bein' stuffed with feathers."

"Ain't you been eatin' nothin' this afternoon?"

"Nothin' but them few cherries before I went out."

"That was jest enough to take your appetite off. I never can taste a thing between meals without feelin' it."

"Well, I dare say that was it. Any of them cherries in the house now?"

"Yes; there's some in the cupboard. Want some?"

"I'll git 'em."

Sarah jumped up and got a plate of beautiful red cherries and set them on the table.

"Let me see, these came off the Sarah-tree," said Abby, meditatively. "There wa'n't any on the Abby one this year."

"No," said Sarah, shortly.

"Kind of queer, wa'n't it? It's always bore, ever since I can remember."

"I don't see nothin' very queer about it. It was frost-bit that cold spell last spring; that's all that ails it."

"Why, the other one wa'n't."

"This one's more exposed."

The two round, symmetrical cherry-trees in the front yard had been called Abby and Sarah ever since the two women could remember. The fancy had originated somehow far back in their childhood, and ever since it had been the "Abby-tree" and the "Sarah-tree." Both had borne plentifully until this season, when the Abby-tree displayed only her fine green leaves in fruit-time, and the Sarah-tree alone was rosy with cherries. Sarah had picked some that evening, standing primly on a chair under the branches, a little basket on her arm, poking her pale inquisitive face into the perennial beauties of her woody namesake. Abby had been used to picking cherries after a more vigorous fashion, with a ladder, but she had not offered to this season.

"I couldn't git many—couldn't reach nothin' but the lowest branches," said Sarah to-night, watching Abby eat the cherries. "I guess you'd better take the ladder out there to-morrow. They're dead ripe, an' the birds are gittin' 'em. I scared off a whole flock to-day."

"Well, I will if I can," said Abby.

"Will if you can! Why, there ain't no reason why you can't, is there?"

"No, not that I know of."

The next morning Abby painfully dragged the long ladder around the house to the tree, and did her appointed task. Sarah came to the door to watch her once, and Abby was coughing distressingly up amongst the green boughs.

"Don't give up to that ticklin' in your throat, for pity's sake, Abby," she called out.

Abby's laugh floated back in answer, like a brave song, from the tree.

Presently Mrs. Dunbar came up the path; she lived alone herself, and was a constant visitor. She stood under the tree, tall and lank and vigorous in her straight-skirted brown cotton gown.

"For the land sake, Abby! you don't mean to say you're pickin' cherries?" she called out. "Are you crazy?"

"Hush!" whispered Abby, between the leaves.

"I don't see why she's crazy," spoke up Sarah; "she always picks 'em."

"You don't catch me givin' up pickin' cherries till I'm a hundred," said Abby, loudly. "I'm a regular cherry bird."

Sarah went into the house soon, and directly Abby crawled down the ladder. She was dripping with perspiration, and trembling.

"Abby Vane, I'm all out of patience," said Mrs. Dunbar.

Abby sank down on the ground. "It's this cherry bird's last season," said she, with a pathetic twinkle in her eyes.

"There ain't no sense in your doin' so."

"Well, I've picked enough for a while, I guess."

"Give me that other basket," said Mrs. Dunbar, harshly, "an' I'll go up an' pick."

"You can pick some for yourself," coughed Abby.

"I don't like 'em," said Mrs. Dunbar, jerking herself up the ladder. "Git up off the ground, an' go in."

Abby obeyed without further words. She sat down in the sitting-room rocker, and leaned her head back. Sarah was stepping about in the kitchen, and did not come in, and she was glad.

In the course of a few months this old-fashioned chair, with its green cushion, held Abby from morning till night. She did not go out any more. She had kept about as long as she could. Every summer Sunday she had sat smartly beside Sarah in church, with those brave red roses on her head. But when the cold weather came her enemy's arrows were too sharp even for her strong mail of love and resolution.

Sarah's behavior seemed inexplicable. Even now that Abby was undeniably helpless, she was constantly goading her to her old tasks. She refused to admit that she was ill. She rebelled when the doctor was called. "No more need of a doctor than nothin' at all," she said.

Affairs went on so till the middle of the winter. Abby grew weaker and weaker, but Sarah seemed to ignore it. One day she went over to Mrs. Dunbar's. One of the other neighbors was sitting with Abby. Sarah walked in suddenly. The outer door opened directly in Mrs. Dunbar's living-room, and a whiff of icy air came in with her.

"How's Abby?" asked Mrs. Dunbar.

"'Bout the same." Sarah stood upright, staring. She had a blue plaid shawl over her head, and she clutched it together with her red bony fingers. "I've got something on my mind," said she, "an' I've got to tell somebody. I'm goin' crazy."

"What do you mean?"

"Abby's goin' to die, an' I've got something on my mind. I 'ain't treated her right."

"Sarah Arnold, do, for pity's sake, sit down, an' keep calm!"

"I'm calm enough. Oh, what shall I do?"

Mrs. Dunbar forced Sarah into a chair, and took her shawl. "You mustn't feel so," said she. "You've been just devoted to Abby all your life, an' everybody knows it. I know when folks die we're very apt to feel as if we hadn't done right by 'em, but there ain't no sense in your feelin' so."

"I know what I'm talkin' about. I've got something awful on my mind. I've got to tell somebody."

"Sarah Arnold, what do you mean?"

"I've got to tell."

There was a puzzled look on the other woman's thin, strong face. "Well, if you've got anything you want to tell, you can tell it, but I can't think what you're drivin' at."

Sarah fixed her eyes on the wall at the right of Mrs. Dunbar. "It begins 'way back when we was girls. You know I went to live with Abby an' her mother after my folks died. Abby an' me had always been together. You remember that John Marshall that used to keep store where Simmons is, about thirty year ago. When Abby was about twenty, he begun waitin' on her. He was a good-lookin' fellar, an' I guess he was smart, though I never took a fancy to him.

"He was crazy after Abby; but her mother didn't like him. She talked again' him from the very first of it, and wouldn't take no notice of him. She declared she shouldn't have him. Abby didn't say much. She'd laugh an' tell her mother not to fret, but she'd treat him pretty well when he came.

"I s'pose she liked him. I used to watch her, an' think she did. An' he kep' comin' an' comin'. All the fellars were crazy 'bout her anyhow. She was the handsomest girl that was ever seen, about. She'd laugh an' talk with all of 'em, but I s'pose Marshall was the one.

"Well, finally Mis' Vane made such a fuss that he stopped comin'. 'Twas along about a year before she died. I never knew, but I s'pose Abby told him. He went right off to Mexico. Abby didn't say a word, but I knew she felt bad. She didn't seem to care much about goin' into company, an' didn't act jest like herself.

"Well, old Mis' Vane died sudden, you know. She'd had the consumption for years, coughed ever since I could remember, but she went real quick at last, an' Abby was away. She'd gone over to her Aunt Abby's in Colebrook to stay a couple of days. Her aunt wa'n't well neither, an' wanted to see her, an' her mother seemed comfortable, so she thought she could go. We sent for her jest as soon as Mis' Vane was took worse, but she couldn't git home in time.

"So I was with Mis' Vane when she died. She had her senses, and she left word for Abby. She said to tell her she'd give her consent to her marryin' John Marshall."

Sarah stopped. Mrs. Dunbar waited, staring.

"I 'ain't told her from that day to this."

"What!"

"I 'ain't never told what her mother said."

"Why, Sarah Arnold, why not?"

"Oh, I couldn't have it nohow—I couldn't—I couldn't, Mis' Dunbar. Seemed as if it would kill me to think of it. I couldn't have her likin' anybody else, an' gittin' married. You don't know what I'd been through. All my own folks had died before I was sixteen years old, an' Mis' Vane was gone, an' she'd been jest like a mother to me. I didn't have nobody in the world but Abby. I couldn't have it so—I couldn't—I couldn't."

"Sarah Arnold, you've been livin' with her all these years, an' been such friends, an' had this shut up in your mind! What are you made of?"

"Oh, I've done everything I could for Abby—everything."

"You couldn't make it up to her in such a way as that."

"She 'ain't seemed as if she fretted much, she 'ain't."

"You can't tell nothin' by that."

"I know it. Oh, Mis' Dunbar, have I got to tell her? Have I?"

Mrs. Dunbar, with her intent, ascetic face, confronted Sarah like an embodied conscience.

"Tell her? Sarah Arnold, don't you let another sun go down over your head before you tell her."

"Oh, it don't seem as if I could."

"Don't you wait another minute. You go right home now an' tell her, if you ever want any more peace in this world."

Sarah stood gazing at her a minute, trembling. Then she pulled her shawl up over her head and turned toward the door.

"Well, I'll see," said she.

"Don't you wait a minute!" Mrs. Dunbar called after her again. Then she stood watching the lean, pitiful figure slink down the street. She wondered a good many times afterward if Sarah had told; she suspected that she had not.

Sarah avoided her, and never alluded to the matter again. She fell back on her old philosophy. "'Tain't nothin' but Abby's goin' to git over," she told people. "'Tain't on her lungs. She'll git up as soon as it comes warmer weather."

She treated Abby now with the greatest tenderness. She toiled for her day and night. Every delicacy which the sick woman had ever fancied stood waiting on the pantry shelves. Sarah went without shoes and flannels to purchase them, though the chance that they would be tasted was small.

Every spare moment which she could get she sewed for Abby, and folded and hung away new garments which would never be worn. If Abby ventured to remonstrate, Sarah was indignant, and sewed the more; sitting up through long winter nights, she stitched and hemmed with fierce zeal. She ransacked her own wardrobe for material, and hardly left herself a whole article to wear.

Toward spring, when her little dividends came in, she bought stuff for a new dress for Abby—soft cashmere of a beautiful blue. She got patterns, and cut and fitted and pleated with the best of her poor country skill.

"There," said she, when it was completed, "you've got a decent dress to put on, Abby, when you get out again."

"It's real handsome, Sarah," said Abby, smiling.

Abby did not die till the last of May. She sat in her chair by the window, and watched feebly the young grass springing up and the green film spreading over the tree boughs. Way over across in a neighbor's garden was a little peach-tree. Abby could just see it.

"Jest see that peach-tree over there," she whispered to Sarah one evening. It was all rosy with bloom. "It's the first tree I've seen blowed out this year. S'pose the Abby-tree's goin' to blossom?"

"I guess so," said Sarah; "it's leavin' out."

Abby seemed to dwell on the blossoming of the Abby-tree. She kept talking about it. One morning she saw some cherry-trees in the next yard had blossomed, and she called Sarah eagerly.

"Sarah, have you looked to see if the Abby-tree's blossomed?"

"Of course it has. What's to hender?"

Abby's face was radiant. "Oh, Sarah, I want to see it."

"Well, you wait till afternoon," said Sarah, with a tremble in her voice. "I'll draw you round to the front-room door after dinner, an' you can look through at it."

People passing that morning stared to see Sarah Arnold doing some curious work in the front yard. Not one blossom was there on the Abby-tree, but the Sarah-tree was white. Its delicate garlanded boughs stirred softly, and gave out a sweet smell. Bees murmured through them. Sarah had a ladder plunged into the roadward side of all this bloom and sweetness, and she was sawing and hacking at the white boughs. Then she would stagger across to the other tree with her arms full of them. They trailed on the green turf, they lay over her shoulders like white bayonets. All the air around her was full of flying petals. She looked like some homely Spring Angel. Then she bound these fair branches and twigs into the houseward side of the Abby-tree. She worked hard and fast. That afternoon one looking at the tree from the house would have been misled. That side of the Abby-tree was brave with bloom.

Sarah drew Abby in her chair a little way into the front room. "There!" said she.

"Oh! ain't it beautiful?" cried Abby.

The white branches waved before the window. Abby sat looking at it with a peaceful smile on her face.

When she was back in her old place in the sitting-room, she gave a bright look up at Sarah.

"It ain't any use to worry," said she, "the Abby-tree is bound to blossom."

Sarah cried out suddenly, "Oh, Abby! Abby! Abby! what shall I do! oh, what shall I do!" She flung herself down by Abby's chair, and put her face on her thin knees. "Oh, Abby! Abby!"

"Why, Sarah, you mustn't," said Abby.

"I ain't goin' to," said Sarah, in a minute. She stood up, and wiped her eyes. "I know you're better, Abby, an' you'll be out pretty soon. All is, you've been sick pretty long, an' it's kind of wore on me, an' it come over me all of a sudden."

"Sarah," said Abby, solemnly, "what's got to come has got to. You've got to look at things reasonable. There's two of us, an' one would have to go before the other one; we've always known it. It ain't goin' to be so bad as you think. Mis' Dunbar is comin' here to live with you. I've got it all fixed with her. She's real strong, an' she can make up the fires, an' git the water an' the tubs. You're fifty years old, an' you're goin' to have some more years to live. But it's just goin' to be gittin' up one day after another an' goin' to bed at night, an' they'll be gone. It can be got through with. There's roads trod out through everything, an' there's folks ahead with lanterns, as it were. You—"

"Oh, Abby! Abby! stop!" Sarah broke in. "If you knew all there was

to it. You don't know—you don't know! I 'ain't treated you right, Abby,
I 'ain't. I've been keepin' something from you."

"What have you been keepin', Sarah?"

Then Abby listened. Sarah told. There had always been an arch
curve to Abby's handsome mouth—a look of sweet amusement at life.
It showed forth plainly toward the close of Sarah's tale. Then it deepened suddenly. The poor sick woman laughed out, with a charming,
gleeful ring.

A look of joyful wonder flashed over Sarah's despairing face. She
stood staring.

"Sarah," said Abby, "I wouldn't have had John Marshall if he'd come
on his knees after me all the way from Mexico!"

How Nancy Jackson Married
Kate Wilson

——•——

Mark Twain

Thomas Furlong was a grizzled and sour bachelor of fifty who lived solitary and alone in a log house which stood remote and lonely in the middle of a great cornfield at the base of the rising spurs of the mountains. At two o'clock on a certain morning he came in out of a drizzling rain, lit his tallow dip, pulled down the cheap oiled shade of the single window, punched up his fire, took off his steaming coat, hung it before the fire to dry, sat down, spread his damp hands in front of the blaze, and said to himself—

"It's a puzzle. I wonder what ever did become of her. Seven hours. Maybe she ain't as much of a fool as people think." He sat silently considering the puzzle for some moments, then added, with energy, "Damn her! damn her whole tribe!"

The wooden latch clicked, the door opened and closed softly, and a fresh and comely young girl, clothed in the sunbonnet and the linsey woolsey of the region, stood before him. The man exhibited amazement. He bent a hostile eye upon her and said—

"You here! I just this minute said you warn't a fool. I take it back."

He rose and made [a] step toward the door. The girl motioned him back.

"Leave it alone," she said, "I'm not going to run away."

She sat down and put her feet to the fire. The man hesitated a moment, then resumed his seat with the air of one who has encountered another puzzle.

"You never had much sense, Nancy Jackson," he growled; "I reckon you've lost what you had."

"You think so, do you? What makes you think so?"

"What makes me?" He flung it out with vexed impatience. "Would anybody but a goose come to a sworn enemy's house when he is being hunted for his life?"

The girl did not seem overcome by the argument.

"Did they go to our house?"

"Of course."

"And didn't find me. Are they hiding around it, waiting to catch me when I come?"

"Of course—any fool could guess that."

"I am one of the fools; I guessed it. Have they hunted all the farmsteads for me for miles around—you and the others?"

"For seven hours. Yes. We've searched every one of them."

"Every one?"

"Yes, every one."

The girl gave a satisfied toss of the head and said—

"No you haven't. You didn't search this one."

The man seemed puzzled again, and said—

"I don't get your idea. Would anybody in his right mind ever think of coming *here* to find a cussed Jackson?"

Nancy laughed.

"I judged you'd all be in your right minds," she said; "so I came straight here."

"Great Scott, you can't mean it!"

"I've been sitting safe and comfortable by the embers in the dark of your kitchen six hours and a half."

Furlong gazed at her in silence a while, then shook his head and said—

"Well, it beats me. Of course it *was* the only place they wouldn't search, come to think." He turned the matter over in his mind a moment or two, then said, reluctantly, "You ain't the fool you look."

"Thanks," she said. "I can return the compliment."

"Er—what do you mean by that?"

"Oh, take it as you please—you people. My idea was, that you are not just the *kind* of fools you look."

Furlong started an angry sentence or two, dropped them in the middle, then brushed the dispute aside with a wave of his hand, and said—

"Come down to business. What are you here for? What's your game?"

The girl's face grew grave. She did not answer at once; after a little she began to word it, carefully, heedfully, and she seemed to watch for effects as the words fell.

"No one—saw me—shoot him—but you." The man's face betrayed nothing. If the girl was fishing for a confirmation of this statement, the project failed. She paused a moment, and seemed a trifle fluttered; then she pulled herself together and began to speak with what looked like good confidence. "Maybe one witness can hang me—I don't know, but I reckon not—it can't be law." A pause; no response from the man. She resumed. "Well, let that be as may be. If I hang, I hang; but I want my chance—I don't want to be lynched. *That* is why I took the risk and came here, where they'll never look for me. You hate me, and you hate all of my name, Thomas Furlong, but a man that's a man couldn't turn a dog out that fled to him for help when it was hunted for its life—hide me three days till the lynching fever's over, and I'll go and stand my trial!"

There was no change in Furlong's face. It had been implacably resentful before; it remained so.

"Did you kill Jim Bradley in self-defence?"

"Ye—s," hesitatingly.

"You did, did you?"

A nod of the head.

"It'll get you off unhung, you think?"

"I—I—it is my hope."

The man slowly crushed a dried tobacco leaf in his hand, loaded his pipe, emptied some embers on it with the shovel, gave a whiff or two, then said with calm conviction—

"Drop the idea. You'll hang, for sure."

"Why?" and the girl shrunk together and her face paled.

"I'll tell you, when I come to it. Didn't you know there'd be blood when Jim Bradley and your brother Floyd met?"

"Why—yes, I believed so."

"Quite likely. Everybody knew it, you knew it, your mother knew it. How did *you* come to be at the cross roads with Floyd just as dark was coming on and Jim was likely to come by?"

No answer.

"You was there to help. You can't deny it. And when Jim got the drop of Floyd and killed him and broke for the woods, you grabbed Floyd's gun and chased him a hundred yards and sent a bullet through his temple when he turned to look back. *He* shot Floyd when Floyd stepped from behind the tree raising his gun—and it was self-defence. Yourn *wasn't,* my girl. What do you say to that?"

Nancy was very white. She put up her hands appealingly, and said—

"Oh, oh, have some pity, Mr. Furlong! You can save me—you are the only witness—"

"There was two others!"

"Two? Oh—"

"And they don't love the Jacksons. I name no names, but when the trial comes off *I* can't save you—couldn't if I wanted to."

Nancy was sobbing now, and wringing her hands miserably.

"Oh, what shall I do! what shall I do!" she said. "My mother's heart will be broken."

At the mention of the mother the anger in Furlong's eyes blazed up fiercely, and he said—

"Let it break! let it break, I say! On the very morning of the day set for our wedding she flung me over and married that low-grade fool your father; humiliated me, made me the joke of the countryside; spoiled my life and made it bitter and lonely and a burden; and the children that should have been mine—but damn these histories, they—look here! Do you want to live?"

"Oh, I do, I do. Let me live!"

"Then you shall! And I'll make it so hard for you, and for *her,* that—"

"Oh, make it anything you like, only let me live, and I will be thankful and she—"

"Then these are the terms. Now listen. You will leave this region, and go far away—for good and all."

"I shall be glad to, God knows. And she may go with me?"

"No."

The word smote like a blow. The girl said faintly—

"Not go with me?"

"I said it."

Nancy rocked her head from side to side, as one in physical pain, and said—

"Oh, it is hard—never to see her again—she never to see me again—oh, she could not bear it, it would kill her—I will not go!"

"As you please. Stay here and hang, if that would suit her better."

"Oh, no, no, no!—I didn't mean it, I didn't indeed; I will go! To know that I am alive will be a comfort to her. She *will* know it, won't she?"

"You will write her every week—in a disguised hand; and for your own safety, see to it that you send the letters under cover to me, who will not be suspected of corresponding with a Jackson. A letter every week, do you understand? If you fail once, I set the dogs of the law on your track."

"I will not fail; oh, I shall be glad to write her and take some of the aches out of her heart."

"Another detail. To-night you are wearing women's clothes for the last time in your life."

"What!"

"For the last time—it is what I said."

"Ah, be merciful; do not require this—say you will not, Mr. Furlong. I—"

"You can't get away from here without a disguise; you can't risk living where you are going without a disguise—"

"But I can dress as a—"

"You will dress as a *man*—that is what you will do. It suits my humor. Say no more about it. Do you agree?"

"I do. There is no help."

"On your honor, now: will you *never* leave off your male dress nor reveal your real sex under any pressure whatever? Promise."

"Oh, must it be—be—always?"

"Absolutely. Promise!"

"Oh, if any other—if—."

"Promise! If in ten seconds you have not pr—"

"I promise! On my honor I promise!"

"Very well, then. Go up in the garret and go to bed. The clothes of the young negro I used to have three years ago before they lynched him on suspicion of stealing two dollars from Jake Carter, who never *had* two dollars that he got honestly, are up there, and they'll fit you. Put them on in the morning, and hide your own or burn them; you won't need that kind anymore. I'll trim your head and make a young fellow of you. Every day you'll practice, and I'll help you; and by and by when you're letter perfect and can walk and act like a male person and the lynch-fever has blown over, I'll take you out of this region some night and see you safe over the border and on your way. You will call yourself Robert Finlay."

After the girl was gone to the garret, Furlong smoked and thought, and listened to the peaceful patter of the rain on the shingles for half an hour; then he muttered—

"Two of them are dead, two of them are miserable from this out. My chance was a long time coming, but it was worth waiting for. I've drunk a lot of bitter in these twenty years, but there's sugar in this."

He was very happy, and smiled the smile of a contented fiend.

Roughly stated, it was like this.

Jacob Wilson was a farmer who owned a hundred acres of good land, and raised hogs, mules and corn for the southern market. He lived half a mile from the village of Hackley, which had a population of three hundred persons, young and old, and had also a store, a blacksmith shop and a small square church which was without steeple or other gaud. Wilson was of middle age, and had a wife and three children—two young boys and a girl. The girl was well along in her eighteenth year, and was trim and pretty, and carried herself in an independent fashion and upon occasion exhibited a masterful spirit. Her name was Catherine, and she was called Kate. For more than two years, now, she had been of marriageable age, and the young fellows of the farmsteads and the village had been paying awkward court to her, but her heart was still untouched. She was quite willing to flirt with them, and she did it, and got great pleasure out of it, encouraging each of the youths in turn to think she was taking him seriously, then discarding him and laughing at him when she was tired of him. She made some sore hearts, and for it she got many reproaches, from her mother, and from other mothers concerned; but she was not troubled, she only tossed her head and curled her lip and baited her traps again. Her mother tried to warn her, tried to reason with her, and feared that a judgment would overtake her; but she laughed a gay laugh and said that on the contrary the judgments seemed to be overtaking those others. The mother was grieved, and asked her if she had no heart. The girl said maybe she had, maybe she hadn't; but if she had, it was her intention to market it to her satisfaction or not at all; meantime perhaps there was no great harm in amusing herself with it.

Then came a stranger along, in the early June days, and he had fine manners, and eastern ways, and tailor-made clothes, and was easy, and at home, and bright in his talk, and the village took him to its heart and was happy in his possession. He soon found his way to the Wilson farm; and Kate rejoiced, and straightway she set a trap for him. He came often, then oftener, and he and the girl roamed the primeval woods and the hills hour by hour in the soft gloaming and the moonlight.

If there had been a doubt as to whether Catherine Wilson had a heart or not, that doubt had now vanished. She had one, and she gave it in its absolute entirety to this young stranger, Alfred Hamilton, and was deeply, passionately, unspeakably happy. She walked on air, she thought herself in heaven. There was a week of this delicious trance, this delirium, then Hamilton bade the family good-bye and left for the east to richly prepare and make beautiful a home for his back-settlements bride. He would telegraph, every day, on his journey, to keep his Kate comforted and enable her to bear the separation, and with every opportunity he would write a letter.

All the countryside were talking about the engagement. The Wilsons did not deny it, but that was as far as they went. However, they looked happy, and that was considered equivalent to a confession.

That first telegram did not come!

Had Hamilton met with an accident? was he sick? The family were in great tribulation, Kate was in a state of pitiable terror. She could not sleep that night, but counted the slow hours and waited for next day's news.

It did not come. There was no telegram.

The third day the same.

Kate could not endure the heart-breaking suspense. Should she telegraph Mr. Hamilton's family for tidings? There was a family consultation over this question. It was finally judged best not to indulge in privacies over the wire; to write would be more judicious. So the letter went, to the Hamilton family's Boston address.

A blank week followed—a wretched week for the Wilsons. No

answer came. What did the silence mean? Suspicions began to rise in the minds of those poor people. They did not voice them; out of charity for each other each kept his own counsel and suffered in silence.

But this could not go on so; something must be done. What should it be? Apparently there was no choice, there was but one thing to do. Mr. Wilson did it. He wrote the Boston police.

There was another blank week. Then came news which the sufferers had been trying hard not to expect: no Hamiltons had ever lived at that address. Kate Wilson swooned away and was carried to her bed. The mother went to the village and visited among her friends, and talked as pleasantly and cheerfully as she could about all sorts of things, waiting meanwhile for the topic of supreme interest to drift into the conversation; then she smiled and said—

"Oh, that girl, she is incurable! We did hope, for a while, that this time she would stick; but no, what's bred in the bone will come out in the flesh, as the saying is. She's flung him over, just as usual."

"It's too bad."

"Yes, it is. She made him promise to keep still and wait a month for his answer, and now she's sent it ahead of time. I've told her time and again she'll bring a judgment on herself some day, but she always laughs and says the judgments seem to fall to the others. What nice weather we're having. Well, good-bye, I must be going."

So, with a shamed spirit and an aching heart she went her rounds under a cheery mask and distributed her pride-saving and excusable lie.

Kate Wilson kept her bed only a day; then she pulled her courage together and went about her affairs as in former days. Exteriorly she seemed unchanged, but her gayeties were not real; she was entertaining a volcano inside. She wanted revenge for the insult which had been put upon her; she had taken a medicine which she had often administered, and had not found it to her taste. Had the others found it to their taste? That was a question of no importance; it did not interest her, perhaps it did not even suggest itself. She wanted revenge. How could she get it? Well, on the whole the old way was good enough. She would resume, at the old stand. She would never marry, for she could not love again, but she would break every heart that came in her way, and try to imagine it was Hamilton's.

When she had been out of bed a couple of days her father brought home at eventide a waif whom he had found wandering the country roads a mile from the house—a comely young fellow of nineteen or twenty. He said his name was Robert Finlay. He was worn out and famishing. They fed him to his stomach's content, then he was palleted for the night on the floor, and promised a home if he was willing to work for it. He was very grateful, and said he would prove himself worthy.

There was an unoccupied log cabin in the edge of the forest a half mile from the house, and next day the Wilsons fitted this up and installed him in it. As the days went by he won his way with the family and they all liked him and were glad he fell to their share. He was not good for very heavy work, but he did all kinds of light work well and handily, and was a willing and diligent soul.

He was very gentle, and very winning in his ways, but inclined to sadness. Mrs. Wilson pitied him, mothered him, loved him, and the gratefulness that shone in his kind eyes and fell caressingly from his tongue was her sufficient reward. He seemed to shrink a little from talking about himself, but a fleeting word dropped here and there and now and then revealed in time a kind of outline of his history. Thus it was perceived that he had come from far away; that his liberty, if not his life, had been in danger because of a crime plausibly laid to his charge but which he said he had not committed; that he could never go back whence he came. If he could stay where he was now he should be safe, and in this house he could be happier than anywhere else in the world. Several times he said, pressing mother Wilson's hand and looking up worshipingly in her good face—

"*You* cannot know what you are doing for me; my life was a terror and a misery to me, and you have taken all that away and made it dear to me and beautiful. I kiss your hands—I could kiss your feet! Do you believe there is any sacrifice I would not make for you and yours? *Any* sacrifice! The harder the better. I wish I could show you. If a time ever comes you shall see, oh, you shall see!"

The only fault papa Wilson could find in him was these outbursts. He was a plain man and destitute of "gush," and these things discomforted him. He kept his thought to himself for a time, but at last, with caution—feeling that the ice was thin—he took a risk and privately suggested to his wife that the young fellow protested too much. It fired a mine! He did not make that venture a second time. He continued to hold his opinion, but he did not air it any more.

Before Robert had been on the place four days Kate had set her trap for him. But there was no result; Robert responded to her advances, and was evidently pleased by them, but he did not respond in the usual way; he radiated gratified friendliness, but nothing warmer. Kate was surprised, dissatisfied, and privately indignant. But she was not troubled; he was human; a few days would change the complexion of things—there was no hurry.

She was soon deeply interested in her enterprise, and found it unusually attractive because it was difficult; which was a new thing in her experience. She got to happening upon Robert accidentally in the fields and all about; she double-charged the batteries of her eyes and let him have the whole load; she sweetly weaned him from calling her Miss Wilson, and beguiled him to call her Kate; she rewarded him by calling him—timorously—Robert, then she watched for the effect—and was vexed to see that there wasn't any.

When Sunday came around she happened by his cabin and took him for a walk through the sweet solitudes of the wooded hills, and talked sentiment and romance and poetry to him; she allowed her elbow to touch his, but could not discover that it communicated a thrill; she gave a little scream at an imaginary snake, and put her hand upon his arm, and forgot it and left it there a while; then took it away with inviting reluctance and slowly, but he did not try to retain it. Finally she said she was weary, and he offered to turn back homeward, "like a fool," she said to herself; but she said a little rest would restore her; so they sat down on a mossy bank and she worked along up to the subject of love, and said, dreamily—

"It may be beautiful—it would be, no doubt—if one could find the right and loyal heart, a heart that could feel and return a deep and sincere affection—but I—I—something tells me I shall never find it."

She paused, to give Robert an opportunity. After reflection, he said, sympathetically—

"Do not say that. You will find it."

"Oh, do you think so—do you?"

"Why, yes—I think it must happen."

"How good of you! And you are *always* so good. So good and so—so—affectionate, if you will let me say it and not think me bold. You *have* an affectionate nature, *haven't* you?"

"Why—I hope I have—I—"

"Oh I *know* you have! It is in your eyes, Robert—I love to look in your eyes; do you love to have me?" She laid her warm soft hand upon his with a gentle pressure. "You do, don't you, Robert?"

"Why, yes, I—I'm sure I—"

Her pouting lips were near to his; languidly she whispered, "Kiss me, Robert," and closed her eyes.

She waited. Nothing happened. She unclosed her eyes; they were spouting anger. He began to explain humbly that she had misunderstood him; that he *liked* her—liked her ever so much, but—

"I hate you!" she burst out, and gathered up her skirts and strode away without looking backward.

The next day she sat brooding over the humiliation which he had put upon her, and over her yesterday's failure to avenge that wrong upon another member of his detested sex. Was this defeat to stand? Well, no. Her resentment against Robert flamed up, and she said she would find a way somehow to make him sorry that he had ever crossed her path. She began to form a plan; as she proceeded with it she grew enamored of it. She finished it to her content, and said it would answer—now let him look to himself.

After a little a new thought came drifting into her brain—and it stopped her breath for a moment. Her lips fell apart; she moistened them with her tongue; her face blenched, her breath began to come in gasps; she muttered a frightened ejaculation, her head drooped, her chin sank upon her breast.

Two days later mother Wilson went to the village and made another house-to-house visitation with news to deliver. Happy news this time: her daughter was engaged to Robert Finlay. She was snowed under with enthusiastic congratulations everywhere she went, and as soon as her back was turned the friends discussed the matter and pitied the bridegroom. They agreed that although he was a tramp and unknown he was manifestly a simple and honest good creature and a better man than Kate Wilson deserved. In their opinion a judgment had fallen again—and on the wrong person, as usual. A few cautious conservatives said it was too early, as yet, to be locating the judgment; Kate could back out before the wedding day, and it was an even bet that she would do it. There was wisdom in this remark, and it sensibly cooled the general joy produced by the prospect of the exasperating flirt's early retirement from her professional industries.

There was a fortnight's suspense, then all doubts and all questionings were put to rest: Kate and Robert were married. The wedding took place at the farm at noonday, and was followed by a barbecue and a dance. It was noticed that Robert, in his wedding clothes, was a surprisingly handsome person; also that fleeting glimpses of his accustomed sadness were catchable through chance rifts in his new happiness; also that Kate's exuberant joy seemed a little overdone, at times; also that there was a haunting and pathetic something in mother Wilson's face that took the strength out of one's congratulations and made them sound almost like words of comfort and compassion; also that papa Wilson's manner was grave, austere, almost gloomy; that when he gave his daughter a deed of half his farm as a wedding present from her parents he did not look at his son-in-law, and did not grace the gift with a speech of any kind; that he then excused himself and took his leave with a general bow and some mumbled words which nobody heard, and was seen no more.

The guests departed at six in the afternoon, observing privately to each other that there was "something wrong there—what can the matter be?" Arrived at their several homes, they reported to their households that they had been at a funeral, they didn't know whose—maybe Kate's, maybe Robert's, maybe the whole family's.

The company gone, the bride, the groom and the mother found themselves sitting together—with liberal spaces between—moody, distraught, silent, each waiting for the others to begin. It was the groom who began, finally. He said—

"You commanded, mother Wilson; I have obeyed. Against my will. I obeyed because I could not help myself; I obeyed because there was no possible way out, and I had to do it; if there had been a way out, I never would have obeyed. I—"

Mother Wilson interrupted him, in a tone of gentle reproach.

"Ah, Robert, you could not honorably and humanely do otherwise than obey. You denied the charge, but obeying was confession, Robert."

The young man rejoined, with almost a groan in his voice—

"Oh, the deadly logic of it! I *know* it looks like that, and there's no answering it; it is *un*answerable, and yet I say again, the charge is not true. It is my misfortune that I cannot at this time explain why I was obliged to obey; and so—"

"Yes, it *is* unfortunate," the bride remarked, tauntingly; "shall you ever be able to explain?"

"That is the worst of it—no! But you! how do you dare to speak? You who sit smirking there—you, Catherine Wil—Finlay—you know I never did you harm. You—"

"I say it again. The charge I made was true."

Finlay tugged at his collar to loosen it; tried to retort; the words choked in his throat. Mother Wilson said, in gentle rebuke—

"You are a stranger, Robert; we love you, but we do not know you yet. It is not reasonable to expect us to believe you against our daughter's word."

"Oh, I know it, I know it! My case is weaker than water; and all because I cannot explain, I cannot *explain*! You believe her; papa Wilson believes her, and both of you are justified—I were a fool to deny it. Papa Wilson thinks me an ungrateful cur, and despises me—and in the circumstances he is right, though I have never done harm to any member of this family, nor meditated it."

"Ah well," said mother Wilson, soothingly, "things are as they are, and we must accept them; they may be blessings in disguise—we cannot know. Let us let bygones be bygones, and think no more about them, resolving to begin a new life and a happy and righteous one. Put your fault behind you, dear and beloved son; it is forgiven, it shall be forgotten. My child will make you a good and loving wife—"

"No—no—no! She is no wife of mine, and never shall be, except in name."

"My dear son! You—"

"You commanded, mother; I have obeyed—because I could not help myself. I have saved your daughter's good name from gossip and wreck—let the sacrifice stop there. I will never live with her—not even so much as a single day."

"My son, oh, my son! What are you saying! Oh—"

"Let him alone, mother," said the new wife, with a serene confidence born of old experience; "if I shall ever desire his society, trust me I shall know how to acquire it."

After supper the new husband betook himself at once to his lonely cabin and sat down and wrote a long letter; sealed it in an envelop directed to "Mrs. Sarah Jackson"; sealed that envelop in a larger one; directed this one to an obscure village in a distant State, and addressed it to "Mr. Thomas Furlong." Then he went to bed and to sleep.

The letter was several days on its road. Mr. Furlong took it from the village postoffice and carried it to his ancient log cabin three or four miles in the country. He was expecting the letter; one came from the same source punctually every week. Furlong stirred up his fire, lit his cob pipe, and made himself comfortable. He exhibited the strong and lively interest of a person who is expecting exhilarating tidings and is proposing to get a deal of enjoyment out of them. Yet he knew that the letter was not for him. He settled himself in his chair and opened both envelops. The letter began—

"DEAR MOTHER: To-day I was married to the girl I have already spoken of."

Furlong put down pipe and letter and threw back his head and delivered himself of crash after crash, gust after gust of delighted laughter; then, middle-aged man as he was, got up, mopping the happy tears from his leathery cheeks, and expended the remaining remnant of his strength in a breakdown of scandalous violence, and finally sank into his chair, heaving and panting, limp and exhausted, and said with what wind he had left—

"Lord, it's just good to be alive!"

He resumed his pipe and Mrs. Jackson's letter, now, and read the latter through to the end, making comments as he proceeded. The story of the marriage, and what brought it about, and what happened after it, was detailed and complete—all the facts, just as we already know them—and they gave Mr. Furlong high satisfaction and amusement, particularly where poor Finlay broke into pathetic lamentations over his miseries and wrongs and humiliations. At these places Furlong slapped his thigh and said with evil glee—

"It's great, it's grand, it's lovely! It couldn't suit me better if I had planned it myself."

The letter closed with—

"And so, as you see, I am married, yet have no wife; for, as I told them at the end of that wretched talk, I shall never live with her for even so much as a single day. Dear mother, pity your poor son. ROBERT FINLAY."

"He's keeping his word," was Furlong's comment. "And damn him he'd better, if he knows what's good for him!"

He put the letter in his pocket without re-enveloping it, and left his cabin, remarking to himself—

"His mamma must have it straight off. Her head's turning gray; I reckon this will help."

At the Wilson farm the months dragged drearily along. The four members of the family ate their meals together, and sometimes they took their food in silence, sometimes they talked, but it was in a constrained and colorless way, and papa Wilson's share in it was exceedingly small, and was confined to the two women as a rule; it was but rarely that he included "Mr. Finlay"—as he called him—in his remarks, and when he did it was not in order to pay him compliments. The young couple called each other "Mr." and "Mrs." Mother Wilson and Robert remained affectionate toward each other, and she continued to call him Robert and "son," and he continued to call her Mother Wilson. The good lady made many attempts to soften and sweeten this arid life, but she got no encouragement and had no success. She mourned much, and shed many tears.

After the free ways of the country, visitors came often—uninvited— and stopped to a meal, to spy out the conditions. On these occasions efforts were made by all the family to seem friendly and content, but those made by papa Wilson were so lame and poor that they spoiled the game and no visitor went away deceived.

Evenings at eight o'clock the family met at family worship for half an hour. Papa Wilson read and prayed, and he always wanted to ignore Robert, and would have done it but for his wife's anguished appeals. Through their influence a compromise was effected—such as it was— and nightly a prayer went up for "mercy" for "the stranger within our gates"; a prayer which always came from the cold-storage closet in the supplicant's heart and changed the temperature of the room. Mother Wilson tried hard to get a blessing put in the place of mercy, but the embittered old man would not have it so. He said—

"I loved this cur and was kind to him; and for pay he . . . drop the subject, I will not listen to it!"

Nightly, after prayers, [Robert] withdrew promptly from the house's depressing atmosphere and betook him to the refuge of his cabin, and was not seen again until morning. Sundays he rode by his wife's side to the village, along with her parents, and by her side he sat through the forenoon service. The keeping up of appearances in public went little or no further than this. All the world knew that the pair did not live together; all the world wondered at it and discussed it, and tried to guess the reason; a former schoolmate of Kate's carried her curiosity so far as to leave hinting and boldly put the straight question—

"If the old friends ask me why things are as they are, what shall I say?"

Kate reflected; seemed to search warily for a safe and diplomatic answer, then laid her hand on the woman's knee, gazed into her face with yearning simplicity and said—

"How would it do to say it is none of their business?"

At last the child was born—a boy.

Paul's Case

A Study in Temperament

Willa Cather

I

It was Paul's afternoon to appear before the faculty of the Pittsburg
High School to account for his various misdemeanors. He had been
suspended a week ago, and his father had called at the principal's office and confessed his perplexity about his son. Paul entered the faculty
room, suave and smiling. His clothes were a trifle outgrown, and the
tan velvet on the collar of his open overcoat was frayed and worn; but,
for all that, there was something of the dandy about him, and he wore
an opal pin in his neatly knotted black four-in-hand, and a red carnation in his buttonhole. This latter adornment the faculty somehow felt
was not properly significant of the contrite spirit befitting a boy under
the ban of suspension.

Paul was tall for his age and very thin, with high, cramped shoulders and a narrow chest. His eyes were remarkable for a certain hysterical brilliancy, and he continually used them in a conscious,
theatrical sort of way, peculiarly offensive in a boy. The pupils were
abnormally large, as though he were addicted to belladonna, but there
was a glassy glitter about them which that drug does not produce.

When questioned by the principal as to why he was there, Paul stated, politely enough, that he wanted to come back to school. This was a lie, but Paul was quite accustomed to lying—found it, indeed, indispensable for overcoming friction. His teachers were asked to state their respective charges, which they did with such a rancor and aggrievedness as evinced that this was not a usual case. Disorder and impertinence were among the offences named, yet each of his instructors felt that it was scarcely possible to put into words the real cause of the trouble, which lay in a sort of hysterically defiant manner of the boy's; in the contempt which they all knew he felt for them, and which he seemingly made not the least effort to conceal. Once, when he had been making a synopsis of a paragraph at the blackboard, his English teacher had stepped to his side and attempted to guide his hand. Paul had started back with a shudder, and thrust his hands violently behind him. The astonished woman could scarcely have been more hurt and embarrassed had he struck at her. The insult was so involuntary and definitely personal as to be unforgettable. In one way and another he had made all his teachers, men and women alike, conscious of the same feeling of physical aversion.

His teachers felt, this afternoon, that his whole attitude was symbolized by his shrug and his flippantly red carnation flower, and they fell upon him without mercy. He stood through it, smiling, his pale lips parted over his white teeth. (His lips were continually twitching, and he had a habit of raising his eyebrows that was contemptuous and irritating to the last degree.) Older boys than Paul had broken down and shed tears under that baptism of fire, but his set smile did not once desert him, and his only sign of discomfort was the nervous trembling of the fingers that toyed with the buttons of his overcoat, and an occasional jerking of the other hand that held his hat. Paul was always smiling, always glancing about him, seeming to feel that people might be watching him and trying to detect something. This conscious expression, since it was as far as possible from boyish mirthfulness, was usually attributed to insolence or "smartness."

As the inquisition proceeded, one of his instructors repeated an impertinent remark of the boy's, and the principal asked him whether he thought that a courteous speech to have made a woman. Paul shrugged his shoulders slightly and his eyebrows twitched.

"I don't know," he replied. "I didn't mean to be polite, or impolite, either. I guess it's a sort of way I have of saying things, regardless."

The principal, who was a sympathetic man, asked him whether he didn't think that a way it would be well to get rid of. Paul grinned and said he guessed so. When he was told that he could go, he bowed gracefully and went out. His bow was but a repetition of the scandalous red carnation.

His teachers were in despair, and his drawing-master voiced the feeling of them all when he declared there was something about the boy which none of them understood. He added: "I don't really believe that smile of his comes altogether from insolence; there's something sort of haunted about it. The boy is not strong, for one thing. I happen to know that he was born in Colorado, only a few months before his mother died out there of a long illness. There is something wrong about the fellow."

The drawing-master had come to realize that, in looking at Paul, one saw only his white teeth and the forced animation of his eyes. One warm afternoon the boy had gone to sleep at his drawing-board, and his master had noted with amazement what a white, blue-veined face it was; drawn and wrinkled like an old man's about the eyes, the lips twitching even in his sleep, and stiff with a nervous tension that drew them back from his teeth.

As for Paul, he ran down the hill, whistling the soldiers' chorus from "Faust," looking wildly behind him, now and then, to see whether some of his teachers were not there to writhe under his light-heartedness. As it was now late in the afternoon, and Paul was on duty that evening as usher in Carnegie Hall, he decided that he would not go home to supper, but would hang about an Oakland tobacconist's shop until it was time to go to the concert hall.

When Paul reached the ushers' dressing-room at about half-past seven that evening, half a dozen boys were there already, and Paul began, excitedly, to tumble into his uniform. It was one of the few that at all approached fitting, and he thought it very becoming, though he knew that the tight, straight coat accentuated his narrow chest, about which he was exceedingly sensitive. He was always considerably excited while he dressed, twanging all over to the tuning of the strings and the preliminary flourishes of the horns in the music-room; but to-night he seemed quite beside himself, and he teased and plagued the boys until, telling him that he was crazy, they put him down on the floor and sat on him.

Somewhat calmed by his suppression, Paul dashed out to the front of the house to seat the early comers.

He was a model usher; gracious and smiling, he ran up and down the aisles; nothing was too much trouble for him; he carried messages and brought programs as though it were his greatest pleasure in life, and all the people in his section thought him a charming boy, feeling that he remembered and admired them. As the house filled, he grew more and more vivacious and animated, and the color came to his cheeks and lips. It was very much as though this were a great reception, and Paul were the host.

When the symphony began, Paul sank into one of the rear seats, with a long sigh of relief. It was not that symphonies, as such, meant anything in particular to Paul, but the first sigh of the instruments seemed to free some hilarious and potent spirit within him—something that struggled there like the Genius in the bottle found by the Arab fisherman. He felt a sudden zest of life; the lights danced before his eyes and the concert hall blazed into unimaginable splendor. When the soprano soloist came on, Paul half closed his eyes, and gave himself up to the peculiar stimulus such personages always had for him. The soloist chanced to be a German woman, by no means in her first youth and the mother of many children; but she wore an elaborate gown and a tiara, and above all, she had that indefinable air of achievement, that world-shine upon her, which, in Paul's eyes, made her a veritable queen of romance.

After a concert was over Paul was always irritable and wretched until he got to sleep, and to-night he was even more than usually restless. He had the feeling of not being able to let down, of its being impossible to give up this delicious excitement which was the only thing that could be called living at all. During the last number he withdrew, and, after hastily changing his clothes in the dressing-room, slipped out to the side door where the soprano's carriage stood. Here he began pacing rapidly up and down the walk, waiting to see her come out.

Over yonder the Schenley, in its vacant stretch, loomed big and square through the fine rain, the windows of its twelve stories glowing like those of a lighted cardboard house under a Christmas tree. All the actors and singers of the better class stayed there when they were in the city, and a number of the big manufacturers of the place lived there in the winter. Paul had often hung about the hotel, watching the people go in and out, longing to enter and leave school-masters and dull care behind him forever.

At last the singer came out, accompanied by the conductor who helped her into her carriage and closed the door with a cordial *auf wiedersehen,* which set Paul to wondering whether she were not an old sweetheart of his. Paul followed the carriage over to the hotel, walking so rapidly as not to be far from the entrance when the singer alighted and disappeared behind the swinging glass doors that were opened by a negro in a tall hat and a long coat. In the moment that the door was ajar, it seemed to Paul that he too entered. He seemed to feel himself go after her up the steps, into the warm, lighted building, into an exotic, a tropical world of shiny, glistening surfaces and basking ease. He reflected upon the mysterious dishes that were brought into the dining-room, the green bottles in buckets of ice, as he had seen them in the supper-party pictures of the Sunday *World* supplement. A quick gust of wind brought the rain down with sudden vehemence, and Paul was startled to find that he was still outside in the slush of the gravel drive-way; that his boots were letting in the water, and his scanty overcoat was clinging wet about him; that the lights in front of the concert hall were out, and that the rain was driving in sheets between him and the orange glow of the windows above him. There it was, what he wanted—tangibly before him, like the fairy world of a Christmas pantomime, but mocking spirits stood guard at the doors, and as the rain beat in his face, Paul wondered whether he were destined always to shiver in the black night outside, looking up at it.

He turned and walked reluctantly toward the car tracks. The end had to come sometime; his father in his night-clothes at the top of the stairs, explanations that did not explain, hastily improvised fictions that were forever tripping him up, his upstairs room and its horrible yellow wall-paper, the creaking bureau with the greasy plush collar box, and over his painted wooden bed the pictures of George Washington and John Calvin, and the framed motto, "Feed my Lambs," which had been worked in red worsted by his mother.

Half an hour later, Paul alighted from his car and went slowly down one of the side streets off the main thoroughfare. It was a highly respectable street, where all the houses were exactly alike, and where business men of moderate means begot and reared large families of children, all of whom went to Sabbath-school and learned the shorter catechism, and were interested in arithmetic; all of whom were as exactly alike as their homes, and of a piece with the monotony in which they lived. Paul never went up Cordelia Street without a shudder of loathing. His home was next to the house of the Cumberland minister. He approached it to-night with the nerveless sense of defeat, the hopeless feeling of sinking back forever into ugliness and commonness that he always had when he came home. The moment he turned into Cordelia Street he felt the waters close above his head. After each of these orgies of living, he experienced all the physical depression which follows a debauch; the loathing of respectable beds, of common food, of a house penetrated by kitchen odors; a shuddering repulsion for the flavorless, colorless mass of every-day existence; a morbid desire for cool things and soft lights and fresh flowers.

The nearer he approached the house, the more absolutely unequal Paul felt to the sight of it all: his ugly sleeping chamber, the cold bathroom, with the grimy zinc tub, the cracked mirror, the dripping spigots, his father at the top of the stairs, his hairy legs sticking out from his night-shirt, his feet thrust into carpet slippers. He was so much later than usual that there would certainly be inquiries and reproaches. Paul stopped short before the door. He felt that he could not be accosted by his father to-night, that he could not toss again on that miserable bed. He would not go in. He would tell his father that he had had no car fare, and it was raining so hard he had gone home with one of the boys and stayed all night.

Meanwhile, he was wet and cold. He went around to the back of the house and tried one of the basement windows, found it open, raised it cautiously, and scrambled down the cellar wall to the floor. There he stood, holding his breath, terrified by the noise he had made, but the floor above him was silent, and there was no creak on the stairs. He found a soap box, and carried it over to the soft ring of light that streamed from the furnace door, and sat down. He was horribly afraid of rats, so he did not try to sleep, but sat looking distrustfully at the dark, still terrified least he might have awakened his father. In such reactions, after one of the experiences which made days and nights out of the dreary blanks of the calendar, when his senses were deadened, Paul's head was always singularly clear. Suppose his father had heard him getting in at the window, and come down and shot him for a burglar? Then, again, suppose his father had come down, pistol in hand,

and he had cried out in time to save himself, and his father had been horrified to think how nearly he had killed him? Then, again, suppose a day should come when his father would remember that night, and wish there had been no warning cry to stay his hand? With this last supposition Paul entertained himself until daybreak.

The following Sunday was fine; the sodden November chill was broken by the last flash of autumnal summer. In the morning Paul had to go to church and Sabbath-school, as always. On seasonable Sunday afternoons the burghers of Cordelia Street always sat out on their front "stoops," and talked to their neighbors on the next stoop, or called to those across the street in neighborly fashion. The men usually sat on gay cushions placed upon the steps that led down to the sidewalk, while the women, in their Sunday "waists," sat in rockers on the cramped porches, pretending to be greatly at their ease. The children played in the streets; there were so many of them that the place resembled the recreation grounds of a kindergarten. The men on the steps— all in their shirt-sleeves, their vests unbuttoned—sat with their legs well apart, their stomachs comfortably protruding, and talked of the prices of things, or told anecdotes of the sagacity of their various chiefs and overlords. They occasionally looked over the multitude of squabbling children, listened affectionately to their high-pitched, nasal voices, smiling to see their own proclivities reproduced in their offspring, and interspersed their legends of the iron kings with remarks about their sons' progress at school, their grades in arithmetic, and the amounts they had saved in their toy banks.

On this last Sunday of November, Paul sat all afternoon on the lowest step of his "stoop," staring into the street, while his sisters, in their rockers, were talking to the minister's daughters next door about how many shirt-waists they had made in the last week, and how many waffles some one had eaten at the last church supper. When the weather was warm, and his father was in a particularly jovial frame of mind, the girls made lemonade, which was always brought out in a red glass pitcher, ornamented with forget-me-nots in blue enamel. This the girls thought very fine, and the neighbors always joked about the suspicious color of the pitcher.

To-day Paul's father sat on the top step, talking to a young man who shifted a restless baby from knee to knee. He happened to be the young man who was daily held up to Paul as a model, and after whom it was his father's dearest hope that he would pattern. This young man was of a ruddy complexion, with a compressed, red mouth, and faded, near-sighted eyes, over which he wore thick spectacles, with gold bows that curved about his ears. He was clerk to one of the magnates of a great steel corporation, and was looked upon in Cordelia Street as a young man with a future. There was a story that, some five years ago—he was now barely twenty-six—he had been a trifle dissipated, but in order to curb his appetites and save the loss of time and strength that a sowing of wild oats might have entailed, he had taken his chief's advice, oft reiterated to his employees, and at twenty-one, had married the first woman whom he could persuade to share his fortunes. She happened to be an angular schoolmistress, much older than he, who also wore thick glasses, and who had now borne him four children, all near-sighted, like herself.

The young man was relating how his chief, now cruising in the Mediterranean, kept in touch with all the details of the business, arranging his office hours on his yacht just as though he were at home, and "knocking off work enough to keep two stenographers busy." His father told, in turn, the plan his corporation was considering, of putting in an electric railway plant at Cairo. Paul snapped his teeth; he had an awful apprehension that they might spoil it all before he got there. Yet he rather liked to hear these legends of the iron kings, that were told and retold on Sundays and holidays; these stories of palaces in Venice, yachts on the Mediterranean, and high play at Monte Carlo appealed to his fancy, and he was interested in the triumphs of these cash-boys who had become famous, though he had no mind for the cash-boy stage.

After supper was over, and he had helped to dry the dishes, Paul nervously asked his father whether he could go to George's to get some help in his geometry, and still more nervously asked for car fare. This latter request he had to repeat, as his father, on principle, did not like to hear requests for money, whether much or little. He asked Paul whether he could not go to some boy who lived nearer, and told him that he ought not to leave his school work until Sunday; but he gave him the dime. He was not a poor man, but he had a worthy ambition to come up in the world. His only reason for allowing Paul to usher was, that he thought a boy ought to be earning a little.

Paul bounded up-stairs, scrubbed the greasy odor of the dish-water from his hands with the ill-smelling soap he hated, and then shook over his fingers a few drops of violet water from the bottle he kept hidden in his drawer. He left the house with his geometry conspicuously under his arm, and the moment he got out of Cordelia Street and boarded a downtown car, he shook off the lethargy of two deadening days, and began to live again.

The leading juvenile of the permanent stock company which played at one of the downtown theaters was an acquaintance of Paul's, and the boy had been invited to drop in at the Sunday-night rehearsals whenever he could. For more than a year Paul had spent every available moment loitering about Charley Edwards's dressing-room. He had won a place among Edwards's following, not only because the young actor, who could not afford to employ the services of a dresser, often found the boy very useful, but because he recognized in Paul something akin to what Churchmen term "vocation."

It was at the theater and at Carnegie Hall that Paul really lived; the rest was but a sleep and a forgetting. This was Paul's fairy tale, and it had for him all the allurement of a secret love. The moment he inhaled the gassy, painty, dusty odor behind the scenes, he breathed like a prisoner set free, and felt within him the possibility of doing or saying splendid, brilliant, poetic things. The moment the cracked orchestra beat out the overture from "Martha," or jerked at the serenade from "Rigoletto," all stupid and ugly things slid from him, and his senses were deliciously, yet delicately fired.

Perhaps it was because, in Paul's world, the natural nearly always wore the guise of ugliness, that a certain element of artificiality seemed to him necessary in beauty. Perhaps it was because his experience of life elsewhere was so full of Sabbath-school picnics, petty economies, wholesome advice as to how to succeed in life, and the unescapable odors of cooking, that he found this existence so alluring, these smartly clad men and women so attractive, that he was so moved by these starry apple orchards that bloomed perennially under the lime-light.

It would be difficult to put strongly enough how convincingly the stage entrance of that theater was for Paul the actual portal of Romance. Certainly none of the company ever suspected it, least of all Charley Edwards. It was very like the old stories that used to float about London of fabulously rich Jews, who had subterranean halls there; with palms, and fountains, and soft lamps, and richly appareled women who never saw the disenchanting light of London day. So, in the midst of that smoke-palled city, enamored of figures and grimy toil, Paul had his secret temple, his wishing carpet, his bit of blue-and-white Mediterranean shore bathed in perpetual sunshine.

Several of Paul's teachers had a theory that his imagination had been perverted by garish fiction, but the truth was that he scarcely ever read at all. The books at home were not such as would either tempt or corrupt a youthful mind, and as for reading the novels that some of his friends urged upon him—well, he got what he wanted much more quickly from music; any sort of music, from an orchestra to a barrel-organ. He needed only the spark, the indescribable thrill that made his imagination master of his senses, and he could make plots and pictures enough of his own. It was equally true that he was not stage-struck—not, at any rate, in the usual acceptation of that expression. He had no desire to become an actor, any more than he had to become a musician. He felt no necessity to do any of these things; what he wanted was to see, to be in the atmosphere, float on the wave of it, to be carried out, blue league after blue league, away from everything.

After a night behind the scenes, Paul found the school-room more than ever repulsive: the bare floors and naked walls, the prosy men who never wore frock-coats, or violets in their button-holes, the women with their dull gowns, shrill voices, and pitiful seriousness about prepositions that govern the dative. He could not bear to have the other pupils think, for a moment, that he took these people seriously; he must convey to them that he considered it all trivial, and was there only by way of a jest, anyway. He had autograph pictures of all the members of the stock company, which he showed his classmates, telling them the most incredible stories of his familiarity with these people, of his acquaintance with the soloists who came to Carnegie Hall, his suppers with them and the flowers he sent them. When these stories lost their effect, and his audience grew listless, he became desperate and would bid all the boys good-night, announcing that he was going to travel for a while, going to Naples, to Venice, to Egypt. Then, next Monday, he would slip back, conscious, and nervously smiling; his sister was ill, and he should have to defer his voyage until spring.

Matters went steadily worse with Paul at school. In the itch to let his instructors know how heartily he despised them and their homilies, and how thoroughly he was appreciated elsewhere, he mentioned once or twice that he had no time to fool with theorems; adding, with a twitch of the eyebrows and a touch of that nervous bravado which so perplexed them, that he was helping the people down at the stock company; they were old friends of his.

The upshot of the matter was, that the principal went to Paul's father, and Paul was taken out of school and put to work. The manager at Carnegie Hall was told to get another usher in his stead, the doorkeeper at the theater was warned not to admit him to the house, and Charley Edwards remorsefully promised the boy's father not to see him again.

The members of the stock company were vastly amused when some of Paul's stories reached them—especially the women. They were hard-working women, most of them supporting indigent husbands or brothers, and they laughed rather bitterly at having stirred the boy to such fervid and florid inventions. They agreed with the faculty and with his father that Paul's was a bad case.

II

The east-bound train was plowing through a January snow-storm; the dull dawn was beginning to show gray, when the engine whistled a mile out of Newark. Paul started up from the seat where he had lain curled in uneasy slumber, rubbed the breath-misted window-glass with his hand, and peered out. The snow was whirling in curling eddies above the white bottom-lands, and the drifts lay already deep in the fields and along the fences, while here and there the long dead grass and dried weed stalks protruded black above it. Lights shone from the scattered houses, and a gang of laborers who stood beside the track waved their lanterns.

Paul had slept very little, and he felt grimy and uncomfortable. He had made the all-night journey in a day-coach, partly because he was ashamed, dressed as he was, to go into a Pullman, and partly because he was afraid of being seen there by some Pittsburg business man, who might have noticed him in Denny & Carson's office. When the whistle awoke him, he clutched quickly at his breast pocket, glancing about him with an uncertain smile. But the little, clay-bespattered Italians were still sleeping, the slatternly women across the aisle were in open-mouthed oblivion, and even the crumby, crying babies were for the nonce stilled. Paul settled back to struggle with his impatience as best he could.

When he arrived at the Jersey City station, Paul hurried through his breakfast, manifestly ill at ease and keeping a sharp eye about him. After he reached the Twenty-third Street station, he consulted a cabman, and had himself driven to a men's furnishing establishment that was just opening for the day. He spent upward of two hours there, buying with endless reconsidering and great care. His new street suit he put on in the fitting-room; the frock-coat and dress-clothes he had bundled into the cab with his linen. Then he drove to a hatter's and a shoe house. His next errand was at Tiffany's, where he selected his silver and a new scarf-pin. He would not wait to have his silver marked, he said. Lastly, he stopped at a trunk shop on Broadway, and had his purchases packed into various traveling bags.

It was a little after one o'clock when he drove up to the Waldorf, and after settling with the cabman, went into the office. He registered from Washington; said his mother and father had been abroad, and that he had come down to await the arrival of their steamer. He told his story plausibly and had no trouble, since he volunteered to pay for them in advance, in engaging his rooms, a sleeping-room, sitting-room and bath.

Not once, but a hundred times, Paul had planned this entry into New York. He had gone over every detail of it with Charley Edwards, and in his scrap-book at home there were pages of description about New York hotels, cut from the Sunday papers. When he was shown to his sitting-room on the eighth floor, he saw at a glance that everything was as it should be; there was but one detail in his mental picture that the place did not realize, so he rang for the bell-boy and sent him down for flowers. He moved about nervously until the boy returned, putting away his new linen and fingering it delightedly as he did so. When the flowers came, he put them hastily into water, and then tumbled into a hot bath. Presently he came out of his white bath-room, resplendent in his new silk underwear, and playing with the tassels of his red robe. The snow was whirling so fiercely outside his windows that he could scarcely see across the street, but within the air was deliciously soft and fragrant. He put the violets and jonquils on the taboret beside the couch, and threw himself down, with a long sigh, covering himself with a Roman blanket. He was thoroughly tired; he had been in such haste, had stood up to such a strain, covered so much ground in the last twenty-four hours, that he wanted to think how it had all come about. Lulled by the sound of the wind, the warm air, and the cool fragrance of the flowers, he sank into deep, drowsy retrospection.

It had been wonderfully simple; when they had shut him out of the theater and concert hall, when they had taken away his bone, the whole thing was virtually determined. The rest was a mere matter of opportunity. The only thing that at all surprised him was his own courage, for he realized well enough that he had always been tormented by fear, a sort of apprehensive dread that, of late years, as the meshes of the lies he had told closed about him, had been pulling the muscles of his body tighter and tighter. Until now, he could not remember the time when he had not been dreading something. Even when he was a little boy, it was always there—behind him, or before, or on either side. There had always been the shadowed corner, the dark place into which he dared not look, but from which something seemed always to be watching him— and Paul had done things that were not pretty to watch, he knew.

But now he had a curious sense of relief, as though he had at last thrown down the gauntlet to the thing in the corner.

Yet it was but a day since he had been sulking in the traces; but yesterday afternoon that he had been sent to the bank with Denny & Carson's deposits as usual—but this time he was instructed to leave the book to be balanced. There were above two thousand dollars in checks, and nearly a thousand in the bank-notes which he had taken from the book and quietly transferred to his pocket. At the bank he had made out a new deposit-slip. His nerves had even been steady enough to permit of his returning to the office, where he had finished his work and asked for a full day's holiday to-morrow, Saturday, giving a perfectly reasonable pretext. The bank-book, he knew, would not be returned before Monday or Tuesday, and his father would be out of town for the next week. From the time he slipped the bank-notes into his pocket until he boarded the night train for New York, he had not known a moment's hesitation. It was not the first time Paul had steered through treacherous waters.

How astonishingly easy it had all been; here he was, the thing done, and this time there would be no awakening, no figure at the top of the stairs. He watched the snow-flakes whirling by his window until he fell asleep.

When he awoke, it was three o'clock in the afternoon. He bounded up with a start; half of one of his precious days gone already! He spent more than an hour in dressing, watching every stage of his toilet carefully in the mirror. Everything was quite perfect; he was exactly the kind of boy he had always wanted to be.

When he went down-stairs, Paul took a carriage and drove up Fifth Avenue toward the Park. The snow had somewhat abated, carriages and tradesmen's wagons were hurrying to and fro in the winter twilight, boys in woolen mufflers were shoveling off the doorsteps, the avenue stages made fine spots of color against the white street. Here and there on the corners were stands, with whole flower gardens blooming under glass cases, against the sides of which the snow-flakes stuck and melted; violets, roses, carnations, lilies of the valley, somehow vastly more lovely and alluring that they blossomed thus unnaturally in the snow. The Park itself was a wonderful stage winter-piece.

When he returned, the pause of the twilight had ceased, and the tune of the streets had changed. The snow was falling faster, lights streamed from the hotels that reared their dozen stories fearlessly up into the storm, defying the raging Atlantic winds. A long, black stream of carriages poured down the avenue, intersected here and there by other streams, tending horizontally. There were a score of cabs about the entrance of his hotel, and his driver had to wait. Boys in livery were running in and out of the awning that was stretched across the sidewalk, up and down the red velvet carpet laid from the door to the street. Above, about, within it all was the rumble and roar, the hurry and toss of thousands of human beings as hot for pleasure as himself, and on every side of him towered the glaring affirmation of the omnipotence of wealth.

The boy set his teeth and drew his shoulders together in a spasm of realization; the plot of all dramas, the text of all romances, the nerve-stuff of all sensations was whirling about him like the snowflakes. He burnt like a faggot in a tempest.

When Paul went down to dinner, the music of the orchestra came floating up the elevator shaft to greet him. His head whirled as he stepped into the thronged corridor, and he sank back into one of the chairs against the wall to get his breath. The lights, the chatter, the perfumes, the bewildering medley of color—he had for a moment the feeling of not being able to stand it. But only for a moment; these were his own people, he told himself. He went slowly about the corridors, through the writing-rooms, smoking-rooms, reception-rooms, as though he was exploring the chambers of an enchanted palace, built and peopled for him alone.

When he reached the dining-room, he sat down at a table near a window. The flowers, the white linen, the many-colored wine glasses, the gay toilettes of the women, the low popping of corks, the undulating repetitions of the "Blue Danube" from the orchestra, all flooded Paul's dream with bewildering radiance. When the rosy tinge of his champagne was added—that cold, precious, bubbling stuff that creamed and foamed in his glass—Paul wondered that there were honest men in the world at all. This was what all the world was fighting for, he reflected; this was what all the struggle was about. He doubted the reality of his past. Had he ever known a place called Cordelia Street, a place where fagged-looking business men got on the early car; mere rivets in a machine, they seemed to Paul—sickening men, with combings of children's hair always hanging to their coats, and the smell of cooking in their clothes. Cordelia Street—Ah! that belonged to another time and country; had he not always been thus, had he not sat here night after night, from as far back as he could remember, looking pensively over just such shimmering textures and slowly twirling the stem of a glass like this one between his thumb and middle finger? He rather thought he had.

He was not in the least abashed or lonely. He had no especial desire to meet or to know any of these people; all he demanded was the right to look on and conjecture, to watch the pageant. The mere stage properties were all he contended for. Nor was he lonely later in the evening, in his *loge* at the Metropolitan. He was now entirely rid of his nervous misgivings, of his forced aggressiveness, of the imperative desire to show himself different from his surroundings. He felt now that his surroundings explained him. Nobody questioned the purple; he had only to wear it passively. He had only to glance down at his attire to reassure himself that here it would be impossible for anyone to humiliate him.

He found it hard to leave his beautiful sitting-room to go to bed that night, and sat long watching the raging storm from his turret window. When he went to sleep, it was with the lights turned on in his bedroom; partly because of his old timidity and partly so that, if he should wake in the night, there would be no wretched moment of doubt, no horrible suspicion of yellow wall-paper, or of Washington and Calvin above his bed.

Sunday morning the city was practically snow-bound. Paul breakfasted late, and in the afternoon he fell in with a wild San Francisco boy, a freshman at Yale, who said he had run down for a "little flyer" over Sunday. The young man offered to show Paul the night side of the town, and the two boys went out together after dinner, not returning to the hotel until seven o'clock the next morning. They had started out in the confiding warmth of a champagne friendship, but their parting in the elevator was singularly cool. The freshman pulled himself together to make his train and Paul went to bed. He awoke at two o'clock in the afternoon, very thirsty and dizzy, and rang for ice-water, coffee, and the Pittsburg papers.

On the part of the hotel management, Paul excited no suspicion. There was this to be said for him, that he wore his spoils with dignity and in no way made himself conspicuous. Even under the glow of his wine he was never boisterous, though he found the stuff like a magician's wand for wonder-building. His chief greediness lay in his ears and eyes, and his excesses were not offensive ones. His dearest pleasures were the gray winter twilights in his sitting-room; his quiet enjoyment of his flowers, his clothes, his wide divan, his cigarette, and his sense of power. He could not remember a time when he had felt so at peace with himself. The mere release from the necessity of petty lying, lying every day and every day, restored his self-respect. He had never lied for pleasure, even at school, but to be noticed and admired, to assert his difference from other Cordelia Street boys; and he felt a good deal more manly, more honest even, now that he had no need for boastful pretensions, now that he could, as his actor friends used to say, "dress the part." It was characteristic that remorse did not occur to him. His golden days went by without a shadow, and he made each as perfect as he could.

On the eighth day after his arrival in New York, he found the whole affair exploited in the Pittsburg papers, exploited with a wealth of detail which indicated that local news of a sensational nature was at a low ebb. The firm of Denny & Carson announced that the boy's father had refunded the full amount of the theft, and that they had no intention of prosecuting. The Cumberland minister had been interviewed, and expressed his hope of yet reclaiming the motherless boy, and his

Sabbath-school teacher declared that she would spare no effort to that end. The rumor had reached Pittsburg that the boy had been seen in a New York hotel, and his father had gone East to find him and bring him home.

Paul had just come in to dress for dinner; he sank into a chair, weak to the knees, and clasped his head in his hands. It was to be worse than jail, even; the tepid waters of Cordelia Street were to close over him finally and forever. The gray monotony stretched before him in hopeless, unrelieved years; Sabbath-school, Young People's Meeting, the yellow-papered room, the damp dish-towels; it all rushed back upon him with a sickening vividness. He had the old feeling that the orchestra had suddenly stopped, the sinking sensation that the play was over. The sweat broke out on his face, and he sprang to his feet, looked about him with his white, conscious smile, and winked at himself in the mirror. With something of the old childish belief in miracles with which he had so often gone to class, all his lessons unlearned, Paul dressed and dashed whistling down the corridor to the elevator.

He had no sooner entered the dining-room and caught the measure of the music than his remembrance was lightened by his old elastic power of claiming the moment, mounting with it, and finding it all-sufficient. The glare and glitter about him, the mere scenic accessories had again, and for the last time, their old potency. He would show himself that he was game, he would finish the thing splendidly. He doubted, more than ever, the existence of Cordelia Street, and for the first time he drank his wine recklessly. Was he not, after all, one of those fortunate beings born to the purple, was he not still himself and in his own place? He drummed a nervous accompaniment to the Pagliacci music and looked about him, telling himself over and over that it had paid.

He reflected drowsily, to the swell of the music and the chill sweetness of his wine, that he might have done it more wisely. He might have caught an outbound steamer and been well out of their clutches before now. But the other side of the world had seemed too far away and too uncertain then; he could not have waited for it; his need had been too sharp. If he had to choose over again, he would do the same thing tomorrow. He looked affectionately about the dining-room, now gilded with a soft mist. Ah, it had paid indeed!

Paul was awakened next morning by a painful throbbing in his head and feet. He had thrown himself across the bed without undressing, and had slept with his shoes on. His limbs and hands were lead heavy, and his tongue and throat were parched and burnt. There came upon him one of those fateful attacks of clear-headedness that never occurred except when he was physically exhausted and his nerves hung loose. He lay still and closed his eyes and let the tide of things wash over him.

His father was in New York; "stopping at some joint or other," he told himself. The memory of successive summers on the front stoop fell upon him like a weight of black water. He had not a hundred dollars left; and he knew now, more than ever, that money was everything, the wall that stood between all he loathed and all he wanted. The thing was winding itself up; he had thought of that on his first glorious day in New York, and had even provided a way to snap the thread. It lay on his dressing-table now; he had got it out last night when he came blindly up from dinner, but the shiny metal hurt his eyes, and he disliked the looks of the thing.

He rose and moved about with a painful effort, succumbing now and again to attacks of nausea. It was the old depression exaggerated; all the world had become Cordelia Street. Yet, somehow, he was not afraid of anything, was absolutely calm; perhaps because he had looked into the dark corner at last and knew. It was bad enough, what he saw there, but somehow not so bad as his long fear of it had been. He saw everything clearly now. He had a feeling that he had made the best of it, that he had lived the sort of life he was meant to live, and for half an hour he sat staring at the revolver. But he told himself that was not the way, so he went down stairs and took a cab to the ferry.

When Paul arrived at Newark, he got off the train and took another cab, directing the driver to follow the Pennsylvania tracks out of the town. The snow lay heavy on the roadways and had drifted deep in the open fields. Only here and there the dead grass or dried weed stalks projected, singularly black, above it. Once well into the country, Paul dismissed the carriage and walked, floundering along the tracks, his mind a medley of irrelevant things. He seemed to hold in his brain an actual picture of everything he had seen that morning. He remembered every feature of both his drivers, of the toothless old woman from whom he had bought the red flowers in his coat, the agent from whom he had got his ticket, and all of his fellow-passengers on the ferry. His mind, unable to cope with vital matters near at hand, worked feverishly and deftly at sorting and grouping these images. They made for him a part of the ugliness of the world, of the ache in his head, and the bitter burning of his tongue. He stooped and put a handful of snow into his mouth as he walked, but that, too, seemed hot. When he reached a little hillside, where the tracks ran through a cut some twenty feet below him, he stopped and sat down.

The carnations in his coat were drooping with the cold, he noticed, their red glory all over. It occurred to him that all the flowers he had seen in the glass cases that first night must have gone the same way, long before this. It was only one splendid breath they had, in spite of their brave mockery at the winter outside the glass, and it was a losing game in the end, it seemed, this revolt against the homilies by which the world is run. Paul took one of the blossoms carefully from his coat and scooped a little hole in the snow, where he covered it up. Then he dozed a little, from his weak condition, seeming insensible to the cold.

The sound of an approaching train awoke him, and he started to his feet, remembering only his resolution, and afraid lest he should be too late. He stood watching the approaching locomotive, his teeth chattering, his lips drawn away from them in a frightened smile; once or twice he glanced nervously sidewise, as though he were being watched. When the right moment came, he jumped. As he fell, the folly of his haste occurred to him with merciless clearness, the vastness of what he had left undone. There flashed through his brain, clearer than ever before, the blue of Adriatic water, the yellow of Algerian sands.

He felt something strike his chest, and that his body was being thrown swiftly through the air, on and on, immeasurably far and fast, while his limbs were gently relaxed. Then, because the picture-making mechanism was crushed, the disturbing visions flashed into black, and Paul dropped back into the immense design of things.

PART III

QUEER ATTACHMENTS

Twin-Love

Bayard Taylor

When John Vincent, after waiting twelve years, married Phebe Etheridge, the whole neighborhood experienced that sense of relief and satisfaction which follows the triumph of the right. Not that the fact of a true love is ever generally recognized and respected when it is first discovered; for there is a perverse quality in American human nature which will not accept the existence of any fine, unselfish passion, until it has been tested and established beyond peradventure. There were two views of the case when John Vincent's love for Phebe, and old Reuben Etheridge's hard prohibition of the match, first became known to the community. The girls and boys, and some of the matrons, ranged themselves at once on the side of the lovers, but a large majority of the older men and a few of the younger supported the tyrannical father.

Reuben Etheridge was rich, and, in addition to what his daughter would naturally inherit from him, she already possessed more than her lover, at the time of their betrothal. This, in the eyes of one class, was a sufficient reason for the father's hostility. When low natures live (as they almost invariably do) wholly in the present, they neither take tenderness from the past nor warning from the possibilities of the future. It is the exceptional men and women who remember their youth.

So, these lovers received a nearly equal amount of sympathy and condemnation; and only slowly, partly through their quiet fidelity and patience, and partly through the improvement in John Vincent's worldly circumstances, was the balance changed. Old Reuben remained an unflinching despot to the last: if any relenting softness touched his heart, he sternly concealed it; and such inference as could be drawn from the fact that he, certainly knowing what would follow his death, bequeathed his daughter her proper share of his goods, was all that could be taken for consent.

They were married: John, a grave man in middle age, weatherbeaten and worn by years of hard work and self-denial, yet not beyond the restoration of a milder second youth; and Phebe a sad, weary woman, whose warmth of longing had been exhausted, from whom youth and its uncalculating surrenders of hope and feeling had gone forever. They began their wedded life under the shadow of the death out of which it grew; and when, after a ceremony in which neither bridesmaid nor groomsman stood by their side, they united their divided homes, it seemed to their neighbors that a separated husband and wife had come together again, not that the relation was new to either.

John Vincent loved his wife with the tenderness of an innocent man, but all his tenderness could not avail to lift the weight of settled melancholy which had gathered upon her. Disappointment, waiting, yearning, indulgence in long lament and self-pity, the morbid cultivation of unhappy fancies,—all this had wrought its work upon her, and it was too late to effect a cure. In the night she awoke to weep at his side, because of the years when she had awakened to weep alone; by day she kept up her old habit of foreboding, although the evening steadily refuted the morning; and there were times when, without any apparent cause, she would fall into a dark, despairing mood, which her husband's greatest care and cunning could only slowly dispel.

Two or three years passed, and new life came to the Vincent farm. One day, between midnight and dawn, the family pair was doubled; the cry of twin sons was heard in the hushed house. The father restrained his happy wonder in his concern for the imperilled life of the mother; he guessed that she had anticipated death, and she now hung by a thread so slight that her simple will might snap it. But her will, fortunately, was as faint as her consciousness; she gradually drifted out of danger, taking her returning strength with a passive acquiescence rather than with joy. She was hardly paler than her wont, but the lurking shadow seemed to have vanished from her eyes, and John Vincent felt that her features had assumed a new expression, the faintly perceptible stamp of some spiritual change.

It was a happy day for him when, propped against his breast and gently held by his warm, strong arm, the twin boys were first brought to be laid upon her lap. Two staring, dark-faced creatures, with restless fists and feet, they were alike in every least feature of their grotesque animality. Phebe placed a hand under the head of each, and looked at them for a long time in silence.

"Why is this?" she said, at last, taking hold of a narrow pink ribbon, which was tied around the wrist of one.

"He's the oldest, sure," the nurse answered. "Only by fifteen minutes or so, but it generally makes a difference when twins come to be named; and you may see with your own eyes that there's no telling of 'em apart, otherways."

"Take off the ribbon, then," said Phebe, quietly; "*I* know them."

"Why, ma'am, it's always done, where they're so like! And I'll never he able to tell which is which; for they sleep and wake and feed by the same clock. And you might mistake, after all, in giving 'em names—"

"There is no oldest or youngest, John; they are two and yet one, this is mine, and this is yours."

"I see no difference at all, Phebe," said John; "and how can we divide them?"

"We will not divide," she answered; "I only meant it as a sign."

She smiled, for the first time in many days. He was glad of heart, but did not understand her. "What shall we call them?" he asked. "Elias and Reuben, after our fathers?"

"No, John: their names must be David and Jonathan."

And so they were called. And they grew, not less, but more alike, in passing through the stages of babyhood. The ribbon of the older one had been removed, and the nurse would have been distracted, but for Phebe's almost miraculous instinct. The former comforted herself with the hope that teething would bring a variation to the two identical mouths; but no! they teethed as one child. John, after desperate attempts, which always failed in spite of the headaches they gave him, postponed the idea of distinguishing one from the other, until they should be old enough to develop some dissimilarity of speech, or gait, or habit. All trouble might have been avoided, had Phebe consented to the least variation in their dresses; but herein she was mildly immovable.

"Not yet," was her set reply to her husband; and one day, when he manifested a little annoyance at her persistence, she turned to him, holding a child on each knee, and said with a gravity which silenced him thenceforth: "John, can you not see that our burden has passed into them? Is there no meaning in this,—that two children who are one in body and face and nature, should be given to us at our time of life, after such long disappointment and trouble? Our lives were held apart; theirs were united before they were born, and I dare not turn them in different directions. Perhaps I do not know all that the Lord intended to say to us, in sending them; but his hand is here!"

"I was only thinking of their good," John meekly answered. "If they are spared to grow up, there must be some way of knowing one from the other."

"*They* will not need it, and I, too, think only of them. They have taken the cross from my heart, and I will lay none on theirs. I am reconciled to my life through them, John; you have been very patient and good with me, and I will yield to you in all things but in this. I do not think I shall live to see them as men grown; yet, while we are together, I feel clearly what it is right to do. Can you not, just once, have a little faith without knowledge, John?"

"I'll try, Phebe," he said. "Any way, I'll grant that the boys belong to you more than to me."

Phebe Vincent's character had verily changed. Her attacks of semi-hysterical despondency never returned; her gloomy prophecies ceased. She was still grave, and the trouble of so many years never wholly vanished from her face; but she performed every duty of her life with at least a quiet willingness, and her home became the abode of peace; for passive content wears longer than demonstrative happiness.

David and Jonathan grew as one boy: the taste and temper of one was repeated in the other, even as the voice and features. Sleeping or waking, grieved or joyous, well or ill, they lived a single life, and it seemed so natural for one to answer to the other's name, that they probably would have themselves confused their own identities, but for their mother's unerring knowledge. Perhaps unconsciously guided by her, perhaps through the voluntary action of their own natures, each quietly took the other's place when called upon, even to the sharing of praise or blame at school, the friendships and quarrels of the playground. They were healthy and happy lads, and John Vincent was accustomed to say to his neighbors, "They're no more trouble than one would be, and yet they're four hands instead of two."

Phebe died when they were fourteen, saying to them, with almost her latest breath, "Be one, always!" Before her husband could decide whether to change her plan of domestic education, they were passing out of boyhood, changing in voice, stature, and character with a continued likeness which bewildered and almost terrified him. He procured garments of different colors, but they were accustomed to wear each article in common, and the result was only a mixture of tints for both. They were sent to different schools, to be returned the next day, equally pale, suffering, and incapable of study. Whatever device was employed, they evaded it by a mutual instinct which rendered all external measures unavailing. To John Vincent's mind their resemblance was an accidental misfortune, which had been confirmed through their mother's fancy. He felt that they were bound by some deep, mysterious tie, which, inasmuch as it might interfere with all practical aspects of life, ought to be gradually weakened. Two bodies, to him, implied two distinct men, and it was wrong to permit a mutual dependence which prevented either from exercising his own separate will and judgment.

But, while he was planning and pondering, the boys became young men, and he was an old man. Old, and prematurely broken; for he had worked much, borne much, and his large frame held only a moderate measure of vital force. A great weariness fell upon him, and his powers began to give way, at first slowly, but then with accelerated failure. He saw the end coming, long before his sons suspected it; his doubt, for their sakes, was the only thing which made it unwelcome. It was "upon his mind" (as his Quaker neighbors would say) to speak to them of the future, and at last the proper moment came.

It was a stormy November evening. Wind and rain whirled and drove among the trees outside, but the sitting-room of the old farmhouse was bright and warm. David and Jonathan, at the table, with their arms over each other's backs and their brown locks mixed together, read from the same book: their father sat in the ancient rocking-chair before the fire, with his feet upon a stool. The house-keeper and hired man had gone to bed, and all was still in the house.

John waited until he heard the volume closed, and then spoke.

"Boys," he said, "let me have a bit of talk with you. I don't seem to get over my ailments rightly,—never will, maybe. A man must think of things while there's time, and say them, when they *have* to be said. I don't know as there's any particular hurry in my case; only, we never can tell, from one day to another. When I die, everything will belong to you two, share and share alike, either to buy another farm with the money out, or divide this: I won't tie you up in any way. But two of you will need two farms for two families; for you won't have to wait twelve years, like your mother and me.

"We don't want another farm, father!" said David and Jonathan together.

"I know you don't think so, now. A wife seemed far enough off from me, when I was your age. You've always been satisfied to be with each other, but that can't last. It was partly your mother's notion; I remember her saying that our burden had passed into you. I never quite understood what she meant, but I suppose it must rather be the opposite of what *we* had to bear."

The twins listened with breathless attention while their father, suddenly stirred by the past, told them the story of his long betrothal.

"And now," he exclaimed, in conclusion, "it may be putting wild ideas into your two heads, but I must say it! *That* was where I did wrong,—wrong to her and to me,—in waiting! I had no right to spoil the best of our lives; I ought to have gone boldly, in broad day, to her father's house, taken her by the hand, and led her forth to be my wife. Boys, if either of you comes to love a woman truly, and she to love you, and there is no reason why God (I don't say man) should put you asunder, do as I ought to have done, not as I did! And, maybe, this advice is the best legacy I can leave you."

"But, father," said David, speaking for both, "we have never thought of marrying."

"Likely enough," their father answered; "we hardly ever think of what surely comes. But to me, looking back, it's plain. And this is the reason why I want you to make me a promise, and as solemn as if I was on my death-bed. Maybe I shall be, soon."

Tears gathered in the eyes of the twins. "What is it, father?" they both said.

"Nothing at all to any other two boys, but I don't know how *you*'ll take it. What if I was to ask you to live apart for a while?"

"O father!" both cried. They leaned together, cheek pressing cheek, and hand clasping hand, growing white and trembling. John Vincent, gazing into the fire, did not see their faces, or his purpose might have been shaken.

"I don't say *now*," he went on. "After a while, when—well, when I'm dead. And I only mean a beginning, to help you toward what *has* to be. Only a month; I don't want to seem hard to you; but that's little, in all conscience. Give me your word: say, 'For mother's sake!'"

There was a long pause. Then David and Jonathan said, in low, faltering voices, "For mother's sake, I promise."

"Remember that you were only boys to her. She might have made all this seem easier, for women have reasons for things no man can answer. Mind, within a year after I'm gone!"

He rose, and tottered out of the room.

The twins looked at each other: David said, "Must we?" and Jonathan, "How can we?" Then they both thought, "It may be a long while yet." Here was a present comfort, and each seemed to hold it firmly in holding the hand of the other, as they fell asleep side by side.

The trial was nearer than they imagined. Their father died before the winter was over; the farm and other property was theirs, and they might have allowed life to solve its mysteries as it rolled onwards, but for their promise to the dead. This must be fulfilled, and then—one thing was certain; they would never again separate.

"The sooner the better," said David. "It shall be the visit to our uncle and cousins in Indiana. You will come with me as far as Harrisburg; it may be easier to part there than here. And our new neighbors, the Bradleys, will want your help for a day or two, after getting home."

"It is less than death," Jonathan answered, "and why should it seem to be more? We must think of father and mother, and all those twelve years; now I know what the burden was."

"And we have never really borne any part of it! Father must have been right in forcing us to promise."

Every day the discussion was resumed, and always with the same termination. Familiarity with the inevitable step gave them increase of courage; yet, when the moment had come and gone, when, speeding on opposite trains, the hills and valleys multiplied between them with terrible velocity, a pang like death cut to the heart of each, and the divided life became a chill, oppressive dream.

During the separation no letters passed between them. When the neighbors asked Jonathan for news of his brother, he always replied, "He is well," and avoided further speech with such evidence of pain that they spared him. An hour before the month drew to an end, he walked forth alone, taking the road to the nearest railway station. A stranger who passed him at the entrance of a thick wood, three miles from home, was thunderstruck on meeting the same person shortly after entering the wood from the other side; but the farmers in the near fields saw two figures issuing from the shade, hand in hand.

Each knew the other's month, before they slept, and the last thing Jonathan said, with his head on David's shoulder, was, "You must know our neighbors, the Bradleys, and especially Ruth." In the morning, as they dressed, taking each other's garments at random, as of old, Jonathan again said, "I have never seen a girl that I like so well as Ruth Bradley. Do you remember what father said about loving and marrying? It comes into my mind whenever I see Ruth; but she has no sister."

"But we need not both marry," David replied, "that might part us, and this will not. It is for always, now."

"For always, David."

Two or three days later Jonathan said, as he started on an errand to the village: "I shall stop at the Bradleys this evening, so you must walk across and meet me there."

When David approached the house, a slender, girlish figure, with her back towards him, was stooping over a bush of great crimson roses, cautiously clipping a blossom here and there. At the click of the gate-latch she started and turned towards him. Her light gingham bonnet, falling back, disclosed a long oval face, fair and delicate, sweet brown eyes, and brown hair laid smoothly over the temples. A soft flush rose suddenly to her cheeks, and he felt that his own were burning.

"O Jonathan!" she exclaimed, transferring the roses to her left hand, and extending her right, as she came forward.

He was too accustomed to the name to recognize her mistake at once, and the word "Ruth!" came naturally to his lips.

"I should know your brother David has come," she then said; "even if I had not heard so. You look so bright. How glad I am!"

"Is he not here?" David asked.

"No; but there he is now, surely!" She turned towards the lane, where Jonathan was dismounting. "Why, it is yourself over again, Jonathan!"

As they approached, a glance passed between the twins, and a secret transfer of the riding-whip to David set their identity right with Ruth, whose manner towards the latter innocently became shy with all its friendliness, while her frank, familiar speech was given to Jonathan, as was fitting. But David also took the latter to himself, and when they left, Ruth had apparently forgotten that there was any difference in the length of their acquaintance.

On their way homewards David said: "Father was right. We must marry, like others, and Ruth is the wife for us,—I mean for you, Jonathan. Yes, we must learn to say *mine* and *yours,* after all, when we speak of her."

"Even she cannot separate us, it seems," Jonathan answered. "We must give her some sign, and that will also be a sign for others. It will seem strange to divide ourselves; we can never learn it properly; rather let us not think of marriage!"

"We cannot help thinking of it; she stands in mother's place now, as we in father's."

Then both became silent and thoughtful. They felt that something threatened to disturb what seemed to be the only possible life for them, yet were unable to distinguish its features, and therefore powerless to resist it. The same instinct which had been born of their wonderful spiritual likeness told them that Ruth Bradley already loved Jonathan: the duty was established, and they must conform their lives to it. There was, however, this slight difference between their natures,—that David was generally the first to utter the thought which came to the minds of both. So when he said, "We shall learn what to do when the need comes," it was a postponement of all foreboding. They drifted contentedly towards the coming change.

The days went by, and their visits to Ruth Bradley were continued. Sometimes Jonathan went alone, but they were usually together, and the tie which united the three became dearer and sweeter as it was more closely drawn. Ruth learned to distinguish between the two when they were before her: at least she said so, and they were willing to believe it. But she was hardly aware how nearly alike was the happy warmth in her bosom produced by either pair of dark gray eyes and the soft half-smile which played around either mouth. To them she seemed to be drawn within the mystic circle which separated them from others,—she, alone; and they no longer imagined a life in which she should not share.

Then the inevitable step was taken. Jonathan declared his love, and was answered. Alas! he almost forgot David that late summer evening, as they sat in the moonlight, and over and over again assured each other how dear they had grown. He felt the trouble in David's heart when they met.

"Ruth is ours, and I bring her kiss to you," he said, pressing his lips to David's; but the arms flung around him trembled, and David whispered, "Now the change begins."

"O, this cannot be our burden!" Jonathan cried, with all the rapture still warm in his heart.

"If it is, it will be light, or heavy, or none at all, as we shall bear it," David answered, with a smile of infinite tenderness.

For several days he allowed Jonathan to visit the Bradley farm alone, saying that it must be so, on Ruth's account. Her love, he declared, must give her the fine instinct which only their mother had ever possessed, and he must allow it time to be confirmed. Jonathan, however, insisted that Ruth already possessed it; that she was beginning to wonder at his absence, and to fear that she would not be entirely welcome to the home which must always be equally his.

David yielded at once.

"You must go alone," said Jonathan, "to satisfy yourself that she knows us at last."

Ruth came forth from the house as he drew near. Her face beamed: she laid her hands upon his shoulders and kissed him. "Now you cannot doubt me, Ruth!" he said, gently.

"Doubt you, Jonathan!" she exclaimed, with a fond reproach in her eyes. "But you look troubled; is anything the matter?"

"I was thinking of my brother," said David, in a low tone.

"Tell me what it is," she said, drawing him into the little arbor of woodbine near the gate. They took seats, side by side, on the rustic bench. "He thinks I may come between you: is it not that?" she asked. Only one thing was clear to David's mind,—that she would surely speak more frankly and freely of him to the supposed Jonathan than to his real self. This once he would permit the illusion.

"Not more than must be," he answered. "He knew all, from the very beginning. But we have been like one person in two bodies, and any change seems to divide us."

"I feel that as you do," said Ruth. "I would never consent to be your wife, if I could really divide you. I love you both too well for that."

"Do you love me?" he asked, entirely forgetting his representative part.

Again the reproachful look, which faded away as she met his eyes. She fell upon his breast, and gave him kisses which were answered with equal tenderness. Suddenly he covered his face with his hands, and burst into a passion of tears.

"Jonathan! O Jonathan!" she cried, weeping with alarm and sympathetic pain.

It was long before he could speak; but at last, turning away his head, he faltered, "I am David!"

There was a long silence.

When he looked up she was sitting with her hands rigidly clasped in her lap: her face was very pale.

"There it is, Ruth," he said; "we are one heart and one soul. Could he love, and not I? You cannot decide between us, for one is the other. If I had known you first, Jonathan would be now in my place. What follows, then?"

"No marriage," she whispered.

"No!" he answered; "we brothers must learn to be two men instead of one. You will partly take my place with Jonathan; I must live with half my life, unless I can find, somewhere in the world, your other half."

"I cannot part you, David!"

"Something stronger than you or me parts us, Ruth. If it were death, we should bow to God's will: well, it can no more be got away from than death or judgment. Say no more: the pattern of all this was drawn long before we were born, and we cannot do anything but work it out."

He rose and stood before her. "Remember this, Ruth," he said; "it is no blame in us to love each other. Jonathan will see the truth in my

face when we meet, and I speak for him also. You will not see me again
until your wedding-day, and then no more afterwards—but, yes! *once,*
in some far-off time, when you shall know me to be David, and still give
me the kiss you gave to-day."

"Ah, after death!" she thought: "I have parted them forever." She
was about to rise, but fell upon the seat again, fainting. At the same
moment Jonathan appeared at David's side.

No word was said. They bore her forth and supported her between
them until the fresh breeze had restored her to consciousness. Her first
glance rested on the brother's hands, clasping; then, looking from one
to the other, she saw that the cheeks of both were wet.

"Now leave me," she said, "but come to-morrow, Jonathan!" Even
then she turned from one to the other with a painful, touching uncertainty, and stretched out both hands to them in farewell.

How that poor twin-heart struggled with itself is only known to
God. All human voices, and, as they believed, also the Divine Voice,
commanded the division of their interwoven life. Submission would
have seemed easier, could they have taken up equal and similar burdens; but David was unable to deny that his pack was overweighted.
For the first time their thoughts began to diverge.

At last David said: "For mother's sake, Jonathan, as we promised.
She always called you *her* child. And for Ruth's sake, and father's last
advice: they all tell me what I must do."

It was like the struggle between will and desire in the same nature,
and none the less fierce or prolonged because the softer quality fore-
saw its ultimate surrender. Long after he felt the step to be inevitable,
Jonathan sought to postpone it, but he was borne by all combined in-
fluences nearer and nearer to the time.

And now the wedding-day came. David was to leave home the same
evening, after the family dinner under his father's roof. In the morning
he said to Jonathan: "I shall not write until I feel that I have become
other than now, but I shall always be here, in you, as you will be in me,
everywhere. Whenever you want me, I shall know it; and I think I shall
know when to return."

The hearts of all the people went out towards them as they stood
together in the little village church. Both were calm, but very pale and
abstracted in their expression, yet their marvellous likeness was still
unchanged. Ruth's eyes were cast down, so they could not be seen; she

trembled visibly, and her voice was scarcely audible when she spoke the vow. It was only known in the neighborhood that David was going to make another journey. The truth could hardly have been guessed by persons whose ideas followed the narrow round of their own experiences; had it been, there would probably have been more condemnation than sympathy. But in a vague way the presence of some deeper element was felt,—the falling of a shadow, although the outstretched wing was unseen. Far above them, and above the shadow, watched the Infinite Pity, which was not denied to three hearts that day.

It was a long time, more than a year, and Ruth was lulling her first child on her bosom, before a letter came from David. He had wandered westwards, purchased some lands on the outer line of settlement, and appeared to be leading a wild and lonely life. "I know now," he wrote, "just how much there is to bear, and how to bear it. Strange men come between us, but you are not far off when I am alone on these plains. There is a place where I can always meet you, and I know that you have found it,—under the big ash-tree by the barn. I think I am nearly always there about sundown, and on moonshiny nights, because we are then nearest together; and I never sleep without leaving you half my blanket. When I first begin to wake, I always feel your breath, so we are never really parted for long. I do not know that I can change much; it is not easy; it is like making up your mind to have different colored eyes and hair, and I can only get sunburnt and wear a full beard. But we are hardly as unhappy as we feared to be; mother came the other night, in a dream, and took us on her knees. O, come to me, Jonathan, but for one day! No, you will not find me; I am going across the Plains!"

And Jonathan and Ruth? They loved each other tenderly; no external trouble visited them; their home was peaceful and pure; and yet, every room and stairway and chair was haunted by a sorrowful ghost. As a neighbor said after visiting them, "There seemed to be something lost." Ruth saw how constantly and how unconsciously Jonathan turned to see his own every feeling reflected in the missing eyes; how his hand sought another, even while its fellow pressed hers; how half-spoken words, day and night, died upon his lips, because they could not reach the twin-ear. She knew not how it came, but her own nature took upon itself the same habit. She felt that she received a less measure of love than she gave,—not from Jonathan, in whose whole, warm, transparent heart no other woman had ever looked, but something of her own passed beyond him and never returned. To both their life was like one of those conjurer's cups, seemingly filled with red wine, which is held from the lips by the false crystal hollow.

Neither spoke of this: neither dared to speak. The years dragged out their slow length, with rare and brief messages from David. Three children were in the house, and still peace and plenty laid their signs upon its lintels. But at last Ruth, who had been growing thinner and paler ever since the birth of her first boy, became seriously ill. Consumption was hers by inheritance, and it now manifested itself in a form which too surely foretold the result. After the physician had gone, leaving his fatal verdict behind him, she called to Jonathan, who, bewildered by his grief, sank down on his knees at her bedside and sobbed upon her breast.

"Don't grieve," she said; "this is my share of the burden. If I have taken too much from you and David, now comes the atonement. Many things have grown clear to me. David was right when he said that there was no blame. But my time is even less than the doctor thinks: where is David? Can you not bid him come?"

"I can only call him with my heart," he answered. "And will he hear me now, after nearly seven years?"

"Call, then!" she eagerly cried. "Call with all the strength of your love for him and for me, and I believe he will hear you!"

The sun was just setting. Jonathan went to the great ash-tree, behind the barn, fell upon his knees, and covered his face, and the sense of an exceeding bitter cry filled his heart. All the suppressed and baffled longing, the want, the hunger, the unremitting pain of years, came upon him and were crowded into the single prayer, "Come, David, or I die!" Before the twilight faded, while he was still kneeling, an arm came upon his shoulder, and the faint touch of another cheek upon his own. It was hardly for the space of a thought, but he knew the sign.

"David will come!" he said to Ruth.

From that day all was changed. The cloud of coming death which hung over the house was transmuted into fleecy gold. All the lost life came back to Jonathan's face, all the unrestful sweetness of Ruth's brightened into a serene beatitude. Months had passed since David had been heard from; they knew not how to reach him without many delays; yet neither dreamed of doubting his coming.

Two weeks passed, three, and there was neither word nor sign. Jonathan and Ruth thought, "He is near," and one day a singular unrest fell upon the former. Ruth saw it, but said nothing until night came, when she sent Jonathan from her bedside with the words, "Go and meet him!"

An hour afterwards she heard double steps on the stone walk in front of the house. They came slowly to the door; it opened; she heard them along the hall and ascending the stairs; then the chamber-lamp showed her the two faces, bright with a single, unutterable joy.

One brother paused at the foot of the bed; the other drew near and bent over her. She clasped her thin hands around his neck, kissed him fondly, and cried, "Dear, dear David!"

"Dear Ruth," he said, "I came as soon as I could. I was far away, among wild mountains, when I felt that Jonathan was calling me. I knew that I must return, never to leave you more, and there was still a little work to finish. Now we shall all live again!"

"Yes," said Jonathan, coming to her other side, "try to live, Ruth!"

Her voice came clear, strong, and full of authority. "I *do* live, as never before. I shall take all my life with me when I go to wait for the one soul, as I shall find it there! Our love unites, not divides, from this hour!"

The few weeks still left to her were a season of almost superhuman peace. She faded slowly and painlessly, taking the equal love of the twin-hearts, and giving an equal tenderness and gratitude. Then first she saw the mysterious need which united them, the fulness and joy wherewith each completed himself in the other. All the imperfect past was enlightened, and the end, even that now so near, was very good.

Every afternoon they carried her down to a cushioned chair on the veranda, where she could enjoy the quiet of the sunny landscape, the presence of the brothers seated at her feet, and the sports of her children on the grass. Thus, one day, while David and Jonathan held her hands and waited for her to wake from a happy sleep, she went before them, and, ere they guessed the truth, she was waiting for their one soul in the undiscovered land.

And Jonathan's children, now growing into manhood and girlhood, also call David "father." The marks left by their divided lives have long since vanished from their faces; the middle-aged men, whose hairs are turning gray, still walk hand in hand, still sleep upon the same pillow, still have their common wardrobe, as when they were boys. They talk of "our Ruth" with no sadness, for they believe that death will make them one, when, at the same moment, he summons both. And we who know them, to whom they have confided the touching mystery of their nature, believe so too.

OUT OF THE DEEPS

———•·——

Elizabeth Stoddard

H orace Hampden brooded by the fire in his dusky parlor, and his cousin George Hampden sat near him. When a jet of flame darted from the grate and lighted up their faces they saw the grief which was busy at their hearts. For a long time they had been silent, intent upon their cigars; now one moved his hand, and the other his foot, and then each supposed the other was about to speak. Horace and George were cousins. Horace was married, a prosperous man of business, and George was a bachelor, and a lawyer; both were men of means, lived in the same circle, enjoyed the same amusements, and many of their attachments were in common. Consequently they were much in each other's society, and Charlotte Hampden, the wife of Horace, looked upon George as one of her family.

A few weeks before this period, Horace, not able to leave his business, permitted Charlotte to take their only son, a boy of fourteen, to France, to be educated in the college at Amiens. She crossed the sea in safety, left her son, and started on the return voyage in the steamer "Andromeda." When her arrival was nearly due, a terrible gale sprung up, and extended along the Atlantic sea-board, which lasted several days. "Prayers for those at sea" went up from all interested souls, and a raging anxiety devoured both Horace and George. The nominal date of the "Andromeda's" arrival went by. Other steamers came in, more or less ravaged by the storm, news of shipwreck were rife, the underwriters were busy, but nothing was heard of the "Andromeda." At first the papers gave plausible reasons, mentioned the seaworthy character of the steamer, and the ability of her commander—and then became oblivious. Afterwards, when a list of her passengers was published, more than one person read the name of Charlotte Hampden with regret. She was popular in her circle, and deserved to be; still in her brightest prime, handsome, and lovable in all respects. Her friends, in their obituary remarks, said that her life might be compared to a party of pleasure sailing over a calm lake on a summer's day. Now her awful fate had been mysterious—annihilated by the dreadful sea in some sudden spasm of relentless fury, and ingulphed in the dark world of a deep which never gives up its dead! Horace and George watched and waited still, with hopes that hourly turned to despair, and refused to own their fatal dread to each other.

One day a ship came into port with tidings which confirmed the wreck of the "Andromeda." Sailing north of Hatteras she had come in contact with a mass of floating gear, and secured it. There was evidence that a useless effort had been made by some drowning wretches to tie spars and boards together; a portion of a bulk-head was with it. With a coarse brush some ship's hand had drawn the outline of a dromedary with a huge hump, and upon that were the half-effaced letters which composed the name *"Andromeda."* The day this news appeared, Horace and George met on the pier where the ship was moored, with the same errand—that of seeing with their own eyes, and hearing with their own ears, the truth. Hand griping hand they turned away, and brokenly said that all hope was gone.

"Oh!" cried poor Horace, "to have no last service to perform, to know that this loss must be for ever invisible!"

"As if she were merely absent, no last memories to turn to, but one temporary farewell," replied George.

The evening found them together by the deserted fireside. George broke the silence at last.

"Is dinner nearly ready?" he asked.

"Half an hour yet," replied Horace, holding his watch to the firelight. "Will you have the gas lighted?"

"No. Something lies so heavy at my heart, that I have resolved to unburden myself."

"My dear boy," said Horace, surprised that he should choose the present moment for a personal confidence; but thinking that he meant it for his own distraction, he added that he was all attention.

"We are such complicated creatures," began George, "and circumstances so arrange our consciences that all reasoning is baffled. Were Charlotte living, it would be impossible for me to make this confession—though, living or dead, to her I am the same man. I have long loved her, Horace, as no man should love the wife of his friend, or the wife of any man. By the stress of my suffering and my sympathy for you, I tell you, we are one in this loss."

Horace was dumb; another chasm seemed to open in his life. What else should he see

"In the dark backward and abysm of time?"

"Are you amazed?" continued George. "Charlotte has never dreamed of me. To her I have been *your* friend; the reflection of our friendship has chastely fallen on her affectionate heart."

Unconsciously Horace drew a breath of relief, which George, with deep sadness, perceived, and went on.

"I tell you this, partly because if mere abstract love is noble, mine has been, and partly to prove to you that I have entered into your loss as no other being can, and with the hope that my pure and faithful love may prove a bond between us, and an everlasting solace. To all intents and worldly purposes, your son shall be my son, and together, as white-headed old men, we will watch and aid his progress into manhood and the duties of life."

George ended with a hysterical sob. His instincts told him that Horace was less great than himself at this moment, and he was disappointed. Horace, too, was now conscious of a want of magnanimity; but, how was it possible to resist that vital jealousy which invades the soul of a man, when the woman whose sole possession is his own comes in question with another man? He longed to be alone that he might go back over all the past of their mutual lives; but swallowing something, he knew not what, he rose suddenly, offered his hand to George, and in a husky voice said,

"It's all right, my dear boy; such matters scare one at first, you know. But upon my word, I see no occasion to wonder over what you have told me. I have not now to learn how much we are alike."

"Spare me all criticism, Horace; the Judgment Day may be anticipated sometimes. Charlotte was my ideal of all that was noble and beautiful; why should I not pay her this tribute to you now?"

Dinner was announced. Dinner that comes as inexorably as death— dinner that must be prepared, must be eaten; dinner, like the king, "never dies."

Both felt the relief of the announcement. The dinner passed off with a few commonplace remarks, and soon after George withdrew to his own solitary apartments in an adjoining street. When alone, he questioned his course, and condemned himself for sentimentality. Of what use to reveal the inner life, and show the pure flame of the soul burning on a sacred altar, to one whose limitations suggested a dark lantern, the slides of which shut over its own feeble wick at any approach? Calmer than he had been for many nights, however, he fell asleep, and more than once dreamed of the "touch of a vanished hand." The old ways were resumed in Audley Street; George paid his daily visit there, and he and Horace were seen abroad as formerly. People mentioned them as the inseparable mourners—again referring to Charlotte's blighted life, which had been rounded so completely by such a husband, and such a friend.

It was now in the full tide of falling leaves, more than a month since the confirmation of the "Andromeda's" loss. Horace and George, inhabiting the little smoking den upstairs—the rest of the house being closed, for they could not endure yet to be where Charlotte's belongings were—felt an additional melancholy when rain fell, or high winds roared round the walls. The picture of a ghastly sea rose before them, rent and torn by the wind like clouds; figures with despairing gestures tossed wildly to and fro, and agonized cries ascended from an unfathomable depth and distance of space, reaching them, lost, mingled, and spent by the wind, whose merciless errand it was to bring them. This made Horace and George close their teeth, and inwardly strangle the strange noises which stifled their own hearts.

"Suppose we were to shut the house at once?" asked Horace. "It grows too dismal; this howling weather drives my spirits down into my boots, and no tugging at the straps fetches them up again. What do you say to a Canadian trip? I want to see my agent in Toronto."

"As you please," answered George with a sigh. "It is all one to me. It seems to me the most congenial place here; there is distraction in travel, though, and if you want to be distracted, go we will."

"I hardly feel it a duty to try and test my feelings, George. Will you remain if I go?"

"Oh confound it—no! We must Ruth and Naomize it, having begun so—I'll go. I believe I have lost all spring; my days are like zinc, my nights like lead."

And so they grimly talked and laughed. The trip was decided on, two days from that time.

There was a little more bustle than usual in Audley Street, at the appointed hour of departure. Horace and George were to leave by an evening train; dinner was ordered an hour earlier. Some stir of packing the trunk of Horace by the housekeeper made things wear a familiar aspect. When Horace turned his latch-key and entered the hall, seeing open doors, lighted rooms, and a general movement of life, the old familiar sense of home smote his sick heart. He looked up in the empty air, and his soul cried:

"My lost life, and love, and home! Oh treasures mocking my memory—would that I could die this moment!" He was mechanically wiping his hot face when George came in, with an assumption of cheerfulness, speaking loudly, and stepping about as if he liked it.

"Old boy," said Horace, putting away his handkerchief, "Maggie is getting up a first-rate dinner for us; she says we must start on strengthening diet. I declare she is a trump. I feel bound to the servants—they all are trumps—showed so much feeling, by George—"

"Good," interposed George, "I am awfully hungry."

"Of course you are," muttered Horace, "and you have been—eating as much as Charlotte's goldfinch this past month."

"We have a fair night to leave in," said George, as they commenced their soup.

"Yes, we have had a calm day."

"Our Indian summer sets in now."

Both dropped in a reverie, remembering the past.

"What have you here, Pat?" asked Horace.

"Beef, of course, sir."

Horace took his carver, as Pat raised the cover.

A rumbling noise was heard in the street, which they listened to. Wheels were thundering up the street, and horses were galloping.

"Too soon for us," said George, taking his watch out.

"But it stops here," answered Horace.

"Pshaw!" cried George, his face flushing deeply.

A carriage was at the door, and the bell was pulled. Its wire was then a true electric wire; it gave the knowledge of a coming event like lightning. A curious cry and stir came up the stairs, and Horace and George sprang from their chairs, and flew down. They saw Hannah, the maid, supporting Charlotte Hampden—Charlotte, alive, but speechless from emotion—pale, altered, but still herself! Behind her stood a young man, with a big railway rug in one hand, and several packages in the other.

"Bless me," he said, with an affected accent, but half-crying too, "our heroine gives out at the last moment."

Horace took his wife in his arms; not a word was spoken. George slid down the stair in a dead faint. Pat's picking him up made a diversion, and Horace carried Charlotte to the dining room, followed by all, except George, who was rallying from his faint by himself, with a host of sensations which he believed no man had ever felt before.

"What does this wonderful Providence mean?" asked Horace, kneeling by Charlotte, whom he had placed on the sofa. "I am afraid to look away from you, lest I should find myself a madman."

"It means," replied Charlotte's companion leisurely, ridding himself of his traps, "that we kept the boat tolerably dry, and that your wife has more nerve than any other woman upon earth. But what extraordinary introductions do I have to America! The denizens of the coast where we were stranded have a very limited view of the earth, but a very comprehensive one of the sea, and their rights therefrom. Consequently we found it impossible to convey tidings sooner of ourselves."

"Dear Horace," said Charlotte, "Mr. Egremont Moyston may joke as he will—he has saved my life."

Horace fell to shaking his hand violently, and stared at him with eyes full of feeling which he could not express.

"Nonsense," continued Mr. Moyston, "we undoubtedly aided each other. Mr. Hampden, we had a touch of brain fever which delayed us. We were thrown only six miles above the Batto light-house, but we might as well have landed in Patagonia. The white trash who kept us had no sense of what country they were in. 'Pomanco Court House' was the idea of their outside world. No conveyances, no comfort of any sort could we obtain. We were compelled to remain there till I was able to prowl about, and get down to the Batto light, to learn our where-abouts."

From point to point the wonderful narrative went on. Dinner was renewed. The servants, stricken with astonishment and admiration, lost their sense of decorum, and even the cook came up and occupied the edge of a chair, without remembering, as was her duty, that her plane was so much lower than the company that no number of kitchen stairs could measure it.

George had recovered himself, and returned.

"And so you missed your poor Charlotte, dear George?" she asked.

"Very much," he replied.

"Do I look badly?"

"As if you had suffered."

"Yet, dear Mrs. Hampden," said Mr. Moyston, very seriously, "if you and I should consult the glass, we could not find the traces of suffering that we may behold in the faces of your husband and brother."

At the word *brother* Horace felt a violent throb in all his frame. Heavens! George was no brother; he was his wife's devoted, life-long lover. In spite of the situation and the circumstances, the blood flew like birds through every vein. It appeared an inexorable necessity that he should go away by himself, and reflect upon his own feelings, and speculate upon those of George, and guess at the management of the clouded future.

"Why," exclaimed Charlotte, "George's hair has grown white."

So it had. Horace's was not changed a whit, and this he acknowl-edged to himself, when he saw her eyes scanning his ebon locks; he wished they were a dead white.

"No, indeed," laughed George, "being a little worried at your ab-sence, I left off my 'Hair Restorer.' Now that you have returned—" For the life of him he could not utter another word, his lips trembled so. Charlotte rose, went to him, and kissed him, and said softly:

"I thank God more than ever for having restored me to those who so tenderly love me. Now, Horace, I must shut my eyes and sense for the night. Pat, take the best care of Mr. Moyston; this house is his home."

"By Jove, Mr. Hampden," said Mr. Moyston, as Horace withdrew with Charlotte, "is there anything in antiquity to beat our case? I've gone through the Greek tragedies, and fed on our stalwart British classics, but I do not find its match."

"By the way," said George, absently, "I am not the brother of Mrs. Hampden's husband, but his cousin; we are very much together, however."

"Oh," answered Mr. Moyston. "America is the most extraordinary place. Home isn't a flea bite."

"Pray accept my gratitude, Mr. Moyston. I divine, by Mrs. Hampden's manner, what the nature of your service has been." He looked at him with so profound a thankfulness that Mr. Moyston was affected by this praise, and for the first time indicated emotion.

"It is just what you would have done for my sister," he replied hastily; and then they shook hands. Horace re-entered. Charlotte had retired, he said; he had tried to keep up his composure before her, for he saw how shattered her nerves were, but he could have no rest till he heard the full account of the disaster, and rescue.

It was gray dawn before the men separated. The occasion had made them firm friends; Horace was ready to give half his money to Mr. Moyston, and George half his affection. The journey was given up, of course. As George looked round for his valise, Mr. Moyston expressed some surprise.

"Do you go from here at this hour?"

A mighty longing came over George to remain under the roof with her who had been so miraculously restored. He looked at Horace, and Horace made no response. Human failing came over him again: he could not be magnanimous, and George turned away with a sigh. Mr. Moyston perceived there was some hidden fact or feeling between them.

"My apartment is very near," said George carelessly. "And by the way, Mr. Moyston, I hope you will share it a part of the time—bachelors prefer their solitary quarters, you know."

"I hate bachelordom from this out," replied Mr. Moyston. "I have lately seen all the virtues under the sun in Mrs. Hampden. Can I find another in this country?"

"Is he in love with her, too?"—thought poor Horace. "I suppose so—confound him! He is a hero—and George's hair must needs turn white."

"I'm off. Horace, bolt the door, to keep Charlotte in. What will Herbert say to these tidings of his mother?"

Herbert! his son—Horace had not thought of him yet; George was in advance even here.

"Boys are boys," he replied quickly. "I'll warrant you he has played cricket to-day."

"As he ought to," laughed Mr. Moyston, making a move towards the door, feeling an internal uneasiness.

"All this has given me a shock," said Horace, vaguely. "I am not equal to it. George, I tell you, I am not equal to it, and I can't bear it. You always were the strongest, and now your hair's got white. By George, do you know she showed me her arm, with a great scar on it, where she was knocked down on deck! I don't believe she is here at all. The scar is here, nothing else, you know, George." He staggered, and grew frightfully pale; he shook his head from side to side, and groaned pitifully.

"The shock, added to his great sorrow, has been too much for him," said Mr. Moyston. "Fetch some brandy, we must rub him; he is about to have a stroke. Just my luck in America," he said to himself.

George, stricken to the heart, but collected, made use of all available means; but Horace sunk momently—babbling at intervals about Charlotte—whom George would not at present disturb—and finally became wholly insensible.

Whatever Fate changes, or returns, God still disposes. Charlotte, bearing the greatest exposure, suffering, and vicissitude, survived; and Horace, in the ease and comfort of his orderly life, was struck with paralysis. His head and heart were not strong enough for the burdens placed upon them. He lingered two years, a helpless, but gentle, childish man, sedulously tended by George, whose secret was carefully protected from Charlotte. Mr. Moyston alone discovered it.

"I forswear England for the present," he said one day. "I find more character in America. George, noble as you are, you need me for awhile, and as I was the means of bringing Charlotte safely out of a crisis, I shall stay till I see you landed in the haven which shall be your right and rest. Not a word. I love Charlotte as I love no other woman, and I honor and respect you. Hurrah for the Colonies of King George! Just you propose going to England, to leave her now, for the fun."

"I have never proposed anything," answered George, "and I shall never propose."

"It will not be necessary, my dear boy."

IN THE TULES

———•———

Bret Harte

He had never seen a steamboat in his life. Born and reared in one of the Western Territories, far from a navigable river, he had only known the "dug-out" or canoe as a means of conveyance across the scant streams whose fordable waters made even those scarcely a necessity. The long, narrow, hooded waggon, drawn by swaying oxen, known familiarly as a "prairie schooner," in which he journeyed across the plains to California in '53, did not help his conception by that nautical figure. And when at last he dropped upon the land of promise through one of the Southern mountain passes, he halted all unconsciously upon the low banks of a great yellow river amidst a tangled brake of strange, reed-like grasses that were unknown to him. The river, broadening as it debouched through many channels into a lordly bay, seemed to him the *ultima thule* of his journeyings. Unyoking his oxen on the edge of the luxuriant meadows which blended with scarcely any line of demarcation into the great stream itself, he found the prospect "good" according to his lights and prairial experiences, and converting his halted waggon into a temporary cabin, he resolved to rest here and "settle."

There was little difficulty in so doing. The cultivated clearings he had passed were few and far between; the land would be his by discovery and occupation; his habits of loneliness and self-reliance made him independent of neighbours. He took his first meal in his new solitude under a spreading willow, but so near his natural boundary that the waters gurgled and oozed in the reeds but a few feet from him. The sun sank, deepening the gold of the river until it might have been the stream of Pactolus itself. But Martin Morse had no imagination; he was not even a gold-seeker; he had simply obeyed the roving instincts of the frontier-man in coming hither. The land was virgin and unoccupied; it was his; he was alone. These questions settled, he smoked his pipe with less concern over his three thousand miles' transference of habitation than the man of cities who had moved into a next street. When the sun sank he rolled himself in his blankets in the waggon bed and went quietly to sleep.

But he was presently awakened by something which at first he could not determine to be a noise or an intangible sensation. It was a deep throbbing through the silence of the night—a pulsation that seemed even to be communicated to the rude bed whereon he lay. As it came nearer it separated itself into a laboured, monotonous panting, continuous, but distinct from an equally monotonous but fainter beating of the waters, as if the whole track of the river were being coursed and trodden by a multitude of swiftly-trampling feet. A strange feeling took possession of him—half of fear, half of curious expectation. It was coming nearer. He rose, leaped hurriedly from the waggon, and ran to the bank. The night was dark; at first he saw nothing before him but the steel-black sky pierced with far-spaced, irregularly scattered stars. Then there seemed to be approaching him, from the left, another and more symmetrical constellation; a few red and blue stars high above the river, with three compact lines of larger planetary lights flashing towards him and apparently on his own level. It was almost upon him; he involuntarily drew back as the strange phenomenon swept abreast of where he stood, and resolved itself into a dark, yet airy, bulk, whose vagueness, topped by enormous towers, was yet illuminated by those open squares of light that he had taken for stars, but which he saw now were brilliantly-lit windows.

Their vivid rays shot through the reeds and sent broad bands across the meadow, the stationary waggon, and the slumbering oxen. But all this was nothing to the inner life they disclosed through lifted curtains and open blinds, which was the crowning revelation of this strange and wonderful spectacle. Elegantly-dressed men and women moved through brilliantly-lit and elaborately-gilt saloons; in one a banquet seemed to be spread, served by white-jacketed servants; in another were men playing cards around marble-topped tables; in another the light flashed back again from the mirrors and glistening glasses and decanters of a gorgeous refreshment saloon; in smaller openings there was the shy disclosure of dainty, white curtains and velvet lounges of more intimate apartments.

Martin Morse stood enthralled and mystified. It was as if some invisible Asmodeus had revealed to this simple frontier-man a world of which he had never dreamed. It was *the* world—a world of which he knew nothing in his simple, rustic habits and profound Western isolation—sweeping by him with the rush of an unknown planet. In another moment it was gone; a shower of sparks shot up from one of the towers and fell all around him, and then vanished, even as he remembered the set piece of "Fourth of July" fireworks had vanished in his own rural town, when he was a boy. The darkness fell with it too. But such was his utter absorption and breathless preoccupation that only a cold chill recalled him to himself, and he found he was standing mid-leg deep in the surge cast over the low banks by this passage of the first steamboat he had ever seen!

He waited for it the next night, when it appeared a little later from the opposite direction, on its return trip. He watched it the next night and the next. Hereafter he never missed it, coming or going—whatever the hard and weary preoccupations of his new and lonely life. He felt he could not have slept without seeing it go by. Oddly enough, his interest and desire did not go further. Even had he the time and money to spend in a passage on the boat, and thus actively realize the great world of which he had only these rare glimpses, a certain proud, rustic shyness kept him from it. It was not *his* world; he could not affront the snubs that his ignorance and inexperience would have provoked, and he was dimly conscious, as so many of us are in our ignorance, that in mingling with it he would simply lose the easy privileges of alien criticism. For there was much that he did not understand, and some things that grated upon his lonely independence.

One night, a lighter one than those previous, he lingered a little longer in the moonlight to watch the phosphorescent wake of the retreating boat. Suddenly it struck him that there was a certain irregular splashing in the water, quite different from the regular, diagonally crossing surges that the boat swept upon the bank. Looking at it more intently, he saw a black object turning in the water like a porpoise, and then the unmistakable uplifting of a black arm in an unskilful swimmer's overhand stroke. It was a struggling man. But it was quickly evident that the current was too strong and the turbulence of the shallow water too great for his efforts. Without a moment's hesitation, clad as he was in only his shirt and trousers, Morse strode into the reeds, and the next moment, with a call of warning, was swimming towards the now wildly-struggling figure. But from some unknown reason, as Morse approached him nearer, the man uttered some incoherent protest and desperately turned away, throwing off Morse's extended arm.

Attributing this only to the vague convulsions of a drowning man, Morse, a skilled swimmer, managed to clutch his shoulder and propelled him at arm's length, still struggling, apparently with as much reluctance as incapacity, towards the bank. As their feet touched the reeds and slimy bottom, the man's resistance ceased and he lapsed quite listlessly in Morse's arms. Half lifting, half dragging his burden, he succeeded at last in gaining the strip of meadow, and deposited the unconscious man beneath the willow tree. Then he ran to his waggon for whisky.

But to his surprise, on his return the man was already sitting up and wringing the water from his clothes. He then saw for the first time, by the clear moonlight, that the stranger was elegantly dressed and of striking appearance, and was clearly a part of that bright and fascinating world which Morse had been contemplating in his solitude. He eagerly took the proffered tin cup and drank the whisky. Then he rose to his feet, staggered a few steps forward, and glanced curiously around him at the still motionless waggon, the few felled trees and evidence of "clearing," and even at the rude cabin of logs and canvas just beginning to rise from the ground a few paces distant, and said, impatiently:

"Where the deuce am I?"

Morse hesitated. He was unable to name the locality of his dwelling-place. He answered, briefly:—

"On the right bank of the Sacramento."

The stranger turned upon him a look of suspicion not unmingled with resentment. "Oh!" he said, with ironical gravity, "and I suppose that this water you picked me out of was the Sacramento River. Thank you!"

Morse, with slow Western patience, explained that he had only settled there three weeks ago, and the place had no name.

"What's your nearest town, then?"

"Thar ain't any. Thar's a blacksmith's shop and grocery at the cross-roads, twenty miles further on, but it's got no name as I've heard on."

The stranger's look of suspicion passed. "Well," he said, in an imperative fashion, which however seemed as much the result of habit as the occasion, "I want a horse, and pretty quick, too."

"H'ain't got any."

"No horse? How did you get to this place?"

Morse pointed to his slumbering oxen.

The stranger again stared curiously at him. After a pause he said, with a half pitying, half humorous smile: "Pike—aren't you?"

Whether Morse did or did not know that this current California slang for a denizen of the bucolic West implied a certain contempt, he replied, simply:—

"I'm from Pike County, Mizzouri."

"Well," said the stranger, resuming his impatient manner, "you must beg or steal a horse from your neighbours."

"Thar ain't any neighbour nearer than fifteen miles."

"Then send fifteen miles! Stop." He opened his still clinging shirt and drew out a belt pouch, which he threw to Morse. "There! there's two hundred and fifty dollars in that. Now I want a horse. *Sabe?*"

"Thar ain't anyone to send," said Morse, quietly.

"Do you mean to say you are all alone here?"

"Yes."

"And you fished me out—all by yourself?"

"Yes."

The stranger again examined him curiously. Then he suddenly stretched out his hand and grasped his companion's.

"All right; if you can't send, I reckon I can manage to walk over there to-morrow."

"I was goin' on to say," said Morse, simply, "that if you'll lie by to-night, I'll start over at sun up, after puttin' out the cattle, and fetch you back a horse afore noon."

"That's enough." He, however, remained looking curiously at Morse. "Did you never hear," he said, with a singular smile, "that it was about the meanest kind of luck that could happen to you to save a drowning man?"

"No," said Morse, simply. "I reckon it orter be the meanest if you *didn't*."

"That depends upon the man you save," said the stranger, with the same ambiguous smile, "and whether the *saving* him is only putting things off. Look here," he added, with an abrupt return to his imperative style, "can't you give me some dry clothes?"

Morse brought him a pair of overalls and a "hickory shirt," well worn, but smelling strongly of a recent wash with coarse soap. The stranger put them on while his companion busied himself in collecting a pile of sticks and dry leaves.

"What's that for?" said the stranger, suddenly.

"A fire to dry your clothes."

The stranger calmly kicked the pile aside.

"Not any fire to-night if I know it," he said, brusquely. Before Morse could resent his quickly changing moods, he continued, in another tone, dropping to an easy reclining position beneath the tree, "Now, tell me all about yourself, and what you are doing here."

Thus commanded, Morse patiently repeated his story from the time he had left his back-woods cabin to his selection of the river bank for a "location." He pointed out the rich quality of this alluvial bottom and its adaptability for the raising of stock, which he hoped soon to acquire. The stranger smiled grimly, raised himself to a sitting position, and, taking a penknife from his damp clothes began to clean his nails in the bright moonlight—an occupation which made the simple Morse wander vaguely in his narration.

"And you don't know that this hole will give you chills and fever, till you'll shake yourself out of your boots?"

Morse had lived before in aguish districts and had no fear.

"And you never heard that some night the whole river will rise up and walk over you and your cabin and your stock?"

"No. For I reckon to move my shanty farther back."

The man shut up his penknife with a click and rose.

"If you've got to get up at sunrise, we'd better be turning in. I suppose you can give me a pair of blankets?"

Morse pointed to the waggon. "Thar's a shake-down in the waggon bed; you kin lie there." Nevertheless he hesitated, and with the inconsequence and abruptness of a shy man continued the previous conversation.

"I shouldn't like to move far away, for them steamboats is pow'ful kempany o' nights. I never seed one afore I kem here," and then, with the inconsistency of a reserved man, and without a word of further preliminary, he launched into a confidential disclosure of his late experiences. The stranger listened with a singular interest, and a quietly searching eye.

"Then you were watching the boat very closely just now, when you saw me. What else did you see? Anything before that—before you saw me in the water?"

"No—the boat had got well off before I saw you at all."

"Ah," said the stranger. "Well, I'm going to turn in." He walked to the waggon, mounted it, and by the time that Morse had reached it with his wet clothes, he was already wrapped in the blankets. A moment later he seemed to be in a profound slumber.

It was only then, when his guest was lying helplessly at his mercy, that he began to realize his strange experiences. The domination of this man had been so complete, that Morse, although by nature independent and self-reliant, had not permitted himself to question his right or to resent his rudeness. He had accepted his guest's careless or premeditated silence regarding the particulars of his accident as a matter of course, and had never dreamed of questioning him. That it was a natural accident of that great world so apart from his own experiences he did not doubt, and thought no more about it. The advent of the man himself was greater to him than the causes which brought him there. He was as yet quite unconscious of the complete fascination this mysterious stranger held over him, but he found himself shyly pleased with even the slight interest he had displayed in his affairs, and his hand felt yet warm and tingling from his sudden soft, but expressive grasp, as if it had been a woman's. There is a simple intuition of friendship in some lonely, self-abstracted natures that is nearly akin to love at first sight. Even the audacities and insolence of this stranger affected Morse as he might have been touched and captivated by the coquetries or imperiousness of some bucolic virgin. And this reserved and shy frontier-man found himself that night sleepless, and hovering

with an abashed timidity and consciousness around the waggon that
sheltered his guest, as if he had been a very Corydon watching the
moonlit couch of some slumbering Amaryllis.

He was off by daylight—after having placed a rude breakfast by the
side of the still sleeping guest—and before mid-day he had returned
with a horse. When he handed the stranger his pouch less the amount
he had paid for the horse, the man said, curtly:—

"What's that for?"

"Your change. I paid only fifty dollars for the horse."

The stranger regarded him with his peculiar smile. Then, replacing
the pouch in his belt, he shook Morse's hand again and mounted the
horse.

"So your name's Martin Morse! Well—good-bye, Morsey!"

Morse hesitated. A blush rose to his dark cheek. "You didn't tell me
your name," he said. "In case—"

"In case I'm *wanted*? Well, you can call me Captain Jack." He smiled
and, nodding his head, put spurs to his mustang and cantered away.

Morse did not do much work that day, falling into abstracted moods
and living over his experiences of the previous night, until he fancied
he could almost see his strange guest again. The narrow strip of
meadow was haunted by him. There was the tree under which he had
first placed him, and that was where he had seen him sitting up in his
dripping but well-fitting clothes. In the rough garments he had worn
and returned lingered a new scent of some delicate soap, overpower-
ing the strong alkali flavour of his own. He was early by the river side,
having a vague hope, he knew not why, that he should again see him
and recognise him among the passengers. He was wading out among
the reeds in the faint light of the rising moon, recalling the exact spot
where he had first seen the stranger, when he was suddenly startled
by the rolling over in the water of some black object that had caught
against the bank, but had been dislodged by his movements. To his
horror it bore a faint resemblance to his first vision of the preceding
night. But a second glance at the helplessly floating hair and bloated
outline showed him that it was a *dead* man, and of a type and build far
different from his former companion. There was a bruise upon his
matted forehead and an enormous wound in his throat already washed
bloodless, white, and waxen. An inexplicable fear came upon him, not
at the sight of the corpse, for he had been in Indian massacres and had

rescued bodies mutilated beyond recognition; but from some moral dread that, strangely enough, quickened and deepened with the far-off pant of the advancing steamboat. Scarcely knowing why, he dragged the body hurriedly ashore, concealing it in the reeds, as if he were disposing of the evidence of his own crime. Then, to his preposterous terror, he noticed that the panting of the steamboat and the beat of its paddles were "slowing" as the vague bulk came in sight, until a huge wave from the suddenly-arrested wheels sent a surge like an enormous heat-beat pulsating through the sedge that half submerged him. The flashing of three or four lanterns on deck and the motionless line of lights abreast of him dazzled his eyes, but he knew that the low fringe of willows hid his house and waggon completely from view. A vague murmur of voices from the deck was suddenly over-ridden by a sharp order, and to his relief the slowly-revolving wheels again sent a pulsation through the water, and the great fabric moved solemnly away. A sense of relief came over him, he knew not why, and he was conscious that for the first time he had not cared to look at the boat.

When the moon arose he again examined the body, and took from its clothing a few articles of identification and some papers of formality and precision, which he vaguely conjectured to be some law papers from their resemblance to the phrasing of sheriffs' and electors' notices which he had seen in the papers. He then buried the corpse in a shallow trench which he dug by the light of the moon. He had no question of responsibility; his pioneer training had not included coroners' inquests in its experience; in giving the body a speedy and secure burial from predatory animals, he did what one frontier-man would do for another: what he hoped might be done for *him*. If his previous unaccountable feelings returned occasionally it was not from that; but rather from some uneasiness in regard to his late guest's possible feelings and a regret that he had not been here at the finding of the body. That it would in some way have explained his own accident, he did not doubt.

The boat did not "slow up" the next night, but passed as usual; yet three or four days elapsed before he could look forward to its coming with his old extravagant and half-exalted curiosity—which was his nearest approach to imagination. He was then able to examine it more closely, for the appearance of the stranger whom he now began to call "his friend" in his verbal communings with himself—but whom he did not seem destined to again discover; until one day, to his astonishment, a couple of fine horses were brought to his clearing by a stock-drover. They had been "ordered" to be left there. In vain Morse expostulated and questioned.

"Your name's Martin Morse, ain't it?" said the drover, with business brusqueness; "and I reckon there ain't no other man o' that name around here?"

"No," said Morse.

"Well, then, they're *your's*."

"But who sent them?" insisted Morse. "What was his name, and where does he live?"

"I didn't know ez I was called upon to give the pedigree o' buyers," said the drover, drily; "but the horses is 'Morgan,' you kin bet your life," he grinned as he rode away.

That Captain Jack sent them, and that it was a natural prelude to his again visiting him, Morse did not doubt, and for a few days he lived in that dream. But Captain Jack did not come. The animals were of great service to him in "rounding up" the stock he now easily took in for pasturage, and saved him the necessity of having a partner or a hired man. The idea that this superior gentleman in fine clothes might ever appear to him in the former capacity had even flitted through his brain, but he had rejected it with a sigh. But the thought that, with luck and industry, he himself might, in course of time, approximate to Captain Jack's evident station, *did* occur to him, and was an incentive to energy. Yet it was quite distinct from the ordinary working-man's ambition of wealth and state. It was only that it might make him more worthy of his friend. The great world was still as it had appeared to him in the passing boat—a thing to wonder at—to be above—and to criticise.

For all that, he prospered in his occupation. But one day he awoke with listless limbs and feet that scarcely carried him through his daily labours. At night his listlessness changed to active pain and a feverishness that seemed to impel him towards the fateful river, as if his one aim in life was to drink up its waters and bathe in its yellow stream. But whenever he seemed to attempt it, strange dreams assailed him of dead bodies arising with swollen and distorted lips to touch his own as he strove to drink, or of his mysterious guest battling with him in its current, and driving him ashore. Again, when he essayed to bathe his parched and crackling limbs in its flood, he would be confronted with the dazzling lights of the motionless steamboat and the glare of stony eyes—until he fled in aimless terror. How long this lasted he knew not, until one morning he awoke in his new cabin with a strange man sitting by his bed, and a negress in the doorway.

"You've had a sharp attack of 'tule fever,'" said the stranger, dropping Morse's listless wrist, and answering his questioning eyes, "but you're all right now, and will pull through."

"Who are you?" stammered Morse, feebly.

"Dr. Deukesne, of Sacramento."

"How did you come here?"

"I was ordered to come to you and bring a nurse, as you were alone. There she is." He pointed to the smiling negress.

"*Who* ordered you?"

The doctor smiled with professional tolerance. "One of your friends, of course."

"But what was his name?"

"Really I don't remember. But don't distress yourself. He has settled for everything right royally. You have only to get strong now. My duty is ended, and I can safely leave you with the nurse. Only when you are strong again, I say—and *he* says—keep back farther from the river."

And that was all he knew. For even the nurse who attended him through the first days of his brief convalescence would tell him nothing more. He quickly got rid of her and resumed his work, for a new and strange phase of his simple, childish affection for his benefactor, partly superinduced by his illness, was affecting him. He was beginning to feel the pain of an unequal friendship; he was dimly conscious that his mysterious guest was only coldly returning his hospitality and benefits, while holding aloof from any association with him—and indicating the immeasurable distance that separated their future intercourse. He had withheld any kind message or sympathetic greeting; he had kept back even his *name*. The shy, proud, ignorant heart of the frontier-man swelled beneath the fancied slight, which left him helpless alike of reproach or resentment. He could not return the horses, although in a fit of childish indignation he had resolved not to use them; he could not reimburse him for the doctor's bill, although he had sent away the nurse.

He took a foolish satisfaction in not moving back from the river, with a faint hope that his ignoring of Captain Jack's advice might mysteriously be conveyed to him. He even thought of selling out his location and abandoning it, that he might escape the cold surveillance of his heartless friend. All this was undoubtedly childish—but there is an irrepressible simplicity of youth in all deep feeling, and the worldly inexperience of the frontier-man left him as innocent as a child. In this phase of his unrequited affection he even went so far as to seek some news of Captain Jack at Sacramento, and following out his foolish quest, to even take the steamboat from thence to Stockton.

What happened to him then was perhaps the common experience of such natures. Once upon the boat the illusion of the great world it contained for him utterly vanished. He found it noisy, formal, insincere, and had he ever understood or used the word in his limited vocabulary—*vulgar*. Rather, perhaps, it seemed to him that the prevailing sentiment and action of those who frequented it—and for whom it was built—were of a lower grade than his own. And, strangely enough, this gave him none of his former sense of critical superiority, but only of his own utter and complete isolation. He wandered in his rough frontier-man's clothes from deck to cabin, from airy galleries to long saloons, alone, unchallenged, unrecognised, as if he were again haunting it only in spirit, as he had so often done in his dreams.

His presence on the fringe of some voluble crowd caused no interruption; to him this speech was almost foreign in its allusions to things he did not understand, or, worse, seemed inconsistent with their eagerness and excitement. How different from all this was his recollection of the slowly oncoming teams, uplifted above the level horizon of the plains in his old wanderings; the few sauntering figures that met him as man to man, and exchanged the chronicle of the road; the record of Indian tracks; the finding of a spring; the discovery of pasturage, with the lazy, restful hospitality of the night. And how fierce here this continual struggle for dominance and existence, even in this lull of passage. For, above all and through all, he was conscious of the feverish haste of speed and exertion.

The boat trembled, vibrated, and shook with every stroke of the ponderous piston. The laughter of the crowd, the exchange of gossip and news, the banquet at the long table, the newspapers and books in the reading-room, even the luxurious couches in the state-rooms, were all dominated, thrilled, and pulsating with the perpetual throb of the demon of hurry and unrest. And when at last a horrible fascination dragged him into the engine-room, and he saw the cruel, relentless machinery at work, he seemed to recognise and understand some intelligent but pitiless Moloch, who was dragging this feverish world at its heels.

Later he was seated in a corner of the hurricane deck, whence he could view the monotonous banks of the river; yet, perhaps by certain signs unobservable to others, he knew he was approaching his own locality. He knew that his cabin and clearing would be undiscernible behind the fringe of willows on the bank, but he already distinguished the points where a few cotton woods struggled into a promontory of lighter foliage beyond them. Here voices fell upon his ear, and he was suddenly aware that two men had lazily crossed over from the other side of the boat, and were standing before him looking upon the bank.

"It was about here, I reckon," said one, listlessly, as if continuing a previous lagging conversation, "that it must have happened. For it was after we were making for the bend we've just passed, that the deputy, goin' to the state-room below us, found the door locked and the window open. But both men—Jack Despard and Seth Hall, the sheriff—weren't to be found. Not a trace of 'em. The boat was searched, but all for nothing. The idea is that the sheriff, arter getting his prisoner comf'ble in the state-room, took off Jack's handcuffs and locked the door; that Jack, who was mighty desp'rate, bolted through the window into the river, and the sheriff, who wasn't a slouch, arter him. Others allow—for the chairs and things was all tossed about in the state-room—that the two men clinched *thar*, and Jack choked Hall and chucked him out, and then slipped cl'ar into the water himself; for the state-room window was just ahead of the paddle-box, and the cap'n allows that no man or men would fall afore the paddles and live. Anyhow, that was all they ever knew of it."

"And there wasn't no trace of them found?" said the second man, after a long pause.

"No. Cap'n says them paddles would hev' just snatched 'em and slung 'em round and round and buried 'em 'way down in the ooze of the river bed with all the silt of the current atop of 'em, and they mightn't come up for ages, or else the wheels might have waltzed 'em 'way up to Sacramento, until there wasn't enough left of 'em to float, and dropped 'em when the boat stopped."

"It was a mighty fool risk for a man like Despard to take," resumed the second speaker, as he turned away with a slight yawn.

"Bet your life! but he was desp'rate, and the sheriff had got him safe! And they *do* say that he was superstitious like all them gamblers, and allowed that a man who was fixed to die by a rope or a pistol wasn't to be washed out of life by water."

The two figures drifted lazily away, but Morse sat rigid and motionless. Yet, strange to say, only one idea came to him clearly out of this awful revelation—the thought that his friend was still true to him—and that his strange absence and mysterious silence were fully accounted for and explained. And with it came the more thrilling fancy that this man was alive now to *him* alone. *He* was the sole custodian of his secret. The morality of the question, while it profoundly disturbed him, was rather in reference to its effect upon the chances of Captain Jack and the power it gave his enemies, than his own conscience. He would rather that his friend should have proven the prescribed outlaw who retained an unselfish interest in him, than the superior gentleman who was coldly wiping out his gratitude. He thought he understood now the reason of his strange and varying moods; even his bitter superstitious warning in regard to the probable curse entailed upon himself for saving a drowning man. Of this he recked little; enough that he fancied that Captain Jack's concern in his illness was heightened by that fear, and this assurance of his protecting friendship thrilled him with pleasure.

There was no reason now why he should not at once go back to his farm, where, at least, Captain Jack would always find him; and he did so, returning on the same boat. He was now fully recovered from his illness, and calmer in mind; he redoubled his labours to put himself in a position to help the mysterious fugitive when the time should come. The remote farm should always be a haven of refuge for him, and in this hope he forbore to take any outside help, remaining solitary and alone that Captain Jack's retreat should be inviolate. And so the long, dry season passed, the hay was gathered, the pasturing herds sent home, and the first rains dimpling like shot the broadening surface of the river were all that broke his unending solitude. In this enforced attitude of waiting and expectancy he was exalted and strengthened by a new idea. He was not a religious man, but dimly remembering the exhortations of some camp meeting of his boyhood, he conceived the idea that he might have been selected to work out the regeneration of Captain Jack. What might not come of this meeting and communing together in this lonely spot? That anything was due to the memory of the murdered sheriff, whose bones were rotting in the trench he daily but unconcernedly passed, did not occur to him. Perhaps his mind was not large enough for the double consideration. Friendship and love— and, for the matter of that, religion—are eminently one-ideaed.

But one night he awakened with a start. His hand, which was hanging out of his bunk, was dabbling idly in water. He had barely time to spring to his middle in what seemed to be a slowly filling tank, before the door fell out as from that inward pressure, and his whole shanty collapsed like a pack of cards. But it fell outwards; the roof sliding from over his head like a withdrawn canopy, and he was swept from his feet against it and thence out into what might have been another world! For the rain had ceased and the full moon revealed only one vast, illimitable expanse of water. It was not an overflow, but the whole rushing river magnified and repeated a thousand times, which, even as he gasped for breath and clung to the roof, was bearing him away he knew not whither. But it was bearing him away upon its centre, for as he cast one swift glance towards his meadows he saw they were covered by the same sweeping torrent, dotted with his sailing hay-ricks and reaching to the wooded foot-hills. It was the great flood of '54. In its awe-inspiring completeness it might have seemed to him the primeval Deluge.

As his frail raft swept under a cotton wood he caught at one of the overhanging limbs, and working his way desperately along the bough, at last reached a secure position in the fork of the tree. Here he was for the moment safe. But the devastation viewed from this height was only the more appalling. Every sign of his clearing, all evidence of his past year's industry, had disappeared. He was now conscious, for the first time, of the lowing of the few cattle he had kept as, huddled together on a slight eminence, they one by one slipped over struggling into the flood. The shining bodies of his dead horses rolled by him as he gazed. The lower-lying limbs of the sycamore near him were bending with the burden of the lighter articles from his overturned waggon and cabin which they had caught and retained, and a rake was securely lodged in a bough. The habitual solitude of his locality was now strangely invaded by drifting sheds, agricultural implements, and fence rails from unknown and remote neighbours, and he could faintly hear the far calling of some unhappy farmer adrift upon a spar of his wrecked and shattered house. When day broke he was cold and hungry.

Hours passed in hopeless monotony, with no slackening or diminution of the waters. Even the drifts became less, and a vacant sea at last spread before him on which nothing moved. An awful silence impressed him. In the afternoon, rain again began to fall on this grey, nebulous expanse, until the whole world seemed made of aqueous vapour. He had but one idea now—the coming of the evening boat, and he would reserve his strength to swim to it. He did not know until later that it could no longer follow the old channel of the river, and passed far beyond his sight and hearing. With his disappointment and exposure that night came a return of his old fever. His limbs were alternately racked with pain, or benumbed and lifeless. He could scarcely retain his position—at times he scarcely cared to—and speculated upon ending his sufferings by a quick plunge downwards. In other moments of lucid misery he was conscious of having wandered in his mind; of having seen the dead face of the murdered sheriff, washed out of the shallow grave by the flood, staring at him from the water; to this was added the hallucination of noises. He heard voices, his own name called by a voice he knew—Captain Jack's!

Suddenly he started, but in that fatal movement lost his balance and plunged downwards. But before the water closed above his head he had had a cruel glimpse of help near him; of a flashing light—of the black hull of a tug not many yards away—of moving figures—the sensation of a sudden plunge following his own, the grip of a strong hand upon his collar, and—unconsciousness!

When he came to he was being lifted in a boat from the tug and rowed through the deserted streets of a large city, until he was taken in through the second-story window of a half-submerged hotel and cared for. But all his questions yielded only the information that the tug—a privately procured one, not belonging to the Public Relief Association—had been dispatched for him with special directions, by a man who acted as one of the crew, and who was the one who had plunged in for him at the last moment. The man had left the boat at Stockton. There was nothing more? Yes!—he had left a letter. Morse seized it feverishly. It contained only a few lines:—

"We are quits now. You are all right. I have saved *you* from drowning, and shifted the curse to my own shoulders. Good-bye.

"CAPTAIN JACK."

The astounded man attempted to rise—to utter an exclamation—but fell back, unconscious.

Weeks passed before he was able to leave his bed—and then only as an impoverished and physically shattered man. He had no means to re-stock the farm left bare by the subsiding water. A kindly train-packer offered him a situation as muleteer in a pack-train going to the mountains—for he knew tracks and passes and could ride. The mountains gave him back a little of the vigour he had lost in the river valley, but none of its dreams and ambitions. One day, while tracking a lost mule, he stopped to slake his thirst in a water-hole—all that the summer had left of a lonely mountain torrent. Enlarging the hole to give drink to his beast also, he was obliged to dislodge and throw out with the red soil some bits of honey-comb rock, which were so queer-looking and so heavy as to attract his attention. Two of the largest he took back to camp with him. They were gold. From the locality he took out a fortune. Nobody wondered. To the Californian's superstition it was perfectly natural. It was "nigger luck"—the luck of the stupid, the ignorant, the inexperienced, the non-seeker—the irony of the gods!

But the simple, bucolic nature that had sustained itself against temptation with patient industry and lonely self-concentration, succumbed to rapidly acquired wealth. So it chanced that one day, with a crowd of excitement-loving spendthrifts and companions, he found himself on the outskirts of a lawless mountain town. An eager, frantic crowd had already assembled there—a desperado was to be lynched! Pushing his way through the crowd, for a nearer view of the exciting spectacle, the changed and reckless Morse was stopped by armed men only at the foot of a cart, which upheld a quiet, determined man, who, with a rope around his neck, was scornfully surveying the mob, that held the other end of the rope drawn across the limb of a tree above him. The eyes of the doomed man caught those of Morse—his expression changed—a kindly smile lit his face—he bowed his proud head for the first time, with an easy gesture of farewell.

And then, with a cry, Morse threw himself upon the nearest armed guard, and a fierce struggle began. He had overpowered his adversary and seized another in his hopeless fight towards the cart, when the half-astonished crowd felt that something must be done. It was done: with a sharp report, the upward curl of smoke and the holding back of the guard as Morse staggered forward *free*—with a bullet in his heart. Yet even then he did not fall until he reached the cart, when he lapsed forward, dead, with his arms outstretched and his head at the doomed man's feet.

There was something so supreme and all-powerful in this hopeless act of devotion that the heart of the multitude thrilled and then re-coiled aghast at its work, and a single word or a gesture from the doomed man himself would have set him free. But they say—and it is credibly recorded—that as Captain Jack Despard looked down upon the hopeless sacrifice at his feet, his eyes blazed, and he flung upon the crowd a curse so awful and sweeping, that, hardened as they were, their blood ran cold, and then leaped furiously to their cheeks.

"And now," he said, coolly tightening the rope around his neck with a jerk of his head—"Go on, and be hanged to you! I'm ready."

They did not hesitate this time. And Martin Morse and Captain Jack Despard were buried in the same grave.

Martha's Lady

Sarah Orne Jewett

I

One day, many years ago, the old Judge Pyne house wore an un-wonted look of gayety and youthfulness. The high-fenced green garden beyond was bright with June flowers. In the large shady front yard under the elms you might see some chairs placed near together, as they often used to be when the family were all at home and life was going on gayly with eager talk and pleasure-making; when the elder judge, the grandfather, used to quote his favorite Dr. Johnson and say to his girls, "Be brisk, be splendid, and be public."

One of the chairs had a crimson silk shawl thrown carelessly over its straight back, and a passer-by who looked in through the latticed gate between the tall gate-posts, with their white urns, might think that this piece of shining East Indian color was a huge red lily that had suddenly bloomed against the syringa bush. There were certain win-dows thrown wide open that were usually shut, and their curtains were blowing free in the light wind of a summer afternoon; it looked as if a large household had returned to the old house to fill the prim best rooms and find them pleasant.

It was evident to every one in town that Miss Harriet Pyne, to use the village phrase, had company. She was the last of her family, and was by no means old; but being the last, and wonted to live with people much older than herself, she had formed all the habits of a serious elderly person. Ladies of her age, a little past thirty, often wore discreet caps in those days, especially if they were married, but being single, Miss Harriet clung to youth in this respect, making the one concession of keeping her waving chestnut hair as smooth and stiffly arranged as possible. She had been the dutiful companion of her father and mother in their latest years, all her elder brothers and sisters having married and gone, or died and gone, out of the old house. Now that she was left alone it seemed quite the best thing frankly to accept the fact of age at once, and to turn more resolutely than ever to the companionship of duty and serious books. She was more serious and given to routine than her elders themselves, as sometimes happened when the daughters of New England gentlefolks were brought up wholly in the society of their elders. At thirty she had more reluctance than her mother to face an unforeseen occasion, certainly more than her grandmother, who had preserved some cheerful inheritance of gayety and worldliness from colonial times.

There was something about the look of the crimson silk shawl in the front yard to make one suspect that the sober customs of the best house in a quiet New England village were all being set at defiance, and once when the mistress of the house came to stand in her own doorway she wore the pleased but somewhat apprehensive look of a guest. In these days New England life held the necessity of much dignity and discretion of behavior; there was the truest hospitality and good cheer in all occasional festivities, but it was sometimes a self-conscious hospitality, followed by an inexorable return to asceticism both of diet and of behavior. Miss Harriet Pyne belonged to the very dullest days of New England, those which perhaps held the most priggishness for the learned professions, the most limited interpretation of the word "evangelical," and the pettiest indifference to large things. The outbreak of a desire for larger religious freedom caused at first a most determined reaction toward formalism and even stagnation of thought and behavior, especially in small and quiet villages like Ashford, intently busy with their own concerns. It was high time for a little leaven to begin its work, in this moment when the great impulses of the war for liberty had died away and those of the coming war for patriotism and a new freedom had hardly yet begun, except as a growl of thunder or a flash of lightning draws one's eyes to the gathering clouds through the lifeless air of a summer day.

The dull interior, the changed life of the old house whose former activities seemed to have fallen sound asleep, really typified these larger conditions, and the little leaven had made its easily recognized appearance in the shape of a light-hearted girl. She was Miss Harriet's young Boston cousin, Helena Vernon, who, half-amused and half-impatient at the unnecessary sober-mindedness of her hostess and of Ashford in general, had set herself to the difficult task of gayety. Cousin Harriet looked on at a succession of ingenious and, on the whole, innocent attempts at pleasure, as she might have looked on at the frolics of a kitten who easily substitutes a ball of yarn for the uncertainties of a bird or a wind-blown leaf, and who may at any moment ravel the fringe of a sacred curtain-tassel in preference to either.

Helena, with her mischievous appealing eyes, with her enchanting old songs and her guitar, seemed the more delightful and even reasonable because she was so kind to everybody, and because she was a beauty. She had the gift of most charming manners. There was all the unconscious lovely ease and grace that had come with the good breeding of her city home, where many pleasant persons came and went; she had no fear, one had almost said no respect, of the individual, and she did not need to think of herself. Cousin Harriet turned cold with apprehension when she saw the minister coming in at the front gate, and wondered in agony if Martha were properly attired to go to the door, and would by any chance hear the knocker; it was Helena who, delighted to have anything happen, ran to the door to welcome the Reverend Mr. Crofton as if he were a congenial friend of her own age. She could behave with more or less propriety during the stately first visit, and even contrive to lighten it with modest mirth, and to extort the confession that the guest had a tenor voice though sadly out of practice, but when the minister departed a little flattered, and hoping that he had not expressed himself too strongly for a pastor upon the poems of Emerson, and feeling the unusual stir of gallantry in his proper heart, it was Helena who caught the honored hat of the late Judge Pyne from its last resting-place in the hall, and holding it securely in both hands, mimicked the minister's self-conscious entrance. She copied his pompous and anxious expression in the dim parlor in such delicious fashion, that Miss Harriet, who could not always extinguish a ready spark of the original sin of humor, laughed aloud.

"My dear!" she exclaimed severely the next moment. "I am ashamed of your being so disrespectful!" and then laughed again, and took the affecting old hat and carried it back to its place.

"I would not have had any one else see you for the world," she said sorrowfully as she returned, feeling quite self-possessed again, to the parlor doorway; but Helena still sat in the minister's chair, with her small feet placed as his stiff boots had been, and a copy of his solemn expression before they came to speaking of Emerson and of the guitar. "I wish I had asked him if he would be so kind as to climb the cherry-tree," said Helena, unbending a little at the discovery that her cousin would consent to laugh no more. "There are all those ripe cherries on the top branches. I can climb as high as he, but I can't reach far enough from the last branch that will bear anybody. The minister is so long and thin"—

"I don't know what Mr. Crofton would have thought of you; he is a very serious young man," said cousin Harriet, still ashamed of her laughter. "Martha will get the cherries for you, or one of the men. I should not like to have Mr. Crofton think you were frivolous, a young lady of your opportunities"—but Helena had escaped through the hall and out at the garden door at the mention of Martha's name. Miss Harriet Pyne sighed anxiously, and then smiled, in spite of her deep convictions, as she shut the blinds and tried to make the house look solemn again.

The front door might be shut, but the garden door at the other end of the broad hall was wide open into the large sunshiny garden, where the last of the red and white peonies and the golden lilies, and the first of the tall blue larkspurs lent their colors in generous fashion. The straight box borders were all in fresh and shining green of their new leaves, and there was a fragrance of the old garden's inmost life and soul blowing from the honeysuckle blossoms on a long trellis. Now it was late in the afternoon, and the sun was low behind great apple-trees at the garden's end, which threw their shadows over the short turf of the bleaching-green. The cherry-trees stood at one side in full sunshine still, and Miss Harriet, who presently came to the garden steps to watch like a hen at the water's edge, saw her cousin's pretty figure in its white dress of India muslin hurrying across the grass. She was accompanied by the tall, ungainly shape of Martha the new maid, who, dull and indifferent to every one else, showed a surprising willingness and allegiance to the young guest.

"Martha ought to be in the dining-room already, slow as she is; it wants but half an hour of tea-time," said Miss Harriet, as she turned and went into the shaded house. It was Martha's duty to wait at table, and there had been many trying scenes and defeated efforts toward her education. Martha was certainly very clumsy, and she seemed the clumsier because she had replaced her aunt, a most skillful person, who had but lately married a thriving farm and its prosperous owner. It must be confessed that Miss Harriet was a most bewildering instructor, and that her pupil's brain was easily confused and prone to blunders. The coming of Helena had been somewhat dreaded by reason of this incompetent service, but the guest took no notice of frowns or futile gestures at the first tea-table, except to establish friendly relations with Martha on her own account by a reassuring smile. They were about the same age, and next morning, before cousin Harriet came down, Helena showed by a word and a quick touch the right way to do something that had gone wrong and been impossible to understand the night before. A moment later the anxious mistress came in without suspicion, but Martha's eyes were as affectionate as a dog's, and there was a new look of hopefulness on her face; this dreaded guest was a friend after all, and not a foe come from proud Boston to confound her ignorance and patient efforts.

The two young creatures, mistress and maid, were hurrying across the bleaching-green.

"I can't reach the ripest cherries," explained Helena politely, "and I think that Miss Pyne ought to send some to the minister. He has just made us a call. Why Martha, you haven't been crying again!"

"Yes, 'm," said Martha sadly. "Miss Pyne always loves to send something to the minister," she acknowledged with interest, as if she did not wish to be asked to explain these latest tears.

"We'll arrange some of the best cherries in a pretty dish. I'll show you how, and you shall carry them over to the parsonage after tea," said Helena cheerfully, and Martha accepted the embassy with pleasure. Life was beginning to hold moments of something like delight in the last few days.

"You'll spoil your pretty dress, Miss Helena," Martha gave shy warning, and Miss Helena stood back and held up her skirts with unusual care while the country girl, in her heavy blue checked gingham, began to climb the cherry-tree like a boy.

Down came the scarlet fruit like bright rain into the green grass.

"Break some nice twigs with the cherries and leaves together; oh, you're a duck, Martha!" and Martha, flushed with delight, and looking far more like a thin and solemn blue heron, came rustling down to earth again, and gathered the spoils into her clean apron.

That night at tea, during her handmaiden's temporary absence, Miss Harriet announced, as if by way of apology, that she thought Martha was beginning to understand something about her work. "Her aunt was a treasure, she never had to be told anything twice; but Martha has been as clumsy as a calf," said the precise mistress of the house. "I have been afraid sometimes that I never could teach her anything. I was quite ashamed to have you come just now, and find me so unprepared to entertain a visitor."

"Oh, Martha will learn fast enough because she cares so much," said the visitor eagerly. "I think she is a dear good girl. I do hope that she will never go away. I think she does things better every day, cousin Harriet," added Helena pleadingly, with all her kind young heart. The china-closet door was open a little way, and Martha heard every word. From that moment, she not only knew what love was like, but she knew love's dear ambitions. To have come from a stony hill-farm and a bare small wooden house was like a cave-dweller's coming to make a permanent home in an art museum; such had seemed the elaborateness and elegance of Miss Pyne's fashion of life, and Martha's simple brain was slow enough in its processes and recognitions. But with this sympathetic ally and defender, this exquisite Miss Helena who believed in her, all difficulties appeared to vanish.

Later that evening, no longer homesick or hopeless, Martha returned from her polite errand to the minister, and stood with a sort of triumph before the two ladies who were sitting in the front doorway, as if they were waiting for visitors, Helena still in her white muslin and red ribbons, and Miss Harriet in a thin black silk. Being happily self-forgetful in the greatness of the moment, Martha's manners were perfect, and she looked for once almost pretty and quite as young as she was.

"The minister came to the door himself, and sent his thanks. He said that cherries were always his favorite fruit, and he was much obliged to both Miss Pyne and Miss Vernon. He kept me waiting a few minutes, while he got this book ready to send to you, Miss Helena."

"What are you saying, Martha? I have sent him nothing!" exclaimed Miss Pyne, much astonished. "What does she mean, Helena?"

"Only a few of your cherries," explained Helena. "I thought Mr. Crofton would like them after his afternoon of parish calls. Martha and I arranged them before tea, and I sent them with our compliments."

"Oh, I am very glad you did," said Miss Harriet, wondering, but much relieved. "I was afraid"—

"No, it was none of my mischief," answered Helena daringly. "I did not think that Martha would be ready to go so soon. I should have shown you how pretty they looked among their green leaves. We put them in one of your best white dishes with the openwork edge. Martha shall show you to-morrow; mamma always likes to have them so." Helena's fingers were busy with the hard knot of a parcel.

"See this, cousin Harriet!" she announced proudly, as Martha disappeared round the corner of the house, beaming with the pleasures of adventure and success. "Look! the minister has sent me a book: Sermons on *what?* Sermons—it is so dark that I can't quite see."

"It must be his Sermons on the Seriousness of Life; they are the only ones he has printed, I believe," said Miss Harriet, with much pleasure. "They are considered very fine; remarkably able discourses. He pays you a great compliment, my dear. I feared that he noticed your girlish levity."

"I behaved beautifully while he stayed," insisted Helena. "Ministers are only men," but she blushed with pleasure. It was certainly something to receive a book from its author, and such a tribute made her of more value to the whole reverent household. The minister was not only a man, but a bachelor, and Helena was at the age that best loves conquest; it was at any rate comfortable to be reinstated in cousin Harriet's good graces.

"Do ask the kind gentleman to tea! He needs a little cheering up," begged the siren in India muslin, as she laid the shiny black volume of sermons on the stone doorstep with an air of approval, but as if they had quite finished their mission.

"Perhaps I shall, if Martha improves as much as she has within the last day or two," Miss Harriet promised hopefully. "It is something I always dread a little when I am all alone, but I think Mr. Crofton likes to come. He converses so elegantly."

II

These were the days of long visits, before affectionate friends thought it quite worth while to take a hundred miles' journey merely to dine or to pass a night in one another's houses. Helena lingered through the pleasant weeks of early summer, and departed unwillingly at last to join her family at the White Hills, where they had gone like other households of high social station, to pass the month of August out of town. The happy-hearted young guest left many lamenting friends behind her, and promised each that she would come back again next year. She left the minister a rejected lover, as well as the preceptor of the academy, but with their pride unwounded, and it may have been with wider outlooks upon the world and a less narrow sympathy both for their own work in life and for their neighbors' work and hindrances. Even Miss Harriet Pyne herself had lost some of the unnecessary provincialism and prejudice which had begun to harden a naturally good and open mind and affectionate heart. She was conscious of feeling younger and more free, and not so lonely. Nobody had ever been so gay, so fascinating, or so kind as Helena, so full of social resource, so simple and undemanding in her friendliness. The light of her young life cast no shadow on either young or old companions, her pretty clothes never seemed to make other girls look dull or out of fashion. When she went away up the street in Miss Harriet's carriage to take the slow train toward Boston and the gayeties of the new Profile House, where her mother waited impatiently with a group of Southern friends, it seemed as if there would never be any more picnics or parties in Ashford, and as if society had nothing left to do but to grow old and get ready for winter.

Martha came into Miss Helena's bedroom that last morning, and it was easy to see that she had been crying; she looked just as she did in that first sad week of homesickness and despair. All for love's sake she had

been learning to do many things, and to do them exactly right; her eyes
had grown quick to see the smallest chance for personal service. Nobody could be more humble and devoted; she looked years older than
Helena, and wore already a touching air of caretaking.

"You spoil me, you dear Martha!" said Helena from the bed. "I don't
know what they will say at home, I am so spoiled."

Martha went on opening the blinds to let in the brightness of the
summer morning, but she did not speak.

"You are getting on splendidly, aren't you?" continued the little mistress. "You have tried so hard that you make me ashamed of myself. At
first you crammed all the flowers together, and now you make them
look beautiful. Last night cousin Harriet was so pleased when the table
was so charming, and I told her that you did everything yourself, every
bit. Won't you keep the flowers fresh and pretty in the house until I
come back? It's so much pleasanter for Miss Pyne, and you'll feed my
little sparrows, won't you? They're growing so tame."

"Oh yes, Miss Helena!" and Martha looked almost angry for a moment, then she burst into tears and covered her face with her apron.
"I couldn't understand a single thing when I first came. I never had
been anywhere to see anything, and Miss Pyne frightened me when she
talked. It was you made me think I could ever learn. I wanted to keep
the place, 'count of mother and the little boys; we're dreadful hard
pushed at home. Hepsy has been good in the kitchen; she said she
ought to have patience with me, for she was awkward herself when
she first came."

Helena laughed; she looked so pretty under the tasseled white curtains.

"I dare say Hepsy tells the truth," she said. " I wish you had told me
about your mother. When I come again, some day we'll drive up country, as you call it, to see her. Martha! I wish you would think of me
sometimes after I go away. Won't you promise?" and the bright young
face suddenly grew grave. "I have hard times myself; I don't always
learn things that I ought to learn, I don't always put things straight. I
wish you wouldn't forget me ever, and would just believe in me. I think
it does help more than anything."

"I won't forget," said Martha slowly. "I shall think of you every day."
She spoke almost with indifference, as if she had been asked to dust a
room, but she turned aside quickly and pulled the little mat under the

hot water jug quite out of its former straightness; then she hastened
away down the long white entry, weeping as she went.

III

To lose out of sight the friend whom one has loved and lived to
please is to lose joy out of life. But if love is true, there comes presently
a higher joy of pleasing the ideal, that is to say, the perfect friend. The
same old happiness is lifted to a higher level. As for Martha, the girl
who stayed behind in Ashford, nobody's life could seem duller to those
who could not understand; she was slow of step, and her eyes were
almost always downcast as if intent upon incessant toil; but they startled you when she looked up, with their shining light. She was capable
of the happiness of holding fast to a great sentiment, the ineffable
satisfaction of trying to please one whom she truly loved. She never
thought of trying to make other people pleased with herself; all she
lived for was to do the best she could for others, and to conform to an
ideal, which grew at last to be like a saint's vision, a heavenly figure
painted upon the sky.

On Sunday afternoons in summer, Martha sat by the window of her
chamber, a low-storied little room, which looked into the side yard and
the great branches of an elm-tree. She never sat in the old wooden
rocking-chair except on Sundays like this; it belonged to the day of rest
and to happy meditation. She wore her plain black dress and a clean
white apron, and held in her lap a little wooden box, with a brass hinge
on top for a handle. She was past sixty years of age and looked even
older, but there was the same look on her face that it had sometimes
worn in girlhood. She was the same Martha; her hands were old-
looking and work-worn, but her face still shone. It seemed like yesterday that Helena Vernon had gone away, and it was more than forty
years.

War and peace had brought their changes and great anxieties, the
face of the earth was furrowed by floods and fire, the faces of mistress
and maid were furrowed by smiles and tears, and in the sky the stars
shone on as if nothing had happened. The village of Ashford added a
few pages to its unexciting history, the minister preached, the people
listened; now and then a funeral crept along the street, and now and
then the bright face of a little child rose above the horizon of a family

pew. Miss Harriet Pyne lived on in the large white house, which gained more and more distinction because it suffered no changes, save successive repaintings and a new railing about its stately roof. Miss Harriet herself had moved far beyond the uncertainties of an anxious youth. She had long ago made all her decisions, and settled all necessary questions; her scheme of life was as faultless as the miniature landscape of a Japanese garden, and as easily kept in order. The only important change she would ever be capable of making was the final change to another and a better world; and for that nature itself would gently provide, and her own innocent life.

Hardly any great social event had ruffled the easy current of life since Helena Vernon's marriage. To this Miss Pyne had gone, stately in appearance and carrying gifts of some old family silver which bore the Vernon crest, but not without some protest in her heart against the uncertainties of married life. Helena was so equal to a happy independence and even to the assistance of other lives grown strangely dependent upon her quick sympathies and instinctive decisions, that it was hard to let her sink her personality in the affairs of another. Yet a brilliant English match was not without its attractions to an old-fashioned gentlewoman like Miss Pyne, and Helena herself was amazingly happy; one day there had come a letter to Ashford, in which her very heart seemed to beat with love and self-forgetfulness, to tell cousin Harriet of such new happiness and high hope. "Tell Martha all that I say about my dear Jack," wrote the eager girl; "please show my letter to Martha, and tell her that I shall come home next summer and bring the handsomest and best man in the world to Ashford. I have told him all about the dear house and the dear garden; there never was such a lad to reach for cherries with his six foot two." Miss Pyne, wondering a little, gave the letter to Martha, who took it deliberately and as if she wondered too, and went away to read it slowly by herself. Martha cried over it, and felt a strange sense of loss and pain; it hurt her heart a little to read about the cherry-picking. Her idol seemed to be less her own since she had become the idol of a stranger. She never had taken such a letter in her hands before, but love at last prevailed, since Miss Helena was happy, and she kissed the last page where her name was written, feeling overbold, and laid the envelope on Miss Pyne's secretary without a word.

The most generous love cannot but long for reassurance, and

Martha had the joy of being remembered. She was not forgotten when the day of the wedding drew near, but she never knew that Miss Helena had asked if cousin Harriet would not bring Martha to town; she should like to have Martha there to see her married. "She would help about the flowers," wrote the happy girl; "I know she will like to come, and I'll ask mamma to plan to have some one take her all about Boston and make her have a pleasant time after the hurry of the great day is over."

Cousin Harriet thought it was very kind and exactly like Helena, but Martha would be out of her element; it was most imprudent and girlish to have thought of such a thing. Helena's mother would be far from wishing for any unnecessary guest just then in the busiest part of her household, and it was best not to speak of the invitation. Some day Martha should go to Boston if she did well, but not now. Helena did not forget to ask if Martha had come, and was astonished by the indifference of the answer. It was the first thing which reminded her that she was not a fairy princess having everything her own way in that last day before the wedding. She knew that Martha would have loved to be near, for she could not help understanding in that moment of her own happiness the love that was hidden in another heart. Next day this happy young princess, the bride, cut a piece of the great cake and put it into a pretty box that had held one of her wedding presents. With eager voices calling her, and all her friends about her, and her mother's face growing more and more wistful at the thought of parting, she still lingered and ran to take one or two trifles from her dressing-table, a little mirror and some tiny scissors that Martha would remember, and one of the pretty handkerchiefs marked with her maiden name. These she put in the box too; it was half a girlish freak and fancy, but she could not help trying to share her happiness, and Martha's life was so plain and dull. She whispered a message, and put the little package into cousin Harriet's hand for Martha as she said good-by. She was very fond of cousin Harriet. She smiled with a gleam of her old fun; Martha's puzzled look and tall awkward figure seemed to stand suddenly before her eyes, as she promised to come again to Ashford. Impatient voices called to Helena, her lover was at the door, and she hurried away leaving her old home and her girlhood gladly. If she had only known it, as she kissed cousin Harriet good-by, they were never going to see each other again until they were old women. The first step that she took out of her father's house that day, married, and full of hope and joy, was a step that led her away from the green elms of Boston Common and away from her own country and those she loved best, to a brilliant much-varied foreign life, and to nearly all the sorrows and nearly all the joys that the heart of one woman could hold or know.

On Sunday afternoons Martha used to sit by the window in Ashford and hold the wooden box which a favorite young brother, who afterward died at sea, had made for her, and she used to take out of it the pretty little box with a gilded cover that had held the piece of wedding-cake, and the small scissors, and the blurred bit of a mirror in its silver case; as for the handkerchief with the narrow lace edge, once in two or three years she sprinkled it as if it were a flower, and spread it out in the sun on the old bleaching-green, and sat near by in the shrubbery to watch lest some bold robin or cherry-bird should seize it and fly away.

IV

Miss Harriet Pyne was often congratulated upon the good fortune of having such a helper and friend as Martha. As time went on this tall gaunt woman, always thin, always slow, gained a dignity of behavior and simple affectionateness of look which suited the charm and dignity of the ancient house. She was unconsciously beautiful like a saint, like the picturesqueness of a lonely tree which lives to shelter unnumbered lives and to stand quietly in its place. There was such rustic homeliness and constancy belonging to her, such beautiful powers of apprehension, such reticence, such gentleness for those who were troubled or sick; all these gifts and graces Martha hid in her heart. She never joined the church because she thought she was not good enough, but life was such a passion and happiness of service that it was impossible not to be devout, and she was always in her humble place on Sundays, in the back pew next the door. She had been educated by a remembrance; Helena's young eyes forever looked at her reassuringly from a gay girlish face. Helena's sweet patience in teaching her own awkwardness could never be forgotten.

"I owe everything to Miss Helena," said Martha half aloud as she sat alone by the window; she had said it to herself a thousand times. When she looked in the little keepsake mirror she always hoped to see some faint reflection of Helena Vernon, but there was only her own brown old New England face to look back at her wonderingly.

Miss Pyne went less and less often to pay visits to her friends in Boston; there were very few friends left to come to Ashford and make long visits in the summer, and life grew more and more monotonous. Now and then there came news from across the sea and messages of remembrance, letters that were closely written on thin sheets of paper, and that spoke of lords and ladies, of great journeys, of the death of little children and the proud successes of boys at school, of the wedding of Mrs. Dysart's only daughter; but even that had happened years ago. These things seemed far away and vague, as if they belonged to a story and not to life itself; the true links with the past were quite different. There was the unvarying flock of ground-sparrows that Helena had begun to feed; every morning Martha scattered crumbs for them from the side doorsteps while Miss Pyne watched from the dining-room window, and they were counted and cherished year by year.

Miss Pyne herself had many fixed habits, but little ideality or imagination, and so at last it was Martha who took thought for her mistress, and gave freedom to her own good taste. After a while, without any one's observing the change, the everyday ways of doing things in the house came to be the stately ways that had once belonged only to the entertainment of guests. Happily both mistress and maid seized all possible chances for hospitality, yet Miss Harriet nearly always sat alone at her exquisitely served table with its fresh flowers, and the beautiful old china which Martha handled so lovingly that there was no good excuse for keeping it hidden on closet shelves. Every year when the old cherry-trees were in fruit, Martha carried the round white Limoges dish with a fretwork edge, full of pointed green leaves and scarlet cherries, to the minister, and his wife never quite understood why every year he blushed and looked so conscious of the pleasure, and thanked Martha as if he had received a very particular attention. There was no pretty suggestion toward the pursuit of the fine art of housekeeping in Martha's limited acquaintance with newspapers that she did not adopt; there was no refined old custom of the Pyne housekeeping that she consented to let go. And every day, as she had promised, she thought of Miss Helena,—oh, many times in every day: whether this thing would please her, or that be likely to fall in with her fancy or ideas of fitness. As far as was possible the rare news that reached Ashford through an occasional letter or the talk of guests was made part of Martha's own life, the history of her own heart. A worn old geography often stood open at the map of Europe on the light-stand in her room, and a little old-fashioned gilt button, set with a piece of glass like a ruby, that had broken and fallen from the trimming of one of Helena's dresses, was used to mark the city of her dwelling-place. In the changes of a diplomatic life Martha followed her lady all about the map. Sometimes the button was at Paris, and sometimes at Madrid; once, to her great anxiety, it remained long at St. Petersburg. For such a slow scholar Martha was not unlearned at last, since everything about life in these foreign towns was of interest to her faithful heart. She satisfied her own mind as she threw crumbs to the tame sparrows; it was all part of the same thing and for the same affectionate reasons.

V

One Sunday afternoon in early summer Miss Harriet Pyne came hurrying along the entry that led to Martha's room and called two or three times before its inhabitant could reach the door. Miss Harriet looked unusually cheerful and excited, and she held something in her hand. "Where are you, Martha?" she called again. "Come quick, I have something to tell you!"

"Here I am, Miss Pyne," said Martha, who had only stopped to put her precious box in the drawer, and to shut the geography.

"Who do you think is coming this very night at half past six? We must have everything as nice as we can; I must see Hannah at once. Do you remember my cousin Helena who has lived abroad so long? Miss Helena Vernon, the Honorable Mrs. Dysart, she is now."

"Yes, I remember her," answered Martha, turning a little pale.

"I knew that she was in this country, and I had written to ask her to come for a long visit," continued Miss Harriet, who did not often explain things, even to Martha, though she was always conscientious about the kind messages that were sent back by grateful guests. "She telegraphs that she means to anticipate her visit by a few days and come to me at once. The heat is beginning in town, I suppose. I daresay, having been a foreigner so long, she does not mind traveling on Sunday. Do you think Hannah will be prepared? We must have tea a little later."

"Yes, Miss Harriet," said Martha. She wondered that she could speak as usual, there was such a ringing in her ears. "I shall have time to pick some fresh strawberries; Miss Helena is so fond of our strawberries."

"Why, I had forgotten," said Miss Pyne, a little puzzled by something quite unusual in Martha's face. "We must expect to find Mrs. Dysart a good deal changed, Martha; it is a great many years since she was here; I have not seen her since her wedding, and she has had a great deal of trouble, poor girl. You had better open the parlor chamber, and make it ready before you go down."

"It is all ready, I think," said Martha. "I can bring some of those little sweet-brier roses upstairs before she comes."

"Yes, you are always thoughtful," said Miss Pyne, with unwonted feeling.

Martha did not answer. She glanced at the telegram wistfully. She had never really suspected before that Miss Pyne knew nothing of the love that had been in her heart all these years; it was half a pain and half a golden joy to keep such a secret; she could hardly bear this moment of surprise.

Presently the news gave wings to her willing feet. When Hannah the cook, who never had known Miss Helena, went to the parlor an hour later on some errand to her old mistress, she discovered that this stranger guest must be a very important person. She had never seen the tea-table look exactly as it did that night, and in the parlor itself there were fresh blossoming boughs in the old East Indian jars, and lilies in the paneled hall, and flowers everywhere, as if there were some high festivity.

Miss Pyne sat by the window watching, in her best dress, looking stately and calm; she seldom went out now, and it was almost time for the carriage. Martha was just coming in from the garden with the strawberries, and with more flowers in her apron. It was a bright cool evening in June, the golden robins sang in the elms, and the sun was going down behind the apple-trees at the foot of the garden. The beautiful old house stood wide open to the long expected guest.

"I think that I shall go down to the gate," said Miss Pyne, looking at Martha for approval, and Martha nodded and they went together slowly down the broad front walk.

There was a sound of horses and wheels on the roadside turf: Martha could not see at first; she stood back inside the gate behind the white lilacs as the carriage came. Miss Pyne was there; she was holding out both arms and taking a tired, bent little figure in black to her heart. "Oh, my Miss Helena is an old woman like me!" and Martha gave a pitiful sob; she had never dreamed it would be like this; this was the one thing she could not bear.

"Where are you, Martha?" called Miss Pyne. "Martha will bring these in; you have not forgotten my good Martha, Helena?" Then Helena looked up and smiled just as she used to smile in the old days. The young eyes were there still in the changed face, and Miss Helena had come.

That night Martha waited in her lady's room just as she used, humble and silent, and went through with the old unforgotten loving services. The long years seemed like days. At last she lingered a moment trying to think of something else that might be done, then she was going silently away, but Helena called her back.

"You have always remembered, haven't you, Martha dear?" she said. "Won't you please kiss me good-night?"

THE HEART'S DESIRE

Sui Sin Far

She was dainty, slender, and of waxen pallor. Her eyes were long and drooping, her eyebrows finely arched. She had the tiniest Golden Lily feet and the glossiest black hair. Her name was Li Chung O'Yam, and she lived in a sad, beautiful, old palace surrounded by a sad, beautiful, old garden, situated on a charming island in the middle of a lake. This lake was spanned by marble bridges, entwined with green creepers, reaching to the mainland. No boats were ever seen on its waters, but the pink lotus lily floated thereon and swans of marvelous whiteness.

Li Chung O'Yam wore priceless silks and radiant jewels. The rarest flowers bloomed for her alone. Her food and drink were of the finest flavors and served in the purest gold and silver plates and goblets. The sweetest music lulled her to sleep.

Yet Li Chung O'Yam was not happy. In the midst of the grandeur of her enchanted palace she sighed for she knew not what.

"She is weary of being alone," said one of the attendants. And he who ruled all within the palace save Li Chung O'Yam said, "Bring her a father!"

A portly old mandarin was brought to O'Yam. She made humble obeisance and her august father inquired ceremoniously as to the state of her health, but she sighed and was still weary.

"We have made a mistake; it is a mother she needs," said they.

A comely matron, robed in rich silks and waving a beautiful pea-cock feather fan, was presented to O'Yam as her mother. The lady de-livered herself of much good advice and wise instruction as to deportment and speech, but O'Yam turned herself on her silken cush-ions and wished to say good-bye to her mother.

Then they led O'Yam into a courtyard which was profusely illumi-nated with brilliant lanterns and flaring torches. There were a number of little boys of about her own age dancing on stilts. One little fellow, dressed all in scarlet and flourishing a small sword, was pointed out to her as her brother. O'Yam was amused for a few moments, but in a little while she was tired of the noise and confusion.

In despair, they who lived but to please her consulted amongst themselves. O'Yam, overhearing them, said, "Trouble not your minds. I will find my own hearts-ease."

Then she called for her carrier dove and had an attendant bind under its wing a note which she had written. The dove went forth and flew with the note to where a little girl named Ku Yum, with a face as round as a harvest moon and a mouth like a red vine leaf, was hugging a cat to keep her warm and sucking her finger to prevent her from being hungry. To this little girl the dove delivered O'Yam's message, then returned to its mistress.

"Bring me my dolls and my cats, and attire me in my brightest and best," cried O'Yam.

When Ku Yum came slowly over one of the marble bridges towards the palace wherein dwelt Li Chung O'Yam, she wore a blue cotton blouse, carried a peg in one hand and her cat in another. O'Yam ran to greet her and brought her into the castle hall. Ku Yum looked at O'Yam, at her radiant apparel, at her cats and her dolls.

"Ah," she exclaimed, "how beautifully you are robed! In the same col-ors as I. And behold, your dolls and your cat, are they not much like mine?"

"Indeed they are," replied O'Yam, lifting carefully the peg doll and patting the rough fur of Ku Yum's cat.

Then she called her people together and said to them:

"Behold, I have found my heart's desire—a little sister."

And forever after O'Yam and Ku Yum lived happily together in a glad, beautiful, old palace surrounded by a glad, beautiful, old garden, on a charming little island in the middle of a lake.

PART IV

QUEER THINGS

I AND MY CHIMNEY

Herman Melville

I and my chimney, two grey-headed old smokers, reside in the country. We are, I may say, old settlers here; particularly my old chimney,
which settles more and more every day.

Though I always say, *I and my chimney*, as Cardinal Wolsey used to
say, *I and my King*, yet this egotistic way of speaking, wherein I take
precedence of my chimney, is hereby borne out by the facts; in everything, except the above phrase, my chimney taking precedence of me.

Within thirty feet of the turf-sided road, my chimney—a huge, cor-
pulent old Harry VIII. of a chimney—rises full in front of me and all my
possessions. Standing well up a hill-side, my chimney, like Lord Rosse's
monster telescope, swung vertical to hit the meridian moon, is the first
object to greet the approaching traveler's eye, nor is it the last which
the sun salutes. My chimney, too, is before me in receiving the first-
fruits of the seasons. The snow is on its head ere on my hat; and every
spring, as in a hollow beech tree, the first swallows build their nests
in it.

But it is within doors that the preëminence of my chimney is most
manifest. When in the rear room, set apart for that object, I stand to
receive my guests (who, by the way call more, I suspect, to see my
chimney than me), I then stand, not so much before, as, strictly

speaking, behind my chimney, which is, indeed, the true host. Not that I demur. In the presence of my betters, I hope I know my place.

From this habitual precedence of my chimney over me, some even think that I have got into a sad rearward way altogether; in short, from standing behind my old-fashioned chimney so much, I have got to be quite behind the age too, as well as running behind-hand in everything else. But to tell the truth, I never was a very forward old fellow, nor what my farming neighbors call a forehanded one. Indeed, those rumors about my behindhandedness are so far correct, that I have an odd sauntering way with me sometimes of going about with my hands behind my back. As for my belonging to the rear-guard in general, certain it is, I bring up the rear of my chimney—which, by the way, is this moment before me—and that, too, both in fancy and fact. In brief, my chimney is my superior; my superior by I know not how many heads and shoulders; my superior, too, in that humbly bowing over with shovel and tongs, I much minister to it; yet never does it minister, or incline over to me; but, if any thing, in its settlings, rather leans the other way.

My chimney is grand seignior here—the one great domineering object, not more of the landscape, than of the house; all the rest of which house, in each architectural arrangement, as may shortly appear, is, in the most marked manner, accommodated, not to my wants, but to my chimney's, which, among other things, has the centre of the house to himself, leaving but the odd holes and corners to me.

But I and my chimney must explain; and as we are both rather obese, we may have to expatiate.

In those houses which are strictly double houses—that is, where the hall is in the middle—the fire-places usually are on opposite sides; so that while one member of the household is warming himself at a fire built into a recess of the north wall, say another member, the former's own brother, perhaps, may be holding his feet to the blaze before a hearth in the south wall—the two thus fairly sitting back to back. Is this well? Be it put to any man who has a proper fraternal feeling. Has it not a sort of sulky appearance? But very probably this style of chimney building originated with some architect afflicted with a quarrelsome family.

Then again, almost every modern fire-place has its separate flue—separate throughout, from hearth to chimney-top. At least such an arrangement is deemed desirable. Does not this look egotistical, self-ish? But still more, all these separate flues, instead of having indepen-dent masonry establishments of their own, or instead of being grouped together in one federal stock in the middle of the house—instead of this, I say, each flue is surreptitiously honey-combed into the walls; so that these last are here and there, or indeed almost anywhere, treach-erously hollow, and, in consequence, more or less weak. Of course, the main reason of this style of chimney building is to economize room. In cities, where lots are sold by the inch, small space is to spare for a chimney constructed on magnanimous principles; and, as with most thin men, who are generally tall, so with such houses, what is lacking in breadth must be made up in height. This remark holds true even with regard to many very stylish abodes, built by the most stylish of gentlemen. And yet, when that stylish gentleman, Louis le Grand of France, would build a palace for his lady friend, Madame de Main-tenon, he built it but one story high—in fact in the cottage style. But then how uncommonly quadrangular, spacious, and broad—horizontal acres, not vertical ones. Such is the palace, which, in all its one-storied magnificence of Languedoc marble, in the garden of Versailles, still remains to this day. Any man can buy a square foot of land and plant a liberty-pole on it; but it takes a king to set apart whole acres for a grand Trianon.

But nowadays it is different; and furthermore, what originated in a necessity has been mounted into a vaunt. In towns there is large ri-valry in building tall houses. If one gentleman builds his house four stories high, and another gentleman comes next door and builds five stories high, then the former, not to be looked down upon that way, immediately sends for his architect and claps a fifth and a sixth story on top of his previous four. And, not till the gentleman has achieved his aspiration, not till he has stolen over the way by twilight and observed how his sixth story soars beyond his neighbor's fifth—not till then does he retire to his rest with satisfaction.

Such folks, it seems to me, need mountains for neighbors, to take this emulous conceit of soaring out of them.

If, considering that mine is a very wide house, and by no means lofty, aught in the above may appear like interested pleading, as if I did but fold myself about in the cloak of a general proposition, cunningly to tickle my individual vanity beneath it, such misconception must vanish upon my frankly conceding, that land adjoining my alder swamp was sold last month for ten dollars an acre, and thought a rash purchase at that; so that for wide houses hereabouts there is plenty of room, and cheap. Indeed so cheap—dirt cheap—is the soil, that our elms thrust out their roots in it, and hang their great boughs over it, in the most lavish and reckless way. Almost all our crops, too, are sown broadcast, even peas and turnips. A farmer among us, who should go about his twenty-acre field, poking his finger into it here and there, and dropping down a mustard seed, would be thought a penurious, narrow-minded husbandman. The dandelions in the river-meadows, and the forget-me-nots along the mountain roads, you see at once they are put to no economy in space. Some seasons, too, our rye comes up, here and there a spear, sole and single like a church-spire. It doesn't care to crowd itself where it knows there is such a deal of room. The world is wide, the world is all before us, says the rye. Weeds, too, it is amazing how they spread. No such thing as arresting them—some of our pastures being a sort of Alsatia for the weeds. As for the grass, every spring it is like Kossuth's rising of what he calls the peoples. Mountains, too, a regular camp-meeting of them. For the same reason, the same all-sufficiency of room, our shadows march and countermarch, going through their various drills and masterly evolutions, like the old imperial guard on the Champs de Mars. As for the hills, especially where the roads cross them, the supervisors of our various towns have given notice to all concerned, that they can come and dig them down and cart them off, and never a cent to pay, no more than for the privilege of picking blackberries. The stranger who is buried here, what liberal-hearted landed proprietor among us grudges him his six feet of rocky pasture?

Nevertheless, cheap, after all, as our land is, and much as it is trodden under foot, I, for one, am proud of it for what it bears; and chiefly for its three great lions—the Great Oak, Ogg Mountain, and my chimney.

Most houses, here, are but one and a half stories high; few exceed two. That in which I and my chimney dwell, is in width nearly twice its height, from sill to eaves—which accounts for the magnitude of its main content—besides, showing that in this house, as in this country at large, there is abundance of space, and to spare, for both of us.

The frame of the old house is of wood—which but the more sets forth the solidity of the chimney, which is of brick. And as the great wrought nails, binding the clapboards, are unknown in these degenerate days, so are the huge bricks in the chimney walls. The architect of the chimney must have had the pyramid of Cheops before him; for, after that famous structure, it seems modeled, only its rate of decrease towards the summit is considerably less, and it is truncated. From the exact middle of the mansion it soars from the cellar, right up through each successive floor, till, four feet square, it breaks water from the ridge-pole of the roof, like an anvil-headed whale, through the crest of a billow. Most people, though, liken it, in that part, to a razeed observatory, masoned up.

The reason for its peculiar appearance above the roof touches upon rather delicate ground. How shall I reveal that, forasmuch as many years ago the original gable roof of the old house had become very leaky, a temporary proprietor hired a band of woodmen, with their huge, cross-cut saws, and went to sawing the old gable roof clean off. Off it went, with all its birds' nests, and dormer windows. It was replaced with a modern roof, more fit for a railway wood-house than an old country gentleman's abode. This operation—razeeing the structure some fifteen feet—was, in effect upon the chimney, something like the falling of the great spring tides. It left uncommon low water all about the chimney—to abate which appearance, the same person now proceeds to slice fifteen feet off the chimney itself, actually beheading my royal old chimney—a regicidal act, which, were it not for the palliating fact, that he was a poulterer by trade, and, therefore, hardened to such neck-wringings, should send that former proprietor down to posterity in the same cart with Cromwell.

Owing to its pyramidal shape, the reduction of the chimney inordinately widened its razeed summit. Inordinately, I say, but only in the estimation of such as have no eye to the picturesque. What care I, if, unaware that my chimney, as a free citizen of this free land, stands upon an independent basis of its own, people passing it, wonder how such a brick-kiln, as they call it, is supported upon mere joists and rafters? What care I? I will give a traveler a cup of switchel, if he want it; but am I bound to supply him with a sweet taste? Men of cultivated minds see, in my old house and chimney, a goodly old elephant-and-castle.

All feeling hearts will sympathize with me in what I am now about to add. The surgical operation, above referred to, necessarily brought into the open air a part of the chimney previously under cover, and intended to remain so, and, therefore, not built of what are called weather-bricks. In consequence, the chimney, though of a vigorous constitution, suffered not a little, from so naked an exposure; and, unable to acclimate itself, ere long began to fail—showing blotchy symptoms akin to those in measles. Whereupon travelers, passing my way, would wag their heads, laughing: "See that wax nose—how it melts off!" But what cared I? The same travelers would travel across the sea to view Kenilworth peeling away, and for a very good reason: that of all artists of the picturesque, decay wears the palm—I would say, the ivy. In fact, I've often thought that the proper place for my old chimney is ivied old England.

In vain my wife—with what probable ulterior intent will, ere long, appear—solemnly warned me, that unless something were done, and speedily, we should be burnt to the ground, owing to the holes crumbling through the aforesaid blotchy parts, where the chimney joined the roof. "Wife," said I, "far better that my house should burn down, than that my chimney should be pulled down, though but a few feet. They call it a wax nose; very good; not for me to tweak the nose of my superior." But at last the man who has a mortgage on the house dropped me a note, reminding me that, if my chimney was allowed to stand in that invalid condition, my policy of insurance would be void. This was a sort of hint not to be neglected. All the world over, the picturesque yields to the pocketesque. The mortgagor cared not, but the mortgagee did.

So another operation was performed. The wax nose was taken off, and a new one fitted on. Unfortunately for the expression—being put up by a squint-eyed mason, who, at the time, had a bad stitch in the same side—the new nose stands a little awry, in the same direction.

Of one thing, however, I am proud. The horizontal dimensions of the new part are unreduced.

Large as the chimney appears upon the roof, that is nothing to its spaciousness below. At its base in the cellar, it is precisely twelve feet square; and hence covers precisely one hundred and forty-four superficial feet. What an appropriation of terra firma for a chimney, and what a huge load for this earth! In fact, it was only because I and my chimney formed no part of his ancient burden, that that stout peddler,

Atlas of old, was enabled to stand up so bravely under his pack. The dimensions given may, perhaps, seem fabulous. But, like those stones at Gilgal, which Joshua set up for a memorial of having passed over Jordan, does not my chimney remain, even unto this day?

Very often I go down into my cellar, and attentively survey that vast square of masonry. I stand long, and ponder over, and wonder at it. It has a druidical look, away down in the umbrageous cellar there, whose numerous vaulted passages, and far glens of gloom, resemble the dark, damp depths of primeval woods. So strongly did this conceit steal over me, so deeply was I penetrated with wonder at the chimney, that one day—when I was a little out of my mind, I now think—getting a spade from the garden, I set to work, digging round the foundation, especially at the corners thereof, obscurely prompted by dreams of striking upon some old, earthen-worn memorial of that by-gone day, when, into all this gloom, the light of heaven entered, as the masons laid the foundation-stones, peradventure sweltering under an August sun, or pelted by a March storm. Plying my blunted spade, how vexed was I by that ungracious interruption of a neighbor, who, calling to see me upon some business, and being informed that I was below, said I need not be troubled to come up, but he would go down to me; and so, without ceremony, and without my having been forewarned, suddenly discovered me, digging in my cellar.

"Gold digging, sir?"

"Nay, sir," answered I, starting, "I was merely—ahem!—merely—I say I was merely digging—round my chimney."

"Ah, loosening the soil, to make it grow. Your chimney, sir, you regard as too small, I suppose; needing further development, especially at the top?"

"Sir!" said I, throwing down the spade, "do not be personal. I and my chimney—"

"Personal?"

"Sir, I look upon this chimney less as a pile of masonry than as a personage. It is the king of the house. I am but a suffered and inferior subject."

In fact, I would permit no gibes to be cast at either myself or my chimney; and never again did my visitor refer to it in my hearing, without coupling some compliment with the mention. It well deserves a respectful consideration. There it stands, solitary and alone—not a council-of-ten flues, but, like his sacred majesty of Russia, a unit of an autocrat.

Even to me, its dimensions, at times, seem incredible. It does not look so big—no, not even in the cellar. By the mere eye, its magnitude can be but imperfectly comprehended, because only one side can be received at one time; and said side can only present twelve feet, linear measure. But then, each other side also is twelve feet long; and the whole obviously forms a square; and twelve times twelve is one hundred and forty-four. And so, an adequate conception of the magnitude of this chimney is only to be got at by a sort of process in the higher mathematics, by a method somewhat akin to those whereby the surprising distances of fixed stars are computed.

It need hardly be said, that the walls of my house are entirely free from fire-places. These all congregate in the middle—in the one grand central chimney, upon all four sides of which are hearths—two tiers of hearths—so that when, in the various chambers, my family and guests are warming themselves of a cold winter's night, just before retiring, then, though at the time they may not be thinking so, all their faces mutually look towards each other, yea, all their feet point to one centre; and, when they go to sleep in their beds, they all sleep round one warm chimney, like so many Iroquois Indians, in the woods, round their one heap of embers. And just as the Indians' fire serves, not only to keep them comfortable, but also to keep off wolves, and other savage monsters, so my chimney, by its obvious smoke at top, keeps off prowling burglars from the towns—for what burglar or murderer would dare break into an abode from whose chimney issues such a continual smoke—betokening that if the inmates are not stirring, at least fires are, and in case of an alarm, candles may readily be lighted, to say nothing of muskets.

But stately as is the chimney—yea, grand high altar as it is, right worthy for the celebration of high mass before the Pope of Rome, and all his cardinals—yet what is there perfect in this world? Caius Julius Cæsar, had he not been so inordinately great, they say that Brutus, Cassius, Antony, and the rest, had been greater. My chimney, were it not so mighty in its magnitude, my chambers had been larger. How often has my wife ruefully told me, that my chimney, like the English aristocracy, casts a contracting shade all round it. She avers that endless domestic inconveniences arise—more particularly from the chimney's stubborn central locality. The grand objection with her is, that it stands midway in the place where a fine entrance-hall ought to be. In truth, there is no hall whatever to the house—nothing but a sort of square landing-place, as you enter from the wide front door. A roomy enough landing-place, I admit, but not attaining to the dignity of a hall. Now, as the front door is precisely in the middle of the front of the house, inwards it faces the chimney. In fact, the opposite wall of the landing-place is formed solely by the chimney; and hence—owing to the gradual tapering of the chimney—is a little less than twelve feet in width. Climbing the chimney in this part, is the principal stair-case— which, by three abrupt turns, and three minor landing-places, mounts to the second floor, where, over the front door, runs a sort of narrow gallery, something less than twelve feet long, leading to chambers on either hand. This gallery, of course, is railed; and so, looking down upon the stairs, and all those landing-places together, with the main one at bottom, resembles not a little a balcony for musicians, in some jolly old abode, in times Elizabethan. Shall I tell a weakness? I cherish the cobwebs there, and many a time arrest Biddy in the act of brushing them with her broom, and have many a quarrel with my wife and daughters about it.

Now the ceiling, so to speak, of the place where you enter the house, that ceiling is, in fact, the ceiling of the second floor, not the first. The two floors are made one here; so that ascending this turning stairs, you seem going up into a kind of soaring tower, or light-house. At the second landing, midway up the chimney, is a mysterious door, entering to a mysterious closet; and here I keep mysterious cordials, of a choice, mysterious flavor, made so by the constant nurturing and subtle ripening of the chimney's gentle heat, distilled through that warm mass of masonry. Better for wines is it than voyages to the Indies; my chimney itself a tropic. A chair by my chimney in a November day is as good for an invalid as a long season spent in Cuba. Often I think how grapes might ripen against my chimney. How my wife's geraniums bud there! Bud in December. Her eggs, too—can't keep them near the chimney, on account of the hatching. Ah, a warm heart has my chimney.

How often my wife was at me about that projected grand entrance-hall of hers, which was to be knocked clean through the chimney, from one end of the house to the other, and astonish all guests by its generous amplitude. "But, wife," said I, "the chimney—consider the chimney:

if you demolish the foundation, what is to support the superstructure?"
"Oh, that will rest on the second floor." The truth is, women know next
to nothing about the realities of architecture. However, my wife still
talked of running her entries and partitions. She spent many long
nights elaborating her plans; in imagination building her boasted hall
through the chimney, as though its high mightiness were a mere spear
of sorrel-top. At last, I gently reminded her that, little as she might
fancy it, the chimney was a fact—a sober, substantial fact, which, in all
her plannings, it would be well to take into full consideration. But this
was not of much avail.

And here, respectfully craving her permission, I must say a few
words about this enterprising wife of mine. Though in years nearly old
as myself, in spirit she is young as my little sorrel mare, Trigger, that
threw me last fall. What is extraordinary, though she comes of a rheu-
matic family, she is straight as a pine, never has any aches; while for
me with the sciatica, I am sometimes as crippled up as any old apple
tree. But she has not so much as a toothache. As for her hearing—let
me enter the house in my dusty boots, and she away up in the attic.
And for her sight—Biddy, the housemaid, tells other people's house-
maids, that her mistress will spy a spot on the dresser straight through
the pewter platter, put up on purpose to hide it. Her faculties are alert
as her limbs and her senses. No danger of my spouse dying of torpor.
The longest night in the year I've known her lie awake, planning her
campaign for the morrow. She is a natural projector. The maxim,
"Whatever is, is right," is not hers. Her maxim is, Whatever is, is wrong;
and what is more, must be altered; and what is still more, must be altered right away. Dreadful maxim for the wife of a dozy old dreamer
like me, who dote on seventh days as days of rest, and out of a sabbat-
ical horror of industry, will, on a week day, go out of my road a quarter
of a mile, to avoid the sight of a man at work.

That matches are made in heaven, may be, but my wife would have
been just the wife for Peter the Great, or Peter the Piper. How she
would have set in order that huge littered empire of the one, and with
indefatigable painstaking picked the peck of pickled peppers for the
other.

But the most wonderful thing is, my wife never thinks of her end.
Her youthful incredulity, as to the plain theory, and still plainer fact of
death, hardly seems Christian. Advanced in years, as she knows she

must be, my wife seems to think that she is to teem on, and be inexhaustible forever. She doesn't believe in old age. At that strange promise in the plain of Mamre, my old wife, unlike old Abraham's, would not have jeeringly laughed within herself.

Judge how to me, who, sitting in the comfortable shadow of my chimney, smoking my comfortable pipe, with ashes not unwelcome at my feet, and ashes not unwelcome all but in my mouth; and who am thus in a comfortable sort of not unwelcome, though, indeed, ashy enough way, reminded of the ultimate exhaustion even of the most fiery life; judge how to me this unwarrantable vitality in my wife must come, sometimes, it is true, with a moral and a calm, but oftener with a breeze and a ruffle.

If the doctrine be true, that in wedlock contraries attract, by how cogent a fatality must I have been drawn to my wife! While spicily impatient of present and past, like a glass of ginger-beer she overflows with her schemes; and, with like energy as she puts down her foot, puts down her preserves and her pickles, and lives with them in a continual future; or ever full of expectations both from time and space, is ever restless for newspapers, and ravenous for letters. Content with the years that are gone, taking no thought for the morrow, and looking for no new thing from any person or quarter whatever, I have not a single scheme or expectation on earth, save in unequal resistance of the undue encroachment of hers.

Old myself, I take to oldness in things; for that cause mainly loving old Montaigne, and old cheese, and old wine; and eschewing young people, hot rolls, new books, and early potatoes, and very fond of my old claw-footed chair, and old club-footed Deacon White, my neighbor, and that still nigher old neighbor, my betwisted old grape-vine, that of a summer evening leans in his elbow for cosy company at my windowsill, while I, within doors, lean over mine to meet his; and above all, high above all, am fond of my high-mantled old chimney. But she, out of that infatuate juvenility of hers, takes to nothing but newness; for that cause mainly, loving new cider in autumn, and in spring, as if she were own daughter of Nebuchadnezzar, fairly raving after all sorts of salads and spinages, and more particularly green cucumbers (though all the time nature rebukes such unsuitable young hankerings in so elderly a person, by never permitting such things to agree with her), and has an itch after recently-discovered fine prospects (so no grave-yard be in the background), and also after Swedenborgianism, and the Spirit Rapping philosophy, with other new views, alike in things natural and unnatural; and immortally hopeful, is forever making new flower-beds even on the north side of the house, where the bleak mountain wind would scarce allow the wiry weed called hard-hack to gain a thorough footing; and on the road-side sets out mere pipe-stems of young elms; though there is no hope of any shade from them, except over the ruins of her great granddaughter's grave-stones; and won't wear caps, but plaits her gray hair; and takes the Ladies' Magazine for the fashions; and always buys her new almanac a month before the new year; and rises at dawn; and to the warmest sunset turns a cold shoulder; and still goes on at odd hours with her new course of history, and her French, and her music; and likes young company; and offers to ride young colts; and sets out young suckers in the orchard; and has a spite against my elbowed old grape-vine, and my club-footed old neighbor, and my claw-footed old chair, and above all, high above all, would fain persecute, until death, my high-mantled old chimney. By what perverse magic, I a thousand times think, does such a very autumnal old lady have such a very vernal young soul? When I would remonstrate at times, she spins round on me with, "Oh, don't you grumble, old man (she always calls me old man), it's I, young I, that keep you from stagnating." Well, I suppose it is so. Yea, after all, these things are well ordered. My wife, as one of her poor relations, good soul, intimates, is the salt of the earth, and none the less the salt of my sea, which otherwise were unwholesome. She is its monsoon, too, blowing a brisk gale over it, in the one steady direction of my chimney.

Not insensible of her superior energies, my wife has frequently made me propositions to take upon herself all the responsibilities of my affairs. She is desirous that, domestically, I should abdicate; that, renouncing further rule, like the venerable Charles V., I should retire into some sort of monastery. But indeed, the chimney excepted, I have little authority to lay down. By my wife's ingenious application of the principle that certain things belong of right to female jurisdiction, I find myself, through my easy compliances, insensibly stripped by degrees of one masculine prerogative after another. In a dream I go about my fields, a sort of lazy, happy-go-lucky, good-for-nothing, loafing, old Lear. Only by some sudden revelation am I reminded who is over me; as year before last, one day seeing in one corner of the premises fresh deposits of mysterious boards and timbers, the oddity of the incident at length begat serious meditation. "Wife," said I, "whose boards and timbers are those I see near the orchard there? Do you know any thing about them, wife? Who put them there? You know I do not like the neighbors to use my land that way; they should ask permission first."

She regarded me with a pitying smile.

"Why, old man, don't you know I am building a new barn? Didn't you know that, old man?"

This is the poor old lady that was accusing me of tyrannizing over her.

To return now to the chimney. Upon being assured of the futility of her proposed hall, so long as the obstacle remained, for a time my wife was for a modified project. But I could never exactly comprehend it. As far as I could see through it, it seemed to involve the general idea of a sort of irregular archway, or elbowed tunnel, which was to penetrate the chimney at some convenient point under the staircase, and carefully avoiding dangerous contact with the fire-places, and particularly steering clear of the great interior flue, was to conduct the enterprising traveler from the front door all the way into the dining-room in the remote rear of the mansion. Doubtless it was a bold stroke of genius, that plan of hers, and so was Nero's when he schemed his grand canal through the Isthmus of Corinth. Nor will I take oath, that, had her project been accomplished, then, by help of lights hung at judicious intervals through the tunnel, some Belzoni or other might have succeeded in future ages in penetrating through the masonry, and actually emerging into the dining-room, and once there, it would have been inhospitable treatment of such a traveler to have denied him a recruiting meal.

But my bustling wife did not restrict her objections, nor in the end confine her proposed alterations to the first floor. Her ambition was of the mounting order. She ascended with her schemes to the second floor, and so to the attic. Perhaps there was some small ground for her discontent with things as they were. The truth is, there was no regular passage-way up stairs or down, unless we again except that little orchestra-gallery before mentioned. And all this was owing to the chimney, which my gamesome spouse seemed despitefully to regard as the bully of the house. On all its four sides, nearly all the chambers sidled up to the chimney for the benefit of a fire-place. The chimney would not go to them; they must needs go to it. The consequence was, almost every room, like a philosophical system, was in itself an entry, or passage-way to other rooms, and systems of rooms—a whole suite of entries, in fact. Going through the house, you seem to be forever going somewhere, and getting nowhere. It is like losing one's self in the woods; round and round the chimney you go, and if you arrive at all, it is just where you started, and so you begin again, and again get no-where. Indeed—though I say it not in the way of fault-finding at all—never was there so labyrinthine an abode. Guests will tarry with me several weeks and every now and then, be anew astonished at some unforeseen apartment.

The puzzling nature of the mansion, resulting from the chimney, is peculiarly noticeable in the dining-room, which has no less than nine doors, opening in all directions, and into all sorts of places. A stranger for the first time entering this dining-room, and naturally taking no special heed at what door he entered, will, upon rising to depart, com-mit the strangest blunders. Such, for instance, as opening the first door that comes handy, and finding himself stealing up stairs by the back passage. Shutting that door, he will proceed to another, and be aghast at the cellar yawning at his feet. Trying a third, he surprises the house-maid at her work. In the end, no more relying on his own unaided ef-forts, he procures a trusty guide in some passing person, and in good time successfully emerges. Perhaps as curious a blunder as any, was that of a certain stylish young gentleman, a great exquisite, in whose judicious eyes my daughter Anna had found especial favor. He called upon the young lady one evening, and found her alone in the dining-room at her needle-work. He stayed rather late; and after abundance of superfine discourse, all the while retaining his hat and cane, made his profuse adieus, and with repeated graceful bows proceeded to de-part, after the fashion of courtiers from the Queen, and by so doing, opening a door at random, with one hand placed behind, very effectu-ally succeeded in backing himself into a dark pantry, where be care-fully shut himself up, wondering there was no light in the entry. After several strange noises as of a cat among the crockery, he reappeared through the same door, looking uncommonly crest-fallen, and, with a deeply embarrassed air, requested my daughter to designate at which of the nine he should find exit. When the mischievous Anna told me the story, she said it was surprising how unaffected and matter-of-fact the young gentleman's manner was after his reappearance. He was more candid than ever, to be sure; having inadvertently thrust his white kids into an open drawer of Havana sugar, under the impression, probably, that being what they call "a sweet fellow," his route might possibly lie in that direction.

Another inconvenience resulting from the chimney is, the bewilderment of a guest in gaining his chamber, many strange doors lying between him and it. To direct him by finger-posts would look rather queer; and just as queer in him to be knocking at every door on his route, like London's city guest, the king, at Temple Bar.

Now, of all these things and many, many more, my family continually complained. At last my wife came out with her sweeping proposition—in toto to abolish the chimney.

"What!" said I, "abolish the chimney? To take out the back-bone of anything, wife, is a hazardous affair. Spines out of backs, and chimneys out of houses, are not to be taken like frosted lead-pipes from the ground. Besides," added I, "the chimney is the one grand permanence of this abode. If undisturbed by innovators, then in future ages, when all the house shall have crumbled from it, this chimney will still survive—a Bunker Hill monument. No, no, wife, I can't abolish my back-bone."

So said I then. But who is sure of himself, especially an old man, with both wife and daughters ever at his elbow and ear? In time, I was persuaded to think a little better of it; in short, to take the matter into preliminary consideration. At length it came to pass that a master-mason—a rough sort of architect—one Mr. Scribe, was summoned to a conference. I formally introduced him to my chimney. A previous introduction from my wife had introduced him to myself. He had been not a little employed by that lady, in preparing plans and estimates for some of her extensive operations in drainage. Having, with much ado, extorted from my spouse the promise that she would leave us to an unmolested survey, I began by leading Mr. Scribe down to the root of the matter, in the cellar. Lamp in hand, I descended; for though up stairs it was noon, below it was night.

We seemed in the pyramids; and I, with one hand holding my lamp over head, and with the other pointing out, in the obscurity, the hoar mass of the chimney, seemed some Arab guide, showing the cobwebbed mausoleum of the great god Apis.

"This is a most remarkable structure, sir," said the master-mason, after long contemplating it in silence, "a most remarkable structure, sir."

"Yes," said I complacently, "every one says so."

"But large as it appears above the roof, I would not have inferred the magnitude of this foundation, sir," eyeing it critically.

Then taking out his rule, he measured it.

"Twelve feet square; one hundred and forty-four square feet! sir, this house would appear to have been built simply for the accommodation of your chimney."

"Yes, my chimney and me. Tell me candidly, now," I added, "would you have such a famous chimney abolished?"

"I wouldn't have it in a house of mine, sir, for a gift," was the reply. "It's a losing affair altogether, sir. Do you know, sir, that in retaining this chimney, you are losing, not only one hundred and forty-four square feet of good ground, but likewise a considerable interest upon a considerable principal?"

"How?"

"Look, sir!" said he, taking a bit of red chalk from his pocket, and figuring against a whitewashed wall, "twenty times eight is so and so; then forty-two times thirty-nine is so and so—aint it, sir? Well, add those together, and subtract this here, then that makes so and so," still chalking away.

To be brief, after no small ciphering, Mr. Scribe informed me that my chimney contained, I am ashamed to say how many thousand and odd valuable bricks.

"No more," said I fidgeting. "Pray now, let us have a look above."

In that upper zone we made two more circumnavigations for the first and second floors. That done, we stood together at the foot of the stairway by the front door; my hand upon the knob, and Mr. Scribe hat in hand.

"Well, sir," said he, a sort of feeling his way, and, to help himself, fumbling with his hat, "well, sir, I think it can be done."

"What, pray, Mr. Scribe; *what* can be done?"

"Your chimney, sir; it can without rashness be removed, I think."

"*I* will think of it, too, Mr. Scribe," said I, turning the knob and bowing him towards the open space without, "I will *think* of it, sir; it demands consideration; much obliged to ye; good morning, Mr. Scribe."

"It is all arranged, then," cried my wife with great glee, bursting from the nighest room.

"When will they begin?" demanded my daughter Julia.

"To-morrow?" asked Anna.

"Patience, patience, my dears," said I, "such a big chimney is not to be abolished in a minute."

Next morning it began again.

"You remember the chimney," said my wife.

"Wife," said I, "it is never out of my house, and never out of my mind."

"But when is Mr. Scribe to begin to pull it down?" asked Anna.

"Not to-day, Anna," said I.

"*When*, then?" demanded Julia, in alarm.

Now, if this chimney of mine was, for size, a sort of belfry, for ding-donging at me about it, my wife and daughters were a sort of bells, always chiming together, or taking up each other's melodies at every pause, my wife the key-clapper of all. A very sweet ringing, and pealing, and chiming, I confess; but then, the most silvery of bells may, sometimes, dismally toll, as well as merrily play. And as touching the subject in question, it became so now. Perceiving a strange relapse of opposition in me, wife and daughters began a soft and dirge-like, melancholy tolling over it.

At length my wife, getting much excited, declared to me, with pointed finger, that so long as that chimney stood, she should regard it as the monument of what she called my broken pledge. But finding this did not answer, the next day, she gave me to understand that either she or the chimney must quit the house.

Finding matters coming to such a pass, I and my pipe philosophized over them awhile, and finally concluded between us, that little as our hearts went with the plan, yet for peace' sake, I might write out the chimney's death-warrant, and, while my hand was in, scratch a note to Mr. Scribe.

Considering that I, and my chimney, and my pipe, from having been so much together, were three great cronies, the facility with which my pipe consented to a project so fatal to the goodliest of our trio; or rather, the way in which I and my pipe, in secret, conspired togetber, as it were, against our unsuspicious old comrade—this may seem rather strange, if not suggestive of sad reflections upon us two. But, indeed, we, sons of clay, that is my pipe and I, are no whit better than the rest. Far from us, indeed, to have volunteered the betrayal of our crony. We are of a peaceable nature, too. But that love of peace it was which made us false to a mutual friend, as soon as his cause demanded a vigorous vindication. But I rejoice to add, that better and braver thoughts soon returned, as will now briefly be set forth.

To my note, Mr. Scribe replied in person.

Once more we made a survey, mainly now with a view to a pecuniary estimate.

"I will do it for five hundred dollars," said Mr. Scribe at last, again hat in hand.

"Very well, Mr. Scribe, I will think of it," replied I, again bowing him to the door.

Not unvexed by this, for the second time, unexpected response, again he withdrew, and from my wife and daughters again burst the old exclamations.

The truth is, resolved how I would, at the last pinch I and my chimney could not be parted.

"So Holofernes will have his way, never mind whose heart breaks for it," said my wife next morning, at breakfast, in that half-didactic, half-reproachful way of hers, which is harder to bear than her most energetic assault, Holofernes, too, is with her a pet name for any fell domestic despot. So, whenever, against her most ambitious innovations, those which saw me quite across the grain, I, as in the present instance, stand with however little steadfastness on the defence, she is sure to call me Holofernes, and ten to one takes the first opportunity to read aloud, with a suppressed emphasis, of an evening, the first newspaper paragraph about some tyrannic day-laborer, who, after being for many years the Caligula of his family, ends by beating his long-suffering spouse to death, with a garret door wrenched off its hinges, and then, pitching his little innocents out of the window, suicidally turns inward towards the broken wall scored with the butcher's and baker's bills, and so rushes headlong to his dreadful account.

Nevertheless, for a few days, not a little to my surprise, I heard no further reproaches. An intense calm pervaded my wife, but beneath which, as in the sea, there was no knowing what portentous movements might be going on. She frequently went abroad, and in a direction which I thought not unsuspicious; namely, in the direction of New

Petra, a griffin-like house of wood and stucco, in the highest style of ornamental art, graced with four chimneys in the form of erect dragons spouting smoke from their nostrils; the elegant modern residence of Mr. Scribe, which he had built for the purpose of a standing advertisement, not more of his taste as an architect, than his solidity as a master-mason.

At last, smoking my pipe one morning, I heard a rap at the door, and my wife, with an air unusually quiet for her, brought me a note. As I have no correspondents except Solomon, with whom, in his sentiments, at least, I entirely correspond, the note occasioned me some little surprise, which was not diminished upon reading the following:—

"NEW PETRA, April 1st.

"SIR:—During my last examination of your chimney, possibly you may have noted that I frequently applied my rule to it in a manner apparently unnecessary. Possibly also, at the same time, you might have observed in me more or less of perplexity, to which, however, I refrained from giving any verbal expression.

"I now feel it obligatory upon me to inform you of what was then but a dim suspicion, and as such would have been unwise to give utterance to, but which now, from various subsequent calculations assuming no little probability, it may be important that you should not remain in further ignorance of.

"It is my solemn duty to warn you, sir, that there is architectural cause to conjecture that somewhere concealed in your chimney is a reserved space, hermetically closed, in short, a secret chamber, or rather closet. How long it has been there, it is for me impossible to say. What it contains is hid, with itself, in darkness. But probably a secret closet would not have been contrived except for some extraordinary object, whether for the concealment of treasure, or what other purpose, may be left to those better acquainted with the history of the house to guess.

"But enough: in making this disclosure, sir, my conscience is eased. Whatever step you choose to take upon it, is of course a matter of indifference to me; though, I confess, as respects the character of the closet, I cannot but share in a natural curiosity.

"Trusting that you may be guided aright, in determining

whether it is Christian-like knowingly to reside in a house, hidden in which is a secret closet,

"I remain,

"With much respect,

"Yours very humbly,

"HIRAM SCRIBE."

My first thought upon reading this note was, not of the alleged mystery of manner to which, at the outset, it alluded—for none such had I at all observed in the master-mason during his surveys—but of my late kinsman, Captain Julian Dacres, long a ship-master and merchant in the Indian trade, who, about thirty years ago, and at the ripe age of ninety, died a bachelor, and in this very house, which he had built. He was supposed to have retired into this country with a large fortune. But to the general surprise, after being at great cost in building himself this mansion, he settled down into a sedate, reserved, and inexpensive old age, which by the neighbors was thought all the better for his heirs: but lo! upon opening the will, his property was found to consist but of the house and grounds, and some ten thousand dollars in stocks; but the place, being found heavily mortgaged, was in consequence sold. Gossip had its day, and left the grass quietly to creep over the captain's grave, where he still slumbers in a privacy as unmolested as if the billows of the Indian Ocean, instead of the billows of inland verdure, rolled over him. Still, I remembered long ago, hearing strange solutions whispered by the country people for the mystery involving his will, and, by reflex, himself; and that, too, as well in conscience as purse. But people who could circulate the report (which they did), that Captain Julian Dacres had, in his day, been a Borneo pirate, surely were not worthy of credence in their collateral notions. It is queer what wild whimsies of rumors will, like toadstools, spring up about any eccentric stranger, who, settling down among a rustic population, keeps quietly to himself. With some, inoffensiveness would seem a prime cause of offense. But what chiefly had led me to scout at these rumors, particularly as referring to concealed treasure, was the circumstance, that the stranger (the same who razeed the roof and the chimney) into whose hands the estate had passed on my kinsman's death, was of that sort of character, that had there been the least ground for those reports, he would speedily have tested them, by tearing down and rummaging the walls.

Nevertheless, the note of Mr. Scribe, so strangely recalling the memory of my kinsman, very naturally chimed in with what had been mysterious, or at least unexplained, about him; vague flashings of ingots united in my mind with vague gleamings of skulls. But the first cool thought soon dismissed such chimeras; and, with a calm smile, I turned towards my wife, who, meantime, had been sitting near by, impatient enough, I dare say, to know who could have taken it into his head to write me a letter.

"Well, old man," said she, "who is it from, and what is it about?"

"Read it, wife," said I, handing it.

Read it she did, and then—such an explosion! I will not pretend to describe her emotions, or repeat her expressions. Enough that my daughters were quickly called in to share the excitement. Although they had never before dreamed of such a revelation as Mr. Scribe's; yet upon the first suggestion they instinctively saw the extreme likelihood of it. In corroboration, they cited first my kinsman, and second, my chimney; alleging that the profound mystery involving the former, and the equally profound masonry involving the latter, though both acknowledged facts, were alike preposterous on any other supposition than the secret closet.

But all this time I was quietly thinking to myself: Could it be hidden from me that my credulity in this instance would operate very favorably to a certain plan of theirs? How to get to the secret closet, or how to have any certainty about it at all, without making such fell work with the chimney as to render its set destruction superfluous? That my wife wished to get rid of the chimney, it needed no reflection to show; and that Mr. Scribe, for all his pretended disinterestedness, was not opposed to pocketing five hundred dollars by the operation, seemed equally evident. That my wife had, in secret, laid heads together with Mr. Scribe, I at present refrain from affirming. But when I consider her enmity against my chimney, and the steadiness with which at the last she is wont to carry out her schemes, if by hook or by crook she can, especially after having been once baffled, why, I scarcely knew at what step of hers to be surprised.

Of one thing only was I resolved, that I and my chimney should not budge.

In vain all protests. Next morning I went out into the road, where I had noticed a diabolical-looking old gander, that, for its doughty exploits in the way of scratching into forbidden enclosures, had been rewarded by its master with a portentous, four-pronged, wooden decoration, in the shape of a collar of the Order of the Garotte. This gander I cornered, and rummaging out its stiffest quill, plucked it, took it home, and making a stiff pen, inscribed the following stiff note:

"CHIMNEY SIDE, April 2.

"MR. SCRIBE.

"Sir:—For your conjecture, we return you our joint thanks and compliments, and beg leave to assure you, that
"We shall remain,
"Very faithfully,
"The same,
"I and my Chimney."

Of course, for this epistle we had to endure some pretty sharp raps. But having at last explicitly understood from me that Mr. Scribe's note had not altered my mind one jot, my wife, to move me, among other things said, that if she remembered aright, there was a statute placing the keeping in private houses of secret closets on the same unlawful footing with the keeping of gunpowder. But it had no effect.

A few days after, my spouse changed her key.

It was nearly midnight, and all were in bed but ourselves, who sat up, one in each chimney-corner; she, needles in hand, indefatigably knitting a sock; I, pipe in mouth, indolently weaving my vapors.

It was one of the first of the chill nights in autumn. There was a fire on the hearth, burning low. The air without was torpid and heavy; the wood, by an oversight, of the sort called soggy.

"Do look at the chimney," she began; "can't you see that something must be in it?"

"Yes, wife. Truly there is smoke in the chimney, as in Mr. Scribe's note."

"Smoke? Yes, indeed, and in my eyes, too. How you two wicked old sinners do smoke!—this wicked old chimney and you."

"Wife," said I, "I and my chimney like to have a quiet smoke together, it is true, but we don't like to be called names."

"Now, dear old man," said she, softening down, and a little shifting the subject, "when you think of that old kinsman of yours, you *know* there must be a secret closet in this chimney."

"Secret ash-hole, wife, why don't you have it? Yes, I dare say there is a secret ash-hole in the chimney; for where do all the ashes go to that we drop down the queer hole yonder?"

"I know where they go to; I've been there almost as many times as the cat."

"What devil, wife, prompted you to crawl into the ash-hole! Don't you know that St. Dunstan's devil emerged from the ash-hole? You will get your death one of these days, exploring all about as you do. But supposing there be a secret closet, what then?"

"What, then? why what should be in a secret closet but—"

"Dry bones, wife," broke in I with a puff, while the sociable old chimney broke in with another.

"There again! Oh, how this wretched old chimney smokes," wiping her eyes with her handkerchief. "I've no doubt the reason it smokes so is, because that secret closet interferes with the flue. Do see, too, how the jams here keep settling; and it's down hill all the way from the door to this hearth. This horrid old chimney will fall on our heads yet; depend upon it, old man."

"Yes, wife, I do depend on it; yes, indeed, I place every dependence on my chimney. As for its settling, I like it. I, too, am settling, you know, in my gait. I and my chimney are settling together, and shall keep settling, too, till, as in a great feather-bed, we shall both have settled away clean out of sight. But this secret oven; I mean, secret closet of yours, wife; where exactly do you suppose that secret closet is?"

"That is for Mr. Scribe to say."

"But suppose he cannot say exactly; what, then?"

"Why then he can prove, I am sure, that it must be somewhere or other in this horrid old chimney."

"And if he can't prove that; what, then?"

"Why then, old man," with a stately air, "I shall say little more about it."

"Agreed, wife," returned I, knocking my pipe-bowl against the jam, "and now, to-morrow, I will a third time send for Mr. Scribe. Wife, the sciatica takes me; be so good as to put this pipe on the mantel."

"If you get the step-ladder for me, I will. This shocking old chimney, this abominable old-fashioned old chimney's mantels are so high, I can't reach them."

No opportunity, however trivial, was overlooked for a subordinate fling at the pile.

Here, by way of introduction, it should be mentioned, that besides the fire-places all round it, the chimney was, in the most hap-hazard way, excavated on each floor for certain curious out-of-the-way cupboards and closets, of all sorts and sizes, clinging here and there, like nests in the crotches of some old oak. On the second floor these closets were by far the most irregular and numerous. And yet this should hardly have been so, since the theory of the chimney was, that it pyramidically diminished as it ascended. The abridgment of its square on the roof was obvious enough; and it was supposed that the reduction must be methodically graduated from bottom to top.

"Mr. Scribe," said I when, the next day, with an eager aspect, that individual again came, "my object in sending for you this morning is, not to arrange for the demolition of my chimney, nor to have any particular conversation about it, but simply to allow you every reasonable facility for verifying, if you can, the conjecture communicated in your note."

Though in secret not a little crestfallen, it may be, by my phlegmatic reception, so different from what he had looked for; with much apparent alacrity he commenced the survey; throwing open the cupboards on the first floor, and peering into the closets on the second; measuring one within, and then comparing that measurement with the measurement without. Removing the fire-boards, he would gaze up the flues. But no sign of the hidden work yet.

Now, on the second floor the rooms were the most rambling conceivable. They, as it were, dovetailed into each other. They were of all shapes; not one mathematically square room among them all—a peculiarity which by the master-mason had not been unobserved. With a significant, not to say portentous expression, he took a circuit of the chimney, measuring the area of each room around it; then going down stairs, and out of doors, he measured the entire ground area; then compared the sum total of all the areas of all the rooms on the second floor with the ground area; then, returning to me in no small excitement, announced that there was a difference of no less than two hundred and odd square feet—room enough, in all conscience, for a secret closet.

"But, Mr. Scribe," said I stroking my chin, "have you allowed for the walls, both main and sectional? They take up some space, you know."

"Ah, I had forgotten that," tapping his forehead; "but," still ciphering on his paper, "that will not make up the deficiency."

"But, Mr. Scribe, have you allowed for the recesses of so many fireplaces on a floor, and for the fire-walls, and the flues; in short, Mr. Scribe, have you allowed for the legitimate chimney itself—some one hundred and forty-four square feet or thereabouts, Mr. Scribe?"

"How unaccountable. That slipped my mind, too."

"Did it, indeed, Mr. Scribe?"

He faltered a little, and burst forth with, "But we must now allow one hundred and forty-four square feet for the legitimate chimney. My position is, that within those undue limits the secret closet is contained."

I eyed him in silence a moment; then spoke:

"Your survey is concluded, Mr. Scribe; be so good now as to lay your finger upon the exact part of the chimney wall where you believe this secret closet to be; or would a witch-hazel wand assist you, Mr. Scribe?"

"No, Sir, but a crow-bar would," he, with temper, rejoined.

Here, now, thought I to myself, the cat leaps out of the bag. I looked at him with a calm glance, under which he seemed somewhat uneasy. More than ever now I suspected a plot. I remembered what my wife had said about abiding by the decision of Mr. Scribe. In a bland way, I resolved to buy up the decision of Mr. Scribe.

"Sir," said I, "really, I am much obliged to you for this survey. It has quite set my mind at rest. And no doubt you, too, Mr. Scribe, must feel much relieved. Sir," I added, "you have made three visits to the chimney. With a business man, time is money. Here are fifty dollars, Mr. Scribe. Nay, take it. You have earned it. Your opinion is worth it. And by the way,"—as he modestly received the money—"have you any objections to give me a—a—little certificate—something, say, like a steamboat certificate, certifying that you, a competent surveyor, have surveyed my chimney, and found no reason to believe any unsoundness; in short, any—any secret closet in it. Would you be so kind, Mr. Scribe?"

"But, but, sir," stammered he with honest hesitation.

"Here, here are pen and paper," said I, with entire assurance. Enough.

That evening I had the certificate framed and hung over the dining-room fire-place, trusting that the continual sight of it would forever put at rest at once the dreams and stratagems of my household.

But, no. Inveterately bent upon the extirpation of that noble old chimney, still to this day my wife goes about it, with my daughter Anna's geological hammer, tapping the wall all over, and then holding her ear against it, as I have seen the physicians of life insurance companies tap a man's chest, and then incline over for the echo. Sometimes of nights she almost frightens one, going about on this phantom errand, and still following the sepulchral response of the chimney, round and round, as if it were leading her to the threshold of the secret closet.

"How hollow it sounds," she will hollowly cry. "Yes, I declare," with an emphatic tap, "there is a secret closet here. Here, in this very spot. Hark! How hollow!"

"Psha! wife, of course it is hollow. Who ever heard of a solid chimney?"

But nothing avails. And my daughters take after, not me, but their mother.

Sometimes all three abandon the theory of the secret closet, and return to the genuine ground of attack—the unsightliness of so cumbrous a pile, with comments upon the great addition of room to be gained by its demolition, and the fine effect of the projected grand hall, and the convenience resulting from the collateral running in one direction and another of their various partitions. Not more ruthlessly did the Three Powers partition away poor Poland, than my wife and daughters would fain partition away my chimney.

But seeing that, despite all, I and my chimney still smoke our pipes, my wife reoccupies the ground of the secret closet, enlarging upon what wonders are there, and what a shame it is, not to seek it out and explore it.

"Wife," said I, upon one of these occasions, "why speak more of that secret closet, when there before you hangs contrary testimony of a master-mason, elected by yourself to decide. Besides, even if there were a secret closet, secret it should remain, and secret it shall. Yes, wife, here for once I must say my say. Infinite sad mischief has resulted from the profane bursting open of secret recesses. Though standing in the heart of this house, though hitherto we have all nestled about it, unsuspicious of aught hidden within, this chimney may or may not have a secret closet. But if it have, it is my kinsman's. To break into that wall, would be to break into his breast. And that wall-breaking wish of Momus I account the wish of a church-robbing gossip and knave. Yes, wife, a vile eaves-dropping varlet was Momus."

"Moses? Mumps? Stuff with your mumps and Moses!"

The truth is, my wife, like all the rest of the world, cares not a fig for my philosophical jabber. In dearth of other philosophical companionship, I and my chimney have to smoke and philosophize together. And sitting up so late as we do at it, a mighty smoke it is that we two smoky old philosophers make.

But my spouse, who likes the smoke of my tobacco as little as she does that of the soot, carries on her war against both. I live in continual dread lest, like the golden bowl, the pipes of me and my chimney shall yet be broken. To stay that mad project of my wife's, naught answers. Or, rather, she herself is incessantly answering, incessantly besetting me with her terrible alacrity for improvement, which is a softer name for destruction. Scarce a day I do not find her with her tape-measure, measuring for her grand hall, while Anna holds a yard-stick on one side, and Julia looks approvingly on from the other. Mysterious intimations appear in the nearest village paper, signed "Claude," to the effect that a certain structure, standing on a certain hill, is a sad blemish to an otherwise lovely landscape. Anonymous letters arrive, threatening me with I know not what, unless I remove my chimney. Is it my wife, too, or who, that sets up the neighbors to badgering me on the same subject, and hinting to me that my chimney, like a huge elm, absorbs all moisture from my garden? At night, also, my wife will start as from sleep, professing to hear ghostly noises from the secret closet. Assailed on all sides, and in all ways, small peace have I and my chimney.

Were it not for the baggage, we would together pack up, and remove from the country.

What narrow escapes have been ours! Once I found in a drawer a whole portfolio of plans and estimates. Another time, upon returning after a day's absence, I discovered my wife standing before the chimney in earnest conversation with a person whom I at once recognized as a meddlesome architectural reformer, who, because he had no gift for putting up anything, was ever intent upon pulling down; in various parts of the country having prevailed upon half-witted old folks to destroy their old-fashioned houses, particularly the chimneys.

But worst of all was, that time I unexpectedly returned at early morning from a visit to the city, and upon approaching the house, narrowly escaped three brickbats which fell, from high aloft, at my feet. Glancing up, what was my horror to see three savages, in blue jean overalls, in the very act of commencing the long-threatened attack. Aye, indeed, thinking of those three brickbats, I and my chimney have had narrow escapes.

It is now some seven years since I have stirred from home. My city friends all wonder why I don't come to see them, as in former times. They think I am getting sour and unsocial. Some say that I have become a sort of mossy old misanthrope, while all the time the fact is, I am simply standing guard over my mossy old chimney; for it is resolved between me and my chimney, that I and my chimney will never surrender.

THE CANDY COUNTRY

Louisa May Alcott

"I shall take Mamma's red sun-umbrella; it is so warm,—and none of the children at school will have one like it," said Lilly, one day, as she went through the hall.

"The wind is very high; I'm afraid you'll be blown away if you carry that big thing," called nurse from the window.

"I wish I could be blown away; I always wanted to go up in a balloon," answered Lilly, as she struggled out of the gate.

She managed quite well until she came to the bridge, where she stopped to look over the railing at the fast-running water below, and the turtles sunning themselves on the rocks. Lilly was fond of throwing stones at the turtles; she thought it funny to watch them tumble with a headlong splash into the water. Now, when she saw three big fellows close by, she stooped for a stone, but just at that very minute a gale of wind nearly took the umbrella out of her hand. She clutched it tightly; and away she went like a thistle-down, right up in the air, over river and hill, houses and trees, faster and faster and faster, till her head spun around, her breath was all gone, and she had to let go. The dear red umbrella flew away like a leaf; and Lilly fell down, down, till she came crash into a tree which grew in so curious a place that she forgot her fright as she sat looking about her.

The tree looked as if it were made of glass or colored sugar; for she could look through the red cherries, the green leaves, and the brown branches. An agreeable aroma came to her nose. "Oh," she cried at once, as would any child have said, "I smell candy!" She picked a cherry and ate it. Oh, how good it was!—all sugar and no stone. The next discovery was so delightful that she nearly fell off her perch; for by touching her tongue here and there, she found the whole tree was made of candy. What a pleasure to sit and break off twigs of barley sugar, candied cherries, and leaves that tasted like peppermint and sassafras!

Lilly rocked in the branches and ate away until she had finished the top of the little tree; then she climbed down and strolled along, making more surprising and agreeable discoveries as she went.

What looked like snow under her feet was white sugar; the rocks were lumps of chocolate; the flowers were of all colors and tastes; and every sort of fruit grew on those delightful trees. Little white houses soon appeared; and in them lived the dainty candy people, all made from the best sugar, and painted to look like real people. Dear little men and women, looking as if they had stepped off of cakes and bonbons, went about in their gay sugar clothes, laughing and talking in sweet-toned voices. Bits of babies rocked in open-work cradles and sugar boys and girls played with sugar toys in a very natural way. Carriages rolled along the jujube streets, drawn by red and yellow barley horses; cows fed in the green fields, and sugar birds sang in the candy trees.

Lilly listened, and in a moment she understood, in some way, just what the song said,—

"Sweet! Sweet!
Come, come and eat
Dear little girls
With yellow curls;
For here you'll find
Sweets to your mind.
On every tree
Sugar-plums you'll see;
In every dell
Grows the caramel;

Over every wall
Gum-drops fall;
Molasses flows
Where our river goes;
Under your feet
Lies sugar sweet;
Over your head
Grow almonds red.
Our lilly and rose
Are not for the nose;
Our flowers we pluck
To eat or suck;
And, oh! what bliss
When two friends kiss,
For they honey sip
From lip to lip!
And all you meet,
In house or street,
At work or at play,
Sweethearts are they.

So, little dear,
Pray feel no fear;
Go where you will;
Eat, eat your fill;
Here is a feast
From west to east;
And you can say,
Ere you go away:
'At last I stand
In dear Candy-land.'
Sweet! Sweet!
Tweet! Tweet!
Tweedle-dee!
Tweedle-dee!"

"That is the most interesting song I ever heard," said Lilly, clapping
her hands and dancing along toward a fine palace of white cream

candy, with pillars of striped peppermint-stick, and a roof of frosting that made it look like Milan Cathedral.

"I'll live here, and eat candy all day long, with no tiresome school or patchwork to spoil my fun," said Lilly.

So she ran up the chocolate steps into the pretty rooms, where all the chairs and tables were of every colored candy, and the beds of spun sugar. A fountain of lemonade supplied drink; and floors of ice-cream that never melted kept people and things from sticking together, as they would have done, had it been warm.

For some time Lilly was quite happy, in going about, tasting the many different kinds of sweets, talking to the little people, who were very amiable, and finding out curious things about them and their country.

The babies were plain sugar, but the grown people had different flavors. The young ladies were mostly violet, rose, or orange; the gentlemen were apt to have cordials of some sort inside of them, as she found when she slyly ate one now and then, and as a punishment had her tongue bitten by the hot, strong taste. The old people were peppermint, clove, and such comfortable flavors, good for pain; but the old maids were lemon, flag-root, and all sorts of sour, bitter things, and were not eaten much. Lilly soon learned to know the characters of her new friends by a single taste, and some she never touched but once. The dear babies melted in her mouth, and the delicately flavored young ladies she was very fond of. Dr. Ginger was called to her more than once when so much candy made her teeth ache, and she found him a very hot-tempered little man; but he stopped the pain, so she was glad to see him.

A lime-drop boy and a little pink checkerberry girl were her favorite playmates; and they had fine times making mud-pies by scraping the chocolate rocks and mixing this dust with honey from the wells near by. These pies they could eat; and Lilly thought this much better than throwing them away, as she had to do at home. They had candy-pulls very often, and made swings of long loops of molasses candy, and birds'-nests with almond eggs, out of which came birds that sang sweetly. They played foot-ball with big bull's-eyes, sailed in sugar boats on lakes of syrup, fished in rivers of molasses, and rode the barley horses all over the country.

Lilly discovered that it never rained, but that it white-sugared.

There was no sun, as it would have been too hot; but a large yellow
lozenge made a nice moon, and there were red and white comfits for
the stars.

All the people lived on sugar, and never quarreled. No one was ill;
and if any one was broken, as sometimes happened with so brittle
creatures, the fractured parts were just stuck together and all was
right again. When they grew old they became thinner and thinner, till
there was danger of their vanishing. Then the friends of the old person
bore him to the great golden urn, always full of a certain fine syrup,
which stood in their largest temple; and into that he was dipped and
dipped till he was stout and strong again, and went home as good as
new, to enjoy himself for a long time.

This was very interesting to Lilly, and she went to many such reju-
venations. But the weddings were better still; for the lovely white
brides were so sweet that Lilly longed to eat them. The feasts were
delicious; the guests all went in their best clothes, and danced at the
ball till they grew so warm that half-a-dozen would stick together and
would have to be taken to the ice-cream room to cool off. Then the
happy pair would drive away in a fine carriage with white horses to a
new palace in some other part of the country, and Lilly would have
another pleasant place to visit.

But by and by, when she had seen everything, and eaten so many
sweet things that at last she longed for plain bread and butter, she
began to be cross, as children always are when they live on candy; and
the little people wished she would go away, for they were afraid of her.
No wonder, for she would sometimes catch up a dear sugar baby and
eat it, or break some respectable old grand-mamma all into bits because she reproved her for her naughty ways. Finally, Lilly calmly sat
down on the biggest church, crushing it flat, and one day in a pet, she
even tried to poke the moon out of the sky. The King ordered her to go
home; but she said, "I wont!" and, with a petulant motion, she knocked
off his head, crown and all.

Such a wail went up at this awful deed that she ran away out of the
city, fearing that some one would put poison in her candy, since she
had no other food.

"I suppose I shall bring up somewhere if I keep on walking; and I
can't starve, though I hate the sight of this horrid stuff," she said to
herself, as she hurried over the mountains of Gibraltar rock that

divided the city of Saccharissa behind her from the great desert of brown sugar that lay beyond.

Lilly marched bravely across this desert for a long time, and saw at last a great smoke in the sky, smelt a spicy smell, and felt a hot wind blowing toward her.

"I wonder if there are sugar savages here, roasting and eating some poor traveler like me," she said, thinking of Robinson Crusoe and other wanderers in strange lands.

She crept carefully along till she saw a settlement of little huts very like mushrooms, for they were made of cookies set on lumps of brown sugar. Queer people, looking as if made of gingerbread, were working very busily around several stoves which seemed to be baking away at a great rate.

"I'll creep nearer and see what sort of people they are before I show myself," thought Lilly, going into a grove of spice trees and sitting down on a stone which proved to be the plummy sort of cake we used to call Brighton Rock.

Presently one of the tallest men came striding toward the trees with a pan, evidently to get spice; and before Lilly could run away he saw her.

"Hullo, what do you want?" he asked, staring at her with his black-currant eyes, while he briskly picked the bark off a cinnamon tree.

"I'm traveling, and should like to know what place this is, if you please," answered Lilly, very politely, as she was rather frightened.

"Cake-land. Where did you come from?" asked the gingerbread man, in a crisp tone of voice.

"I was blown into the Candy country, and have been there a long time; but I grew tired of it and ran away to find something better."

"Sensible child!" and the man smiled till Lilly thought his cheeks would crumble. "You'll like it better here with us Cake-folk than with the lazy Bonbons, who never work and are all for show. They wont recognize us, though we all are related through our grandparents Sugar and Molasses. We are busy folk; so they turn up their noses and don't speak when we meet at parties. Poor creatures,—silly, and sweet, and unsubstantial! I pity 'em."

"Could I make you a visit? I'd like to see how you live and what you do. I'm sure it must be interesting," said Lilly, picking herself up after a tumble, having eaten nearly all the cake she was sitting on, she was so hungry.

"Of course you can," said her friend. "Come on! I can talk while I work."

And the funny gingerbread man trotted away toward his kitchen, which was full of pans, rolling-pins, and molasses jugs.

"Sit down. I shall be at leisure as soon as this batch is baked. There are still some wise people down below who like gingerbread, and I have my hands full," he said, dashing about, stirring, rolling out, and slapping the brown dough into pans, which he whisked into the oven and out again so fast that Lilly knew there must be magic about it somewhere.

Every now and then he threw her a delicious cookie warm from the oven. She liked the queer fellow, and soon began to ask all sorts of questions, as she was very curious about this country.

"What is your name, sir?" she ventured, first.

"Ginger-Snap," he answered, briskly.

Lilly thought it a good name; for he was very quick, and she fancied he could be short and sharp if he liked.

"Where does all this cake go?" she asked, after she had watched a great many other kitchens full of workers, who all were of different kinds of cake, and each making its own sort.

"I'll show you by and by," answered Snap, beginning to pile up the heaps of gingerbread on a little car that ran along a track leading to some distant store-room, Lilly thought.

"Don't you become tired of doing this all the time?" she asked.

"Yes; but I wish to be promoted, and I never shall be till I've done my best, and won the prize here," Snap explained.

"Oh, tell me about it!" cried Lilly. "What is the prize, and how are you promoted? Is this a cooking-school?"

"Yes; the prize for best gingerbread is a cake of condensed yeast," said Snap. "That puts a soul into me, and I begin to rise until I am able to float over the hills yonder into the blessed land of bread, and be one of the happy creatures who are always wholesome, always needed, and without which the world below would be in a bad way."

"Dear me! that is the queerest thing I've heard yet!" said Lilly. "But I don't wonder you want to go; I'm tired of sweets myself, and just long for a good piece of bread, though I always used to want cake and candy at home."

"Ah, my dear, you'll learn a great deal here; and you are lucky not to have fallen into the clutches of Giant Dyspepsia, who always gets people if they eat too much of such rubbish as cake and candy, and scorn wholesome bread. I leave my ginger behind when I go, and become white and round and beautiful, as you will see. The Gingerbread family have never been as foolish as some of the other cakes. Wedding-cake is the worst; such extravagance in the way of wine and spice and fruit I never saw, and such a mess to eat when it's done! I don't wonder it makes people sick; serves 'em right." And Snap flung down a pan with a bang that made Lilly jump.

"Sponge-cake isn't bad, is it? Mamma lets me eat it, but I like frosted pound-cake better," she said, looking over to the next kitchen, where piles of that sort of cake were being iced.

"Poor stuff. No substance. Ladies' fingers will do for babies, but Pound has too much butter to be wholesome. Let it alone, and eat cookies or seed-cakes, my dear. Now, come along; I'm ready." And Snap trundled away his car-load at a great pace.

Lilly ran behind to pick up whatever fell, and looked about her as she went, for this was certainly a very queer country. Lakes of eggs all beaten up, and hot springs of saleratus foamed here and there, ready for use. The earth was brown sugar or ground spice; and the only fruits were raisins, dried currants, citron, and lemon peel. It was a very busy place; for every one cooked all the time, and never failed and never seemed tired, though they were always so hot that they only wore sheets of paper for clothes. There were piles of it to put over the cake, so it shouldn't burn; and they made cooks' white caps and aprons of it, which looked very fine. A large clock made of a flat pancake, with cloves to mark the hours and two toothpicks for hands, showed them how long to bake things; and in one place an ice wall was built around a lake of butter, which they cut in lumps as they wanted it.

"Here we are. Now, stand aside while I pitch 'em down," said Snap, stopping at last before a hole in the ground where a dumb-waiter, with a name over it, hung ready.

There were many holes all about, and many dumb-waiters, each with a special name; and Lilly was amazed when she read "Weber," "Copeland," "Dooling,"* and others, which she knew very well.

Over Snap's place was the name "Newmarch," and Lilly said: "Why,

---

* Well-known Boston caterers.

that's where Mamma gets her hard gingerbread, and Weber's is where
we go for ice-cream. Do *you* make cake for them?"

"Yes, but no one knows it. It's one of the secrets of the trade. We
cook for all the confectioners, and people think the good things come
out of the cellars under their shops. Good joke, isn't it?" And Snap
laughed till a crack came in his neck and made him cough.

Lilly was so surprised that she sat down on a warm queen's-cake
that happened to be near, and watched Snap send down load after load
of gingerbread to be eaten by children, who would have liked it much
better if they had only known, as did she, where it all came from.

As she sat on the queen's-cake there came up through the nearest
hole, which was marked "Copeland," the clatter of many spoons, the
smell of many dinners, and the sound of many voices calling:—"One
vanilla, two strawberries, and a Charlotte Russe"; "Three stews, cup
coffee, dry toast"; "Roast chicken and apple without!"

"Dear me! it seems as if I were there," said Lilly, longing to hop
down, but afraid of the bump at the other end.

"That's done. Come along. I'll ride you back," called Snap, shying
the last cookie after the dumb-waiter as it went slowly out of sight with
its spicy load.

"I wish you'd teach me to cook. It must be great fun, and Mamma
wants me to learn; only our cook hates to have me around the kitchen,
and she is so cross that I don't like to try, at home," said Lilly as she
went trundling back on Snap's car.

"Better wait till you go to Bread-land, and learn to make bread. It's
a great art, and worth knowing. Don't waste your time on cake, though
plain gingerbread isn't bad to have in the house. I'll teach you that in
a jiffy, if the clock doesn't strike my hour too soon," answered Snap,
helping her down.

"What hour?" inquired Lilly.

"Why, the hour of my freedom. I shall never know when I've done
my task until I'm called by the chimes and go to get my soul," answered
Snap, turning his currant eyes anxiously toward the clock.

"I hope you *will* have time," said Lilly as she fell to work with all her
might, after Snap had fitted her with a paper apron and a cap like his.

It was not hard; for when she was about to make a mistake, a spark
flew out of the fire and burnt her in time to remind her to look at the
recipe, which was hung up before her on a sheet of gingerbread in a

frame of pie-crust; the directions had been written on it while it was soft and baked in. The third sheet she made came out of the oven spicy, light, and brown; and Snap, giving it one poke with his finger, said, "That's all right. Now you know. Here's your reward."

He handed her a recipe-book made of thin sheets of sugar gingerbread held together by a gelatine binding, with her name stamped on the back, and each leaf crimped with a cake-cutter in a very delightful manner.

Lilly was charmed with it, but had no time to read all it contained; for just then the clock began to strike, and a chime of bells to ring:

"Gingerbread,
Go to the head.
Your task is done:
A soul is won.
Take it and go
Where muffins grow,
Where sweet loaves rise
To the very skies,
And biscuits fair
Perfume the air.
Away, away!
Make no delay;
Into the Flour
Sea, plunge this hour.
Safe in your breast
Let the yeast-cake rest,
Till you rise in joy,
A white-bread boy!"

"Ha, ha! I'm free! I'm free!" cried Snap, catching up a square silver-covered cake that seemed to fall from somewhere above; and running to the great white sea of flour, he dashed in, head first, holding the yeast-cake clasped to his breast as if his life depended on it.

Lilly watched breathlessly, while a curious working and bubbling went on, as if Snap were tumbling about down there like a small earthquake. The other cake-folk stood with her upon the shore; for it was a great event, and all were glad that the dear fellow had been promoted so soon. Suddenly a cry was heard, and on the farther side of the sea up rose a beautiful white figure. It waved its hand as if bidding all "Good-bye," and ran over the hills so fast they had only time to see how plump and fair it was, with a little knob on the top of its head like a crown.

"He's gone to the happy Land of Bread, and we shall miss him; but we'll follow his example and soon find him again," said a gentle Sponge-cake, with a sigh, as they all went back to their work; while Lilly hurried after Snap, eager to see the new country, which she was sure must be the best of all.

A delicious odor of fresh bread blew up from the valley as she stood on the hill-top and looked down on the peaceful scene below. Fields of yellow grain waved in the breeze; hop-vines grew from tree to tree; and the white sails of many windmills whirled around as they ground the different grains into fresh, sweet meal, for the loaves of bread with which the houses were built and the streets paved, and which in many shapes formed the people, furniture, and animals. A river of milk flowed through the peaceful land, and fountains of yeast rose and fell with a pleasant foam and fizz. The ground was a mixture of many meals, and the paths were golden Indian, which gave a very gay look to the scene. Buckwheat flowers bloomed on their rosy stems, and tall corn-stalks rustled their leaves in the warm air that came from the ovens hidden in the hill-sides; for bread needs a slow fire, and an oblig-ing volcano did the baking there.

"What a lovely place!" cried Lilly, feeling the charm of the home-like landscape, in spite of the funny, plump people moving about.

Two of these figures came running to meet her as she slowly walked down the yellow path from the hill. One was a golden boy, with a beam-ing face; the other a little girl in a shiny brown cloak, who looked as if she would taste very nice. They each put a warm hand into Lilly's, and the boy said: "We are glad to see you. Muffin told us you were coming."

"I thank you. But who is Muffin?" asked Lilly, feeling as if she had seen both these little people before, and liked them. The boy answered her question immediately:

"He was Ginger-Snap once, but he's a Muffin now. We begin in that way, and work by degrees up to the perfect loaf. My name is Johnny-Cake, and here's Sally Lunn. You know us; so come on and have a race."

Lilly burst out laughing at the idea of playing with these old friends of hers; and away ran all three as fast as they could tear, down the hill, over a bridge, into the middle of the village, where they stopped, panting, and sat down on some very soft rolls to rest.

"What do you all do here?" asked Lilly, when she got her breath again.

"We farm, we study, we bake, we brew, and are merry as crickets all day long. It's school-time now, and we must go; will you come?" said Sally, jumping up as if she liked going to school.

"Our schools are not like yours; we study only two things—grain and yeast. I think you'll like it. We have yeast to-day, and the experiments are very jolly," added Johnny, trotting off to a tall brown tower of rye and Indian bread, where the school was kept.

Lilly never liked to go to school, but she was ashamed to own it; so she went along with Sally, and was so amused with all she saw that she was glad she had come. The brown loaf was hollow, and had no roof; and when she asked why they used a ruin, Sally told her to wait and see why they chose strong walls and plenty of room overhead. All around was a circle of very small biscuits like cushions, and on these the Bread-children sat. A square loaf in the middle was the teacher's desk, and on it lay an ear of wheat, with several bottles of yeast well corked up. The teacher was a pleasant, plump lady from Vienna, very wise, and so famous for her good bread that she was a Professor of Grainology.

When all were seated, she began her lesson with the wheat ear, and told all about it in so interesting a way that Lilly felt as if she had never before known anything about the bread she ate. The experiments with the yeast were quite exciting,—for Fraulein Pretzel showed them how it would work until it blew the cork out, and went fizzing up to the sky. If it were kept too long; how it would turn sour or flat, and spoil the bread if care were not taken to use it at just the right moment; and how too much would cause the loaf to rise until there was no substance to it.

The children were very bright; for they were fed on the best kinds of oatmeal and Graham bread, with very little white or hot cakes to spoil their young stomachs. Hearty, happy boys and girls they were, and their yeasty souls were very lively in them; for they danced and sang, and seemed as bright and gay as if acidity, heaviness, and mold were quite unknown.

Lilly was very happy with them, and when school was done raced

home with Sally, and ate for dinner the best bread and milk that she had
ever tasted. In the afternoon Johnny took her to the corn-field, and
showed her how they kept the growing ears free from mildew and
worms. Then she went to the bake-house, and here she found her old
friend Muffin hard at work making Parker House rolls, for he was so
good a cook that he was set to work at once on the lighter kinds of bread.

"Well, isn't this better than Saccharissa or even Cake-land?" he
asked, as he rolled and folded his bits of dough with a dab of butter
tucked inside.

"Ever so much!" cried Lilly. "I feel better already, and I mean to
learn all I can. Mamma will be so pleased if I can make good bread
when I go home! She is rather old-fashioned, and wishes me to be a
good housekeeper. I never could think bread interesting, then, but I do,
now; and Johnny's mother is going to teach me to make Indian cakes
to-morrow."

"Glad to hear it!" said Snap. "Learn all you can, and tell other people how to make healthy bodies and happy souls by eating good plain
food. Not like this, though these rolls are better than cake. I have to
work my way up to the perfect loaf, you know; and then, oh, then, I
shall be a happy thing!"

"What happens then? Do you go on to some other wonderful
place?" asked Lilly, as Muffin paused, with a smile on his face.

"Yes; I am eaten by some wise, good human being, and become a
part of him or her. That is my happy destiny; for I may nourish a poet
and help him sing, or feed a good woman who makes the world better
for being in it, or be crumbed into the golden porringer of a baby
prince who is to rule a kingdom. Isn't that a noble hope to have, and
an end worth working for?" asked Muffin, in a tone that made Lilly feel
as if she had some sort of fine yeast inside her, which was setting her
brain to work with quite new thoughts.

"Yes, it is. I suppose that all things are made for some such purpose,
if we only knew it; and people should be glad to do anything to help the
world along, if only by making good bread in a kitchen," answered Lilly
in a sober way.

She staid in Bread-land a long time, and enjoyed and learned a
great deal that she never forgot. But at last, when she had made the
perfect loaf, she wished to go home, that her mother might see it and
taste it.

"I've put a great deal of myself into it, and I'd love to think I had given her strength or pleasure by my work," she said, as she and Sally stood looking at the handsome loaf.

"You can go whenever you like; just take the bread in your hands and wish three times, and you'll be wherever you desire to be. I'm sorry you must go, but I don't wonder you want to see your mother. Don't forget what you have learned, and you will always be glad that you came to us," said Sally, kissing her good-bye.

"Where is Muffin? I can't go without seeing him—my dear old friend," answered Lilly, looking around for him.

"He is here," said Sally, touching the loaf. "He was ready to go, and chose to pass into your bread rather than any other; for he said he loved you, and would be glad to help feed so good a little girl."

"How kind of him! I must be careful to grow wise and excellent, or he will be disappointed and will have lived in vain," said Lilly, touched by his devotion.

Then bidding them all farewell, she hugged her loaf close, wished three times to be at her own home, and like a flash she was there.

Whether her friends believed the wonderful tale of her adventures, I can not tell; but I know that she was a nice little housekeeper from that day, and made bread so good that other girls came to learn of her. She also grew from a sickly, fretful child into a fine, strong, healthy woman, because she ate very little cake and candy, except at Christmastime, when the oldest and the wisest of us like to make a short visit to Candy-land.

Dave's Neckliss

Charles W. Chesnutt

"Have some dinner, Uncle Julius?" said my wife.
It was a Sunday afternoon in early autumn. Our two women-servants had gone to a camp-meeting some miles away, and would not return until evening. My wife had served the dinner, and we were just rising from the table, when Julius came up the lane, and, taking off his hat, seated himself on the piazza.

The old man glanced through the open door at the dinner-table, and his eyes rested lovingly upon a large sugar-cured ham, from which several slices had been cut, exposing a rich pink expanse that would have appealed strongly to the appetite of any hungry Christian.

"Thanky, Miss Annie," he said, after a momentary hesitation, "I dunno ez I keers ef I does tas'e a piece er dat ham, ef yer'll cut me off a slice un it."

"No," said Annie, "I won't. Just sit down to the table and help your-self; eat all you want, and don't be bashful."

Julius drew a chair up to the table, while my wife and I went out on the piazza. Julius was in my employment; he took his meals with his own family, but when he happened to be about our house at meal-times, my wife never let him go away hungry.

I threw myself into a hammock, from which I could see Julius through an open window. He ate with evident relish, devoting his attention chiefly to the ham, slice after slice of which disappeared in the spacious cavity of his mouth. At first the old man ate rapidly, but after the edge of his appetite had been taken off he proceeded in a more leisurely manner. When he had cut the sixth slice of ham (I kept count of them from a lazy curiosity to see how much he *could* eat) I saw him lay it on his plate; as he adjusted the knife and fork to cut it into smaller pieces, he paused, as if struck by a sudden thought, and a tear rolled down his rugged cheek and fell upon the slice of ham before him. But the emotion, whatever the thought that caused it, was transitory, and in a moment he continued his dinner. When he was through eating, he came out on the porch, and resumed his seat with the satisfied expression of countenance that usually follows a good dinner.

"Julius," I said, "you seemed to be affected by something, a moment ago. Was the mustard so strong that it moved you to tears?"

"No, suh, it wa'n't de mustard; I wuz studyin' 'bout Dave."

"Who was Dave, and what about him?" I asked.

The conditions were all favorable to story-telling. There was an autumnal languor in the air, and a dreamy haze softened the dark green of the distant pines and the deep blue of the Southern sky. The generous meal he had made had put the old man in a very good humor. He was not always so, for his curiously undeveloped nature was subject to moods which were almost childish in their variableness. It was only now and then that we were able to study, through the medium of his recollection, the simple but intensely human inner life of slavery. His way of looking at the past seemed very strange to us; his view of certain sides of life was essentially different from ours. He never indulged in any regrets for the Arcadian joyousness and irresponsibility which was a somewhat popular conception of slavery; his had not been the lot of the petted house-servant, but that of the toiling field-hand. While he mentioned with a warm appreciation the acts of kindness which those in authority had shown to him and his people, he would speak of a cruel deed, not with the indignation of one accustomed to quick feeling and spontaneous expression, but with a furtive disapproval which suggested to us a doubt in his own mind as to whether he had a right to think or to feel, and presented to us the curious psychological spectacle of a mind enslaved long after the shackles had been struck off from the limbs of its possessor. Whether the sacred name of liberty ever set his soul aglow with a generous fire; whether he had more than the most elementary ideas of love, friendship, patriotism, religion,—things which are half, and the better half, of life to us; whether he even realized, except in a vague, uncertain way, his own degradation, I do not know. I fear not; and if not, then centuries of repression had borne their legitimate fruit. But in the simple human feeling, and still more in the undertone of sadness, which pervaded his stories, I thought I could see a spark which, fanned by favoring breezes and fed by the memories of the past, might become in his children's children a glowing flame of sensibility, alive to every thrill of human happiness or human woe.

"Dave use' ter b'long ter my ole marster," said Julius; "he wuz raise' on dis yer plantation, en I kin 'member all erbout 'im, fer I wuz ole 'nuff ter chop cotton w'en it all happen'. Dave wuz a tall man, en monst'us strong: he could do mo' wuk in a day dan any yuther two niggers on de plantation. He wuz one er dese yer solemn kine er men, en nebber run on wid much foolishness, like de yuther darkies. He use' ter go out in de woods en pray; en w'en he hear de han's on de plantation cussin' en gwine on wid dere dancin' en foolishness, he use' ter tell 'em 'bout religion en jedgmen'-day, w'en dey would haf ter gin account fer eve'y idle word en all dey yuther sinful kyarin's-on.

"Dave had l'arn' how ter read de Bible. Dey wuz a free nigger boy in de settlement w'at wuz monst'us smart, en could write en cipher, en wuz alluz readin' books er papers. En Dave had hi'ed dis free boy fer ter l'arn 'im how ter read. Hit wuz 'g'in de law, but co'se none er de niggers didn' say nuffin ter de w'ite folks 'bout it. Howsomedever, one day Mars Walker—he wuz de oberseah—foun' out Dave could read. Mars Walker wa'n't nuffin but a po' bockrah, en folks said he couldn' read ner write hisse'f, en co'se he didn' lack ter see a nigger w'at knowed mo' d'n he did; so he went en tole Mars Dugal'. Mars Dugal' sont fer Dave, en ax' 'im 'bout it.

"Dave didn't hardly knowed w'at ter do; but he couldn' tell no lie, so he 'fessed he could read de Bible a little by spellin' out de words. Mars Dugal' look' mighty solemn.

"'Dis yer is a se'ious matter,' sezee; 'it's 'g'in de law ter l'arn niggers how ter read, er 'low 'em ter hab books. But w'at yer l'arn out'n dat Bible, Dave?'

"Dave wa'n't no fool, ef he wuz a nigger, en sezee:—

"'Marster, I l'arns dat it's a sin fer ter steal, er ter lie, er fer ter want w'at doan b'long ter yer; en I l'arns fer ter love de Lawd en ter 'bey my marster.'

"Mars Dugal' sorter smile' en laf' ter hisse'f, like he 'uz might'ly tickle' 'bout sump'n, en sezee:—

"'Doan 'pear ter me lack readin' de Bible done yer much harm, Dave. Dat's w'at I wants all my niggers fer ter know. Yer keep right on readin', en tell de yuther han's w'at yer be'n tellin' me. How would yer lack fer ter preach ter de niggers on Sunday?'

"Dave say he'd be glad fer ter do w'at he could. So Mars Dugal' tole de oberseah fer ter let Dave preach ter de niggers, en tell 'em w'at wuz in de Bible, en it would he'p ter keep 'em fum stealin' er runnin' erway.

"So Dave 'mence' ter preach, en done de han's on de plantation a heap er good, en most un 'em lef' off dey wicked ways, en 'mence' ter love ter hear 'bout God, en religion, en de Bible; en dey done dey wuk better, en didn' gib de oberseah but mighty little trouble fer ter manage 'em.

"Dave wuz one er dese yer men w'at didn' keer much fer de gals,— leastways he didn' tel Dilsey come ter de plantation. Dilsey wuz a monst'us peart, good-lookin', gingybread-colored gal,—one er dese yer high-steppin' gals w'at hol's dey heads up, en won' stan' no foolishness fum no man. She had b'long' ter a gemman over on Rockfish, w'at died, en whose 'state ha' ter be sol' fer ter pay his debts. En Mars Dugal' had b'en ter de oction, en w'en he seed dis gal a-cryin' en gwine on 'bout bein' sol' erway fum her ole mammy, Aun' Mahaly, Mars Dugal' bid 'em bofe in, en fotch 'em ober ter our plantation.

"De young nigger men on de plantation wuz des wil' atter Dilsey, but it didn' do no good, en none un 'em couldn' git Dilsey fer dey june-sey,* 'tel Dave 'mence' fer ter go roun' Aun' Mahaly's cabin. Dey wuz a fine-lookin' couple, Dave en Dilsey wuz, bofe tall, en well-shape', en soopl'. En dey sot a heap by one ernudder. Mars Dugal' seed 'em tergedder one Sunday, en de nex' time he seed Dave atter dat, sezee:—

"'Dave, w'en yer en Dilsey gits ready fer ter git married, I ain' got no rejections. Dey's a poun' er so er chawin'- terbacker up at de house, en I reckon yo' mist'iss kin fine a frock en a ribbin er two fer Dilsey. Youer bofe good niggers, en yer neenter be feared er bein' sol' 'way fum one

---

* Sweetheart.

ernudder long ez I owns dis plantation; en I 'spec's ter own it fer a long time yit.'

"But dere wuz one man on de plantation w'at didn' lack ter see Dave en Dilsey tergedder ez much ez ole marster did. W'en Mars Dugal' went ter de sale whar he got Dilsey en Mahaly, he bought ernudder han', by de name er Wiley. Wiley wuz one er dese yer shiny-eyed, double-headed little niggers, sha'p ez a steel trap, en sly ez de fox w'at keep out'n it. Dis yer Wiley had be'n pesterin' Dilsey 'fo' she come ter our plantation, en had nigh 'bout worried de life out'n her. She didn' keer nuffin fer 'im, but he pestered her so she ha' ter th'eaten ter tell her marster fer ter make Wiley let her 'lone. W'en he come ober to our place it wuz des ez bad, 'tel bimeby Wiley seed dat Dilsey had got ter thinkin' a heap 'bout Dave, en den he sorter hilt off aw'ile, en purten' lack he gin Dilsey up. But he wuz one er dese yer 'ceitful niggers, en w'ile he wuz laffin' en jokin' wid de yuther han's 'bout Dave en Dilsey, he wuz settin' a trap fer ter ketch Dave en git Dilsey back fer hisse'f.

"Dave en Dilsey made up dere min's fer ter git married long 'bout Christmas time, w'en dey'd hab mo' time fer a weddin'. But 'long 'bout two weeks befo' dat time ole mars 'mence' ter lose a heap er bacon. Eve'y night er so somebody 'ud steal a side er bacon, er a ham, er a shoulder, er sump'n, fum one er de smoke-'ouses. De smoke-'ouses wuz lock', but somebody had a key, en manage' ter git in some way er 'nudder. Dey's mo' ways 'n one ter skin a cat, en dey's mo' d'n one way ter git in a smoke-'ouse,—leastways dat's w'at I hearn say. Folks w'at had bacon fer ter sell didn' hab no trouble 'bout gittin' rid un it. Hit wuz 'g'in' de law fer ter buy things fum slabes; but Lawd! dat law didn' 'mount ter a hill er peas. Eve'y week er so one er dese yer big covered waggins would come 'long de road, peddlin' terbacker en w'iskey. Dey wuz a sight er room in one er dem big waggins, en it wuz monst'us easy fer ter swop off bacon fer sump'n ter chaw er ter wa'm yer up in de winter-time. I s'pose de peddlers didn' knowed dey wuz breakin' de law, caze de niggers alluz went at night, en stayed on de dark side er de waggin; en it wuz mighty hard fer ter tell *w'at* kine er folks dey wuz.

"Atter two er th'ee hund'ed er meat had be'n stole', Mars Walker call all de niggers up one ebenin', en tol' 'em dat de fus' nigger he cot stealin' bacon on dat plantation would git sump'n fer ter 'member it by long ez he lib'. En he say he'd gin fi' dollars ter de nigger w'at 'skiver' de rogue. Mars Walker say he s'picion' one er two er de niggers, but he couldn' tell fer sho, en co'se dey all 'nied it w'en he 'cuse em un it.

"Dey wa'n't no bacon stole' fer a week er so, 'tel one dark night w'en somebody tuk a ham fum one er de smoke-'ouses. Mars Walker des cusst awful w'en he foun' out de ham wuz gone, en say he gwine ter sarch all de niggers' cabins; w'en dis yer Wiley I wuz tellin' yer 'bout up'n say he s'picion' who tuk de ham, fer he seed Dave comin' 'cross de plantation fum to'ds de smoke-'ouse de night befo'. W'en Mars Walker hearn dis fum Wiley, he went en sarch' Dave's cabin, en foun' de ham hid under de flo'.

"Eve'ybody wuz 'stonish'; but dere wuz de ham. Co'se Dave 'nied it ter de las', but dere wuz de ham. Mars Walker say it wuz des ez he 'spected: he didn' b'lieve in dese yer readin' en prayin' niggers; it wuz all 'pocrisy, en sarve' Mars Dugal' right fer 'lowin' Dave ter be readin' books w'en it wuz 'g'in de law.

"W'en Mars Dugal' hearn 'bout de ham, he say he wuz might'ly 'ceived en disapp'inted in Dave. He say he wouldn' nebber hab no mo' conferdence in no nigger, en Mars Walker could do des ez he wuz a mineter wid Dave er any er de res' er de niggers. So Mars Walker tuk'n tied Dave up en gin 'im forty; en den he got some er dis yer wire clof w'at dey uses fer ter make sifters out'n, en tuk'n wrap' it roun' de ham en fasten it tergedder at de little een'. Den he tuk Dave down ter de blacksmif-shop, en had Unker Silas, de plantation blacksmif, fasten a chain ter de ham, en den fasten de yuther een' er de chain roun' Dave's neck. En den he says ter Dave, sezee:—

"'Now, suh, yer'll wear dat neckliss fer de nex' six mont's; en I 'spec's yer ner none er de yuther niggers on dis plantation won' steal no mo' bacon dyoin' er dat time.'

"Well, it des 'peared ez if fum dat time Dave didn' hab nuffin but trouble. De niggers all turnt ag'in' 'im, caze he be'n de 'casion er Mars Dugal' turnin' 'em all ober ter Mars Walker. Mars Dugal' wa'n't a bad marster hisse'f, but Mars Walker wuz hard ez a rock. Dave kep' on sayin' he didn' take de ham, but none un 'em didn' b'lieve 'im.

"Dilsey wa'n't on de plantation w'en Dave wuz 'cused er stealin' de bacon. Ole mist'iss had sont her ter town fer a week er so fer ter wait on one er her darters w'at had a young baby, en she didn' fine out nuffin 'bout Dave's trouble 'tel she got back ter de plantation. Dave had patien'ly endyoed de finger er scawn, en all de hard words w'at de

niggers pile' on 'im, caze he wuz sho' Dilsey would stan' by 'im, en
wouldn' b'lieve he wuz a rogue, ner none er de yuther tales de darkies
wuz tellin' 'bout 'im.

"W'en Dilsey come back fum town, en got down fum behine de
buggy whar she be'n ridin' wid ole mars, de fus' nigger 'ooman she met
says ter her,—

"'Is yer seed Dave, Dilsey?'

"'No, I ain' seed Dave,' says Dilsey.

"'Yer des oughter look at dat nigger; reckon yer wouldn' want 'im
fer yo' junesey no mo'. Mars Walker cotch 'im stealin' bacon, en gone
en fasten' a ham roun' his neck, so he can't git it off'n hisse'f. He sut'nly
do look quare.' En den de 'ooman bus' out laffin' fit ter kill herse'f.
W'en she got thoo laffin' she up'n tole Dilsey all 'bout de ham, en all de
yuther lies w'at de niggers be'n tellin' on Dave.

"W'en Dilsey started down ter de quarters, who should she meet
but Dave, comin' in fum de cotton-fiel'. She turnt her head ter one side,
en purten' lack she didn' seed Dave.

"'Dilsey!' sezee.

"Dilsey walk' right on, en didn' notice 'im.

"'*Oh*, Dilsey!'

"Dilsey didn' paid no 'tention ter 'im, en den Dave knowed some er
de niggers be'n tellin' her 'bout de ham. He felt monst'us bad, but he
'lowed ef he could des git Dilsey fer ter listen ter 'im fer a minute er so,
he could make her b'lieve he didn' stole de bacon. It wuz a week er two
befo' he could git a chance ter speak ter her ag'in; but fine'ly he cotch
her down by de spring one day, en sezee:—

"'Dilsey, w'at fer yer won' speak ter me, en purten' lack yer doan
see me? Dilsey, yer knows me too well fer ter b'lieve I'd steal, er do dis
yuther wick'ness de niggers is all layin' ter me,—yer *knows* I wouldn'
do dat, Dilsey. Yer ain' gwine back on yo' Dave, is yer?'

"But w'at Dave say didn' hab no 'fec' on Dilsey. Dem lies folks b'en
tellin' her had p'isen' her min' 'g'in' Dave.

"'I doan wanter talk ter no nigger,' says she, 'w'at be'n whip' fer
stealin', en w'at gwine roun' wid sich a lookin' thing ez dat hung roun'
his neck. I's a 'spectable gal, *I* is. W'at yer call dat, Dave? Is dat a cha'm
fer ter keep off witches, er is it a noo kine er neckliss yer got?'

"Po' Dave didn' knowed w'at ter do. De las' one he had 'pended on
fer ter stan' by 'im had gone back on 'im, en dey didn' 'pear ter be

nuffin mo' wuf libbin' fer. He couldn' hol' no mo' pra'r-meetin's, fer Mars Walker wouldn' 'low 'im ter preach, en de darkies wouldn' 'a' listen' ter 'im ef he had preach'. He didn' eben hab his Bible fer ter comfort hisse'f wid, fer Mars Walker had tuk it erway fum 'im en burnt it up, en say ef he ketch any mo' niggers wid Bibles on de plantation he'd do 'em wuss'n he done Dave.

"En ter make it still harder fer Dave, Dilsey tuk up wid Wiley. Dave could see him gwine up ter Aun' Mahaly's cabin, en settin' out on de bench in de moonlight wid Dilsey, en singin' sinful songs en playin' de banjer. Dave use' ter scrouch down behine de bushes, en wonder w'at de Lawd sen' 'im all dem tribberlations fer.

"But all er Dave's yuther troubles wa'n't nuffin side er dat ham. He had wrap' de chain roun' wid a rag, so it didn' hurt his neck; but w'en-eber he went ter wuk, dat ham would be in his way; he had ter do his task, howsomedever, des de same ez ef he didn' hab de ham. W'eneber he went ter lay down, dat ham would be in de way. Ef he turn ober in his sleep, dat ham would be tuggin' at his neck. It wuz de las' thing he seed at night, en de fus' thing he seed in de mawnin'. W'eneber he met a stranger, de ham would be de fus' thing de stranger would see. Most un 'em would 'mence' ter laf, en whareber Dave went he could see folks p'intin' at him, en year 'em sayin':—

"'W'at kine er collar dat nigger got roun' his neck?' er, ef dey knowed 'im, 'Is yer stole any mo' hams lately?' er 'W'at yer take fer yo' neckliss, Dave?' er some joke er 'nuther 'bout dat ham.

"Fus' Dave didn' mine it so much, caze he knowed he hadn' done nuffin. But bimeby he got so he couldn' stan' it no longer, en he'd hide hisse'f in de bushes w'eneber he seed anybody comin', en alluz kep' hisse'f shet up in his cabin atter he come in fum wuk.

"It wuz monst'us hard on Dave, en bimeby, w'at wid dat ham eber-lastin' en etarnally draggin' roun' his neck, he 'mence' fer ter do en say quare things, en make de niggers wonder ef he wa'n't gittin' out'n his mine. He got ter gwine roun' talkin' ter hisse'f, en singin' corn-shuckin' songs, en laffin' fit ter kill 'bout nuffin. En one day he tole one er de niggers he had 'skivered a noo way fer ter raise hams,—gwine ter pick 'em off'n trees, en save de expense er smoke-'ouses by kyoin' 'em in de sun. En one day he up'n tole Mars Walker he got sump'n pertickler fer ter say ter 'im; en he tuk Mars Walker off ter one side, en tole 'im he wuz gwine ter show 'im a place in de swamp whar dey wuz a whole trac' er lan' covered wid ham-trees.

"W'en Mars Walker hearn Dave talkin' dis kine er fool-talk, en w'en he seed how Dave wuz 'mencin' ter git behine in his wuk, en w'en he ax' de niggers en dey tole 'im how Dave be'n gwine on, he 'lowed he reckon' he'd punish' Dave ernuff, en it mou't do mo' harm dan good fer ter keep de ham on his neck any longer. So he sont Dave down ter de blacksmif-shop en had de ham tuk off. Dey wa'n't much er de ham lef' by dat time, fer de sun had melt all de fat, en de lean had all swivel' up, so dey wa'n't but th'ee er fo' poun's lef'.

"W'en de ham had be'n tuk off'n Dave, folks kinder stopped talkin' 'bout 'im so much. But de ham had be'n on his neck so long dat Dave had sorter got use' ter it. He look des lack he'd los' sump'n fer a day er so atter de ham wuz tuk off, en didn' 'pear ter know w'at ter do wid hisse'f; en fine'ly he up'n tuk'n tied a lighterd-knot ter a string, en hid it under de flo' er his cabin, en w'en nobody wuzn' lookin' he'd take it out en hang it roun' his neck, en go off in de woods en holler en sing; en he allus tied it roun' his neck w'en he went ter sleep. Fac', it 'peared lack Dave done gone clean out'n his mine. En atter a w'ile he got one er de quarest notions you eber hearn tell un. It wuz 'bout dat time dat I come back ter de plantation fer ter wuk,—I had be'n out ter Mars Dugal's yuther place on Beaver Crick for a mont' er so. I had hearn 'bout Dave en de bacon, en 'bout w'at wuz gwine on on de plantation; but I didn' b'lieve w'at dey all say 'bout Dave, fer I knowed Dave wa'n't dat kine er man. One day atter I come back, me'n Dave wuz choppin' cotton tergedder, w'en Dave lean' on his hoe, en motion' fer me ter come ober close ter 'im; en den he retch' ober en w'ispered ter me.

"'Julius,' sezee, 'did yer knowed yer wuz wukkin' long yer wid a ham?'

"I couldn' 'magine w'at he meant. 'G'way fum yer, Dave,' says I. 'Yer ain' wearin' no ham no mo'; try en fergit 'bout dat; 't ain' gwine ter do yer no good fer ter 'member it.'

"'Look a-yer, Julius,' sezee, 'kin yer keep a secret?'

"'Co'se I kin, Dave,' says I. 'I doan go roun' tellin' people w'at yuther folks says ter me.'

"'Kin I trus' yer, Julius? Will yer cross yo' heart?'

"I cross' my heart. 'Wush I may die ef I tells a soul,' says I.

"Dave look' at me des lack he wuz lookin' thoo me en 'way on de yuther side er me, en sezee:—

"'Did yer knowed I wuz turnin' ter a ham, Julius?'

"I tried ter 'suade Dave dat dat wuz all foolishness, en dat he oughtn't ter be talkin' dat-a-way,—hit wa'n't right. En I tole 'im ef he'd des be patien', de time would sho'ly come w'en eve'ything would be straighten' out, en folks would fine out who de rale rogue wuz w'at stole de bacon. Dave 'peared ter listen ter w'at I say, en promise' ter do better, en stop gwine on dat-a-way; en it seem lack he pick' up a bit w'en he seed dey wuz one pusson didn' b'lieve dem tales 'bout 'im.

"Hit wa'n't long atter dat befo' Mars Archie McIntyre, ober on de Wimbleton road, 'mence' ter complain 'bout somebody stealin' chickens fum his hen-'ouse. De chickens kep' on gwine, en at las' Mars Archie tole de han's on his plantation dat he gwine ter shoot de fus' man he ketch in his hen-'ouse. In less'n a week atter he gin dis warnin', he cotch a nigger in de hen-'ouse, en fill' 'im full er squir'l-shot. W'en he got a light, he 'skivered it wuz a strange nigger; en w'en he call' one er his own sarven's, de nigger tole 'im it wuz our Wiley. W'en Mars Archie foun' dat out, he sont ober ter our plantation fer ter tell Mars Dugal' he had shot one er his niggers, en dat he could sen' ober dere en git w'at wuz lef' un 'im.

"Mars Dugal' wuz mad at fus'; but w'en he got ober dere en hearn how it all happen', he didn' hab much ter say. Wiley wuz shot so bad he wuz sho' he wuz gwine ter die, so he up'n says ter ole marster:—

"'Mars Dugal',' sezee, 'I knows I's be'n a monst'us bad nigger, but befo' I go I wanter git sump'n off'n my mine. Dave didn' steal dat bacon w'at wuz tuk out'n de smoke-'ouse. *I* stole it all, en I hid de ham under Dave's cabin fer ter th'ow de blame on him—en may de good Lawd fergib me fer it.'

"Mars Dugal' had Wiley tuk back ter de plantation, en sont fer a doctor fer ter pick de shot out'n 'im. En de ve'y nex' mawnin' Mars Dugal' sont fer Dave ter come up ter de big house; he felt kinder sorry fer de way Dave had be'n treated. Co'se it wa'n't no fault er Mars Dugal's, but he wuz gwine ter do w'at he could fer ter make up fer it. So he sont word down ter de quarters fer Dave en all de yuther han's ter 'semble up in de yard befo' de big house at sun-up nex' mawnin'.

"Yearly in de mawnin' de niggers all swarm' up in de yard. Mars Dugal' wuz feelin' so kine dat he had brung up a bairl er cider, en tole de niggers all fer ter he'p deyselves.

"All de han's on de plantation come but Dave; en bimeby, w'en it seem lack he wa'n't comin', Mars Dugal' sont a nigger down ter de quarters ter look fer 'im. De sun wuz gittin' up, en dey wuz a heap er wuk ter be done, en Mars Dugal' sorter got ti'ed waitin'; so he up'n says:—

"'Well, boys en gals, I sont fer yer all up yer fer ter tell yer dat all dat 'bout Dave's stealin' er de bacon wuz a mistake, ez I s'pose yer all done hearn befo' now, en I's mighty sorry it happen'. I wants ter treat all my niggers right, en I wants yer all ter know dat I sets a heap by all er my han's w'at is hones' en smart. En I want yer all ter treat Dave des lack yer did befo' dis thing happen', en mine w'at he preach ter yer; fer Dave is a good nigger, en has had a hard row ter hoe. En de fus' one I ketch sayin' anythin' 'g'in' Dave, I'll tell Mister Walker ter gin 'im forty. Now take ernudder drink er cider all roun', en den git at dat cotton, fer I wanter git dat Persimmon Hill trac' all pick' ober ter-day.'

"W'en de niggers wuz gwine 'way, Mars Dugal' tole me fer ter go en hunt up Dave, en bring 'im up ter de house. I went down ter Dave's cabin, but couldn' fine 'im dere. Den I look' roun' de plantation, en in de aidge er de woods, en 'long de road; but I couldn' fine no sign er Dave. I wuz 'bout ter gin up de sarch, w'en I happen' fer ter run 'cross a foot-track w'at look' lack Dave's. I had wukked 'long wid Dave so much dat I knowed his tracks: he had a monst'us long foot, wid a holler instep, w'ich wuz sump'n skase 'mongs' black folks. So I follered dat track 'cross de fiel' fum de quarters 'tel I got ter de smoke-'ouse. De fus' thing I notice' wuz smoke comin' out'n de cracks: it wuz cu'ous, caze dey hadn' be'n no hogs kill' on de plantation fer six mont' er so, en all de bacon in de smoke-'ouse wuz done kyoed. I couldn' 'magine fer ter sabe my life w'at Dave wuz doin' in dat smoke-'ouse. I went up ter de do' en hollered:—

"'Dave!'

"Dey didn' nobody answer. I didn' wanter open de do', fer w'ite folks is monst'us pertickler 'bout dey smoke-'ouses; en ef de oberseah had a-come up en cotch me in dere, he mou't not wanter b'lieve I wuz des lookin' fer Dave. So I sorter knock at de do' en call' out ag'in:—

"'O Dave, hit's me—Julius! Doan be skeered. Mars Dugal' wants yer ter come up ter de big house,—he done 'skivered who stole de ham.'

"But Dave didn' answer. En w'en I look' roun' ag'in en didn' seed none er his tracks gwine way fum de smoke-'ouse, I knowed he wuz in dere yit, en I wuz 'termine' fer ter fetch 'im out; so I push de do' open en look in.

"Dey wuz a pile er bark burnin' in de middle er de flo', en right ober de fier, hangin' fum one er de rafters, wuz Dave; dey wuz a rope roun' his neck, en I didn' haf ter look at his face mo' d'n once fer ter see he wuz dead.

"Den I knowed how it all happen'. Dave had kep' on gittin' wusser en wusser in his mine, 'tel he des got ter b'lievin' he wuz all done turnt ter a ham; en den he had gone en built a fier, en tied a rope roun' his neck, des lack de hams wuz tied, en had hung hisse'f up in de smoke-'ouse fer ter kyo.

"Dave wuz buried down by de swamp, in de plantation buryin'-groun'. Wiley didn' died fum de woun' he got in Mars McIntyre's hen-'ouse; he got well atter a w'ile, but Dilsey wouldn' hab nuffin mo' ter do wid 'im, en 't wa'n't long 'fo' Mars Dugal' sol' 'im ter a spekilater on his way souf,—he say he didn' want no sich a nigger on de plantation, ner in de county, ef he could he'p it. En w'en de een' er de year come, Mars Dugal' turnt Mars Walker off, en run de plantation hisse'f atter dat.

"Eber sence den," said Julius in conclusion, "w'eneber I eats ham, it min's me er Dave. I lacks ham, but I nebber kin eat mo' d'n two er th'ee poun's befo' I gits ter studyin' 'bout Dave, en den I has ter stop en leab de res' fer ernudder time."

There was a short silence after the old man had finished his story, and then my wife began to talk to him about the weather, on which subject he was an authority. I went into the house. When I came out, half an hour later, I saw Julius disappearing down the lane, with a basket on his arm.

At breakfast, next morning, it occurred to me that I should like a slice of ham. I said as much to my wife.

"Oh, no, John," she responded, "you shouldn't eat anything so heavy for breakfast."

I insisted.

"The fact is," she said, pensively, "I couldn't have eaten any more of that ham, and so I gave it to Julius."

Schopenhauer in the Air

Sadakichi Hartmann

It was a dismal grey-in-grey evening, the atmosphere laden with moisture as if it had not the energy to condense into rain, like forlorn moods of world strangeness and nostalgia when the human soul would seek relief in weeping and finds itself incapable of tears.

Under an old battered lamp post whose head was bent to one side as if weary of its vain endeavor to brighten that cheerless scene, a little girl with folded arms and crouching head crouched on the curbstones. Only when a slight draught floated through the broken panes of the lantern, the flickering flame shed a vague, hasty glare over the dry, haggard form of the little minx, whose dull eyes were seen to throw searching glances along the gutter, as if in quest of some unknown treasure hidden in the mud.

Suddenly she started up, her eyes, growing wide, had caught sight of something lying within her hand's reach,—a little pale green lump; she stretched out her foot and examined it with her toes. It was a single grape, slightly rotten on one side, that had dropped into the gutter. On recognizing what it was, she picked it up with greedy fingers, while her homely, careworn face became distorted with a grinning grimace, which was meant for joy. She began to suck the little fruit, and her harsh features assumed an air of gentleness for the moment, that relaxed, as soon as the pleasure was over, into that phlegmatic expression of despair, which in older beings interprets disgust of life.

The occasional passers-by hardly noticed her; the picture she made was so insignificant in composition, so faded in tone, without the slightest suggestion of brightness in her dirty face, streaky hair, and ragged, patched clothes, that it disappeared entirely in the background of the muddy pavement, on which the reflections of the lantern glimmered like luring gold.

Had she been older, one would have supposed she was thinking, but the little girl had not yet learned to think, nor was she really conscious of or responsible for the stammering expressions of her soul battered like the lamp post. In her mind one blurred picture followed the other, and these impressions made out her life, as they make out that of every child, and also of many grown-up persons, but hers were all steeped in mud like her feet. They were like figures we see with closed eyes, weaving to and fro in a room deprived of light, the forms and meanings of which we cannot define. Only now and then some object stood out distinctly in that chaos of sombre colors,—a huge beer pitcher which she could hardly carry when filled—rings of spilt liquor—a broken pipe—a hairy fist on the table—two drunken forms in a squalid room, a stagnant atmosphere never purified by sunshine, and with them all the associations of sound, familiar to her, coarse laughter, hoarse voices, curses and bestial exclamations.

A stout, blear-eyed wench stepped off the sidewalk to cross the street, brushing the face of the little girl with her greasy, rose-colored wrapper. She saw that spot of color waddling across the sunken filthy pavement and disappearing in the frivolity of a nocturnal scene formed by a loafing crowd before a lighted saloon on the opposite sidewalk. For a moment she felt like following that luring apparition and, after wading through the mire of sin, losing herself in that deluding brightness. But she did not give away to the temptation and remained as before in her crouching position, with gloomy face. Her unconscious meditation returned to the former pictures, which grew darker and still darker, the web of her consciousness being spun without the former threads of blackish blue and red.

The shrill sound of a bell! An ambulance dashed through the street. Men and women interrupted their flirtation and craned their necks with curious astonishment to witness an event so commonplace in a large city, but, nevertheless, an excitement, a vibration, a break in the appalling, unbearable monotony of routine life.

The little girl had also risen, but slowly, not like the others, and now moved along slowly, as if by mere accident, in the same direction. Her thin legs gradually moved in a quicker rhythm, and, aimless, she pressed forward with her head still crouching and swaying abruptly from side to side, along the long street with its dark rows of tenement houses, one looking exactly like the other, and indicating by their dismal similarity that they also shelter human beings, leading, one exactly like the other, a monotonous routine life, minute for minute, and score for score, void of all ideal pleasures, and growing darker and more deserted towards its end, like the street as the little outcast neared the river.

The oppressive atmosphere, spreading like a veil of despondency over the city and seeming to absorb all sounds and colors, bored itself without pity, deeper and deeper into every sensitive soul. Poets and artists hastened into the taverns or to their own humble homes, for to abandon oneself, like the little girl, to the atmosphere of such a night might prove dangerous to one's pulse.

Suddenly she found herself at the end of the wharf, looking down into the water, lapping against the framework like the soft caresses of living hands. Before her lay the river, a dark, sluggishly floating mass, on whose surface the convulsive play of rising and falling waves was hardly perceptible. In the distance a few forlorn lights blinked like the solitary moments of joy in our life of disappointment. The outlines of huge storehouses, looking like medieval castles with towers and turrets in the dim atmosphere, suggested vague reveries to her, never felt before. Profound silence lay on the river. Only far from the distance a melancholy melody was wafted over; some boatsman playing on a harmonica. Then a ferryboat with its many lighted windows floated by like a phantom. Was it a vision of our life, so full of delusion, so beautiful, and yet nothing but a passing show—transparent glass and artificial light?

The little girl stood for a long time on the extreme edge of the framework; she had raised her head and breathed slowly and calmly; her face looked less gloomy. Suddenly she straightened herself, opened her arms as if to embrace that night with all its dark dreams and desires—a little black figure fell—a splash in the water—a suppressed scream that almost sounded like a laugh of satisfaction—then everything grew silent as before, only where the child had disappeared the circles on the dark and desolate flood became wider and wider until they met with the foaming keel water of the phantom boat of happiness, that invariably glides by on the gray river of our life.

Lilacs

Kate Chopin

M me. Adrienne Farival never announced her coming; but the good
nuns knew very well when to look for her. When the scent of the
lilac blossoms began to permeate the air, Sister Agathe would turn
many times during the day to the window; upon her face the happy,
beatific expression with which pure and simple souls watch for the
coming of those they love.

But it was not Sister Agathe; it was Sister Marceline who first espied
her crossing the beautiful lawn that sloped up to the convent. Her arms
were filled with great bunches of lilacs which she had gathered along
her path. She was clad all in brown; like one of the birds that come with
the spring, the nuns used to say. Her figure was rounded and graceful,
and she walked with a happy, buoyant step. The cabriolet which had
conveyed her to the convent moved slowly up the gravel drive that led
to the imposing entrance. Beside the driver was her modest little black
trunk, with her name and address printed in white letters upon it:
"Mme. A. Farival, Paris." It was the crunching of the gravel which had
attracted Sister Marceline's attention. And then the commotion began.

White-capped heads appeared suddenly at the windows; she waved
her parasol and her bunch of lilacs at them. Sister Marceline and Sister
Marie Anne appeared, fluttered and expectant at the doorway. But

Sister Agathe, more daring and impulsive than all, descended the steps and flew across the grass to meet her. What embraces, in which the lilacs were crushed between them! What ardent kisses! What pink flushes of happiness mounting the cheeks of the two women!

Once within the convent Adrienne's soft brown eyes moistened with tenderness as they dwelt caressingly upon the familiar objects about her, and noted the most trifling details. The white, bare boards of the floor had lost nothing of their lustre. The stiff, wooden chairs, standing in rows against the walls of hall and parlor, seemed to have taken on an extra polish since she had seen them, last lilac time. And there was a new picture of the Sacré Coeur hanging over the hall table. What had they done with Ste. Catharine de Sienne, who had occupied that position of honor for so many years? In the chapel—it was no use trying to deceive her—she saw at a glance that St. Joseph's mantle had been embellished with a new coat of blue, and the aureole about his head freshly gilded. And the Blessed Virgin there neglected! Still wearing her garb of last spring, which looked almost dingy by contrast. It was not just—such partiality! The Holy Mother had reason to be jealous and to complain.

But Adrienne did not delay to pay her respects to the Mother Superior, whose dignity would not permit her to so much as step outside the door of her private apartments to welcome this old pupil. Indeed, she was dignity in person; large, uncompromising, unbending. She kissed Adrienne without warmth, and discussed conventional themes learnedly and prosaically during the quarter of an hour which the young woman remained in her company.

It was then that Adrienne's latest gift was brought in for inspection. For Adrienne always brought a handsome present for the chapel in her little black trunk. Last year it was a necklace of gems for the Blessed Virgin, which the Good Mother was only permitted to wear on extra occasions, such as great feast days of obligation. The year before it had been a precious crucifix—an ivory figure of Christ suspended from an ebony cross, whose extremities were tipped with wrought silver. This time it was a linen embroidered altar-cloth of such rare and delicate workmanship that the Mother Superior, who knew the value of such things, chided Adrienne for the extravagance.

"But, dear Mother, you know it is the greatest pleasure I have in life—to be with you all once a year, and to bring some such trifling token of my regard."

The Mother Superior dismissed her with the rejoinder: "Make your-self at home, my child. Sister Thérèse will see to your wants. You will occupy Sister Marceline's bed in the end room, over the chapel. You will share the room with Sister Agathe."

There was always one of the nuns detailed to keep Adrienne com-pany during her fortnight's stay at the convent. This had become al-most a fixed regulation. It was only during the hours of recreation that she found herself with them all together. Those were hours of much harmless merrymaking under the trees or in the nuns' refectory.

This time it was Sister Agathe who waited for her outside of the Mother Superior's door. She was taller and slenderer than Adrienne, and perhaps ten years older. Her fair blonde face flushed and paled with every passing emotion that visited her soul. The two women linked arms and went together out into the open air.

There was so much which Sister Agathe felt that Adrienne must see. To begin with, the enlarged poultry yard, with its dozens upon dozens of new inmates. It took now all the time of one of the lay-sisters to attend to them. There had been no change made in the vegetable garden, but—yes, there had; Adrienne's quick eye at once detected it. Last year old Philippe had planted his cabbages in a large square to the right. This year they were set out in an oblong bed to the left. How it made Sister Agathe laugh to think Adrienne should have noticed such a trifle! And old Philippe, who was nailing a broken trellis not far off, was called forward to be told about it.

He never failed to tell Adrienne how well she looked, and how she was growing younger each year. And it was his delight to recall certain of her youthful and mischievous escapades. Never would he forget that day she disappeared; and the whole convent in a hubbub about it! And how at last it was he who discovered her perched among the tallest branches of the highest tree on the grounds, where she had climbed to see if she could get a glimpse of Paris! And her punishment afterward!— half of the Gospel of Palm Sunday to learn by heart!

"We may laugh over it, my good Philippe, but we must remember that Madame is older and wiser now."

"I know well, Sister Agathe, that one ceases to commit follies after the first days of youth." And Adrienne seemed greatly impressed by the wisdom of Sister Agathe and old Philippe, the convent gardener.

A little later when they sat upon a rustic bench which overlooked the smiling landscape about them, Adrienne was saying to Sister Agathe, who held her hand and stroked it fondly:

"Do you remember my first visit, four years ago, Sister Agathe? and what a surprise it was to you all!"

"As if I could forget it, dear child!"

"And I! Always shall I remember that morning as I walked along the boulevard with a heaviness of heart—oh, a heaviness which I hate to recall. Suddenly there was wafted to me the sweet odor of lilac blossoms. A young girl had passed me by, carrying a great bunch of them. Did you ever know, Sister Agathe, that there is nothing which so keenly revives a memory as a perfume—an odor?"

"I believe you are right, Adrienne. For now that you speak of it, I can feel how the odor of fresh bread—when Sister Jeanne bakes—always makes me think of the great kitchen of ma tante de Sierge, and crippled Julie, who sat always knitting at the sunny window. And I never smell the sweet scented honeysuckle without living again through the blessed day of my first communion."

"Well, that is how it was with me, Sister Agathe, when the scent of the lilacs at once changed the whole current of my thoughts and my despondency. The boulevard, its noises, its passing throng, vanished from before my senses as completely as if they had been spirited away. I was standing here with my feet sunk in the green sward as they are now. I could see the sunlight glancing from that old white stone wall, could hear the notes of birds, just as we hear them now, and the humming of insects in the air. And through all I could see and could smell the lilac blossoms, nodding invitingly to me from their thick-leaved branches. It seems to me they are richer than ever this year, Sister Agathe. And do you know, I became like an enragée; nothing could have kept me back. I do not remember now where I was going; but I turned and retraced my steps homeward in a perfect fever of agitation: 'Sophie! my little trunk—quick—the black one! A mere handful of clothes! I am going away. Don't ask me any questions. I shall be back in a fortnight.' And every year since then it is the same. At the very first whiff of a lilac blossom, I am gone! There is no holding me back."

"And how I wait for you, and watch those lilac bushes, Adrienne! If you should once fail to come, it would be like the spring coming without the sunshine or the song of birds.

"But do you know, dear child, I have sometimes feared that in moments of despondency such as you have just described, I fear that you do not turn as you might to our Blessed Mother in heaven, who is ever ready to comfort and solace an afflicted heart with the precious balm of her sympathy and love."

"Perhaps I do not, dear Sister Agathe. But you cannot picture the annoyances which I am constantly submitted to. That Sophie alone, with her detestable ways! I assure you she of herself is enough to drive me to St. Lazare."

"Indeed, I do understand that the trials of one living in the world must be very great, Adrienne; particularly for you, my poor child, who have to bear them alone, since Almighty God was pleased to call to himself your dear husband. But on the other hand, to live one's life along the lines which our dear Lord traces for each one of us, must bring with it resignation and even a certain comfort. You have your household duties, Adrienne, and your music, to which, you say, you continue to devote yourself. And then, there are always good works— the poor—who are always with us—to be relieved; the afflicted to be comforted."

"But, Sister Agathe! Will you listen! Is it not La Rose that I hear moving down there at the edge of the pasture? I fancy she is reproaching me with being an ingrate, not to have pressed a kiss yet on that white forehead of hers. Come, let us go."

The two women arose and walked again, hand in hand this time, over the tufted grass down the gentle decline where it sloped toward the broad, flat meadow, and the limpid stream that flowed cool and fresh from the woods. Sister Agathe walked with her composed, nun-like tread; Adrienne with a balancing motion, a bounding step, as though the earth responded to her light footfall with some subtle impulse all its own.

They lingered long upon the foot-bridge that spanned the narrow stream which divided the convent grounds from the meadow beyond. It was to Adrienne indescribably sweet to rest there in soft, low converse with this gentle-faced nun, watching the approach of evening. The gurgle of the running water beneath them; the lowing of cattle approaching in the distance, were the only sounds that broke upon the stillness, until the clear tones of the angelus bell pealed out from the convent tower. At the sound both women instinctively sank to their knees, signing themselves with the sign of the cross. And Sister Agathe repeated the customary invocation, Adrienne responding in musical tones:

"The Angel of the Lord declared unto Mary,
And she conceived by the Holy Ghost—"

and so forth, to the end of the brief prayer, after which they arose and retraced their steps toward the convent.

It was with subtle and naive pleasure that Adrienne prepared herself that night for bed. The room which she shared with Sister Agathe was immaculately white. The walls were a dead white, relieved only by one florid print depicting Jacob's dream at the foot of the ladder, upon which angels mounted and descended. The bare floors, a soft yellow-white, with two little patches of gray carpet beside each spotless bed. At the head of the white-draped beds were two benitiers containing holy water absorbed in sponges.

Sister Agathe disrobed noiselessly behind her curtains and glided into bed without having revealed, in the faint candle light, so much as a shadow of herself. Adrienne pattered about the room, shook and folded her garments with great care, placing them on the back of a chair as she had been taught to do when a child at the convent. It secretly pleased Sister Agathe to feel that her dear Adrienne clung to the habits acquired in her youth.

But Adrienne could not sleep. She did not greatly desire to do so. These hours seemed too precious to be cast into the oblivion of slumber.

"Are you not asleep, Adrienne?"

"No, Sister Agathe. You know it is always so the first night. The excitement of my arrival—I don't know what—keeps me awake."

"Say your 'Hail, Mary,' dear child, over and over."

"I have done so, Sister Agathe; it does not help."

"Then lie quite still on your side and think of nothing but your own respiration. I have heard that such inducement to sleep seldom fails."

"I will try. Good night, Sister Agathe."

"Good night, dear child. May the Holy Virgin guard you."

An hour later Adrienne was still lying with wide, wakeful eyes, listening to the regular breathing of Sister Agathe. The trailing of the passing wind through the treetops, the ceaseless babble of the rivulet were some of the sounds that came to her faintly through the night.

The days of the fortnight which followed were in character much like the first peaceful, uneventful day of her arrival, with the exception only that she devoutly heard mass every morning at an early hour in the convent chapel, and on Sundays sang in the choir in her agreeable, cultivated voice, which was heard with delight and the warmest appreciation.

When the day of her departure came, Sister Agathe was not satisfied to say good-by at the portal as the others did. She walked down the drive beside the creeping old cabriolet, chattering her pleasant last words. And then she stood—it was as far as she might go—at the edge of the road, waving good-by in response to the fluttering of Adrienne's handkerchief.

Four hours later Sister Agathe, who was instructing a class of little girls for their first communion, looked up at the classroom clock and murmured: "Adrienne is at home now."

Yes, Adrienne was at home. Paris had engulfed her.

II.

At the very hour when Sister Agathe looked up at the clock, Adrienne, clad in a charming négligé, was reclining indolently in the depths of a luxurious armchair. The bright room was in its accustomed state of picturesque disorder. Musical scores were scattered upon the open piano. Thrown carelessly over the backs of chairs were puzzling and astonishing-looking garments.

In a large gilded cage near the window perched a clumsy green parrot. He blinked stupidly at a young girl in street dress who was exerting herself to make him talk.

In the centre of the room stood Sophie, that thorn in her mistress' side. With hands plunged in the deep pockets of her apron, her white starched cap quivering with each emphatic motion of her grizzled head, she was holding forth, to the evident ennui of the two young women. She was saying:

"Heaven knows I have stood enough in the six years I have been with Mademoiselle; but never such indignities as I have had to endure in the past two weeks at the hands of that man who calls himself a manager! The very first day—and I, good enough to notify him at once of Mademoiselle's flight—he arrives like a lion; I tell you, like a lion. He insists upon knowing Mademoiselle's whereabouts. How can I tell him any more than the statue out there in the square? He calls me a liar! Me, me—a liar! He declares he is ruined. The public will not stand La Petite Gilberta in the role which Mademoiselle has made so famous— La Petite Gilberta, who dances like a jointed wooden figure and sings like a trainée of a café chantant. If I were to tell La Gilberta that, as I easily might, I guarantee it would not be well for the few straggling hairs which he has left on that miserable head of his!

"What could he do? He was obliged to inform the public that Mademoiselle was ill; and then began my real torment! Answering this one and that one with their cards, their flowers, their dainties in covered dishes! which, I must admit, saved Florine and me much cooking. And all the while having to tell them that the physician had advised for Mademoiselle a rest of two weeks at some watering-place, the name of which I had forgotten!"

Adrienne had been contemplating old Sophie with quizzical, half-closed eyes, and pelting her with hothouse roses which lay in her lap, and which she nipped off short from their graceful stems for that purpose. Each rose struck Sophie full in the face; but they did not disconcert her or once stem the torrent of her talk.

"Oh, Adrienne!" entreated the young girl at the parrot's cage. "Make her hush; please do something. How can you ever expect Zozo to talk? A dozen times he has been on the point of saying something! I tell you, she stupefies him with her chatter."

"My good Sophie," remarked Adrienne, not changing her attitude, "you see the roses are all used up. But I assure you, anything at hand goes," carelessly picking up a book from the table beside her. "What is this? Mons. Zola! Now I warn you, Sophie, the weightiness, the heaviness of Mons. Zola are such that they cannot fail to prostrate you; thankful you may be if they leave you with energy to regain your feet."

"Mademoiselle's pleasantries are all very well; but if I am to be shown the door for it—if I am to be crippled for it—I shall say that I think Mademoiselle is a woman without conscience and without heart. To torture a man as she does! A man? No, an angel!

"Each day he has come with sad visage and drooping mien. 'No news, Sophie?'

"'None, Monsieur Henri.' 'Have you no idea where she has gone?' 'Not any more than the statue in the square, Monsieur.' 'Is it perhaps possible that she may not return at all?' with his face blanching like that curtain.

"I assure him you will be back at the end of the fortnight. I entreat him to have patience. He drags himself, désolé, about the room, picking up Mademoiselle's fan, her gloves, her music, and turning them over and over in his hands. Mademoiselle's slipper, which she took off to throw at me in the impatience of her departure, and which I purposely left lying where it fell on the chiffonier—he kissed it—I saw him do it—and thrust it into his pocket, thinking himself unobserved.

"The same song each day. I beg him to eat a little good soup which I have prepared. 'I cannot eat, my dear Sophie.' The other night he came and stood long gazing out of the window at the stars. When he turned he was wiping his eyes; they were red. He said he had been riding in the dust, which had inflamed them. But I knew better; he had been crying.

"Ma foi! in his place I would snap my finger at such cruelty. I would go out and amuse myself. What is the use of being young!"

Adrienne arose with a laugh. She went and seizing old Sophie by the shoulders shook her till the white cap wobbled on her head.

"What is the use of all this litany, my good Sophie? Year after year the same! Have you forgotten that I have come a long, dusty journey by rail, and that I am perishing of hunger and thirst? Bring us a bottle of Chateau Yquem and a biscuit and my box of cigarettes." Sophie had freed herself, and was retreating toward the door. "And, Sophie! If Monsieur Henri is still waiting, tell him to come up."

III.

It was precisely a year later. The spring had come again, and Paris was intoxicated.

Old Sophie sat in her kitchen discoursing to a neighbor who had come in to borrow some trifling kitchen utensil from the old bonne.

"You know, Rosalie, I begin to believe it is an attack of lunacy which seizes her once a year. I wouldn't say it to everyone, but with you I know it will go no further. She ought to be treated for it; a physician should be consulted; it is not well to neglect such things and let them run on.

"It came this morning like a thunder clap. As I am sitting here, there had been no thought or mention of a journey. The baker had come into the kitchen—you know what a gallant he is—with always a girl in his eye. He laid the bread down upon the table and beside it a bunch of lilacs. I didn't know they had bloomed yet. 'For Mam'selle Florine, with my regards,' he said with his foolish simper.

"Now, you know I was not going to call Florine from her work in order to present her the baker's flowers. All the same, it would not do to let them wither. I went with them in my hand into the dining room to get a majolica pitcher which I had put away in the closet there, on an upper shelf, because the handle was broken. Mademoiselle, who rises early, had just come from her bath, and was crossing the hall that opens into the dining room. Just as she was, in her white peignoir, she thrust her head into the dining room, snuffing the air and exclaiming, 'What do I smell?'

"She espied the flowers in my hand and pounced upon them like a cat upon a mouse. She held them up to her, burying her face in them for the longest time, only uttering a long 'Ah!'

"'Sophie, I am going away. Get out the little black trunk; a few of the plainest garments I have; my brown dress that I have not yet worn.'

"'But, Mademoiselle,' I protested, 'you forget that you have ordered a breakfast of a hundred francs for to-morrow.'

"'Shut up!' she cried, stamping her foot.

"'You forget how the manager will rave,' I persisted, 'and vilify me. And you will go like that without a word of adieu to Monsieur Paul, who is an angel if ever one trod the earth.'

"I tell you, Rosalie, her eyes flamed.

"'Do as I tell you this instant,' she exclaimed, 'or I will strangle you—with your Monsieur Paul and your manager and your hundred francs!'"

"Yes," affirmed Rosalie, "it is insanity. I had a cousin seized in the same way one morning, when she smelled calf's liver frying with onions. Before night it took two men to hold her."

"I could well see it was insanity, my dear Rosalie, and I uttered not another word as I feared for my life. I simply obeyed her every command in silence. And now—whiff, she is gone! God knows where. But between us, Rosalie—I wouldn't say it to Florine—but I believe it is for no good. I, in Monsieur Paul's place, should have her watched. I would put a detective upon her track.

"Now I am going to close up; barricade the entire establishment.

Monsieur Paul, the manager, visitors, all—all may ring and knock and shout themselves hoarse. I am tired of it all. To be vilified and called a liar—at my age, Rosalie!"

IV.

Adrienne left her trunk at the small railway station, as the old cabriolet was not at the moment available; and she gladly walked the mile or two of pleasant roadway which led to the convent. How infinitely calm, peaceful, penetrating was the charm of the verdant, undulating country spreading out on all sides of her! She walked along the clear smooth road, twirling her parasol; humming a gay tune; nipping here and there a bud or a wax-like leaf from the hedges along the way; and all the while drinking deep draughts of complacency and content.

She stopped, as she had always done, to pluck lilacs in her path.

As she approached the convent she fancied that a white-capped face had glanced fleetingly from a window; but she must have been mistaken. Evidently she had not been seen, and this time would take them by surprise. She smiled to think how Sister Agathe would utter a little joyous cry of amazement, and in fancy she already felt the warmth and tenderness of the nun's embrace. And how Sister Marceline and the others would laugh, and make game of her puffed sleeves! For puffed sleeves had come into fashion since last year; and the vagaries of fashion always afforded infinite merriment to the nuns. No, they surely had not seen her.

She ascended lightly the stone steps and rang the bell. She could hear the sharp metallic sound reverberate through the halls. Before its last note had died away the door was opened very slightly, very cautiously by a lay Sister who stood there with downcast eyes and flaming cheeks. Through the narrow opening she thrust forward toward Adrienne a package and a letter, saying, in confused tones: "By order of our Mother Superior." After which she closed the door hastily and turned the heavy key in the great lock.

Adrienne remained stunned. She could not gather her faculties to grasp the meaning of this singular reception. The lilacs fell from her arms to the stone portico on which she was standing. She turned the note and the parcel stupidly over in her hands, instinctively dreading what their contents might disclose.

The outlines of the crucifix were plainly to be felt through the wrapper of the bundle, and she guessed, without having courage to assure herself, that the jeweled necklace and the altar cloth accompanied it.

Leaning against the heavy oaken door for support, Adrienne opened the letter. She did not seem to read the few bitter reproachful lines word by word—the lines that banished her forever from this haven of peace, where her soul was wont to come and refresh itself. They imprinted themselves as a whole upon her brain, in all their seeming cruelty—she did not dare to say injustice.

There was no anger in her heart; that would doubtless possess her later, when her nimble intelligence would begin to seek out the origin of this treacherous turn. Now, there was only room for tears. She leaned her forehead against the heavy oaken panel of the door and wept with the abandonment of a little child.

She descended the steps with a nerveless and dragging tread. Once as she was walking away, she turned to look back at the imposing facade of the convent, hoping to see a familiar face, or a hand, even, giving a faint token that she was still cherished by some one faithful heart. But she saw only the polished windows looking down at her like so many cold and glittering and reproachful eyes.

In the little white room above the chapel, a woman knelt beside the bed on which Adrienne had slept. Her face was pressed deep in the pillow in her efforts to smother the sobs that convulsed her frame. It was Sister Agathe.

After a short while, a lay Sister came out of the door with a broom, and swept away the lilac blossoms which Adrienne had let fall upon the portico.

NOTES

The notes to the Introduction are numbered sequentially. The annotations to the short stories that follow are keyed to page numbers; identify quotations and literary allusions; provide biographical, historical, classical, biblical, and other references; and provide various other kinds of supplementary information. Some of the notes (for Whitman's "The Child's Champion," Cather's "Paul's Case," and Jewett's "Martha's Lady") provide information on significant revisions the authors made to subsequent printings of the stories.

INTRODUCTION

1. Alfred Bendixen, "The Emergence and Development of the American Short Story," in *A Companion to the American Short Story*, ed. Alfred Bendixen and James Nagel (Malden, Mass.: Wiley-Blackwell, 2010), 1; Axel Nissen, "The Queer Short Story," in *The Art of Brevity: Excursions in Short Fiction Theory and Analysis*, ed. Per Winther, Jakob Lothe, and Hans H. Skei (Columbia: University of South Carolina Press, 2004), 181.

2. Nissen's argument here builds upon the broad claims made by Eve Kosofsky Sedgwick, who argued that the homo/heterosexual definitional binary has had a chronic and powerful effect on many other categorical binaries, including notably the literary categories of "canonic/noncanonic." See Sedgwick, *Epistemology of the Closet* (Berkeley: University of California Press, 1990), 11.

3. See, among others, Judith Roof, *Come as You Are: Sexuality and Narrative* (New York: Columbia University Press, 1996); Annamarie Jagose, *Inconsequence: Lesbian Representation and the Logic of Sexual Sequence* (Ithaca: Cornell University Press, 2002); *Narrative Theory Unbound: Queer and Feminist Interventions,* ed. Robyn Warhol and Susan S. Lanser (Columbus: Ohio State University Press, 2015).

4. On Irving see, for example, Michael Warner, "Irving's Posterity," *ELH* 67, no. 3 (2000), 773–99; David Greven, "Troubling Our Heads About Ichabod: 'The Legend of Sleepy Hollow,' Classic American Literature, and the Politics of Homosocial Brotherhood," *American Quarterly* 56, no. 1 (2004), 83–11. On Poe see, among others, Gustavus T. Stadler, "Poe and Queer Studies," Poe Studies/Dark Romanticism: History, Theory, Interpretation 33, nos. 1–2 (2000), 19–22; Valerie Rohy, "Ahistorical," *GLQ: A Journal of Lesbian and Gay Studies* 12, no. 1 (2006), 125–47; Leland S. Person, "Queer Poe: The Tell-Tale Heart of His Fiction," *Poe Studies/Dark Romanticism: History, Theory, Interpretation* 41, no. 1 (2008), 7–30.

5. I here acknowledge my profound debt to the pioneering scholar Susan Koppelman, whose important anthology has served as an inspiring model for the present collection. See *Two Friends and Other Nineteenth-Century Lesbian Stories by American Women Writers*, ed. Susan Koppelman (New York: Meridian, 1994). Of note also is Axel Nissen's excellent anthology, *The Romantic Friendship Reader*, although (with a few exceptions) it reprints mostly excerpts from longer works rather than short stories proper. See *The Romantic Friendship Reader: Love Stories Between Men in Victorian America*, ed. Axel Nissen (Boston: Northeastern University Press, 2003).

6. The classic theoretical account of the historical emergence of sexuality remains Michel Foucault, *The History of Sexuality, Volume 1: An Introduction*, trans. Robert Hurley (New York: Vintage, 1990). See also Jonathan Ned Katz, *The Invention of Heterosexuality* (Chicago: University of Chicago Press, 2007), and Hanne Blank, *Straight: The Surprisingly Short History of Heterosexuality* (Boston: Beacon Press, 2012).

7. Foucault, *History of Sexuality*, 75ff.

8. Benjamin Kahan, *Celibacies: American Modernism and Sexual Life* (Durham, N.C.: Duke University Press, 2013).

9. Stephen Bruhm and Natasha Hurley, eds., *Curiouser: On the Queerness of Children* (Minneapolis: University of Minnesota Press, 2004); Katherine Bond Stockton, *The Queer Child, or Growing Sideways in the Twentieth Century* (Durham, N.C.: Duke University Press, 2009).

10. I am here adapting the idea of "rogue circulation" (85, 105) articulated by Nat Hurley. See Hurley, "The Queer Traffic in Literature: Or, Reading Anthologically," *ESC: English Studies in Canada* 36, no. 1 (March 2010), 81–108.

11. See James Creech, *Closet Writing/Gay Reading: The Case of Melville's Pierre* (Chicago: University of Chicago Press, 1994), for a fascinating exploration of the possibility that queer erotic content might be encrypted by an author in anticipation of a later queer-sensitive reader's understanding.

12. Ralph Werther, *The Female-Impersonators* (New York: Medico-Legal Journal, 1922; repr. New York: Arno, 1975), 6.

13. Charles Warren Stoddard to Walt Whitman, 2 March 1869, Charles E. Feinberg Collection of the Papers of Walt Whitman, 1839–1919, Library of Congress, Washington, D.C. http://www.whitmanarchive.org/biography/correspondence/tei/loc.01943.html (accessed 4 Sept. 2015).

14. Leo Bersani, *Homos* (Cambridge, Mass.: Harvard University Press, 1995). Many others have discussed and disputed Bersani's "antisocial thesis." See the forum, "The Antisocial Thesis in Queer Theory," *PMLA* 121, no. 3 (May 2006), 819–28, featuring contributions by Robert Caserio, Tim Dean, Lee Edelman, Judith Halberstam, and José Esteban Muñoz.

15. A very few of the most well-known examples, not including those collected here, would be Constance Fenimore Woolson, "Miss Grief" (1880); Herman Melville, *Billy Budd* (written 1888–91, published 1924); Kate Chopin, *The Awakening* (1899); Blair Niles, *Strange Brother* (1931); James Baldwin, *Giovanni's Room* (1956).

16. The distinction between "symptomatic" and "reparative" reading is usually traced to the late work of Eve Kosofsky Sedgwick. See *Touching Feeling: Affect, Pedagogy, Performativity* (Durham, N.C.: Duke University Press, 2003). More recent discussions include Heather Love, "Truth and Consequences: On Paranoid Reading and Reparative Reading," *Criticism* 52, no. 2 (Spring 2010), 235–41; Ellis Hanson, "The Future's Eve: Reparative Reading After Sedgwick," *South Atlantic Quarterly* 110, no. 1 (Winter 2011), 101–19.

17. Richmond Beatty, *Bayard Taylor: Laureate of the Gilded Age* (Norman: University of Oklahoma Press, 1936), 288.

18. Paul C. Wermuth, *Bayard Taylor* (New York: Twayne, 1973), 99. I have gratefully borrowed these references from the original research of Joe Miranda.

WALT WHITMAN, "THE CHILD'S CHAMPION" (1841)

Walter Whitman, "The Child's Champion," *New World; a Weekly Family Journal of Popular Literature, Science, Art and News* (Nov. 20, 1841), 321–22.

3   **The Child's Champion:** Whitman revised this story after it first appeared in 1841 in the *New World* and republished it as "The Child and the Profligate," *Columbian Lady's and Gentleman's Magazine, Embracing Literature in Every Department . . .* (Oct. 1844), 149–53. As Michael Moon has argued (*Disseminating Whitman: Revision and Corporeality in Leaves of Grass* (Cambridge, Mass.: Harvard University Press, 1991), Whitman's revisions reflected his awareness of "the strong homoerotic quality" of the story as well as his wary observation of "the cultural boundaries along which the official proscription of erotic love between males is maintained" (Moon, 29). According to Moon, Whitman's revisions amounted to "self-censorship" (Moon, 31). Among his changes was the addition of a verse epigraph, from Nathaniel Parker Willis's much-reprinted temperance poem, "Look not upon the wine when it is red" (published, among other places, in John Espy Lovell, ed., *The United States Speaker: A Copious Selection of Exercises in Elocution . . .* [Charleston: S. Babcock, 1836], 204), which helped convert the story into a more properly monitory temperance tale. The added epigraph read: "They say 'tis pleasant on the lip, / And merry on the brain— / They say it stirs the sluggish blood, / And dulls the tooth of pain. / Ay—but within its gloomy deeps / A stinging serpent, unseen, sleeps" ("The Child and the Profligate," 149). The following notes detailing some of Whitman's most significant revisions rely upon Moon (26–36, 53–54, 160, 190).

7   **and with the young men of the place who were very fond of him:** Whitman
     deleted the reference to the specific and intense fondness of the young men
     for the boy, changing this to "and at the parties of the place" ("The Child and
     the Profligate," 151).

8   **Why was it that from the first moment of seeing him, the young man's heart
     had moved with a strange feeling of kindness toward the boy? He felt anx-
     ious to know more of him—he felt that he should love him:** After Whitman's
     revisions this passage became markedly less passionate and more moralistic:
     "Why was it, too, that the young man's heart moved with a feeling of kindness
     toward the somewhat harshly treated child? Was it that his associations had
     hitherto been among the vile, and the contrast was now so strikingly great?"
     ("The Child and the Profligate," 151).

8   **He seized the child with a grip of iron; he bent Charles half way over, and
     with the side of his heavy foot, gave him a sharp and solid kick:** Whitman
     revised this sentence, eliminating the suggestive bending of Charles over, to
     read as follows: "He seized Charles with a grip of iron, and with the side of his
     heavy boot gave him a sharp and solid kick" ("The Child and the Profligate,"
     151).

10   **they two held communion together:** Whitman revised this to "they two con-
     versed together" ("The Child and the Profligate," 152).

10   **for the present night, he said, it would perhaps be best for the boy to stay
     and share his bed at the inn; and little persuading did the child need to do
     so:** Whitman altered this to "for the present night the landlord would probably
     give him a lodging at the inn—and little persuading did the host need for that"
     ("The Child and the Profligate," 152).

10   **As they retired to sleep:** Whitman changed this, in keeping with his bedtime
     segregation of Lankton and Charles, to "As he retired to sleep" ("The Child and
     the Profligate," 152).

10   **All his imaginings . . . his desires!:** Whitman removed these sentences when
     he revised the story.

11   **No sound was heard but the slight breathing of those who slumbered there
     in each others arms:** Whitman altered this passage and much of the surround-
     ing text extensively—deleting the phrase "slumbered there in each others
     arms"—to eliminate the representation of Lankton and Charles sleeping to-
     gether in the same bed ("The Child and the Profligate," 153).

12   **the close knit love of the boy and him:** Whitman modified this phrase to "the
     friendship of Charles and himself" ("The Child and the Profligate," 153).

CHARLES WARREN STODDARD, "A SOUTH-SEA IDYL" (1869)

Charles Warren Stoddard, "A South-Sea Idyl," *Overland Monthly and Out West
Magazine* 3, no. 3 (Sept. 1869), 257–64. This story had a sequel, "How I Converted My
Cannibal," *Overland Monthly and Out West Magazine* 3, no. 5 (Nov. 1869), 455–60.

17   **It was big enough for a Mormon:** Humorous reference to the Mormon prac-
     tice of polygamy.

21   **the prodigal lived riotously and wasted his substance:** Allusion to the parable of the Prodigal Son, Luke 15:13, "The younger son gathered all together, and took his journey into a far country, and there wasted his substance with riotous living" (King James Version). Antimasturbation advocates in the nineteenth century often used the phrase "waste one's substance" in reference to the loss of semen via involuntary nocturnal emissions or self-stimulation.

AMBROSE BIERCE, "THE HAUNTED VALLEY" (1871)

Ambrose Bierce, "The Haunted Valley," *Overland Monthly and Out West Magazine* 7, no. 1 (July 1871), 88–95.

26   **Greaser:** Derogatory term for a Mexican; the slur was in common usage in the American Southwest during the nineteenth century.

26   *riata:* Spanish, lariat or lasso, long looped rope used to catch animals.

27   **Titan:** In Greek mythology, Titans were a primeval race of powerful deities, giants of massive strength.

34   **derned Borgy:** Dialect corruption of *Borgia*, referring to a prominent and powerful family in Renaissance Italy; the Borgias were suspected by their enemies of various crimes, including murder by poisoning.

CONSTANCE FENIMORE WOOLSON, "FELIPA" (1876)

Constance Fenimore Woolson, "Felipa," *Lippincott's Magazine of Popular Literature and Science* 17 (June 1876), 702–13.

38   **Minorcans:** Minorca is a Spanish island in the Mediterranean Sea.

47   **Mr. Aldrich:** In Thomas Bailey Aldrich's short story "Marjorie Daw," John Flemming writes to Edward Delaney, "Cynicism is a small brass field-piece that eventually bursts and kills the artilleryman" (*Atlantic Monthly* 31, no. 186 [April 1873], 407–17; quotation 411–12).

51   **Somebody says somewhere:** P. G. Patmore, criticizing William Hazlitt's lack of hope in the future, wrote chastisingly: "Hope is more than a blessing—it is a duty and a virtue." See Patmore, *My Friends and Acquaintance: Being Memorials, Mind-Portraits, and Personal Recollections of Deceased Celebrities of the Nineteenth Century . . . ,* vol. 2 (London, 1845), 326.

53   **"Have you felt the wool of the beaver . . . so sweet is she!":** Ben Jonson (1572–1637), "A Celebration of Charis: IV. Her Triumph," ll. 25–26.

OCTAVE THANET, "MY LORELEI: A HEIDELBERG ROMANCE" (1880)

Octave Thanet [Alice French], "My Lorelei: A Heidelberg Romance," *The Western,* new series, 6, no. 1 (Jan. 1880), 1–22.

56   **where the White Caps hold their Kneipen:** The White Caps were a corps of Prussian students of noble descent; *kneipen* were their drinking bouts.

57   **German Lorelei:** A lorelei is a feminine water spirit, most famously depicted by Heinrich Heine in his 1824 poem, "Die Lorelei," where she is a siren sitting on a rock above the Rhine, distracting sailors with her beauty and her enchanting song.

59   *restauration*: French, "restaurant."

62   **Du hast Diamenten und Perlen . . . was willst du mehr?**: Heinrich Heine, "Du hast Diamenten und Perlen" (1827). In George McDonald's translation, "Diamonds hast thou and pearls, / And all by which men set store, / And of eyes hast thou the finest— / Darling, what wouldst thou more?"

62   *Undine*: Friedrich de la Motte Fouqué, *Undine* (1811), a fairy tale in which Undine, a water spirit, marries a human in order to gain a soul.

65   *cretins*: Once-current term (now considered derogatory) used to describe a congenital condition of stunted physical and mental development due to an insufficiency of thyroid hormones.

65   **"Gahen snell! Ich haben nix!"**: Imperfect German: "Go away quickly! I have nothing!"

66   **droschky**: Russian, "cab."

66   *beauté de diable*: French, "devilish beauty."

66   **"Blague!"**: French, "joke."

68   **Schwetzingen**: A German town southwest of Heidelberg.

68   **"Ich weiss nicht . . . so traurig bin!"**: Heinrich Heine, "Die Lorelei," "I know not what it means / That I am so sad!" (McDonald's translation).

68   *haus fraus*: German (*Hausfrauen*), "housewives."

72   **Franco-Prussian war**: 1870–71 conflict between the Second French Empire and the North German Confederation (led by the Kingdom of Prussia). There is a small problem with chronology here, as Von Reibnitz, if he died in this war, would not have been alive in 1874 when Constance's diary entries begin.

SAMUEL L. KNAPP, "THE BACHELORS" (1836)

Samuel L. Knapp, "The Bachelors," *The Bachelors, and Other Tales, Founded on American Incidents and Characters* (New York: J. and W. Sandford, 1836), 9–30.

77   **"One impulse . . . all the sages can."**: William Wordsworth, "The Tables Turned; an Evening Scene, on the same subject."

78   **feast, like Scarron's**: In Paul Scarron's *Roman comique* (1649–57), guests were invited to bring their own dishes to the feast.

78   **embargo of 1807**: The U.S. Congress passed the Embargo Act of 1807, forbidding trade with the United Kingdom and France, in response to violations of U.S. neutrality, including the impressment of American seamen and the seizure of cargo as contraband of war (among other issues). In anticipation of this embargo, the bachelors pool their money to invest in goods that will soon be in short supply and can then be sold for higher prices.

78   **war of 1812**: The United States declared war on the United Kingdom for various reasons, including the British impressment of U.S. sailors and other perceived humiliations.

80   **Mandeville . . . Bruce . . . Ledyard**: The somewhat fantastical *Travels of Sir John Mandeville* was translated and circulated widely in the fourteenth century and thereafter; James Bruce (1730–94) was a Scottish traveler in Africa who traced the origins of the Blue Nile; John Ledyard (1751–89) was an in-

trepid American explorer of the Pacific Ocean, the North American continent, Africa, and Eurasia.

80 **mines of Golconda:** Diamond mines in the region of Golconda, in southern India; the name has taken on a generic meaning, referring to a source great wealth.

80 **supper for Lucullus:** Lucius Licinius Lucullus, a politician of the late Roman Republic, was famous as a gastronome; his lavish banquets made the word *lucullan* a synonym for luxurious dining excess.

81 **son of Crispin:** Saint Crispin is the patron saint of cobblers, tanners, and leather workers.

83 **Sir James Mackintosh:** Mackintosh (1765–1832) was a Scottish doctor, barrister, historian, and philosopher; he was appointed Recorder (chief judge) of Bombay, serving there from 1804 to 1811.

83 **Mocha:** Port city on the Red Sea coast of the Arabian Peninsula, in what is now Yemen; renowned as a major center of the coffee trade.

87 **Mussulman:** Synonym for Muslim, now considered archaic.

88 **Oriental language of flowers:** Nineteenth-century Americans took a great interest in this purported ancient code, which considered different flowers to have inherent meanings that constituted a natural language; this language of flowers could thus be used between friends and lovers to communicate messages and sentiments through the exchange of bouquets. Many flower dictionaries were published that correlated specific feelings with particular flowers.

90 **tricolored violet . . . *pansey*:** "Pansy" only later became a derogatory epithet for a homosexual or an unmanly man. But like the reference to "Urania" below (see following note), it seems oddly prescient here in its anticipation of later semantic modifications.

91 **"*Urania*":** In ancient Greek mythology, Urania was the muse of astronomy. It was not until later in the nineteenth century that the German term *Urning* (and its English adaptation, *Uranian*) came to refer to members of an ostensible "third sex," that is, those allegedly possessed of a female psyche trapped in a male body (and, more loosely, to refer to male homosexual love). Even later this coinage led to a school of English homosexual/pederastic poets known as the Uranians. It is curious that Knapp as early as 1836 should have placed the term *urania* in proximity to male sentimental attachment, and in conjunction with poetry as well.

91 **"How often, from the steep . . . thoughts to heaven.":** John Milton, *Paradise Lost*, book 4, ll. 680–88.

ANONYMOUS, "THE MAN WHO THOUGHT HIMSELF A WOMAN" (1857)

Anonymous, "The Man Who Thought Himself a Woman," *Knickerbocker; or New-York Monthly Magazine* 50, no. 6 (Dec. 1857), 599–610. The author of this story has not been identified. For some discussion, see Christopher Looby, "Sexuality, History, Difficulty, Pleasure," *J19: The Journal of Nineteenth-Century Americanists* 1, no. 1 (2013), 253–58; see also Elisabeth Reis, "Transgender Identity at a Crossroads: A Close Reading of a 'Queer' Story from 1857," *Early American Studies* 12, no. 3 (Fall 2014), 652–65.

95   **Grahamites:** The Reverend Sylvester Graham (1794–1851), inventor of the Graham Cracker, was a well-known dietary reformer and sexual-purity advocate who recommended a vegetarian diet, which he believed would promote health, help cure alcoholism, and curb sexual urges. He was especially opposed to masturbation, believing that it led inevitably to insanity.

95   **manes:** In Roman mythology, the deified souls of deceased ancestors.

96   **"abs" and "ebs":** Connotes the fundamentals of Latin grammar.

96   **phrenologist:** Phrenology was an accepted science of the mind in the nineteenth century; by measuring and palpitating the human skull phrenologists believed they could identify and evaluate an individual's particular talents and propensities.

MARY WILKINS FREEMAN, "TWO FRIENDS" (1887)

Mary Wilkins Freeman, "Two Friends," *Harper's Bazaar* 20, no. 26 (June 25, 1887), 450–51. [This story appeared originally under the author's unmarried name, Mary E. Wilkins.]

110   **consumption:** Outdated name for pulmonary tuberculosis, an infectious bacterial disease that was endemic in the nineteenth century.

MARK TWAIN, "HOW NANCY JACKSON MARRIED KATE WILSON" (C. 1900–1903)

Mark Twain, "How Nancy Jackson Married Kate Wilson," *Missouri Review* 10, no. 1 (1987), 99–112. Published by the University of California Press. Unpublished during Twain's lifetime, the manuscript was prepared for publication and introduced by Robert Sattelmeyer. Permission to republish has been granted by the *Missouri Review* and by the University of California Press (*Miscellaneous Writings: Previously Unpublished Letters, Manuscript Letters, and Literary Manuscripts Available in the Mark Twain Papers*, by Mark Twain, © 2001 by the Mark Twain Foundation).

123   **Great Scott:** Colloquial exclamation expressing surprise or alarm. Its origins are uncertain; one possibility is that it refers to General Winfield Scott, commander in chief of the U.S. Army during the Civil War, who weighed three hundred pounds and was consequently unable to ride a horse.

135   **breakdown:** In the nineteenth century this usually referred to a lively, shuffling dance, often associated with the holiday celebrations of plantation slaves or with the stage performances of blackface minstrels.

WILLA CATHER, "PAUL'S CASE: A STUDY IN TEMPERAMENT" (1905)

Willa Cather, "Paul's Case: A Study in Temperament," *McClure's Magazine* 35, no. 1 (May 1905), 74–83.

138   **A Study in Temperament:** Cather revised this story after its first publication when she included it in a collection of her stories. This subtitle is present in the version of "Paul's Case" that appeared in *The Troll Garden* (1905), the collection of stories that was published in the same year as the story's publication in *McClure's Magazine*; but Cather deleted the subtitle when she later republished the story again, in *Youth and the Bright Medusa* (New York: Alfred

A. Knopf, 1920), 199–234. Cather's revisions are discussed in David A. Carpenter, "Why Willa Cather Revised 'Paul's Case': The Work in Art and Those Sunday Afternoons," *American Literature* 59, no. 4 (Dec. 1987), 590–608. Although the question of Cather's representation of and attitude toward Paul's sexuality is not the focus of Carpenter's essay, some of the changes bear upon the question The notes below (at 92, 98, 100) detailing some of the most significant revisions are indebted to Carpenter's scholarship.

138 **belladonna:** *Belladonna*, which means "beautiful lady" in Italian, is a plant from which medicines are sometimes made; the juice of its berries was sometimes ingested (dangerously) to enlarge the pupils of the eyes and thereby give a woman a dramatically striking appearance.

140 **I happen to know that he was born in Colorado, only a few months before his mother died out there of a long illness:** Cather revised this passage for *Youth and the Bright Medusa*, eliminating this sentence, whereupon the passage read: "The boy is not strong, for one thing. There is something wrong about the fellow" (202). Carpenter argues that this revision reflects Cather's loss of belief in the effect of heredity on a person's character. It might be added that Cather also diminished the possible implication that Paul's sexual orientation, which some sexologists at the time would have traced to hereditary debility, was due to some kind of biological cause.

140 **and stiff with a nervous tension that drew them back from his teeth:** Cather omitted these words when she revised the story for *Youth and the Bright Medusa* (220), arguably making Paul's behavior seem less determined by animal instincts.

140 **soldiers' chorus from "Faust":** From act 4 of Charles Gounod's opera *Faust* (1859), this is a rousing chorus that is perhaps the best-known composition of Gounod.

140 **Carnegie Hall:** Andrew Carnegie (1835–1919), the steel magnate who lived and made his fortune in Pittsburgh, and then became a philanthropist, endowed several music halls in the Pittsburgh area, including the Carnegie Music Hall.

141 **the Genius in the bottle found by the Arab fisherman:** In the traditional Arab folktale, the genius (genie), who is released from the bottle or vase in which he was enclosed, must kill the person who releases him; but he allows the victim to choose the manner of his death.

141 **Schenley:** Built in 1898 as an elegant hotel in Pittsburgh, close to the Carnegie Music Hall, it now serves as the William Pitt Union, the student union building at the University of Pittsburgh.

142 *auf wiedersehen:* German, goodbye ("until we meet again"; literally, "until seeing again").

144 **their Sunday "waists":** Fashionable blouses, tailored like a shirt, with a collar and with buttons down the front. Also called "shirt-waists," as in the next paragraph.

145 **Cairo:** Presumably Cairo, the capital of Egypt, given that the "chief" of the corporation was doing business while he was "cruising the Mediterranean."

146 **a sleep and a forgetting:** From William Wordsworth, "Ode: Intimations of Immortality from Recollections of Early Childhood" (1807): "Our birth is but a sleep and a forgetting" (l. 59).

146 **overture from "Martha" . . . serenade from "Rigoletto":** Friedrich von Flotow, *Martha* (1847); Giuseppe Verdi, *Rigoletto* (1851).

149 **Waldorf:** The Waldorf Hotel opened in 1893 at Fifth Avenue and Thirty-third Street; in 1897 it was joined by the adjacent Astoria Hotel. In 1929 the Waldorf-Astoria at this location—considered by some to be the grandest hotel in the world—was closed and demolished, and the land was sold to the builders of the Empire State Building.

149 **Roman blanket:** Brightly colored decorative blanket or throw.

151 **Here and there on the corners . . . snow-flakes stuck and melted:** Cather revised this passage for *Youth and the Bright Medusa* to read as follows: "Here and there on the corners whole flower gardens blooming behind glass windows, against which the snow flakes stuck and melted" (224). David A. Carpenter argues that Paul is identified with flowers throughout the story, and that changing "glass cases" to "glass windows" seems to limit "the possible interpretations of the story's title, 'Paul's Case'" (595). Carpenter does not make this inference, but using the word "case" less emphatically may also have had the purpose of de-emphasizing the framing of Paul's sexual condition as a medical "case study."

152 **"Blue Danube":** Waltz composed by Johann Strauss Jr. in 1866.

152 **his *loge* at the Metropolitan:** The Metropolitan was an opera house that opened in 1883 on Broadway at Thirty-ninth Street, where it was the home of the Metropolitan Opera Company; it was demolished in 1967. *Loge* often refers, as it seems to do here, to a private box.

154 **Pagliacci music:** *Pagliacci* (1892) is an opera by the Italian composer Ruggero Leoncavallo.

156 **all the flowers he had seen in the glass cases:** For consistency with her previous revision (see note at 151 above), Cather changed "glass cases" here to "show windows" when she revised the story for *Youth and the Bright Medusa* (233).

BAYARD TAYLOR, "TWIN-LOVE" (1871)

Bayard Taylor, "Twin-Love," *Atlantic Monthly: A Magazine of Literature, Science, Art and Politics* 28, no. 167 (Sept. 1871), 257–66.

161 **David and Jonathan:** The biblical figures David and Jonathan were commonly taken to be exemplars of devoted "platonic" friendship; some later scholars have considered their relationship to partake of the romantic or homoerotic. David's praise for Jonathan in 2 Samuel 1:26, "Thy love to me was wonderful, passing the love of women" (King James Version), was often cited in defenses of homosexuality.

172 **Consumption:** See note at 110 above.

ELIZABETH STODDARD, "OUT OF THE DEEPS" (1872)

Elizabeth Stoddard, "Out of the Deeps," *Aldine* 5, no. 5 (May 1872), 94–95.

176 **Hatteras:** Cape Hatteras, a barrier island along the coast of North Carolina.

177 **"In the dark backward and abysm of time?":** William Shakespeare, *The Tempest* (1610–11), I.ii.50.

178 **dinner, like the king, "never dies":** Traditionally it was believed that, while the natural body of a given king might die, the body politic never dies (that is, the monarchy as such was imperishable).

178 **"touch of a vanished hand":** From Alfred, Lord Tennyson, "Break, Break, Break" (1842), an elegy for his deceased intimate friend Arthur Hallam. Quoting this well-known line, Stoddard's story secretes a reference to a legendary same-sex friendship inside what is depicted as George's dreamful yearning for the dead Charlotte.

179 **Ruth and Naomize:** The biblical figures Ruth and Naomi (like David and Jonathan—see note at 104 above) were taken as exemplars of devoted friendship. In Ruth 1:16, Ruth promises Naomi (her mother-in-law), "Whither thou goest, I will go; and where thou lodgest, I will lodge." In 1:17 she continues, "Where thou diest, will I die, and there will I be buried" (King James Version). "Naomize" has been corrected from "Noamize."

181 **Batto light-house:** Presumably a fictional name for a lighthouse on the coast of North Carolina, somewhere in the vicinity of Cape Hatteras.

181 **"Hair Restorer":** A product designed to restore gray hair to its original color.

BRET HARTE, "IN THE TULES" (1895)

Bret Harte, "In the Tules," *Strand Magazine* 10, no. 95 (1895), 753–64.

185 **Tules:** Tules are a giant species of sedge, or marsh grass, common in the wetlands bordering the San Joaquin and Sacramento Rivers in California, among other places. They give rise to a meteorological phenomenon known as "tule fog," a dense, low fog that in the nineteenth century was considered a dangerous miasma apt to breed disease (see note at 195 below). The phrase "in the tules" or "out in the tules" is also a local California idiom indicating a place where no one would want to live, something like "out in the boondocks" or "nowheresville."

186 **stream of Pactolus:** Sardis, capital of the ancient kingdom of Lydia (in western Asia Minor, now part of Turkey), overlooked a stream known as the Pactolus, renowned as the location of an especially rich gold strike.

187 **Asmodeus:** In various ancient traditions, Asmodeus was considered the demon of lust.

192 **Corydon . . . Amaryllis:** Corydon is the name of a shepherd in Virgil's *Eclogues* (II), as well as several other ancient pastorals, including Theocritus's *Idylls* (IV). As represented by Virgil, Corydon loves a beautiful slave boy, Alexis, who does not return his love; he complains to the cruel Alexis that he, Corydon, might be better off with the temperamental Amaryllis—or with another male, the swarthy Menalcas.

194   **the horses is 'Morgan':** Morgan horses were one of the earliest breeds developed in America, all descended from a sire named Figure (whose owner was named Justin Morgan); the versatile breed was used for racing, for pulling coaches, for military purposes, and by gold miners in California and Nevada in the mid-nineteenth century.

195   **'tule fever':** Harte refers in other places in his writings to "tule fever," but it is not clear in retrospect to what this disease (or set of diseases) would now correspond. Nineteenth-century medical authorities considered the tule marshes of the San Joaquin River and lower Sacramento River and their thick fogs to be dangerous incubators of illness. "Where the tule grows the rankest," wrote Dr. Washington Ayer, "we shall always find the most positive type of intermittent fever." Dr. James Tyson referred to the tule marshes as "nurseries of disease." Both are quoted in Linda Lorraine Nash, *Inescapable Ecologies: A History of Environment, Disease, and Knowledge* (Berkeley: University of California Press, 2006), 66.

197   **pitiless Moloch:** Moloch was an ancient Ammonite god, whose name later became a synecdoche for a person or a thing demanding a very costly sacrifice.

199   **great flood of '54:** A series of floods devastated Sacramento in 1854, the year the city became the state capital.

SARAH ORNE JEWETT, "MARTHA'S LADY" (1897)

Sarah Orne Jewett, "Martha's Lady," *Atlantic Monthly: A Magazine of Literature, Science, Art and Politics* 80, no. 480 (Oct. 1897), 523-33.

203   **Martha's Lady:** Jewett revised the ending of this story in a small but consequential way when it was later republished in her collection of stories *The Queen's Twin and Other Stories* (Boston: Houghton Mifflin, 1899), 100-134, as Susan Koppelman noted in *Two Friends and Other Nineteenth-Century Lesbian Short Stories by American Women Writers* (New York: Meridian, 1994), 219n. Jewett's revision has also been recorded in the notes to "Martha's Lady" below; further discussion can be found in Christopher Looby, "Sexuality and American Literary Studies," in *A Companion to American Literary Studies*, ed. Caroline F. Levander and Robert S. Levine (New York: Wiley-Blackwell, 2011), 422-36, esp. 425-33.

203   **Dr. Johnson . . . to his girls:** Annie Adams Fields, Jewett's companion of many years, wrote in her *A Shelf of Old Books* (London: Osgood, McIlvaine, 1894) that William Makepeace Thackeray "loved delightful women always . . . and would have said to his favorites, as Dr. Johnson said to Mrs. Thrale, 'be brisk, and be splendid, and be public'" (213).

204   **outbreak of a desire for larger religious freedom:** In the 1820s and thereafter the movement known as Transcendentalism sought to revitalize religious feeling in reaction against the "corpse-cold Unitarianism" (Ralph Waldo Emerson's 1846 phrase) that afflicted religious practice at Harvard specifically and in the eastern United States more generally.

204   **war for liberty:** The American Revolution, 1776-83.

204–5 **coming war for patriotism and a new freedom:** The American Civil War, 1861–65.

205 **Emerson:** Ralph Waldo Emerson (1803–82), American poet, philosopher, essayist, intellectual leader of the Transcendentalist movement.

206 **cherry-trees:** Possibly a friendly allusion to the role of the cherry trees in Mary Wilkins Freeman's 1887 story, "Two Friends," also included in the present volume.

219 **Helena called her back:** Jewett revised this story for republication in her collection *The Queen's Twin, and Other Stories* (Boston: Houghton Mifflin, 1899), at which time she added a pregnant sentence here at the end of the paragraph: "She suddenly knew the whole story and could hardly speak" (134). This note, and the one below, detailing Jewett's revisions, are indebted to the research of Susan Koppelman in *Two Friends and Other Nineteenth-Century Lesbian Short Stories by American Women Writers* (219n).

219 **"You have always remembered . . . kiss me good-night?":** When Jewett revised the story for inclusion in *The Queen's Twin*, she altered this speech as follows, making it more emphatically plaintive, and arguably making the passionate subtext—or Helena's recognition of the kind and degree of Martha's love—more evident: "'Oh, my dear Martha!' she cried, 'won't you kiss me good-night? Oh, Martha, have you remembered like this, all these long years!'" (134).

SUI SIN FAR, "THE HEART'S DESIRE" (1908)

Sui Sin Far, "The Heart's Desire," *Good Housekeeping* 46, no. 5 (May 1908), 514–15.

221 **peg:** A simple wooden doll, such as a poor girl like Ku Yum might have; see "peg doll" several lines later.

HERMAN MELVILLE, "I AND MY CHIMNEY" (1856)

Herman Melville, "I and My Chimney," *Putnam's Monthly Magazine of American Literature, Science, and Art* 7, no. 39 (March 1856), 269–83.

225 **Cardinal Wolsey:** Thomas Wolsey (1473–1530), an English political figure and Roman Catholic cardinal, was Lord Chancellor, the chief adviser of King Henry VIII, sometimes called *alter rex*, that is, other king.

225 **Harry VIII:** King Henry VIII (1498–1547) became severely obese as he aged.

225 **Lord Rosse's monster telescope:** William Parsons, 3d Earl of Rosse (1800–1867), Anglo-Irish astronomer who built a seventy-two-inch telescope, the largest one in the world until the twentieth century.

227 **Louis le Grande of France:** Louis XIV (1638–1715), king of France, otherwise known as Louis the Great or the Sun King.

227 **Madame de Maintenon:** Françoise d'Aubigné, marquise de Maintenon (1635–1719). Secretly married to Louis XIV, she exercised great influence over him.

227 **Versailles:** Palace of Versailles, symbol of absolute monarchy during the ancien régime.

227 **liberty-pole:** Tall wooden pole, often surmounted by a liberty cap, originating in ancient Rome and serving as a symbol of republicanism.

228 **the world is all before us:** From John Milton, *Paradise Lost* (1667), book 12, l. 646, describing the expulsion of Adam and Eve from Paradise: "The world was all before them."

228 **Kossuth's rising:** Lajos Kossuth (1802–94), Hungarian political leader, admired in the United States as a freedom fighter, a leader of the Hungarian Revolution of 1848.

228 **Champs de Mars:** Now a large public greenspace in Paris, it was named after the Campus Martius in Rome, and was formerly used as drilling and marching grounds for the French military.

228 **Great Oak:** Perhaps a reference to a large, locally renowned, oak tree.

228 **Ogg Mountain:** Possibly a tongue-in-cheek reference to a (perhaps fictional) local elevation.

229 **pyramid of Cheops:** The Great Pyramid of Giza, the oldest and largest of the three pyramids in the Necropolis of Giza in Egypt.

229 **Cromwell:** Oliver Cromwell (1599–1658), English military and political leader, later Lord Protector of the Commonwealth, one of the signers of the death warrant of King Charles I in 1649.

229 **switchel:** Drink made of water mixed with vinegar, often seasoned with ginger and sweetened with honey, molasses, or maple syrup.

229 **elephant-and-castle:** Byword for an English coaching inn.

230 **Kenilworth:** Kenilworth Castle, in Warwickshire, England, a ruined palace dating from Norman through Tudor times.

231 **Atlas:** In Greek mythology, the primordial Titan who held up the celestial spheres.

231 **stones at Gilgal . . . Joshua:** In Joshua 4:3–24 the Israelites encamp at Gilgal and are commanded to take twelve stones from the Jordan River and set them up as a memorial.

232 **sacred majesty of Russia:** Likely a reference to Peter I, or Peter the Great (1672–1725), czar of Russia. See also note at 143 below.

232 **Caius Julius Caesar:** Gaius Julius Caesar (100–44 BCE), Roman general, statesman, and dictator.

232 **Brutus, Cassius, Antony:** Marcus Junius Brutus and Gaius Cassius Longinus, two of the conspirators and assassins of Julius Caesar; Marcus Antonius, one of the three leaders who defeated Caesar's murderers and shared power as the Triumvirate.

234 **"Whatever is, is right":** Alexander Pope, *An Essay on Man* (1734), l. 292.

234 **Peter the Great:** Peter I, czar of Russia.

234 **Peter the Piper:** A popular English-language tongue-twister nursery rhyme, dating from the early nineteenth century.

235 **plain of Mamre . . . old Abraham's:** In Genesis 18:1, the lord appears to Abraham "in the plains of Mamre" (King James Version).

235 **Montaigne:** Michel de Montaigne (1533–92), French essayist.

235 **daughter of Nebuchadnezzar:** In Daniel 4:25, 32–33, in fulfillment of a dream

Nebuchadnezzar lost his reason, dwelt "with the beasts of the field," and "did eat grass as oxen" (King James Version).

236 **Swedenborgianism:** Religious movement informed by the writings of Emanuel Swedenborg (1688–1772), who claimed to have a new revelation from Jesus Christ received through heavenly visions. The movement had some following in nineteenth-century America.

236 **Spirit Rapping philosophy:** Derisive term for Spiritualism, referring to the Fox sisters of New York, who claimed to communicate with spirits through "rappings," which they later admitted had been a hoax.

236 **Charles V:** Charles V (1500–1558), Holy Roman Emperor, who abdicated in 1556 and retreated to a monastery.

236 **old Lear:** Title character of Shakespeare's *King Lear*, who cedes his kingdom to two of his daughters, expecting to continue to live in his accustomed regal style, but is gradually thereafter stripped of his privileges.

237 **Nero's . . . Corinth:** The roman emperor Nero was the first to attempt (67 CE) construction of a canal through the Isthmus of Corinth, to connect the Gulf of Corinth to the Saronic Gulf in the Aegean Sea.

237 **Belzoni:** Giovanni Battista Belzoni (1778–1823), great Italian archaeologist, first to penetrate into the Second Pyramid of Giza, among other accomplishments.

239 **London's city guest . . . Temple Bar:** Temple Bar is the point in London where the city erected a barrier to regulate trade; there is a custom that the monarch, when entering the city from Westminster, stops ceremonially and asks permission to enter.

239 **Bunker Hill monument:** Tall granite obelisk, erected 1827–43 in Charlestown, Massachusetts, commemorating the Battle of Bunker Hill during the American Revolution.

239 **mausoleum . . . Apis:** In Egyptian mythology, Apis is a bull deity; in 1851, Auguste Mariette discovered the ruins of the serapeum at Saqqara, including the subterranean sarcophagi of the Apis bulls.

242 **Holofernes:** In the deuterocanonical book of Judith, Holofernes serves Nebuchadnezzar as "the chief captain of his army" (Judith 2:4).

242 **Caligula:** Roman emperor from 37 to 41 CE; many sources describe him as a vicious tyrant, cruel and sadistic.

243 **Solomon:** Biblical figure renowned for his incomparable wisdom. In 1 Kings 3:9–12 Solomon asks the Lord for "an understanding heart to judge thy people," and his prayer is granted: "Lo, I have given thee a wise and an understanding heart; so that there was none like thee before thee, neither after thee shall any arise like unto thee."

246 **Order of the Garotte:** A garotte is a cord or wire used for strangling; this gander's owner appears to have wrapped his neck tightly in some sort of device meant to prevent him from squeezing into places where he doesn't belong.

247 **St. Dunstan's devil:** Dunstan (909–88), archbishop of Canterbury, later canonized, and renowned for his ability to defeat the devil.

249 **witch-hazel wand:** A forked branch of the witch-hazel tree was often used for dowsing (or "water-witching"), a magical practice of finding hidden water supplies or other desirable resources buried in the ground by pointing the wand downward and feeling it twitch.

250 **Three Powers . . . Poland:** The Russian Empire, the Kingdom of Prussia, and the Habsburg Empire divided the Polish-Lithuanian Commonwealth three times, in 1772, 1793, and 1795.

251 **Momus:** In Greek mythology, the personification of satire, mockery, and censure, who regretted that men did not have doors in their breasts through which their true thoughts could be seen.

251 **golden bowl:** Ecclesiastes 12:6, "Or ever the silver cord be loosed, or the golden bowl be broken, or the pitcher be broken at the fountain, or the wheel broken at the cistern."

LOUISA MAY ALCOTT, "THE CANDY COUNTRY" (1885)

Louisa M. Alcott, "The Candy Country," *St. Nicholas; an Illustrated Magazine for Young Folks* 13, no. 1 (Nov. 1885), 16–23.

256 **Milan Cathedral:** Cathedral church of Milan, Italy, a flamboyantly ornamented Gothic cathedral.

258 **Brighton Rock:** Hard candy, shaped like a cylindrical rod, often flavored with peppermint or spearmint, frequently sold at seaside resorts like Brighton, England.

263 **Sally Lunn:** A Sally Lunn bun is a large bun or teacake, originating in Bath, England.

264 **Graham bread:** High-fiber and chemical-free bread invented by Sylvester Graham in 1829, it was meant both to support dietary health and to decrease sexual urges. See note at 95 above.

265 **Parker House rolls:** Invented at the Parker House Hotel in Boston in 1870, the Parker House roll is made by flattening a ball of dough and folding it in half before baking.

CHARLES W. CHESNUTT, "DAVE'S NECKLISS" (1889)

Charles W. Chesnutt, "Dave's Neckliss," *Atlantic Monthly: A Magazine of Literature, Science, Art and Politics* 64, no. 384 (Oct. 1889), 500–508.

269 **bockrah:** *Buckra* or *buckrah* was a slang derogatory term used by African Americans to refer to a white boss or overseer.

272 **gin 'im forty:** That is, gave him forty lashes of the whip.

275 **lighterd-knot:** A lighter-knot, sometimes called fatwood, pine knot, or lighter wood, is a piece of resin-impregnated pine heartwood, used as kindling for starting fires.

SADAKICHI HARTMANN, "SCHOPENHAUER IN THE AIR" (1894)

Sadakichi Hartmann, "Schopenhauer in the Air," *Art Critic* 1, no. 3 (Mar. 1894), 56–57.

279 **Schopenhauer:** Arthur Schopenhauer (1788–1860) was a German philosopher

who held that human desiring and willing were perpetually dissatisfied, but that this condition could be temporarily escaped by means of aesthetic contemplation.

KATE CHOPIN, "LILACS" (1896)

Kate Chopin, "Lilacs," *Times-Democrat* (New Orleans), Christmas Art Supplement (Dec. 20, 1896), [1].

284　**picture of the Sacré Coeur:** Image of the Sacred Heart of Jesus, a traditional devotional image showing Christ's heart exposed, shining with light, pierced, bleeding, surmounted by a crown of thorns and a cross.

284　**Ste. Catharine de Sienne:** Saint Catherine of Siena (1347–80), a mystic and spiritual writer, a political ambassador, and a woman whose public activities and interventions were unusual for a woman of her time.

286　**enragée:** French, "fanatic," madwoman.

287　**St. Lazare:** Saint-Lazare was a prison in Paris, at this time for women, populated in large part by prostitutes and other debauched women.

287　**angelus bell:** Bell calling the nuns to recite the angelus, a Christian devotional prayer commemorating the Incarnation, often recited three times daily in convents.

288　**"The Angel . . . Holy Ghost—":** Beginning of the angelus prayer.

288　**bénitiers:** French, vases or basins containing holy water.

290　**traînée of a café chantant:** French, a floozy in a music bar.

290　**désolé:** French, "disconsolate."

291　**Ma foi!:** French, "my goodness!"

291　**Chateau Yquem:** Superior and expensive wine from the Sauternes commune in the Gironde region of France.

291　**bonne:** French, "housemaid."

292　**peignoir:** French, "robe" or wrapper.

Acknowledgments

Many fellow scholars suggested stories for inclusion in this collection (not all of which I was able to accept) or otherwise shared their kind advice. For their ideas and assistance I thank Nancy Bentley, Hester Blum, Christopher Castiglia, King-Kok Cheung, Sarah Chinn, Dawn Coleman, Liam Corley, Joseph Dimuro, Jonathan Eburne, Emily D. Field, Sören Fröhlich, Theresa Strouth Gaul, Mitchell Santine Gould, Sharon Harris, Lauren Heintz, Philip J. Kowalski, Marissa Lopez, Eric Norton, Christian Reed, Rick Rodriguez, Sarah Salter, Michael Snediker, Kyla Wazana Tompkins, Brant Torres, and Robert K. Wallace.